POWERFUL TEACHER EDUCATION

POWERFUL TEACHER EDUCATION

Lessons from Exemplary Programs

Linda Darling-Hammond
in collaboration with
Letitia Fickel, Julia Koppich, Maritza Macdonald,
Kay Merseth, Lynne Miller, Gordon Ruscoe,
David Silvernail, Jon Snyder, Betty Lou Whitford,
and Kenneth Zeichner

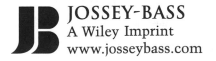
JOSSEY-BASS
A Wiley Imprint
www.josseybass.com

Published by Jossey-Bass
A Wiley Imprint
989 Market Street, San Francisco, CA 94103-1741   www.josseybass.com

Jossey-Bass books and products are available through most bookstores. To contact Jossey-Bass directly call our Customer Care Department within the U.S. at 800-956-7739, outside the U.S. at 317-572-3986, or fax 317-572-4002.

Jossey-Bass also publishes its books in a variety of electronic formats. Some content that appears in print may not be available in electronic books.

Library of Congress Cataloging-in-Publication Data
Darling-Hammond, Linda, date.
Powerful teacher education: lessons from exemplary programs / Linda Darling-Hammond.
p. cm.
Includes bibliographical references and index.
ISBN-13: 978-0-7879-7273-8 (cloth)
ISBN-10: 0-7879-7273-8 (cloth)
1. Teachers—Training of—United States. I. Title.
LB1715.D343 2006
370.71'1—dc22   2006004499

Printed in the United States of America
FIRST EDITION
HB Printing   10 9 8 7 6 5 4 3 2

The Jossey-Bass Education Series

CONTENTS

Preface   ix
Acknowledgments   xv

PART ONE
Introduction

1. Creating Powerful Teacher Education   3
2. Why Teacher Education Is Important—and Difficult   19
3. Addressing the Dilemmas of Teacher Education: 42
   Evidence of Success

PART TWO
Conceptualizing Knowledge, Skills, and Practice

4. Conceptualizing the Knowledge Base for Teaching   77
5. Developing and Assessing Teaching: Constructing   113
   Performances of Understanding
6. Constructing the Clinical Experience: The Glue for   152
   Powerful Preparation

PART THREE
Bringing It All Together

7. The Double Helix of Teaching: Managing the Dialectic   189
   Between Students and Subjects
8. Educating for Equity   222
9. Preparing Teachers to Reach All Students   252

PART FOUR
Issues of Context and Change

10. Transforming Teacher Education: Institutional Challenges   275
11. Developing Professional Policy   313

APPENDIXES

A. Study Methodology   345
B. Survey Results   355
C. Teacher Education Program Structures   363

References   377
About the Author   399
Name Index   401
Subject Index   407

PREFACE

ONE OF THE MOST DAMAGING MYTHS prevailing in American education is the notion that good teachers are born and not made. This superstition has given rise to a set of policies that rely far too much on some kind of prenatal alchemy to produce a cadre of teachers for our nation's schools—and far too little on systematic, sustained initiatives to ensure that all teachers have the opportunity to become well prepared.

A companion myth is the idea that good teacher education programs are virtually nonexistent and perhaps even impossible to construct. As a consequence of the first myth or their own experience, a startling number of policymakers and practitioners appear to believe one or more of these notions: that teaching is mostly telling others what you know and therefore requires little more than subject matter knowledge, that people learn to teach learn primarily from (more or less unguided) experience, or that education schools can offer little more than half-baked "theories" that are unnecessary and perhaps even an impediment in learning the practical requirements of teaching. Thus there is little reason to require much in the way of teacher preparation or to invest in the institutions that are expected to prepare teachers to teach.

The human toll created by these myths was brought home to me in my own experience both as a teacher and as a parent. More than thirty years ago, I entered teaching through one of the many alternative certification programs that proliferated during a previous era of teacher shortages in the early 1970s. I had learned to love working with students as a teacher's aide in an urban district in the Midwest and as an after-school teacher and curriculum director in a program for inner-city students on the East Coast. Armed with this bit of experience, unbounded enthusiasm, and an Ivy League degree (magna cum laude, but *not* in education), I completed a brief summer training, including student teaching at Camden High School in New Jersey, and became a high school teacher the following fall while taking courses toward a master's degree in education.

Quickly I learned what so many unsuspecting recruits discover: how incredibly difficult teaching is if you actually want to reach every single student. Among the more than 150 students who passed through my English classes each day were a number who had gotten to high school without learning how to read, and many more who disliked it or were persuaded that they were not "good at school" and had no reason to try. Many attended school only for the required English class, with the remainder of their courses in a vocational-technical program. What could I do, I wondered, to interest them in the prescribed classical curriculum that meant so little to their daily lives?

Like others before me and many since, I improvised with little assistance. (The alternative program supervisor came once, pronounced me "not nearly as bad off" as some of her other charges, and never came back.) The other teachers were friendly but busy. The assistant principal came by for twenty minutes to evaluate me near the end of the year. My courses at the university were, for the most part, unconnected to my daily travails. I got as far on commitment, common sense, and enthusiasm as one can get; because I was sincere and well meaning and worked hard, most of my students and colleagues thought of me as a "good teacher." I found ways to interest students in material that was close to their experience and got most of them engaged.

However, I was teaching by the seat of my pants with the limited repertoire of teaching strategies I had seen used by my own teachers. I did not know how to help the nonreaders in my classes become literate, how to diagnose the needs of those who struggled, or work most effectively with the special needs students in my classes. I did not know there were ways to organize a classroom, scaffold assignments, or engage students in collaborative work that would have allowed more of my students to achieve at a higher level.

When I later discovered the knowledge bases that would have helped me to meet more of my students' needs and answer the burning questions that kept me awake at night as a beginning teacher, I was perplexed—and then angry—that no one had incorporated this knowledge into a required program of preparation that was available to me (and every other teacher) before entering the classroom. Some of my colleagues, whom I envied, got that kind of preparation, and I was mystified as to why there was so much variation in what teachers had the opportunity to learn and consequently be able to do. At the time, I did not understand that teaching lacked the licensing and accreditation policies that create the greater comparability among professional programs found in more developed professions such as law, medicine, and engineering.

After I went back for a doctorate to study education policy and become a researcher, I reencountered this unevenness years later as a parent. One of my daughters started school in our local elementary school with a new teacher who, like me, was underprepared. This teacher's repertoire was even leaner than my own: a steady diet of workbooks coupled with her attempts to apply the two days of "Assertive Discipline" training she'd received. The Assertive Discipline program assigns rewards (treats or gold stars) or an escalating set of punishments (name on the board, loss of recess, library time, detention, and so on) on the basis of children's behavior. Teachers are never to ask or discuss why a child acts in a particular way in the classroom but merely repeat the consequences (in what is called the "broken record" technique) and apply them mechanically. As the program's founder, Lee Cantor, once explained to me, the simplistic system was designed for teachers who are not skilled enough to engage in more sophisticated diagnosis of children's needs or personalized management of behavior.

When children break the rules—which in this kindergarten class included not talking, moving, or touching other children—they are excluded from class activities. With rules that any normal, active kindergartner would naturally violate, the board was soon full of names with check marks under a heading labeling them as "bad," and the teacher was kept busy administering punishments, which grew more frequent as students reacted to both her poor teaching and her counterproductive disciplinary system. (It is not irrelevant that this neighborhood school was predominantly African American and the students most stigmatized by this system were bright, active black boys.) Within weeks, my daughter, along with some other children in the class, was having daily stomachaches and becoming unwilling to go to school.

In search of an alternative, we found another school for her to attend, where she was taught by another first-year teacher. But what a difference! This teacher ran a seamlessly managed, intellectually exciting classroom in which students read literature, wrote and published their own books, studied hands-on science and mathematics, completed a range of projects within and across subjects, and learned to work collaboratively with one another. No student was ever labeled or stigmatized according to behavior or achievement. The teacher grouped and regrouped students continually in response to their needs and the tasks they were working on. After a few weeks, she diagnosed my daughter's dyslexia, referred her for testing and therapy, and soon developed a set of strategies that taught her to read, without my daughter ever really knowing that she had a disability. I ultimately asked this skillful beginning teacher how she had learned to do all of the things I watched her accomplish. She told me she was a graduate of Teachers College, Columbia University, where she not only completed a rigorous master's degree including a full year of student teaching but also took a set of special education courses, including one on teaching students with reading disabilities. This experience powerfully illustrated how teacher education can give new teachers the knowledge and skills they need to teach effectively.

Later, in my years in New York City (after I joined the faculty of Teachers College), when I was in and out of many classrooms, I found I could almost invariably identify the graduates of distinctive preservice programs, such as those of Bank Street College and Teachers College, by seeing them teach and hearing them discuss their practice. Like the graduates of other programs that our research team discovered by asking practitioners in various parts of the country where the best teachers are prepared, these teachers' deep knowledge of curriculum and assessment, their understanding of individual students, and their capacity to use sophisticated teaching strategies for engaging diverse learners were immediately evident. The regularity with which graduates of these programs were exceptional teachers was striking. Furthermore, I found through my conversations with other educators—and our research team confirmed this systematically—that in many parts of the country there is a high degree of consensus among principals, superintendents, and teachers about which colleges produce the best teachers to work in schools that are successful with diverse learners. These excellent practitioners tend to agree on a short list of colleges in their vicinity (often only one or two) that they find prepare teachers from their very first moments on the job to understand their students' learning and construct productive learning experiences for them.

This study was born from these experiences. Over the years, I heard many castigate the shortcomings of teacher education, and I learned that the strong preparation programs that exist are often a well-kept secret from many policymakers and practitioners. I watched policies emerge aimed at short-circuiting preparation for teachers, on the excuse that most teacher education is just an obstacle to getting into the classroom. These policies are invariably most willing to skip preparation for the teachers of low-income and "minority" students who teach in central cities, allowing these districts to fill their vacancies with underprepared teachers without having to raise salaries or improve working conditions. Paradoxically, I found teachers hungry for access to knowledge and almost evangelical about good preparation when they could find it.

I became convinced that a large part of the answer to poor schooling in this country is to understand what strong preparation for teachers looks like and can do, and to undertake the policy changes needed to ensure that all teachers can have access to such preparation. I was fortunate to work with a group of committed colleagues who also believe that this is possible and necessary, and who have amassed deep knowledge of how teachers learn and how they can be taught.

Lead members of the case study teams were Ken Zeichner, Hoefs-Bascom professor of education at the University of Wisconsin–Madison and an internationally renowned researcher on teacher education nationally and internationally; Jon Snyder, then director of teacher education at UC Santa Barbara and now dean at Bank Street College; Betty Lou Whitford, then professor of education at the University of Louisville and now dean at the University of Southern Maine (USM); Lynne Miller, previously director of teacher education and founder of the Southern Maine Partnership at USM, and David Silvernail, professor of education and director of the Center for Educational Policy at USM; Katherine Merseth, then director of the Harvard Project on Schooling and Children and later director of teacher education at Harvard University; Julia Koppich, then director of Policy Analysis for California Education at the University of California at Berkeley and now president of Koppich Associates; and Maritza Macdonald, then a researcher at the National Center for Restructuring Education, Schools, and Teaching at Teachers College and now director of professional development at the American Museum of Natural History in New York. This team conceptualized and launched the study, and most of us have gone on to act on its findings in many settings. We hope that these findings are as educative to those who read the volume as they have been to those of us who worked on it.

ACKNOWLEDGMENTS

AS IS TRUE WITH ANY ENTERPRISE, many people contributed time, support, and intellectual insights to this book. First and foremost, the book was built from a set of excellent case studies by these authors:

Alverno College—Kenneth Zeichner

Bank Street College of Education—Linda Darling-Hammond and Maritza Macdonald

Trinity University—Julia Koppich

University of California at Berkeley—Jon Snyder

University of Southern Maine—Betty Lou Whitford, Gordon Ruscoe, and Letitia Fickel

University of Virginia—Katherine Merseth and Julia Koppich

Wheelock College—Lynne Miller and David Silvernail

These collaborating authors contributed not only to the individual case studies but also to the initial conceptualization of the study and development of the research instruments and protocols. The individual case studies were published in a three-volume set by the American Association of Colleges of Teacher Educators (AACTE) and the National Commission on Teaching and America's Future in 2000 and are available from AACTE. The volumes are entitled *Studies of Excellence in Teacher Education: Preparation in the Undergraduate Years, Preparation in a Five-Year Program,* and *Preparation at the Graduate Level.*

David Silvernail of the University of Southern Maine ably oversaw production and administration of the surveys and conducted the initial analyses of the data.

Several brilliant doctoral students at Stanford University who participated in a seminar I taught on teacher education read, discussed, and wrote about the case studies and reflected on their meaning for teacher education more broadly. I am grateful to Sue Baker, Janet Coffey, Julie Gainsburg, Morva Macdonald, Daisy Martin, and Misty Sato for their insights, many of which are represented in this book. Fortunately for the field, most of them are now skilled and committed teacher educators themselves.

At various points along the way, research assistance was ably provided by David Ellwood, Maritza Macdonald, Kavemui Murangii, and Patrice Litman, all at Teachers College, Columbia University, as well as Julie Gainsburg at Stanford University.

Karen Hammerness also contributed a great deal to my thinking through a number of studies of teacher education we worked on together over several years when she was a postdoctoral fellow at Stanford. In a major project on teacher education curriculum for the National Academy of Education, she served as a key staff member and author, along with project directors Pamela LePage and Helen Duffy; our joint work on that project intersected with this book in many ways. As cochair of the National Academy Committee with me, John Bransford helped me to think in new ways about the knowledge base for teaching afforded by the learning sciences.

My understanding of teacher education has been informed by many other colleagues over the years, among them Ann Lieberman, Arthur Wise, Gary Sykes, Lee Shulman, Pamela Grossman, Jo Boaler, Rachel Lotan, Rich Shavelson, Gloria Ladson-Billings, Carol Lee, Guadalupe Valdes, Amado Padilla, Kenji Hakuta, Roy Pea, and Nailah Nasir. I thank these colleagues for provoking many insights, and I thank my editors at Jossey-Bass, Lesley Iura and Kate Gagnon, for helping to bring this project to fruition.

The research reported in this book was made possible in part by grants from an anonymous donor and from the Spencer Foundation through a Senior Scholars Grant. The data presented, statements made, and views expressed are solely those of the authors.

I am deeply grateful to the hundreds of teachers, principals, and teacher educators we interviewed and surveyed to learn about their work and to the many more who do this work every day. I am also grateful to my family—Allen, Kia, Elena, and Sean—who have supported me over many years of seeking answers to the mysteries of how to educate all children well and who have contributed to my understanding of these questions on the front lines of their own educational adventures.

Although I thank all of those who contributed to this endeavor, the responsibility for any remaining errors is my own.

L.D.H.

POWERFUL TEACHER EDUCATION

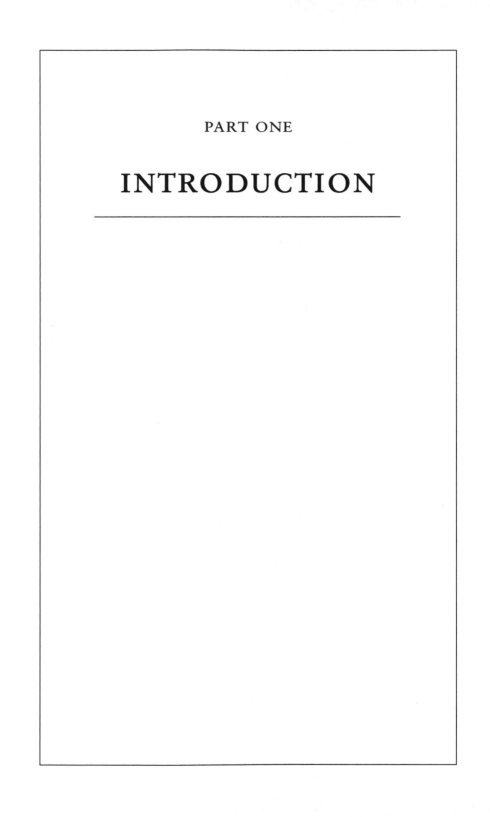

PART ONE

INTRODUCTION

CREATING POWERFUL TEACHER EDUCATION

Wheelock does a better job of preparing early childhood teachers than any place I know.
—Boston school principal

I have sought out Bank Street graduates in all my positions in the last ten years.
—New York City school principal

As I look for teachers, I most immediately look for Alverno applicants. . . . I'll take ten more teachers like the two I've had this year.
—Milwaukee school principal

I take all the DTE grads I can get. . . . They are the best teachers—outstanding, dedicated. It is a program that stands out.
—San Leandro, California, principal, on graduates of the University of California at Berkeley's Developmental Teacher Education Program

UVA's five-year program has made a huge difference. All of the student teachers we have had have been excellent.
—Charlottesville, Virginia, school principal

ETEP graduates are sought out for interviews.
[They] have an excellent success rate in our district.

—Southern Maine principal, on graduates of the University
of Southern Maine's Extended Teacher Education Program (ETEP)

When I hire a Trinity graduate, I know he or she will become
a school leader. These people are smart about curriculum;
they're innovative. They have the torch.

—San Antonio high school principal

IN A WORLD WHERE EDUCATION MATTERS more than it ever has
before, parents and policymakers alike are asking how to find the extraordinary teachers who can help all children acquire the increasingly complex knowledge and skills they need. As the social and economic demands
for education grow, so do expectations of teachers' knowledge and skills.
Teachers must be able to succeed with a wider range of learners than they
were expected to teach in a time when school success was not essential
for employment and participation in society. In the early 1900s, when our
current school system was designed, only 5 percent of jobs required specialized knowledge and skill; today about 70 percent are "knowledge
work" jobs that demand the ability to acquire and use specialized information, manage nonroutine tasks, and employ advanced technologies.
To meet these demands, virtually every state has enacted more ambitious standards for learning tied to new curriculum expectations and assessments. These standards expect students to master more challenging
subject matter content, as well as to think critically, create more sophisticated products, and solve complex problems, rather than merely perform
routine tasks. The standards press for deeper understanding and for student proficiency in applying knowledge that requires far more than rote
recall of facts or application of rules and algorithms.

Teachers are also being asked to achieve these goals for *all* children, not
just the 10–20 percent traditionally siphoned off into gifted and talented
programs or honors courses. Furthermore, students have more extensive
needs: as education becomes more important to life success and schools
both expand the range of students they educate and include more of them
in "regular" classrooms, teachers encounter more students with learning
differences and disabilities; with language learning needs; and with difficult family circumstances, from acute poverty, homelessness, unemployment, and lack of medical care to violence, abuse, and abandonment.
Teachers in many communities need to work as professors of disciplinary

content, facilitators of individual learning, assessors and diagnosticians, counselors, social workers, and community resource managers.

Although it is now widely accepted that teacher quality is a critical component of a successful education, there is little agreement about how to fill the nation's classrooms with teachers who can succeed at the more challenging mission of today's schools. Many still believe that good teachers are born and not made. Others believe that good teachers figure out how to teach on their own over time through classroom experience. This book starts from a different premise: if the nation's classrooms are to be filled with teachers who can teach ambitious skills to all learners, the solution must lie in large part with strong, universal teacher education.

This book is about powerful teacher education programs—programs that prepare teachers to teach a wide range of students successfully, including those who struggle to learn from their first days in the classroom. These are programs whose graduates are sought out by principals and superintendents because they prove consistently capable of creating successful classrooms and helping to lead successful schools, even in circumstances where the deck is traditionally stacked against student success.

The need for such teachers is especially great where schools are the critical lifeline for student success. It may not take much training to teach children who are already skillful learners; who are supported by highly educated parents who build home libraries, take them to museums, pay for summer enrichment programs, and hire tutors when their own knowledge runs out; who have the advantages of steady income, health care, food, and home stability; and whose language and culture are compatible with those of the adults in the school. However, these home and community supports are the exception rather than the rule in most urban (and many suburban and rural) public schools, and teachers who rely on "magical learning" that takes place outside of school are not adequately prepared to meet the real needs of their students.

The programs we describe here have long track records of developing teachers who are strongly committed to all students' learning—and to ensuring especially that students who struggle to learn can succeed. The programs also develop teachers who can *act* on their commitments; who are highly knowledgeable about learning and teaching and who have strong practical skills—teachers who can manage, with grace and purpose, the thousands of interactions that occur in a classroom each day; who know how to teach ambitious subject matter to students who learn in different ways; who can integrate solid teaching of basic skills with support for student invention and inquiry; who can teach language and literacy skills in every grade and across the curriculum; and who can work effectively with parents and colleagues to assemble the resources and motivations needed to help children make progress.

Hide and Seek: Looking for Good Teacher Education Programs

Such powerful teacher education programs are, by most accounts, relatively rare. Indeed, some opponents of professionalization might consider the very notion of an effective teacher education program to be an oxymoron (see, for example, Ballou and Podgursky, 1999). Teacher education has long been criticized as a weak intervention in the life of a teacher, barely able to make a dent in the ideas and behaviors teachers bring with them into the classroom from their own days as students. Since normal schools for training teachers were incorporated into universities in the 1950s, a steady drumbeat of complaints has reiterated the perceptions of program fragmentation, weak content, poor pedagogy, disconnection from schools, and inconsistent oversight of teachers-in-training (see, for example, Conant, 1963; Clifford and Guthrie, 1988; Goodlad, 1990).

Although there are certainly accounts of teachers who have valued their preparation, more popular are stories of teachers who express disdain for their training, suggesting that they learned little in their courses that they could apply to the classroom, or that if there was any benefit to their training it was to be found primarily in student teaching. These views have often led to the perception that if there is anything to be learned about teaching, it can be learned on the job, through trial and error if not with supervision. Indeed, U.S. Secretary of Education Rod Paige argued in his 2002 report on teacher quality that "burdensome requirements" for education coursework that make up "the bulk of current teacher certification regimes" should be removed from teacher certification standards (U.S. Department of Education, 2002, p. 8). The Secretary's report argued that certification should emphasize tests of verbal ability and content knowledge while making most education coursework and student teaching optional (p. 19).

For all the criticism, there is substantial and growing evidence that teacher education matters for teacher effectiveness. (See Chapter Two for discussion of this evidence.) Furthermore, over the many years since Horace Mann created the first normal schools for teachers—and increasingly in the last two decades as teacher education reforms have taken hold—some places where teachers are taught have been known among practitioners as extraordinarily effective.

This book is based on case studies of seven such programs—public and private, large and small, undergraduate and graduate—that, despite their surface differences, share a great deal in terms of how they go about the work of preparing people to teach. Spanning the country, the programs are at Alverno College in Milwaukee; Bank Street College in New York City; Trinity University in San Antonio; the University of California at Berkeley; the University of Southern Maine near Portland; the University of Virginia in Charlottesville; and Wheelock College in Boston. These seven programs are by no means the only ones that could have been studied. They were selected from a much longer list of candidates in order to represent elementary and secondary programs in distinctive institutions serving a variety of clientele in representative parts of the country.

Two of the programs, at Alverno and Wheelock, are undergraduate programs for elementary teaching candidates. Both can be finished in the traditional four years of undergraduate school by those who focus intensely on program requirements, or in an additional semester or two by those who carry a more normal load. Two other programs, at Trinity and UVA, are designed as five-year models that result in a bachelor's degree in the discipline to be taught by their secondary teaching candidates, plus a master's degree in education. Three are graduate-level programs that serve individuals who completed their bachelor's degree and later decided to teach. The Extended Teacher Education Program (ETEP) program at Southern Maine is a one-year internship model. Bank Street College's graduate program, serving mostly midcareer recruits to teaching, can be completed in eighteen months. The Developmental Teacher Education (DTE) program at Berkeley is a two-year graduate-level program.

A team of researchers conducted in-depth case studies of these programs, interviewing and surveying graduates and employers of the graduates (comparing them to a random comparison group of new teachers); observing the programs in action and the practices of graduates in local schools; and studying syllabi, assignments, clinical placements, and other evidence of how the programs work. Through this intensive examination of these places, we set out to learn how good teachers can be "made" and how the critical components of effective preparation can become more widely available.

Better Than Good: The Contemporary Challenge for Teacher Education

Although the seven programs differ markedly in locale and program design, they have in common an approach that prepares teachers to practice in ways that we describe as both *learning-centered* (that is, supportive of focused, in-depth learning that results in powerful thinking and proficient performance on the part of students) and *learner-centered* (responsive to individual students' experiences, interests, talents, needs, and cultural backgrounds). These programs go well beyond preparing teachers to manage a calm classroom and make their way through a standard curriculum by teaching to the middle of the class. They help teachers learn to reach students who experience a range of challenges and teach them for deep understanding. They also help teachers learn not only how to cope with the students they encounter but how to expand children's aspirations as well as accomplishments, thereby enhancing educational opportunity and social justice.

The study was designed to understand the work and outcomes of these programs and to *teach* about the teaching of teachers, by revealing in detail how it is these programs accomplish their goals. Alongside the myths about teaching and teacher education that predominate in our society, the stuff of teacher education is to a great extent a mystery.

Most people tend to think of the act of teaching as largely intuitive: someone knows something and then "teaches" it to others—a fairly straightforward transmission model. From this image, the job of teacher preparation appears equally simple: be sure that candidates know what they are to teach and have some tools of the trade for presenting that information to students. However, as mountains of research now demonstrate, this notion of transmission teaching doesn't actually work most of the time. The reality of effective teaching is much different: successful teachers link what students already know and understand to new information, correcting misimpressions, guiding learners' understanding through a variety of activities, providing opportunities for application of knowledge, giving useful feedback that shapes performance, and individualizing for students' distinctive learning needs. They do all this while juggling the social and academic needs of the group and of individuals, the cognitive and motivational consequences of their moment-to-moment teaching decisions, the cultural and community context within which they teach, and much more.

How does one help people learn to do this impossible task? Considered in this way, teacher education seems even more impossible than teaching itself, especially given the challenge of preparing a wide range of individuals to become teachers who can in turn enable an enormously diverse group of students to meet much higher standards than have ever before been expected of education systems. Thus the goals for teacher education today are not just to prepare teachers to deliver a curriculum or get through the book but actually to ensure learning for students with a broad assortment of needs.

A New Mission for Teaching

The old transmission teaching model (which succeeded for some and left many more behind) is not adequate for a knowledge-based society that increases the cognitive requirements of most employment and of life in general. First of all, the kind of learning required to produce students who are strong thinkers and problem solvers creates greater unpredictability in teaching because it cannot be managed primarily through rote memorization or drill. Students must take on novel problems and learn through their own inquiry to find, synthesize, analyze, and interpret information. As students do this, teachers must be able to understand, monitor, and capitalize on student thinking if they are to support a process of knowledge construction that is unique to each one (Darling-Hammond, 1997).

In addition, formulaic approaches to teaching that do not take into account the experiences and needs of students are less and less successful as student populations become more diverse and expectations for student learning grow more ambitious. The image of the student as an empty vessel who can be filled up with facts, drilled on skills, and thus made into an educated person guided much learning theory for the first half of the twentieth century. In this image, teachers needed only to know what facts to pour in and what skills to drill. However, several decades of research have clearly demonstrated that learning—particularly learning that supports problem solving and transfer of knowledge to new situations—does not occur in this way. As the National Academy of Sciences summary of *How People Learn* notes (Donovan and Bransford, 2005), three fundamental and well-established principles of learning are particularly important for teaching:

1. *Students come to the classroom with prior knowledge that must be addressed if teaching is to be effective.* If what they know and believe is not engaged, learners may fail to grasp the new concepts and information that are taught, or they may learn them for purposes of a test but not be able to apply them elsewhere. This means that teachers must understand what students are thinking and how to connect with their prior knowledge if they are to ensure real learning. Because students from a variety of cultural contexts and language backgrounds come to school with distinctive experiences, they present a range of preconceptions and knowledge bases that teachers must take into account in designing instruction.

2. *Students need to organize and use knowledge conceptually if they are to apply it beyond the classroom.* Memorizing is not enough. To develop competence, they must understand how facts and ideas fit

together within a conceptual framework, and they must apply what they are learning. This means that teachers must structure the material around core ideas and engage students actively in using the material, incorporating applications and problem solving while continually assessing students' understanding. Successful teachers offer carefully designed "scaffolds" to help students take each step in the learning process with assistance appropriate to each student's needs and progress.

3. *Students learn more effectively if they understand how they learn and how to manage their own learning.* A metacognitive approach to instruction can help students learn to take control of their own learning. Through modeling and coaching, students can see how to use a range of learning strategies, such as predicting outcomes, creating explanations to improve understanding, noting areas of confusion, activating background knowledge, planning ahead, and apportioning time and memory.

Why Teachers Must Become Adaptive Experts

Modern learning theory implies that teachers must be diagnosticians, knowledge organizers, and skilled coaches to help students master complex information and skills. Thus the desire to succeed at much more formidable learning goals with a much more varied student population radically changes the nature of teaching and the challenges of teacher preparation.

If all students pursued an identical path to understanding, learning might be ensured by designing the perfect scripted curriculum. Teachers could be prepared to implement a prescribed set of lessons using a limited range of teaching techniques. This is what scientific managers of schooling and inventors of "teacher-proof curriculum" have hoped since the late nineteenth century. However, given human diversity and cognitive complexity, learning cannot be achieved through a single set of activities that presume standardized experiences and approaches to learning. Teaching that aims at deep learning, not merely coverage of material, requires sophisticated judgment about how and what students are learning, what gaps in their understanding need to be addressed, what experiences will allow them to connect what they know to what they need to know, and what instructional adaptations can ensure that they reach common goals.

In fact, the more common the expectations for achievement are, the more variable must be the teaching strategies for reaching these goals with a range of learners. If teaching assumes a single mode and pace of learning, students who start at different places and learn in different ways will end with greatly unequal achievement. This is currently the case in the

United States, where the range in school outcomes is much wider than in other industrialized countries (OECD, 1995). As John Dewey (1929) noted in his *Sources of a Science of Education,* the better prepared teachers are, the more their practice becomes differentiated in response to the needs of individual students, rather than routinized: "Command of scientific methods and systematized subject matter liberates individuals; it enables them to see new problems, devise new procedures, and in general makes for diversification rather than for set uniformity. . . . This knowledge and understanding render [the teacher's] practice more intelligent, more flexible, and better adapted to deal effectively with concrete phenomena of practice. . . . His ability to judge being enriched, he has a wider range of alternatives to select from in dealing with individual situations" (pp. 12, 20–21).

If teachers are to help learners who begin and proceed differently reach similar outcomes, they will need to be able to engage in disciplined experimentation, incisive interpretation of complex events, and rigorous reflection to adjust their teaching based on student outcomes. This means that teachers must become "adaptive experts" (Hatano and Inagaki, 1986; Bransford, Brown, and Cocking, 1999) who cannot only use routines that afford greater efficiency, but also their ability to innovate where routines are not enough—to figure out what the problems are when students are not learning and to adapt materials, teaching strategies, or supports accordingly. Adaptive experts also know how to continuously expand their expertise, restructuring their knowledge and competencies to meet new challenges. Preparing teachers who can learn *from* teaching, as well as learning *for* teaching, is a key challenge for teacher education today, one that these seven programs successfully engage.

Preparing Teachers for Responsive Practice

This book seeks to answer a question not yet addressed in the conversation on education reform: How can we prepare teachers for this daunting mission? Although there has been much discussion about the structures of teacher education programs (four years or five, undergraduate or graduate) and the certification categories into which programs presumably fit ("traditional," "alternative"), there has been much less discussion about what goes on *within* the black box of the program—inside the courses and clinical experiences that candidates encounter—and how the experiences programs design for students cumulatively add up to a set of knowledge, skills, and dispositions that determine what teachers actually do in the classroom. In the coming chapters, we describe the content and processes a set of highly effective programs employ and their outcomes in terms of graduate's feelings of preparedness, their actual practice, and their success with students.

This study confronts some widely shared myths about teaching and teacher education: that good teachers are born and not made, that good practice cannot really be taught but only be intuited through trial and error, and that few can ever master complex teaching practices or attend to individual learners' needs. Those who believe the myths argue that teacher-proof curricula rather than well-trained teachers should be the target of educational investment. (Chapter Two discusses the evidence regarding this issue.)

Perhaps most dangerous is the myth that if high-quality programs of teacher education are lacking, requirements for preparing teachers should be abandoned altogether, since they constitute merely an unnecessary "barrier" to entry. This myth undergirds policy proposals like those put forth by the Fordham Foundation (Kanstoroom and Finn, 1999) that argue for eliminating teacher certification and pursuing alternatives that put would-be teachers directly into classrooms to learn by trial-and-error and to be fired later if they are not successful.

Though lacking empirical grounding, these myths drive much policy work and deflect attention from needed investment in high-quality teacher preparation. Furthermore, proposals to avoid preparing teachers are gaining currency in some states, with at least two dangerous outcomes for children and for the nation. One is that access to knowledge about teaching will never really become widespread; as the need for expert teaching grows exponentially, teachers will not gain access to the knowledge they need to be effective. The other is that students' access to well-trained teachers will continue to be a crapshoot, with the poorest odds going to those with the least clout and the greatest needs.

As was true of medical education in the early 1900s, teacher education ranges widely, from a few weeks of summer orientation to intensive multiyear graduate preparation like that required in France, Germany, Sweden, Finland, and elsewhere. Similarly, when Abraham Flexner conducted his study of medical education between 1908 and 1910, doctors could be prepared in a three-week program of training featuring memorized lists of symptoms and cures, or at the other extreme in a graduate program of medicine (as at Johns Hopkins University) with extensive coursework in the sciences of medicine and clinical training in the newly invented teaching hospital.

In his introduction to the Flexner Report, Henry Pritchett, president of the Carnegie Foundation for the Advancement of Teaching, noted that although there was a growing science of medicine, most doctors did not get access to this knowledge because of the great unevenness in medical training. He observed that "very seldom, under existing conditions, does a patient receive the best aid which it is possible to give him in the present state of medicine, . . . [because] a vast army of men is admitted to the practice of medicine who are untrained in sciences fundamental to the profession and quite without a sufficient experience with disease" (Flexner and Pritchett, 1910, p. x). He attributed this problem to the failure of many universities to incorporate advances in medical education into their curricula.

As in teaching today, some argued against the professionalization of medicine, feeling medical practice could best be learned by following another doctor around in a buggy, learning to apply leeches to reduce fevers and selling tonics that purported to cure everything from baldness to cancer. Flexner's identification of universities he deemed successful in conveying new knowledge about causes and treatment of disease and in creating strong training was the stimulus for reforming medical education. Despite resistance from many would-be doctors and from weaker training sites, the enterprise was transformed over the subsequent two decades, as a common curriculum was adopted by the accrediting bodies that approved all programs and incorporated into the licensing tests used to admit all candidates to practice.

Getting Knowledge to Teachers

Without similar efforts in teacher education, much of what is known about learning and teaching will not reach those most desperate to have it. Although many who enter teaching initially believe they do not need specialized training, most learn quickly that teaching is much more difficult than they thought, and they either desperately seek out additional training, construct a teaching style focused on control (often by "dumbing down" the curriculum to what can be easily managed), or leave in despair. Some, like this recruit who entered teaching after a few weeks of summer training, find that they end up blaming the students for their own lack of skills:

> I stayed one year. I felt it was important for me to see the year out but I didn't necessarily feel like it was a good idea for me to teach again without something else. I knew if I wanted to go on teaching there was no way I could do it without training. I found myself having problems with cross-cultural teaching issues—blaming my

kids because the class was crazy and out of control, blaming the parents as though they didn't care about their kids. It was frustrating to me to get caught up in that. Even after only three-fourths of a semester at Berkeley I have learned so much that would have helped me then.

—A recruit who later entered the teacher
preparation program at University of
California at Berkeley

Inadequate preparation also increases teacher attrition, which exacerbates the revolving door that contributes to teacher shortages. Several studies report beginning teachers who lack professional training are about twice as likely to leave teaching in their first year as those who have had student teaching and preparation in such areas as learning theory, child development, and curriculum (Henke, Chen, and Geis, 2000; NCTAF, 2003; Luczak, 2004).

This has been borne out in the aftermath of the crash courses on teaching many states and districts created to get would-be teachers into classrooms quickly (see, for example, Battenfeld, 2001; Fowler, 2001; Goodnough, 2000). A vivid report in the St. Petersburg (Florida) *Times* in January 2001 reported the loss of nearly one hundred area recruits in the first half of the school year, most of them midcareer alternative certification candidates who lacked education training but were supposed to learn on the job. Microbiologist Bill Gaulman, a fifty-six-year-old African American former Marine and New York City firefighter, left before midyear. He reflected the experience of many: "The word that comes to mind is 'overwhelmed.' People told me 'Just get through that first year.' I was like, 'I don't know if I can get through this week.' I didn't want to shortchange the kids. I didn't want to fake it. I wanted to do it right." Erika Lavrack, a twenty-nine-year-old psychologist without education training who was assigned to teach special education, resigned on her second day. "The kids were nice enough. But they were running all over the place. There was no way I could teach them anything if I couldn't get them to sit down. I didn't know what to do" (Hegarty, 2001).

Contrast these recruits' experiences with those of two young teachers in the tough urban district of Oakland, California. The first attended a program that had been referred to us for our study:

I arrived at my first teaching job five years ago, midyear. . . . The first-grade classroom in which I found myself had some two dozen ancient and tattered books, an incomplete curriculum, and an incomplete collection of outdated content standards. Such a placement is the norm for a beginning teacher in my district. I was prepared for this placement, and later came to thrive in my profession, because of the preparation I received in my credential program. The concrete things Mills College gave me were indispensable to me my first year as they are now: the practice I received developing appropriate curricula, exposure to a wide range of learning theories, training in working with non-English-speaking students and children labeled "at risk. . . ." It is the big things, though, that continue to sustain me as a professional and give me the courage to remain and grow: my understanding of the importance of learning from and continually asking questions about my own practice, the value I recognize in cultivating collegial relationships, and the development of a belief in my moral responsibility to my children and to the institution of public education. . . . I attribute this wholly to the training, education, and support provided to me by Mills.

The second finished the UC Berkeley Developmental Teacher Education program we studied: "I'm miles ahead of other first-year teachers. There are five other first-year teachers here this year. I am more confident. I had a plan for where I was trying to go. The others spent more time filling days. . . . I knew what I was doing and why—from the beginning."

Unfortunately, most students in poor urban schools, especially students of color from low-income families, are much less likely to encounter this kind of confident, well-prepared teacher than they are to meet a string of underprepared teachers who suffer from their lack of training and often leave before they learn how to help students succeed. Nationwide, poor and minority students are far more likely than affluent students to have untrained and inexperienced teachers (NCTAF, 1996, 2003). In states that allow large loopholes in the certification and preparation requirements for teachers, there are schools where few teachers complete formal preparation for their job and where many have only the barest rudiments of initial training (Darling-Hammond, 2003, 2004). In virtually every case, these are segregated schools serving exclusively so-called minority students.

In states opting to reduce standards for teaching rather than promoting incentives to enter the profession, the most vulnerable students—those who most need strong teachers—are least likely to get them. Thus the second outcome of proposals to reduce requirements for teacher preparation is that existing inequities in access to expert teaching for rich and poor students will grow more severe. To advance knowledge about teaching, spread good practice, and enhance equity, strong preparation for teachers must become universal, not a rare occurrence available only to a lucky few.

Studying Successful Programs

The seven programs described in this book were selected after extensive review of evidence, including a nationwide reputational survey of researchers, expert practitioners, and scholars of teacher education; interviews with local employers about whom they prefer to hire and why; and outcomes from prior surveys of program graduates. (Appendix A discusses the study's methodology.) To these data about program outcomes, we added a survey of more than nine hundred beginning teachers about their preparation and practices, including graduates from these programs plus a national random sample of beginning teachers, used as a comparison group. We also surveyed the principals of program graduates about their views of graduates' abilities compared to those of other beginning teachers, and we observed graduates' classroom practice in their early years as teachers.

The study did three things. First, it documented the goals, strategies, content, and processes of programs widely acknowledged as exemplars for preparing prospective teachers to engage in skillful, learner-centered practice. Using a standard set of observation and interview protocols as well as survey instruments, a team of researchers examined all aspects of the program of study and clinical practice engaged in by students, by surveying graduates and their employers; shadowing and interviewing students; visiting classes, seminars, and professional development school sites; collecting record data (syllabi, assignments, student work, program descriptions, statistics); and observing and interviewing university-based and school-based faculty about the intentions, processes, and outcomes of their work.

Second, the study documented the capabilities of the prospective teachers who graduate from these programs. It examined the teachers' own work during teacher education and in the field (direct observations as well as artifacts of practice: portfolios, exhibitions, lesson plans, assignments, samples of students' work); surveys and interviews of graduates about how well prepared they felt in various domains when they entered the classroom; interviews with faculty and administrators in the schools where graduates teach; surveys of principals comparing the knowledge and skills of these candidates to others whom they have hired; and record data from other surveys and accreditation reviews.

Finally, the study examined what policies, organizational features, resources, and relationships enabled these programs to be successful, taking into account university and state policy contexts. The end result is a picture of what good teacher education looks like in practice, what those who have experienced it can do, and what it takes to provide this quality of preparation within and across universities and schools.

The seven institutions use distinctive models of preparation: undergraduate models that can be completed in four or four and a half years, five-year models combining undergraduate and graduate preparation in content and pedagogy, and postbaccalaureate models. Some have created professional development school relationships while others organize student teaching more traditionally; some use cohort models while others do not; some attract current or recent college graduates while others attract midcareer recruits into teaching. Together they represent diverse strategies for teacher education serving a range of clientele in different contexts.

The programs also have strong commonalities that are described in the chapters that follow:

○ In the remainder of Part One, I lay the groundwork for the discussion of program models by discussing how teacher education matters and why it is enormously difficult (Chapter Two). Chapter Three then presents program overviews and evidence of success.

○ The next three chapters, comprising Part Two, describe how these programs organize themselves to impart the knowledge, skills, and practices they value. Chapter Four discusses how they conceptualize the knowledge base for teaching and construct their curriculum, Chapter Five explains how the programs seek to develop and assess this knowledge through performance assessments that connect theory and practice, and Chapter Six illustrates how they construct clinical experiences—tightly interwoven with coursework—that accomplish this.

○ Part Three describes how the programs bring it all together: how they help teachers learn to manage the age-old dialectic between subject matter and students (Chapter Seven), teach in ways that promote equity (Chapter Eight), and develop strategies for reaching all learners, including those with learning differences (Chapter Nine).

○ The final two chapters (Part Four) address the issues that must be confronted if powerful teacher education is to become the norm, rather than the exception. Chapter Ten examines the change processes these programs have undertaken to strengthen their work and the institutional challenges that must be confronted within universities. Chapter Eleven takes up the broader policy issues affecting teacher education, arguing for a professional policy agenda to support teachers' access to knowledge and students' access to well-prepared teachers.

2

WHY TEACHER EDUCATION IS
IMPORTANT—AND DIFFICULT

TEACHERS CLEARLY AFFECT STUDENT LEARNING. Parents have long known, and researchers have recently confirmed, that a child's teacher can make a bigger difference to his or her educational success than most other school variables. Studies using value-added student achievement data find that student achievement gains are much more influenced by a student's assigned teacher than factors such as class size and composition (Sanders and Horn, 1994; Sanders and Rivers, 1996; Wright, Horn, and Sanders, 1997). A recent analysis by Rivkin, Hanushek, and Kain (2000) attributes at least 7 percent of the total variance in test-score gains to differences in teachers. Students who are assigned to a succession of highly effective teachers have significantly greater gains in achievement than those assigned to several ineffective teachers in sequence; the influence of a good or bad teacher affects a student's learning not only in that year but also in later years (Sanders and Rivers, 1996).

Despite a growing consensus that teachers matter, the role of teacher education in teachers' effectiveness is a matter of debate. Education schools have been criticized as ineffective in preparing teachers for their work, unresponsive to new demands, remote from practice, or obstacles to the recruitment of bright college students into teaching. President George H. W. Bush's only education proposal on election in 1988 was to encourage alternative teacher certification that could bypass schools of education. Since 1990, more than forty states have enacted alternate routes to certification to create pathways into teaching other than those provided by traditional undergraduate teacher education programs. Although most of these are university-based and some are carefully structured postbaccalaureate programs, others reduce formal training to only a few weeks. In 1995, Newt Gingrich proposed eliminating teacher certification rules as his major education initiative. In 1999, Chester Finn and the Thomas B. Fordham Foundation issued a manifesto arguing against teacher education requirements as a "barrier" to entering teaching.

Dissatisfaction has been raised from within the profession as well. Over the last two decades, traditional teacher education practices have been critiqued by the Holmes Group of education deans (Holmes Group, 1986) and the Carnegie Task Force on Teaching as a Profession (1986), along with scholars such as John Goodlad (1990), Ken Howey and Nancy Zimpher (1989), and Ken Zeichner (1993), among others. These voices, however, have urged the redesign of teacher education to strengthen its knowledge base, connections to practice and theory, and capacity to support the development of powerful teaching. These critiques have led to substantive reforms in teacher preparation that are reflected in the programs we studied, as well as many others.

Although debates on these questions have been largely ideological, there is a growing body of empirical evidence about the outcomes of different approaches to teacher education and recruitment. This research suggests that the extent and quality of teacher education matter for teachers' effectiveness and add significant value to the general knowledge and skills that teachers with a strong subject matter background bring to the classroom. This may be increasingly true as teachers experience greater demands as a result of the expectation that schools teach a much more diverse group of students for much higher standards. Teaching *all* students for problem solving, invention, and application of knowledge requires teachers with deep and flexible knowledge of subject matter who know how to represent ideas in powerful ways, organize a productive learning process for students who start with different levels and kinds of prior knowledge, assess how and what students are learning, and adapt instruction to different learning approaches. This is no mean feat.

How Teacher Education Matters

Although many people believe that anyone can teach—or, at least, that knowing a subject is enough to allow one to teach it well—the evidence strongly suggests otherwise. Reviews of research conducted since the 1960s have concluded that, even with the admitted shortcomings of current teacher education and licensing, fully prepared and certified teachers are generally better rated and more successful with students (Evertson, Hawley, and Zlotnik, 1985; Ashton and Crocker, 1986; Olsen, 1985; Wilson, Floden, and Ferrini-Mundy, 2001). As Evertson and colleagues concluded in one such review: "The available research suggests that among students who become teachers, those enrolled in formal preservice preparation programs are more likely to be effective than those who do not have such training. Moreover, almost all well planned and executed efforts within teacher preparation programs to teach students specific knowledge or skills seem to succeed, at least in the short run" (Evertson, Hawley, and Zlotnik, 1985, p. 8).

A review commissioned by the U.S. Department of Education, which analyzed fifty-seven studies that met specific research criteria and were published in peer-reviewed journals, found relationships between teacher education and effectiveness in controlled studies across units of analysis and measures of preparation (Wilson, Floden, and Ferrini-Mundy, 2001).

Several aspects of teacher qualifications have been found to bear some relationship to student achievement: (1) general academic and verbal ability, (2) subject matter knowledge, (3) knowledge about teaching and learning as reflected in teacher education courses or preparation experience, (4) teaching experience, and (5) the combined set of qualifications measured by teacher certification, which generally includes the preceding factors. Most state licensure systems now require candidates to earn a minimum grade point average in undergraduate courses or pass tests of academic skills, hold a major or minor in the subject to be taught or pass a test of subject matter knowledge, complete a defined set of teacher education courses and sometimes a test of pedagogical knowledge as well, and complete supervised experience as a student teacher or intern.

Studies using national data and other state data sets have found significant relationships between teacher certification measures and student achievement at the level of the individual teacher (Darling-Hammond, Holtzman, Gatlin, and Heilig, 2005; Goldhaber and Brewer, 2000; Hawk, Coble, and Swanson, 1985); the school (Betts, Rueben, and Danenberg, 2000; Fetler, 1999; Goe, 2002); the school district (Ferguson, 1991; Strauss and Sawyer, 1986); and state (Darling-Hammond, 2000).

Some of these studies have found effects of teacher expertise that match or outweigh the well-known influences of race and family income. For example, Ron Ferguson's analysis (1991) of Texas school districts found that teachers' expertise (including scores on a licensing examination measuring basic skills and teaching knowledge, master's degree, and experience) accounted for more of the interdistrict variation in students' reading and mathematics achievement in grades one through eleven than student socioeconomic status. The effects were so strong and variations in teacher expertise so great that, after controlling for socioeconomic status, the large disparity in achievement between black and white students was almost entirely accounted for by differences in the qualifications of their teachers. This finding contravenes the common presumption that students' backgrounds determine their achievement and that school variables make little difference in educational outcomes.

In North Carolina, Strauss and Sawyer (1986) found a similarly strong influence on average school district test performance of teachers' average score on the National Teacher Examinations that measure subject matter and teaching knowledge. With community wealth and other resources taken into account, teachers' test scores had a strikingly large effect on student success on the state competency examinations: a 1 percent increase in teacher quality (measured by NTE scores) yielded a 3–5 percent decline in the number of students failing the exam. The authors' conclusion was similar to Ferguson's: "Of the inputs which are potentially policy-controllable (teacher quality, teacher numbers via the pupil-teacher ratio and capital stock) our analysis indicates quite clearly that improving the quality of teachers in the classroom will do more for students who are most educationally at risk, those prone to fail, than reducing the class size or improving the capital stock by any reasonable margin which would be available to policy makers" (p. 47).

Other research on teacher certification at the individual teacher level is consistent with these findings. In a comparison group study of 36 middle school mathematics teachers and 826 students in North Carolina, where teachers were matched by years of experience and school setting, Hawk, Coble, and Swanson (1985) found that the students of fully certified mathematics teachers experienced significantly higher gains in achievement than those taught by teachers not certified in mathematics. The differences were greater for algebra classes than general mathematics.

A well-controlled study of high school students' performance in mathematics and science using data from the National Educational Longitudinal Studies of 1988 (NELS) found that fully certified mathematics teachers have a significant positive impact on student test scores compared to those not certified in their subject area, beyond the positive effect of a degree in mathematics or mathematics education (Goldhaber and Brewer, 2000). A longitudinal study of individual student level data in Houston using similar controls found that elementary school students of certified teachers consistently outperformed those of uncertified teachers over six years on six different tests in reading and mathematics (Darling-Hammond, Holtzman, Gatlin, and Heilig, 2005).

In states such as Texas and California, where licensing systems allow many teachers to enter through backdoor loopholes, the association between certification and teachers' effectiveness appears to be particularly strong. A recent set of Texas studies (Fuller, 1998, 2000; Alexander and Fuller, 2004) show students in districts, schools, and classrooms with more fully licensed teachers significantly more likely to pass the Texas state achievement tests, after controlling for student socioeconomic status, school wealth, and teacher experience. Three school-level analyses of student test performance in California found a strong negative relationship between average student scores in reading and mathematics and the percentage of teachers on emergency certificates, after controlling for student poverty (Betts, Rueben, and Danenberg, 2000; Fetler, 1999; Goe, 2002).

Studies also show that teacher qualifications are unequally allocated to students by race, income, and location. These unequal distributions are one important source of the achievement gap. In California (see Figure 2.1), Massachusetts, South Carolina, and Texas, for example, state data used in school finance lawsuits between 2000 and 2004 showed elementary school students in high-minority schools three to five times as likely as those in low-minority schools to have teachers without training or certification (Darling-Hammond, 2003, 2004). Even where students in low-income and minority schools are held to the same standards on state reading and math tests to progress from grade to grade or to graduate from high school, the states gave no guarantee that these students would have teachers prepared to teach them to read, understand mathematics, or succeed in other disciplines.

Figure 2.1. Distribution of Underqualified Teachers in California

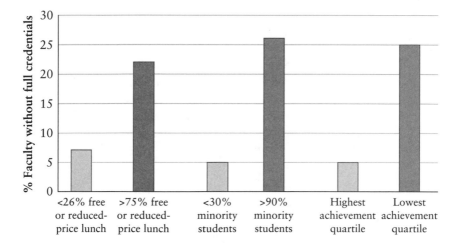

Source: *Shields and others, 2001.*

In California during the late 1990s, a group of schools emerged that might be characterized as "apartheid schools." These schools, serving exclusively students of color in low-income communities, feature crumbling, overcrowded buildings; no libraries and few materials; old and dilapidated texts so scarce that students have to share them in class and cannot take them out for homework; and a revolving-door teaching force, more than half of which are inexperienced and untrained. Not surprisingly, the correlations between student SES, proportion of emergency credentialed teachers, and test score performance are almost perfect under conditions where resources are allocated so unequally by race and class (Figure 2.2). In the most affected schools, lack of preparation for so many teachers compounds the problems individuals experience, as there are too few knowledgeable teachers to give the curriculum guidance, mentoring, and support that untrained and inexperienced teachers need if they are to learn (Shields and others, 2001).

Where the Rubber Meets the Road: How Preparation Matters in the Classroom

There is certainly wide variability in the skills and effectiveness of individuals who have received teacher certification, which is merely a proxy

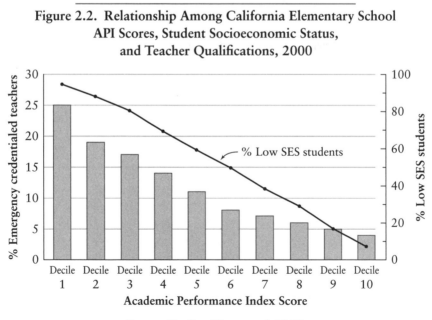

Figure 2.2. Relationship Among California Elementary School API Scores, Student Socioeconomic Status, and Teacher Qualifications, 2000

Source: *Darling-Hammond, 2003.*

for the specific knowledge and skills teachers need. Yet it is striking how much the absence of even the minimal preparation represented by a credential appears to matter, not only in large-scale quantitative studies but also in the experiences of teachers and their students.

In the late 1990s in California, for example, nearly 50 percent of entering teachers did not have a teaching credential, and these teachers were hired in the growing urban districts serving the neediest students. This phenomenon figured prominently in a school equity lawsuit, *Williams* v. *California,* which charged that many students were deprived of their basic right to an education by the lack of expertise represented by the flood of underqualified teachers into these schools. In their testimony in that lawsuit, many principals and teachers were forceful in asserting that certification is an important indicator of teaching ability (Darling-Hammond, 2003).

These witnesses described how, in their experience, credentialed teachers "know what to do and require less assistance" and encounter fewer problems with classroom management and teaching strategies. They called credentialing "as important to teaching as a driver's license is to driving a car" and "as essential as such training is to the qualifications of a dentist." As one principal noted, "I think a lot of people think they can be a teacher because they've gone to school, and I don't necessarily think that that is a fact. For a person to come to the educational setting, they need to be armed, if you will, with various strategies that they are going to use in the classroom. . . . So I would like to see future teachers truly have a year of methodology classes and observation and student teaching under a quality master teacher where they can try things . . . [and] effectively evaluate what [they] are doing" (cited in Darling-Hammond, 2003).

Friedlaender and Frenkel (2002) observed in their study of seventeen hard-to-staff California schools that "school and district officials consider credentialed teachers to be a 'valued commodity' and quickly hired the best qualified credentialed teachers" (p. 8). Uncredentialed teachers they interviewed often commented on their own lack of preparation. At one school, the researchers wrote of three uncredentialed teachers they interviewed:

> All three teachers asserted that they did not feel adequately prepared to teach in their current teaching assignment. They agreed that they had a difficult time with curriculum development and implementation as well as classroom management. All three teachers ascribed their inadequacy to the fact that they had not participated in a formal teacher education program before entering the profession. . . . All of

the teachers also spoke extensively about the fact that most of their students are English learners. The teachers agreed that they were not adequately trained to teach this population of students. They also seemed to resent the fact that the students and their families are not proficient in English because it creates "double the workload" for them as they planned instruction and carried out the required assessment measures [*Williams v. California, Malabed Deposition*, v.2, 308:19–309:17].

Teachers deposed for the lawsuit described how teaching alongside uncredentialed teachers is a problem not only for these novices without training, but also for prepared teachers who must deal with the spillover effects of the lower levels of competence untrained teachers possess:

> [One teacher] was considering a career change and came in and taught our special ed class for a year. During the time she was in that class, she was taking one or two courses out at (State College) to get her credential in teaching special ed, but she wasn't technically qualified and there was no one on the site who was able to advise her or train her or support her appropriately. She had a pretty miserable year and she admitted candidly to many of us that she felt underqualified, sometimes unqualified, and absolutely did not know what she was doing in there. You could tell she was very stressed and very strained. As a peer, it was hard to watch her and it was hard to watch her kids function in the room with somebody who was not experienced and qualified [*Williams v. California, Malabed Deposition*, v.2, 308:19–309:17].

> It was a topic that was . . . discussed at the lunch table about the fact we had a class that had had so many substitutes and had had an uncredentialed teacher who was not able to handle the situation and ended up not returning and the kids were going to struggle and that the . . . teachers who received them the next year would probably have a difficult time with those students because of what they had been through the prior year [*Williams v. California, Salyer Deposition*, v.1, 167:21–168:15].

In addition to many principals who explained why they seek to hire credentialed teachers who know how to manage classes and plan curriculum, many experienced teachers described the difference between the skills of credentialed and uncredentialed teachers they worked with, citing specific teacher education courses and strategies that they saw as essential, particularly with respect to teaching students with learning needs or language needs who flounder or misbehave if they are not skill-fully supported.

Teachers who entered teaching without preparation provided the most eloquent assessment of what they learn from a teacher education program, as this recruit, who entered teaching on an emergency credential and later attended a high-quality preparation program, explained:

> I believe that emergency-credentialed teachers, generally speaking, are not going into classrooms with enough tools, nor are they going in with appropriate lenses for looking at the classroom [*Williams v. California, Medina Deposition,* v.2, 383:3–20].
>
> The best way to do this is to compare myself as a teacher now and myself as a teacher back then. Upon entering . . . my teacher-credentialing program, I've gained a lot of tools how to better address students' needs. As an uncredentialed teacher, I was not aware that I should take literacy into a large consideration into their education. As an uncredentialed teacher, I wasn't emphasizing reading as a skill as the very backbone of communication to my students. As an uncredentialed teacher, I didn't have tools for discipline. I didn't have tools for what good discipline is and what bad discipline looks like. I wasn't taking into consideration the long-term effects of how my classroom policies shifted. As an uncredentialed teacher, I didn't have great record-keeping skills. As an uncredentialed teacher, I had no idea how students were developing biologically, socially during this high time of change. As an uncredentialed teacher, I hadn't looked at or I hadn't compared formally what good teaching looks like and what bad teaching looks like and I've since done so, looking at teachers internationally and just across the state. I didn't have the tools. I wasn't thinking about multiple representations. I wasn't thinking about multiple intelligences. I wasn't thinking about equity. I wasn't thinking about gender equity, racial equity while I was teaching and all of these things really stem from my experience in my credential program and so with these lenses, I'm better able to serve my students. But before those lenses were available to me, I don't think I was doing an adequate job. . . . [*Williams v. California, Medina Deposition,* v.2, 375:17–377:6].

The Debate About Which Aspects of Teacher Knowledge Matter

Much of the debate over teacher quality has been about whether general academic ability and strong subject matter knowledge are sufficient background for effective teaching and whether pedagogical preparation—in learning and development, teaching strategies, curriculum, and assess-ment—is crucial for teacher success or a barrier to entry. Opponents of preparation requirements often note that if Albert Einstein (or any other noted intellect or public official) wanted to teach in a public school, he would not be able to do so, because of credentialing requirements. Those who think this statement is prima facie evidence that certification require-ments are misguided assume that anyone as smart as Einstein could indeed effectively teach a classroom of thirty squirrelly students of diverse abili-ties. But could he?

IS SMART ENOUGH? Some proponents of eliminating pedagogical requirements argue that selecting teachers who score high on tests of gen-eral ability would produce a more effective teaching force. As the previ-ously mentioned secretary's report on teacher quality asserted, "Rigorous research indicates that verbal ability and content knowledge are the most important attributes of highly qualified teachers" (U.S. Department of Education, 2002, p. 19). This statement, however, is not grounded in re-search. Although there is research that finds relationships between student achievement and some measures of verbal ability and content knowledge, there is no evidence that these areas of knowledge are more consequen-tial to student achievement than knowledge of teaching.

The problem with this argument is that studies that look at one side of the question rarely look simultaneously at the other. For example, mea-sures of general academic and verbal ability have been most readily avail-able in large data sets since the 1960s, and a number of studies have suggested that these general teacher abilities are related to student achieve-ment (Bowles and Levin, 1968; Coleman and others, 1966; Hanushek, 1971, 1992; Ferguson and Ladd, 1996). In addition, some researchers have found a relationship between the selectivity of the college a teacher at-tended and students' achievement (Ehrenberg and Brewer, 1994).

Critics of teacher education point to these studies as evidence that ver-bal ability is the most important predictor of teacher effectiveness (Walsh, 2001). However, the datasets used did not include other measures of teacher knowledge and skill. Economist Richard Murnane (1983) pointed out twenty years ago that evidence on the influence of verbal ability was partly a function of the fact that standardized test scores were one of the few variables about teachers available in large-scale databases at that time, which did not include good measures of teacher education. He noted: "Clearly one should not interpret these results as indicating that intellectual ability should be the sole criterion used in recruiting teachers or that formal teacher training cannot make a difference. In fact, the lack of evidence supporting formal pre-service training as a source of competence may be to some extent a result of limitations in the available data" (p. 565).

It is incorrect to infer from these studies that verbal ability trumps preparation as a predictor of effectiveness. More recent data sets that include measures of other kinds of teaching knowledge, including knowledge of content and pedagogy, find that they are significant contributors to teacher effectiveness.

Several studies have sought to examine these questions by looking at the effectiveness of teachers recruited through Teach for America (TFA)—many of whom are from selective universities—who receive a few weeks of training before they begin teaching. The program is often seen as an existence proof for the argument that bright, committed individuals can teach successfully without formal teacher training. For example, Raymond, Fletcher, and Luque (2001), who conducted one study of the program, suggest that "TFA corps members are an admittedly select group of college graduates, culled from the finest universities and often performing near the top of their class. . . . It's possible that traditional certification programs and pedagogical training are less necessary for them than they are for the typical teacher" (p. 68).

Their study did not examine the results of preparation or certification. It found that TFA recruits' students achieved learning gains comparable to or better than those of other beginning teachers in similar schools on the state TAAS tests; however, the other teachers were also largely untrained and uncertified. This study and another comparing TFA recruits to the largely unprepared teachers in their schools (Decker, Mayer, and Glazerman, 2004) also found that the students taught by these underqualified teachers—almost exclusively low-income and minority students in inner-city schools—made little progress in achievement under the teachers they were assigned, whether TFA recruits or not. A competing study using a matched comparison design found that students of uncertified teachers in Arizona (including TFA teachers) did significantly less well than those of comparably experienced certified teachers on mathematics, reading, and language arts tests (Laczko-Kerr and Berliner, 2002). However, that study did not control for prior student achievement.

When teachers' certification for teaching is considered and students' prior achievement is controlled, the answer is much clearer. A replication of the Raymond, Fletcher, and Luque study confirmed that uncertified TFA recruits in Houston were significantly less effective than certified teachers and performed about as well as other uncertified teachers with comparable experience in similar settings. TFA recruits who became certified after two or three years did about as well as other comparably experienced certified teachers in supporting student learning gains. As with other teachers, the effectiveness of these bright young recruits depended substantially on their preparation for teaching (Darling-Hammond, Holtzman, Gatlin, and Heilig, 2005).

General academic ability is helpful and important but insufficient by itself for knowing how to teach students who may struggle to learn. While well-educated people may have the advantage of having had some good teachers whom they can seek to emulate in their own classrooms, the underlying work of teaching is typically invisible to students. What looks easy from the students' vantage point—giving gripping lectures, holding scintillating discussion, assigning challenging tasks, providing insightful feedback—is a function of behind-the-scenes planning, resting on many bodies of knowledge about learning, curriculum, and teaching. It may even be that the problem of not knowing how to support student learning is exacerbated for highly able teachers without training, because they have always learned easily themselves and have few referents in their personal experience regarding how many young people struggle to learn and what might be done to help them. A young TFA recruit who left teaching but later entered a preparation program described this phenomenon poignantly: "I felt very troubled about going into an elementary classroom having had six weeks [of training]. I didn't even know where to start. I was unprepared to deal with every aspect. . . . I had a lot of kids who were frustrated and I was frustrated because I wanted to help them and didn't have the training to do that."

Said another first-year TFA dropout who later went to medical school:

> I could maybe have done a bad job at a suburban high school. I stood to do an awful job at a school where you needed to have special skills. I just didn't have the tools, and I didn't even know I needed them before I went in. I felt like, "OK, I did the workshops; I know science; and I care about these kids." You know, I had the motivation to help, but I didn't have the skill. It's sort of like wanting to fix someone's car and not having any idea how to fix a car. I wasn't equipped to deal with it, and I had no idea.

HOW MUCH DOES KNOWING THE SUBJECT MATTER? A similar debate pits subject matter versus pedagogical knowledge as to their relative value in teacher training. The zero-sum logic that has often characterized this debate is in part a function of the short time typically allocated for training teachers, which has made many wonder whether solid training in both can be accomplished in the time available.

A fair reading of the research concludes that teachers' subject matter knowledge and knowledge of teaching and learning actually appear to interact in determining teacher effectiveness. In separate reviews of research, Ashton and Crocker (1986, 1987) and Evertson, Hawley, and Zlotnik (1985) reported positive effects of subject matter background and teachers' formal education training on supervisory ratings and student learning. Byrne (1983) summarized the results of thirty studies examining the relationship between student achievement and teachers' subject matter knowledge, measured either by a subject knowledge test (standardized or researcher-constructed) or number of college courses taken in the subject area. Among these studies, seventeen showed a positive relationship. Byrne noted that many of the "no relationship" studies had so little variability in the teacher knowledge measure that insignificant findings were almost inevitable. In addition, Byrne suggests that the positive effect is likely mediated by knowledge of how to teach the subject to various kinds of students: "It is surely plausible to suggest that insofar as a teacher's knowledge provides the basis for his or her effectiveness, the most relevant knowledge will be that which concerns the particular topic being taught and the relevant pedagogical strategies for teaching it to the particular types of pupils to whom it will be taught. If the teacher is to teach fractions, then it is knowledge of fractions and perhaps of closely associated topics which is of major importance. . . . Similarly, knowledge of teaching strategies relevant to teaching fractions will be important" (p. 14).

The importance of subject matter knowledge and the additional influence of teaching knowledge and skill are suggested in other research. Goldhaber and Brewer (2000) found positive effects of teachers' subject-matter degrees in mathematics or mathematics education and strong influences of teacher certification on student achievement, with certification having an even stronger influence than a major or minor in the field taught. They report:

> We find that the type (standard, emergency, etc.) of certification a teacher holds is an important determinant of student outcomes. In mathematics, we find that students of teachers who are either not certified in their subject . . . or hold a private school certification do less well than students whose teachers hold a standard, probationary, or emergency certification in math. Roughly speaking, having a teacher with a standard certification in mathematics rather than a private

school certification or a certification out of subject results in at least a 1.3 point increase in the mathematics test. *This is equivalent to about 10% of the standard deviation on the 12th-grade test, a little more than the impact of having a teacher with a BA and MA in mathematics.* Though the effects are not as strong in magnitude or statistical significance, the pattern of results in science mimics that in mathematics [p. 139; emphasis added].

Finding a large effect of certification status even after controlling for teachers' experience and a subject matter degrees (an element of certification in most states) suggests that what teachers learn about teaching in a preparation program adds to what they gain from a strong content background and classroom experience.

Monk (1994) obtained similar findings when he looked at teachers' coursework in content and pedagogy in his analysis of data for 2,829 students from the Longitudinal Study of American Youth (LSAY). Teachers' content preparation, measured by subject field coursework, was usually positively related to student achievement in mathematics and science. In mathematics, teachers' subject matter courses showed diminishing returns above a threshold level (about five courses). In addition, teacher education coursework (e.g., mathematics or science methods courses) had a positive effect on student learning at each grade level in both fields; in mathematics such courses sometimes had "more powerful effects than additional preparation in the content area" (p. 142). Monk concluded that "a good grasp of one's subject area is a necessary but not a sufficient condition for effective teaching" (p. 142).

Monk's findings appear to suggest that subject matter knowledge influences teacher effectiveness up to some level of basic competence but less so thereafter. Begle and Geeslin (1972) also found in their review of research on mathematics teaching that the absolute number of course credits in mathematics was related to teacher performance but not linearly so. It makes sense that knowledge of the material to be taught is essential to good teaching, but also that returns to subject matter expertise might grow smaller beyond some level that exceeds the demands of the curriculum being taught. Like Monk, Begle (1979) found in his review of findings of the National Longitudinal Study of Mathematical Abilities that the number of credits a teacher had in mathematics methods courses was an even stronger correlate of student performance than was the number of credits in mathematics courses.

The strength of the relationship between subject matter knowledge and student performance may also depend on the level of the content being taught. In a multilevel analysis of the LSAY, Monk and King (1994) found small influences of teacher content background on student performance in science and mathematics; the effect of teachers' subject matter background differed for high- and low-achieving students and by grade level.

Similarly, in a review of sixty-five studies of science teachers' characteristics and behaviors, Druva and Anderson (1983) found students' science achievement was positively related to teachers' background in both science coursework and education, with the former showing a stronger relationship to student achievement in higher-level science courses, and the amount of education coursework showing a significant correlation with ratings of teacher effectiveness. Hawk, Coble, and Swanson (1985) also found the effect of having a fully certified teacher in mathematics— one with strong background in the content and knowledge of teaching methods in the subject—greater for algebra courses than for general mathematics courses. Mandeville and Liu (1997) found that teachers' specialized training in mathematics was a more important predictor of seventh grade students' math performance on high-level mathematics problems than on low-level problems. It seems logical that teachers need more subject matter knowledge to teach more complex aspects of the content area.

Using data from the National Assessment of Educational Progress, Wenglinsky (2000, 2002) examined the relationships among teacher training, teaching practices, and student achievement, controlling for student characteristics and other school inputs. He found that eighth grade students did better on the NAEP mathematics assessments if they had teachers with a major or minor in mathematics or mathematics education, more professional training in how to work with diverse student populations (a combined measure of training in cultural diversity, teaching limited-English-proficient students, and teaching students with special needs), more training in how to develop higher-order thinking skills, and who engaged in hands-on learning emphasizing higher-order thinking. Similarly, students did better on the NAEP science assessments when they had teachers who majored in science or science education, who had more training in developing laboratory skills, and who engaged in hands-on learning. The measures of professional training in this study included both preservice coursework and in-service training.

Finally, a recent study conducted by the International Reading Association found that new teacher graduates of eight programs featuring strong preparation for the teaching of reading typically produced larger achievement gains for their students than other novice teachers did.

One lesson of this body of research is that teachers are more effective when they understand how to make subject matter accessible to learners by joining their understanding of a specific domain—such as reading, mathematics, or science—to their understanding of how students learn in that domain. Knowing how students understand (and sometimes *mis-*understand) particular subjects and having a repertoire of strategies to help students engage ideas central to the discipline is at the core of *pedagogical content knowledge* (Shulman, 1987; Grossman and Schoenfeld, 2005). The subject does matter centrally for teachers not only in its own right as the grist for teaching but also as the context for developing understanding of teaching that enables learning.

The Dilemmas of Teacher Education

This research suggests that the *kind* of teacher education matters. For all the evidence that teachers benefit from learning about their craft, it is also true that many teachers feel underprepared for the real challenges they face in their work. Indeed, one survey of three thousand beginning teachers in New York City found they varied widely in how well prepared they felt for teaching (Darling-Hammond, Chung, and Frelow, 2002). Those who entered without training or through an alternative route felt least well prepared, but feelings of preparedness for the tasks of teaching also varied among graduates of different teacher education programs, from just adequate to extremely well prepared.

Developing teacher education that consistently and powerfully influences practice is not an easy matter. Virtually all scholars of professional preparation note the difficulty of helping individuals learn the ways of thinking and acting required by a profession (how to "think like a doctor" or "reason like a lawyer") and then translating those diagnostic and analytic abilities into concrete actions in situations that are nonroutine and require quick but complex judgments and hands-on skills. Professional education must also help clients assume the ethical responsibilities and moral dispositions all professions require—to make decisions in the best interest of the client, acquire new knowledge to help those being served, and seek new solutions when efforts do not succeed.

These complexities pose a challenge to every profession, but teaching may be even more complex than law, medicine, or engineering. Rather than serving one client at a time, teachers work with groups of twenty-five to thirty at once, each with unique needs and proclivities. Teachers must balance these variables, along with a multitude of sometimes competing goals, and negotiate the demands of the content matter along with individual and group needs. They must draw on many kinds of knowledge—

of learning and development, social contexts and culture, language and expression, curriculum and teaching—and integrate what they know to create engaging tasks and solve learning problems for a range of students who learn differently. They must balance the often conflicting desires of school boards, legislators, parents, administrators, colleagues, and students, creating a coherent community within which both learning and social growth can occur. Further, the problem of learning to teach is complicated by the common experience virtually all adults have had of school, which creates strong views among prospective teachers and members of the community alike about what school and teaching are "supposed" to be.

Three Problems in Learning to Teach

Learning to teach—like learning to practice any profession—is no simple matter. In fact, there are some special, perennial challenges in learning to teach. Three in particular stand out. First, learning to teach requires new teachers to understand teaching in ways quite different from their own experience as students. Lortie (1975) called this problem "the apprenticeship of observation," referring to the learning that takes place by virtue of being a student for twelve or more years in traditional classroom settings. Second, learning to teach requires that new teachers not only learn to "think like a teacher" but also to "*act* like a teacher"—what Mary Kennedy (1999) terms "the problem of enactment." Teachers need to *do* a wide variety of things, many of them simultaneously. Finally, learning to teach requires new teachers to understand and respond to the dense and multifaceted nature of the classroom, juggling multiple academic and social goals that set up trade-offs from moment to moment and day to day (Jackson, 1974). They must learn to deal with this "problem of complexity," which derives from the nonroutine and constantly changing nature of teaching and learning in groups.

The Problem of the "Apprenticeship of Observation"

A significant challenge teachers face is that they enter teaching having already had years of experience in schools. Although this prior experience of schools and teaching can be an important source of motivation for teachers, as an "apprenticeship" it has important limits: "Students do not receive invitations to watch the teacher's performance through the wings; they are not privy to the teacher's private intentions and personal reflections on classroom events. Students rarely participate in selecting goals, making preparations or postmortem analysis. Thus they are not pressed to place the teacher's actions in a pedagogically oriented framework" (Lortie, 1975, p. 62).

Indeed, Lortie concludes that such experiences often lead to a "widespread idea that 'anyone can teach'"; meanwhile, the limited vantage point of the student results not in acquisition of professional knowledge but in a tendency to imitate superficial aspects of teaching. Munby, Russell, and Martin (2001) add that even when observing good teaching or experiencing it for oneself, one cannot easily glean a deep understanding of the complexity of the work: "Good teaching tends to reinforce the view that teaching is effortless because the knowledge and experience supporting it are invisible to those taught. Good teaching looks like the ordering and deployment of skills, so learning to teach looks like acquiring the skills" (p. 887).

Therefore individuals often enter teaching assuming they know how to teach and believing all that is required are a few strategies, skills, and some technical routines. Furthermore, many people enter teaching with a conception of *learning* as the simple and rather mechanistic "transfer" of information (Feiman-Nemser and Buchmann, 1989). Preconceptions that teaching is only about transmission make it difficult to prepare teachers to teach in ways that are compatible with what we now know about how people learn (Bransford, Brown, and Cocking, 1999). These more successful methods often differ fundamentally from how student teachers were taught, and sometimes from how the teacher educators themselves learned as students (Borko and Mayfield, 1995). Even more difficult, teacher educators often find themselves trying to develop modes of teaching that are dramatically different from the classrooms in which student teaching occurs (Bramald, Hardman, and Leat, 1995).

Many other beliefs preservice teachers tend to bring to their classrooms hold unexamined assumptions that must be made explicit and explored. These include beliefs that good teaching rests primarily on personality factors (such as caring), teaching styles, and concern for individual children, with little appreciation of the role of social context, subject matter, or pedagogical knowledge (Paine, 1990). If these beliefs are not explicitly addressed, prospective teachers may never learn to incorporate other kinds of knowledge or develop needed skills (Richardson and Placier, 2001).

Countering this apprenticeship of observation and the accompanying naïve beliefs about teaching may be one of the most powerful challenges in learning to teach. To confront this challenge, some teacher educators have reframed their approach to surface and build on the ideas that prospective teachers bring with them. Indeed, Wideen and colleagues

(1998) note that while these beliefs are often considered by teacher educators to be problematic misconceptions, an alternative perspective is to treat them as prior knowledge that must be built on, challenged, or deepened.

The Problem of Enactment

A second challenge teacher educators and novice teachers face is the problem of enactment. This problem often surfaces in complaints that teacher education is too theoretical, by which teachers often mean they have not learned about concrete tools and practices that let them put into action the ideas they have encountered. Teachers-in-training must not only understand how people learn and what teaching strategies may help them; they must also learn to present information clearly, lead discussions that really get at the ideas under study, manage discourse of many kinds, organize groups for learning and give them useful tasks they can do, manage student behavior, weigh difficult dilemmas and make quick decisions, plan well and alter plans for unforeseen circumstances, respond to children, and respond to questions about the material they are teaching.

Some might describe this kind of learning as being able to "apply" knowledge to practice; others suggest that separating theory from practice, even intellectually, creates a false dichotomy. Indeed, Schön (1983) has argued that there are some kinds of professions—including teaching—in which theory is embedded in and inseparable from practice. Learning how to think and act in ways that achieve one's intentions is difficult, particularly if knowledge is embedded in the practice itself. For example, information about what ideas students have developed about a topic, how they understand or misunderstand the material being taught, and how each learns best emerges in the actual work of teaching—and guides the planning and instruction that follows. How strategies work with this or that *group* of students, as well as individuals, also emerges in the course of enacting plans and cannot be fully known ahead of time in the abstract.

Kennedy (1999) attributes the problem of enactment in part to the prior knowledge novices bring from their apprenticeship of observation. She points out that many concepts that educators are interested in helping preservice teachers understand (such as cooperative learning, assessment, or diversity) are things most people already have experience with through their own lengthy schooling. Teacher educators hope to help new teachers develop practical skills tied to a theoretically based understanding of these ideas, but preservice teachers already have clear ideas about these concepts that may interfere with or contradict what they learn in their preservice program. For example, prospective teachers may have participated in successful or unsuccessful group work and have views or strong beliefs about collaborative learning. However, they might *not* know that effective collaboration requires tasks or problems that actually demand diverse perspectives, allocation of time for making sufficient progress, scaffolding of critical skills, and so forth (Brown and Campione, 1996; Cohen and Lotan, 1995). Whether they experienced unguided, poorly planned group work or well-designed collaborative tasks, they may not know what elements made the experience more or less productive.

Novices bring their own frames of reference to the ideas they encounter in teacher education; these may be incompatible with the approaches they are learning about in their coursework and clinical work. In addition, such concepts can be associated with a range of behaviors and, in fitting concepts into what they imagine or have seen before, beginning teachers may enact certain ideals about practice differently from what their preservice program hopes or intends. This is particularly likely if they have no chance to engage in a strong clinical experience where critical concepts are modeled in practice and deconstructed for further study and understanding. Furthermore, individual practices, even when observed and rehearsed, must still be bundled intricately together to accomplish the many goals of teaching.

The Problem of Complexity

A third challenge in learning to teach is that teaching is an incredibly complex and demanding task (Lampert, 2001; McDonald, 1992). As McDonald explains, "Real teaching happens within a wild triangle of relations—among teacher, students, subject—and the points of this triangle shift continuously. What shall I teach amid all that I should teach? How can I grasp it myself so that my grasping might enable theirs? What are they thinking and feeling—toward me, toward each other, toward the thing I am trying to teach? How near should I come, how far off should I stay? How much clutch, how much gas?" (p. 1).

Lampert elaborates on this complexity:

> One reason teaching is a complex practice is that many of the problems a teacher must address to get students to learn occur simultaneously, not one after another. Because of this simultaneity, several different problems must be addressed in a single action. And a

teacher's actions are not taken independently; there are interactions with students, individually and as a group. A teacher acts in different social arrangements in the same time frame. A teacher also acts in different time frames and at different levels of ideas with individuals, groups and the class to make each lesson coherent, to link one lesson to another, and to cover a curriculum over the course of a year. . . .

When I am teaching fifth-grade mathematics, for example, I teach a mathematical idea or procedure to a student while also teaching that student to be civil to classmates and to me, to complete the tasks assigned, and to think of himself and herself and everyone else in the class as capable of learning, no matter what their gender, race or parents' income. As I work to get students to learn something like "improper fractions," I know I will also need to be teaching them the meaning of division, how division relates to other operations, and the nature of our number system. While I take action to get some particular content to be studied by a particular student in a particular moment, I simultaneously have to do the work of engaging all of the students in my class in the lesson as a whole, even as I am paying different kinds of attention to groups of students with diverse characteristics. And I need to act in a way that preserves my potential to keep acting productively day after day, throughout the year [Lampert, 2001, p. 2].

Lampert's account of multiple considerations shaping her teaching of fifth-grade mathematics suggests at least four elements of complexity:

1. *Teaching is never routine.* The "wild triangle" to which McDonald refers is constantly shifting; teachers must cope with changing situations, learning needs, challenges, questions, and dilemmas.

2. *Teaching has multiple goals* that must be addressed simultaneously. At the same time Lampert is teaching content, she is teaching social and intellectual development, paying attention to children's individual needs.

3. *Teaching is done in relationship to diverse groups of students* who differ in cultural background and prior experience as well as learning needs, strengths, areas of challenge, and range of abilities.

4. *Teaching requires multiple kinds of knowledge to be integrated.* For instance, to advance the learning of all their students, teachers must constantly integrate their knowledge of child development; subject matter; group interaction; students' cultures and backgrounds; and their particular students' interests, needs, and strengths.

In sum, helping new teachers appreciate the multidimensionality and simultaneity of teaching (Jackson, 1974) is clearly no easy task.

Two other things make effective teaching more complex than ever before. First, because the mission of contemporary schools is to prepare a diverse set of students for highly ambitious learning, teachers must learn to enact a more complicated *kind* of teaching than in the past. They must be guided by curriculum goals that prepare students to think critically and perform at high levels, but they cannot achieve these goals by teaching a standardized curriculum. Teaching for deep understanding requires open-ended tasks and student-initiated inquiries whose course cannot be fully scripted; teachers must elicit and follow students' thinking and manage an active learning process that goes beyond direct transmission of facts and information to development of analytic skills and performance abilities. While being clear on the curriculum goals to be taught, teachers must also respond to the needs, backgrounds, and experiences of students themselves, combining relevance with rigor in their teaching.

Thus teachers must learn how to maintain a healthy dialectic between the goals of teaching subject matter toward a common set of curriculum objectives and teaching students in ways that attend to their diverse interests, abilities, starting points, and pathways. This is like simultaneously pursuing both sides of a double helix that repeatedly intertwines and separates and intertwines again: the teacher bends the curriculum toward the students by making connections and adaptations and then nudges students toward the curriculum by scaffolding and motivating their learning. Attending to the demands of the curriculum and the needs of the child without losing sight of either requires deep understanding of subject matter and students, and the potential for connections between the two. Doing this when the curriculum presses for deep understanding rather than rote recognition and recall adds to the challenge by requiring flexible content knowledge and a process of teaching that combines direct instruction with skillfully constructed problem solving that helps students develop strategies for independent learning and apply what they are learning to novel situations. Learning to teach for this kind of practice is far from formulaic. The teacher must develop analytic skills that allow her both to investigate curriculum to understand its demands and study students to understand their needs.

Lastly, teaching for this new educational mission is more complex today because teacher educators must prepare teachers for schooling as it should be, while enabling them to cope with schooling as it is.

Common Components of Powerful Teacher Education

How do strong programs of teacher preparation confront these and other problems of learning to teach? Our research on seven distinctive programs demonstrates that there is no cookie-cutter approach to excellence. Nonetheless, though they conduct their work differently we found that the programs had many common features (explored in the chapters to come):

- A common, clear vision of good teaching permeates all coursework and clinical experiences.
- Well-defined standards of practice and performance are used to guide and evaluate coursework and clinical work.
- Curriculum is grounded in knowledge of child and adolescent development, learning, social contexts, and subject matter pedagogy, taught in the context of practice.
- Extended clinical experiences are carefully developed to support the ideas and practices presented in simultaneous, closely interwoven coursework.
- Explicit strategies help students (1) confront their own deep-seated beliefs and assumptions about learning and students and (2) learn about the experiences of people different from themselves.
- Strong relationships, common knowledge, and shared beliefs link school- and university-based faculty.
- Case study methods, teacher research, performance assessments, and portfolio evaluation apply learning to real problems of practice.

These features help the programs productively confront many core dilemmas of teacher education: the strong influence of the apprenticeship of observation candidates bring with them from their years as students in elementary and secondary school, the presumed divide between theory and practice, the limitations of personal and cultural perspectives each person brings to the task of teaching, and the difficult process of helping people learn to enact their intentions in complex settings.

In what follows, we discuss these program features and illustrate what difference they make in the lives of teachers and children.

3

ADDRESSING THE DILEMMAS OF TEACHER EDUCATION

EVIDENCE OF SUCCESS

BECAUSE THE DILEMMAS OF LEARNING TO TEACH, described in the previous chapter, are not always addressed in teacher education, the conventional wisdom about beginning teachers' capabilities is that they are "overwhelmed," focusing primarily on basic survival and classroom management rather than student learning. The aim of classroom management training for such beginning teachers is generally to keep students relatively still and engaged, not necessarily learning powerfully. Qualitative and quantitative evidence about the practice of most beginning teachers suggests that they are indeed less confident and effective than most teachers with three or more years of experience (Feiman-Nemser, 2001; Hanushek, Kain, and Rivkin, 1998).

But as our team observed first-year teachers who had graduated from the programs we studied, we saw something very different. We saw new teachers who constructed well-functioning communities of students engaged in serious intellectual learning.

For example, on the day we visited "Lisa Bransford," a first-year teacher who had just graduated from Bank Street, at Midtown West Elementary School in New York City, she was holding a meeting with her twenty-nine very diverse kindergartners and first graders. Bransford and her students were discussing the message conveyed by children's author Vera Williams. They debated whether Williams's stories always or only sometimes portray children and families saving money for something special or overcoming a family dilemma. The children and their teacher looked for evidence of literary style by reviewing her books, characters, plots, and illustrations. The chart in front of the class indicated that author studies were common in this class. Williams's books were cited along with all of Eric Carl's books, evaluated by the children several months earlier.

As she listened intently and carefully guided the conversation to engage as many children as possible with each other on the topic at hand, it was clear Lisa had moved past the rudimentary concerns of many first-year teachers for classroom discipline. Not only were her kindergarten and first-grade students interacting respectfully and attentively with one another, they were becoming competent readers, tackling serious literary questions not usually addressed until middle school. In later conversations, Lisa credited her preservice program, her principal and colleagues (also Bank Street graduates), and the professional development liaison between the school and college with helping her learn to create a thoughtful literacy curriculum, engage in skillful teaching of reading, and keep her large class simultaneously interested and on task.

Asked how she acquired these skills, Lisa referred to various teacher education courses. She described foundations courses that helped her see and understand issues of equity that she now uses in selecting curriculum resources and topics (like the work by Williams, for example) to help children find themselves in their books. She recalled the value of assignments that asked her to find evidence of how children act and think by following a child over a long time and in a variety of contexts. She noted the specific tools gained from curriculum and methods courses in reading, mathematics, science, social studies, and the arts.

Refuting the conventional wisdom that prospective teachers gain little from teacher education, most graduates of the programs we studied were able to practice in their first year of teaching as though they were much more seasoned veterans; they attributed their success primarily to what they learned in their preparation programs. These were typical comments from graduates in the field:

> *I had a very challenging classroom with many diverse needs in my first year of teaching. I feel that because of my education at Wheelock, I was able to be successful.*

> *Somebody who comes out of the Curry School [at the University of Virginia] is going to be able to walk into a classroom prepared for almost anything. They'll be knowledgeable in the subject area, knowledgeable in a variety of strategies of teaching methods, of classroom procedures and discipline.*

The beginning teachers we observed and interviewed would point to specific preparation experiences that enabled them to mature as teachers and surmount the dilemmas of teacher education. For example, candidates often described how their extended clinical experiences, interwoven with coursework, helped them learn how to conceptualize teaching and enact their ideas in practice. As a Trinity University graduate noted, "The full-year intern teaching experience was the best part. I loved finding my philosophy of teaching. I was truly ready for my own classroom." A graduate of the UC Berkeley Developmental Teacher Education program related how the program's two-year process of coursework, interwoven with four student teaching placements, helped her progress from focusing on herself to focusing on students and their learning—usually a developmental process that takes several years of teaching: "In the second year [of my teacher education program], the theory became mine so I could tell if something was happening or not happening in the classroom. I had enough experience in classrooms not to focus on me."

Graduates pointed to specific courses as practical guides in meeting serious classroom needs. Many, of course, recalled methods courses offering specific strategies for instruction and classroom management. Just as many mentioned courses in child development and learning as essential to their success. As one Bank Street graduate noted:

> *Child Development has probably been the most relevant course in my practice. I got to know where kids are in terms of their social interactions and stages of sociability. . . . That's been really helpful. In fact, it's the kind of thing I want to revisit, to keep up with it and reread all those books. I was committed to making my kids feel respected . . . and I think 95 percent of the time I've succeeded. . . . I suspect and I hope that my students feel that I respect them and take what they feel and think seriously. That's important to me.*

Some even spoke about foundations courses—which are not generally thought of as practical or valued by teachers and are often caricatured as too theoretical. Said one beginning New York City teacher and Bank Street graduate: "The Foundations class was very helpful to me for the kind of children that I'm encountering in this school. There are a lot of children in this school from homeless shelters who have a lot of emotional and behavioral needs. In this class, we studied a lot about children from these types of environments and the effect that it has on them, the types of education they respond best to, what they need, and what helps them. The class helped me come to a whole new understanding of how to deal with them."

What the Programs Do: Distinctive Models of Success

This chapter briefly describes each of the programs, graduates' views of their preparation, and the views of their principals and supervisors about their preparedness for practice. Later chapters discuss how the programs develop these skills and abilities.

Alverno College

Alverno College is an undergraduate model organized around a sophisticated performance assessment strategy. The overall curriculum is built on opportunities for students to master eight general education abilities (expected of all students in the college) and five advanced education abilities (specific to teacher education students). These abilities clearly state what program graduates are expected to know, be like, and be able to do to complete the program successfully and attain certification as teachers. A complex series of performance assessments and portfolios anchor the entire program, from admission through graduation. Students produce demonstrations of skills, essays, letters, position papers, case study analyses, observations of events, presentations to various audiences, videos of practice, and curriculum materials. They also engage in simulated and actual parent-teacher conferences, teacher planning sessions, and the like. There are no grades at Alverno; students receive "validation" of their competence in particular levels of specific abilities during each course. On graduation they receive narrative transcripts describing the nature and quality of their work in relation to the abilities required.

Alverno has always had a strong teacher preparation mission. Founded in Milwaukee in 1887 as a Catholic normal school for women preparing to teach in parochial schools, it became a four-year liberal arts college in 1946. As a commuter college with a strong social mission, Alverno serves mostly first-generation college students and a high proportion of students of color. The college continues to serve only women in its undergraduate program, but men are admitted to the postbaccalaureate teacher certification program. About three hundred of Alverno's twenty-three hundred students are enrolled in teacher education programs (early childhood, elementary, secondary, bilingual, music, art, and adult education). Just over two hundred are in elementary education, the focus of this study; one-third of these complete the postbaccalaureate program. The undergraduate program is so demanding (eighteen credits a semester to finish in four years) that most students complete their studies over four and a half to five years.

The goals of Alverno's program are expressed by overarching themes that focus on the developmental needs of learners; an appreciation for diversity; a view of professionalism that includes ongoing inquiry to inform teaching; a concern for democratic education; and commitment to the use of media and technology. Teachers are prepared to succeed in Milwaukee's urban school settings where more than 75 percent of students are minority and low-income. Faculty agree that their major concern is to produce teachers who "look at the child as an individual and look at what the child's strengths are—knowing about backgrounds and about how they can support them as learners" (Alverno College Faculty, 1994). Giving all pupils access to powerful learning experiences is emphasized. Faculty want their students to see that "ability is abundant" among pupils, and they strongly reject the cultural deficit view that some pupils cannot learn high-level problem solving and thinking skills. As one student in the program told us: "We were taught not to label, to try to recognize differences rather than saying this person can't do X, Y, or Z. We were taught to learn to work with differences."

Alverno faculty are deeply involved in curriculum and teaching projects in many Milwaukee public schools and have close professional development relationships with teams of teachers and schools where student teachers are placed. These include three elementary school partnerships that resemble professional development schools supporting novice and veteran teacher learning, inquiry, and school reform.

Principals perceive Alverno graduates as reflective, open and accepting of diverse points of view, capable of reaching out to families and of using pupils' prior knowledge in their teaching, and very competent and serious about their work. As one observed:

> Alverno graduates come into the Milwaukee city schools "a step ahead" of graduates from other teacher preparation institutions because of the careful way in which they are nurtured and supported in their program by Alverno faculty. I think it is the structure of the program that makes the difference. Alverno . . . takes its students and actually follows them from the freshman year. They are really supported by their supervisors and advisors.

Wheelock College

Much like Alverno, Wheelock College was established with preparation of teachers at the heart of its mission. Founded in Boston in 1888 by Lucy Wheelock, its original charge was to "plant in the land of children whatever you wish to put into the life of our times" (Wheelock College, 1995), and its original goal—improving the quality of life for children and their families—remains unchanged today. Then, as now, it offered programs in only three areas: teaching, social work, and child life (hospital-based child services). With a yearlong curriculum steeped in the tradition of Froebel and the developmental psychology of G. Stanley Hall, Miss Wheelock's Kindergarten Training School graduated its first class of six women in 1889. Known for its progressive approach and commitment to urban education, the college now graduates about 150 students annually from its undergraduate teacher education programs and about 200 from its graduate division. Because all Massachusetts teachers must complete a master's degree within five years to gain a full professional license, many undergraduates start the graduate program immediately; others return after a year or two of teaching.

The program in early childhood care and education, which we studied, prepares teachers to work with children from birth to age eight and to earn a K–3 teaching credential. It is designed to prepare "children-centered, family-focused, and community-oriented" teachers by combining subject matter knowledge, study in pedagogy, and supervised clinical practice. Like the College's other programs, it is firmly rooted in a developmental point of view. In the words of then-president Marjorie Bakken: "Everything grows for the child. You are the curriculum builders. You watch, you look, and you see, you create. You allow the child to create. Methods are not so important as the child. The child comes first. The curriculum of the college clearly reflects the commitment to a human development perspective."

All of Wheelock's undergraduate teacher preparation programs focus on subject matter preparation and pedagogic mastery. The former is enacted through collegewide courses, traditional distribution requirements, and completion of an academic art and science major. All students must satisfy the distribution requirement of thirty-six credit hours by taking courses in arts and humanities, natural sciences and mathematics, social sciences, and multiculturalism, developing problem-solving skills, visual and performing arts, and human growth and development. The major consists of thirty-two hours of coursework in one of four interdisciplinary fields (arts, human development, humanities, mathematics and sciences), each designed to give students common interdisciplinary experiences and develop individual interests and concentrations. All of the majors include a set of multicultural courses and experiences along with an eight-credit course sequence in human development and a course on Children and Their Environment. Those continuing or returning for a master's take additional courses in human development, multicultural education, and teaching methods, continuing their growth as reflective practitioners by undertaking an action research project. Students and faculty describe "the Wheelock Way" as characterized by:

- Learning from one's students and developing curriculum from knowledge of students, families, and cultures; being flexible, responsive, and resourceful
- Using community resources to follow up on children's interests
- Knowing how to observe and listen to children
- Being sensitive to diversity and knowing how to teach multiculturally
- Integrating curriculum across disciplines, using themes and projects to teach content
- Identifying and working on student strengths, and advocating for inclusion
- Working hard, planning well, researching thoroughly
- Being professional all the time

The tightly integrated curriculum explicitly links theory and practice, emphasizing the needs and strengths of diverse learners. It results in teachers feeling well prepared. As one Wheelock graduate claimed: "Wheelock College was the best possible place I could have attended. I feel more prepared than most of my colleagues who went other places, especially when it comes to teaching students from backgrounds that are different from my own."

Ninety-four percent of graduates are snapped up immediately after graduation. As one urban elementary school principal remarked: "If Wheelock College is part of someone's background, I put the application at the top of the pile. I've been connected with Wheelock since 1974 and what has always impressed me is the quality of the teaching. Wheelock is rooted in what it means to be looking at early childhood education from a developmental perspective and to build a program from that."

Bank Street College

Bank Street College engenders the same kind of response from principals in New York City. Its graduate school program is known for a long-standing commitment to progressive, democratic practice. Located just a half block from the hustle and bustle of Broadway on 112th Street, the nine-story building houses a family day care center for infants and toddlers;

the School for Children, an on-site lab school serving children ages three to thirteen; the Graduate School of Education; and a large Continuing Education division. Host to thousands of visitors annually from across the United States and around the world, Bank Street College and its famed School for Children have been wellsprings for developmentally appropriate, "constructivist" teaching for ninety years—long before these terms found their way onto the educational landscape. Founded by Lucy Sprague Mitchell in 1916, Bank Street focuses on developing teaching responsive to human development and learning and supportive of social responsibility and social justice within schools and the broader community.

We studied the preservice programs that prepare early childhood, elementary, and middle school teachers. These master's programs include thirty credits of graduate level coursework plus twelve credits of fieldwork. Students complete a bachelor's degree prior to entry; they then undertake a full academic year of advisement and practicum experiences incorporating several student teaching placements alongside intensive coursework focused on child development, language and literacy development, and content-specific teaching methods. Students who pursue concentrated coursework can complete the program in twelve to fifteen months; however, most take two years. Some begin courses a year before they engage in the full year of student teaching and associated core coursework. Others start with the fieldwork year and begin teaching during the second year while finishing course requirements. In the year we conducted our fieldwork, the preservice programs served some two hundred teachers; about sixty were in the required full year of advisement, field-based practicum, and coursework.

Classrooms of the School for Children are shared with the graduate school. Most graduate courses are taught in this laboratory-like setting, filled with teaching resources and evidence of children's and teachers' work. The School for Children describes itself as a progressive demonstration school where teachers educate children and teachers simultaneously. In its multiage classrooms, each combining two grade levels, teachers develop strong relationships with students whom they teach for two years. Older students help youngsters in an activity-based curriculum that emphasizes exploration of the classroom and community environment; investigations into the physical and social world; and individual and group production of projects, experiments, models, books, plays, and other evidence of complex learning.

During the day, when school is in session, student teachers and interns work side by side with experienced teachers in virtually every classroom.

In the evening, the same classrooms are inhabited by graduate students taking courses. They merge theory and practice by constantly connecting what they learn in courses with what they observe in children's classrooms and field placements in local public schools. Bank Street graduate students typically complete one student teaching placement here, along with many observations of classrooms, and then complete other placements in local public schools, several of which have been designed and almost entirely staffed by Bank Street graduates.

Based on theory and evidence that people build knowledge from a combination of direct experience, reflection, and guided study, Bank Street's program emphasizes the careful construction of settings for learning in which learners can move back and forth between "book learning" and firsthand experience. Earlier in the century, Lucy Sprague Mitchell took children and teachers on extended field trips across the country to study particular places, themes, and social concerns, convinced that such experiences enabled deeper learning than intellectual inquiry alone. Today children in the School for Children and other Bank Street–influenced schools undertake community studies of their neighborhoods and of local environmental and social issues, while reading about them in literature, primary historical or scientific documents, and textbooks. They plant gardens and observe the outcomes while studying plant biology. They build and measure structures while they study measurement and geometry. Whatever is to be learned is approached from a base of experience with opportunities for reflection, not just abstraction.

The teacher education program is also based on a careful combination of experience, reflection, and study. An admissions brochure asking "What makes Bank Street a unique place for graduate work?" offers this reply: "We believe that children and teachers learn best through their own experience—and so do graduate students. Here you will find a special blend of theory and practice that will challenge you intellectually while you learn hands-on approaches to help support and develop students and teachers in the learning process."

Graduate students are placed in classrooms with cooperating teachers who model Bank Street practices throughout their year of full-time study, while they take courses in child development, teaching methods, and social foundations. Thus teaching and study about teaching are continuously cross-referenced, fostering an analytical and practical approach to the development of practice. Teachers develop and try out curriculum to understand its goals and effects. They write children's books to understand the relationship between literature and experience. They solve mathematical problems to understand the thinking and problem-solving processes children undergo. They act and observe the consequences of their actions, interpreted in light of other research and theory, to refine their work in the classroom, emphasizing development of the whole child. As the Bank Street-trained principal of one famous New York City public school explained: "I think [Bank Street graduates] are the best-trained teachers in progressive education that I can find. The Bank Street philosophy and methodology is closely connected with ours. Socialization of children always seems to be related to the balance between the cognitive and the affective, as well as between the individual and the group. Our school emphasizes supporting the individual and also helping [him or her] relate to a community."

University of California at Berkeley

The University of California at Berkeley's Developmental Teacher Education program is also strongly focused on application of developmental psychology to practice. DTE recommends credentials for about twenty-five elementary school teachers each year; UC Berkeley's secondary English and math programs prepare an additional forty to fifty teachers annually. In essence, DTE's goal is that its students become teachers who can mesh the developmental needs of children with the cognitive demands of the curriculum. As the program's state accreditation document explains: "Children are inherently active, self-motivated learners, who bring to the classroom a wealth of prior understandings that are relevant to schooling. They also bring a desire to become competent and to have that competence acknowledged by others. . . . The teacher's task is to channel children's inherent interests, motivation, and developing competencies to the goals of the classroom, recognizing that part of that task is to establish conditions for the child to accept the goals of schooling as personally valuable— to see them as a means for acquiring competence and self-esteem."

The two-year postbaccalaureate program includes a year focused substantially on coursework and observation in classrooms and a year of intensive clinical experience with ongoing connected coursework. Five student-teaching placements are distributed over the two years (the first two are each nine weeks in length and the last three are each eighteen weeks), creating a gradual introduction to teaching and experiences in diverse settings where teaching issues can be addressed from increasingly higher levels of competence. Individual clinical supervision is provided by highly experienced staff. Although the introduction to teaching is gradual, the amount of supervision remains relatively constant over the five placements to support reflection on teaching success and failure and to monitor the development of teaching competencies.

A carefully designed and sequenced set of courses creates a spiral curriculum that enables repeated consideration of teaching issues at higher levels of understanding over the two years. At the core is a four-semester sequence of seminars on human development that aims, as the program's accrediting document explains, to help teachers "establish principles of classroom organization that promote social and psychological development while also promoting the acquisition of knowledge in the various subject areas." Methods courses help students learn to engage children in active learning. Some of the courses have been taught through the Lawrence Hall of Science and the Bay Area Writing Project, both housed at Berkeley. A weekly student teaching seminar promotes integration of theory and practice, small-group problem solving, and interaction between first- and second-year students. The student cohorts develop strong collegial and cooperative relationships early in the teaching career.

The program also has a prominent research orientation. Professional preparation is integrated with pursuit of a master's degree culminating in an individual research project relating developmental theory to teaching practice. Research faculty participate as instructors, and research and program evaluation are ongoing. Asked where the program addresses the balance between theory and practice, a faculty member responded, "Everywhere. And it has to, because the students are always in classrooms." Articulating a rationale for the program's design and sequence, another professor paraphrased Kant: "Percept without concept is blind. Concept without percept is empty." As students work in an array of classrooms, the courses focus intensively on enabling them to use research and theory to see more clearly the children with whom they work.

Finally, the program focuses on helping its student teachers learn to work effectively with diverse learners in urban schools. Alongside student teaching placements with expert teachers in urban schools with mostly minority and recent immigrant students (often DTE graduates), DTE participants take courses such as Teaching Linguistic and Cultural Minority Students, and Education in Inner Cities. A principal of a central city school in Oakland who had recently hired eight DTE graduates noted: "I take all the DTE grads I can get. They are the best teachers—outstanding, dedicated. . . . [The program] is current, research-based, and really attuned to the California Curriculum Frameworks. Their graduates understand development. They have warmth, love, and craziness—the essentials of teaching."

Like other principals who seek out DTE graduates, he noted they have deep commitment to their students and respect for students' experiences, families, and communities, and he credited them with major contributions to his school's success.

University of Southern Maine

The University of Southern Maine's Extended Teacher Education Program (ETEP) is, like Bank Street and UC Berkeley, a graduate-level program. Along with Trinity's program (described next), ETEP is substantially school-based. The program's faculty comprises both school-based and university-based educators, who jointly prepare approximately seventy-five students each year for elementary and secondary schools. Almost all fieldwork and much coursework takes place in professional development partnership schools. At the time of this study they operated in five surrounding school district clusters: Portland, Western Maine, Yarmouth, Wells/Ogunquit and Kennebunk, and Gorham, each of which admitted a cohort of fifteen to twenty students who progress through the internship as a group. In recent years, several other districts have joined as ETEP's size has grown to about one hundred candidates annually.

A key theme of the program is collaborative inquiry to develop learner-centered practice. Interns work together as a team on projects designed to help them learn to collaborate, engage in ongoing assessment and improvement, and continuously reflect on the outcomes of their work. At the institutional level, the program grew out of collaboration among public school and university educators who founded the Southern Maine Partnership to work on a shared agenda of school reform and teacher education reform. This intensive collaboration has created new organizational roles, arrangements, and distributions of responsibility and resources among schools, districts, and the university. In 1995, NCATE cited the program as "representing exemplary practice in the delivery of an extended field-based model for preparing teachers for initial certification" (A. Wise, personal communication, Oct. 1995).

Another key theme is the program's focus on authentic, standards-based teaching and learning for both interns and their students, organized around performance assessments. Maine's work on standards for both students and teachers has emphasized critical thinking, inquiry, and authentic assessment, and the districts that are part of the Southern Maine Partnership often use portfolios and performance assessments to guide their work with children. Meanwhile, ETEP piloted standards-based teacher certification in Maine, based on the state's outcome standards for teaching derived from the work of INTASC. ETEP uses eleven outcomes as categories to guide the collection of evidence from an intern's practice during the year. Observation and evaluation instruments used by cooperating teachers are derived from the outcomes, and the evidence generated is the basis for both formal assessment meetings held during the year and the culminating portfolio.

Students enter the thirty-three-credit-hour ETEP internship year having completed an undergraduate degree (and often having pursued other careers). When they complete this nine-month experience, they can receive a credential. Most also complete an additional eighteen hours of graduate-level work to receive a master of teaching and learning degree. Some continue full-time toward the master's degree after the internship year; others complete the additional coursework at a slower pace while launching teaching careers.

The ETEP schedule is grueling, with full days working in schools followed by courses three to five afternoons each week, all of which draw heavily on developmental and learning theory and link closely to interns' work in classrooms. An integrating internship seminar addresses learning, curriculum, and assessment; in addition, elementary interns take an intensive literacy course, courses in mathematics, science, and social studies methods, and courses in exceptionality and life span development. Most courses are held in the partnering district's schools. In some cases, university faculty members and school district teachers or administrators coteach a course. In each site, a university teacher educator and a teacher employed at the site share responsibility for co-directing that site's overall program.

The clinical portion of the internship—daily practice with cooperating teachers in partnership school classrooms—comprises two separate semester-long placements during which interns assume increasing responsibility for the classroom and maintain an ongoing dialogue journal in which cooperating teachers and site coordinators write comments or questions. The site team manages expectations for the intern's role in instructional planning, how interns' work is assessed, required videotaping of teaching episodes, and cooperating teacher participation in the intern's portfolio presentation and recommendation for certification.

Beyond daily feedback from the cooperating teacher, the site coordinators make weekly visits to each intern to provide feedback and document each intern's progress, informed by the interns' action plans, both coordinators' previous observations of teaching, reports from cooperating teachers, dialogue journals, and materials interns have developed during the week, whether for the classroom or their courses. These weekly visits also help interns learn how to reflect on the outcomes of their efforts and identify evidence from their work that indicates improvement as well as areas for continued work in terms of the eleven ETEP "outcomes."

At the end of this intense, well-integrated, and carefully focused set of experiences, teachers are clearly ready to teach effectively and reflectively from their first day on the job. As one principal said of the many ETEP graduates he hires, "They induct quickly into our school culture." Others observe that ETEP graduates are "professional," "team players," "learner-centered," and "reflective." Graduates' leadership abilities are frequently noted. As one principal remarked: "I look to ETEP grads to help change the culture of this school. They have the big picture."

Trinity University

Trinity University also emphasizes school-based preparation for teaching, but it does so in a five-year program that begins in the undergraduate years and culminates in a master of arts in teaching (MAT). Seeking to develop reform-oriented teachers, the program accepts about fifty candidates each year and offers preparation for elementary and secondary education. Students can also earn license endorsement in special education and in English as a second language. Trinity also offers a one-year postbaccalaureate program, but 75 percent of teachers-to-be take the five-year program.

Modeled explicitly on the reform proposals of the Holmes Group of education deans (Holmes Group, 1986), teacher education at Trinity is grounded in a coherent vision of teacher education, anchored by a network of cooperative university-school partnerships and aimed at producing teachers who act as education change agents. The program offers:

- A required bachelor's degree in humanities for prospective elementary teachers and in one or more academic disciplines for secondary teaching candidates
- Undergraduate education coursework in areas such as child and adolescent development, education reform and policy, and schools and the community
- A minimum of 135 undergraduate hours of study, observation, tutoring, and student teaching in Professional Development School (PDS) settings
- A yearlong postgraduate (fifth year) internship in a PDS under the tutelage of mentors who serve as Trinity clinical faculty
- Concurrent graduate-level coursework emphasizing the connection between theory and practice

At the time of our study, five San Antonio–area schools constituted the Alliance for Better Schools, Trinity's PDS network. (There are now six PDS sites.) Each served well a large population of low-income and minority students, modeling diverse approaches to education reform. Hawthorne Elementary is a core knowledge school offering a thematic interdisciplinary K–5 curriculum; Jackson-Keller Elementary reflects the "whole child" philosophy of Ernest Boyer's basic school initiative; Mark Twain Middle School adopted a comprehensive set of middle-grades reforms consistent with national research findings about healthy adolescent development; Lee High School undertook curriculum reforms that include more intensive use of technology as well as organizational reforms; and the International School for the Americas, developed collaboratively with the university, is a small innovative high school of choice focused on international commerce and technology.

These schools serve as learning laboratories for children and adults, modeling innovative teaching strategies, cooperative faculty relationships, strong university links, intensive efforts to induct teachers-in-training into the profession, and ongoing professional development for experienced and novice teachers alike. Trinity students spend their field time, as undergraduates and as fifth-year interns, in the classrooms of PDS master teachers, all of whom have been designated as mentors by the university and are appointed as Trinity adjunct faculty. In their role as clinical faculty, mentors teach classes conducted at the PDS and are responsible for methods teaching. The scope of the classes is developed cooperatively with Trinity faculty; the conduct of the classes is the province of the mentors.

At the university, students make their way through a sequenced set of courses, beginning with general exploration of school and community issues in freshman year and in the next three years focusing on child development, learning, teaching, and school reform in courses linked to practica experiences. The practicum seminars help students link what they are learning in university courses with the practical realities of teaching. Formal admission to the teacher education program occurs at the end of the sophomore year after the first practicum, based on evidence of both academic ability and potential teaching ability.

The fifth year is a full-year internship in the PDS. Students assume graduated responsibility for work in classrooms under the guidance of mentor teachers and regularly observe, reflect on, and critique one another's practice. This experience is coupled with coursework on teaching methods, clinical supervision, and educational research, as well as a major research paper and a professional portfolio. By the end of the intern year, Trinity students have a clear understanding of the standards of competent professional practice and the ethics of good teaching. They have experienced both success and frustration in the classroom; they have had an opportunity to talk over—with one another, their mentors, and university faculty—the relative merits of various pedagogies and models of teaching. They know what they already do well and are aware of areas needing improvement; and their conversations are grounded in research and practical experience.

Students praise the intern experience but do not minimize its challenge. "The full-year teaching experience was the best part," says a recent graduate. "I loved finding my philosophy of teaching. I was truly ready for my own classroom." Says another, "I'm not going to have the typical first year. I've already had it."

The not-so-hidden agenda of the internship year is achieved as well. Students understand the importance of building and sustaining a professional culture: conferring with colleagues, attending conferences, writing and presenting papers, developing curricula, and keeping current with research. They have already become professional teachers.

University of Virginia

The University of Virginia's BA/MT program is a five-year dual-degree program like Trinity's. Students earn both a baccalaureate and a master's degree as well as a teaching license. During at least three years of the program, students simultaneously take courses in their subject fields while pursuing professional studies. The programs in English and mathematics are particularly noteworthy examples of high-quality secondary teacher education that blends strong preparation in the discipline with connected preparation in pedagogy—a combination still relatively rare across the country.

Although students are not formally admitted to the teacher education program until their junior year, they must enroll in the first course of the dual (BA/MT) program by the midpoint of their second year of college. This requirement begins to build the linkage between professional and academic skills. Taking advanced courses in specific disciplines concurrently with professional studies keeps the importance of subject matter foremost in students' minds. Ongoing communication between faculty at the Curry School of Education and liberal arts faculty helps integrate disciplinary studies with professional courses. This encourages students to explore disciplinary knowledge along with ways to translate that knowledge immediately into secondary education settings. The advising structure also provides a dual focus on liberal arts and professional studies.

Students declare their academic major at the beginning of their junior year, when they also begin the highly selective teacher education program. The approximately ninety students admitted each year are assigned two advisors, one in the teacher education program and one in their academic field.

As sophomores, students in the program participate in an array of field placements designed to expose them to various elements of teaching. During this year, all prospective teachers, regardless of their intended level of teaching, observe in elementary and middle schools. This initial focus is on school organization rather than individual classrooms. Students are asked to interview teachers, students, and administrators to learn about professional roles in schools, experience a number of settings within a school (including the library, media center, special education classrooms, and principal's office), and observe formal instruction in regular and special education classrooms. Students spend approximately thirty hours each semester in such placements.

During the junior year, the focus of field placement is on individual learners. Coupled with the courses Learning and Development and The Exceptional Individual, which afford basic knowledge of learning principles and human development, the field experience requires students to serve as tutors, generally with students with special educational needs. In the fourth year, field experiences require that students observe, describe, and analyze teaching and learning behaviors in the classroom, develop and teach model lessons in peer sessions and in the classroom, identify an organizing theme for a unit of instruction, develop the unit, and teach it in a classroom. Students typically spend two hours weekly in fall and two weeks in spring in the classroom.

This work in the classroom, directly related to the academic major and areas of certification, is concurrent with a two-course sequence of general methods focusing on instruction, assessment, and classroom management, in which students often practice techniques for use in field placement. Finally, in fall of the fifth year, students teach full-time as "teacher associates." In the spring, they take further graduate coursework. Field experiences are closely integrated with coursework at the university.

This progressively intense work with learners combined with coursework enables Curry students to develop well-grounded theory about learning and learners. They embark on student teaching having had extensive, well-structured opportunities to observe teachers and learners in the field and having already taught lessons and at least one unit under the supervision of an experienced classroom teacher, the university special methods faculty member, and a graduate student supervisor. As one program graduate recalled, "Time in the classrooms was key; actively participating with kids for four years is the best way to prepare teachers for teaching."

The influence of these well-structured field experiences is evident. One student observed: "Every year you are put into a school to observe or to tutor or to teach. . . . I can assure you that if I hadn't had a touch of that (communication with the students) at every point in the four years of the five-year program, I would have given up long ago, because the reason I want to be a teacher is to deal with children." External observers frequently comment on the learner-centered focus of the program's graduates. As a former superintendent of the Charlottesville Public Schools observed, UVA graduates "know who we have in our schools. They are particularly well-prepared to work with the urban child. . . ."

What the Graduates Say: Perceptions of Preparedness

To find out how graduates felt about their preparation once they got into the field, we surveyed all the graduates of each of the seven programs within the prior three years, plus a comparison group of teachers with three or fewer years of experience, drawn as a random sample from a list supplied by the National Education Association, the nation's largest teacher association. (For details about the survey, see Silvernail, 1997, and Appendix B.) The resulting sample of 971 teachers included 551 from the research sites and 420 from the comparison group. In addition to demographic questions and questions about the schools in which they taught, we asked these teachers how well they had been prepared across thirty-six dimensions of teaching, what kinds of practices they engaged in, and how efficacious they felt.

We also surveyed 301 principals who employed graduates of the study sites in the last three years, asking them how they perceived graduates' abilities on the same dimensions of teaching compared to other beginning teachers they had hired. Both surveys gave evidence of the programs' success: graduates felt significantly better prepared for teaching than their peers, and they were viewed as more competent than other new teachers by their principals.

The Samples

In the research sample and comparison group of beginning teachers we surveyed, about 86 percent of the respondents were women and about three-fourths were white, non-Hispanic, as is true of the teaching force as a whole. However, our study programs included an older population of teachers, since several were graduate programs serving midcareer recruits. Whereas 68 percent of the comparison group sample were under twenty-five years of age, fully 75 percent of the research sample were *over* twenty-five, and 18 percent were over thirty-five. The research group graduates were almost twice as likely to be teaching in urban schools— 49 percent versus 25 percent—and significantly less likely to be teaching in rural schools (14 percent versus 38 percent).

Program reputations were apparently known to the recruits, and the reasons candidates offered for attending a program differed for the research group and the comparison group. Graduates of our study sites were more likely than comparison teachers to have chosen their program for reasons of reputation (80 percent versus 62 percent) or program philosophy (45 percent versus 16 percent), whereas comparison teachers were more likely to have chosen their program for geographical convenience (55 percent versus 43 percent) or cost (36 percent versus 12 percent).

For example, at Bank Street College, where 90 percent of candidates enter from other careers, most choose the school for its well-known brand of teaching and learning. As one student told us: "I started to get information about Bank Street about ten years ago. Finally I decided to just quit my job (in a technology field) and go to Bank Street full-time and pursue a degree. I chose Bank Street because I had known many people who went there. My children had gone to a school in Brooklyn with many Bank Street-trained teachers. My son is now a writer. I think having that kind of teaching had a big impact on him."

Students from the other programs we studied also typically chose their college because of the kind of teaching they knew its graduates had learned to enact. A representative comment: "If you were to go into Minneapolis Public Schools, anything that you saw that excited you probably was started by an Alverno grad."

Perceptions of Preparation

The survey results showed that, even though graduates of our programs were more likely than others to be teaching in urban schools, they felt significantly better prepared for their work than the random sample of beginning teachers. Overall, 86 percent of these recent graduates felt well prepared for teaching, as compared to 65 percent of the comparison teachers. Furthermore, as a group they felt significantly better prepared on thirty-five of thirty-six separate dimensions of teaching skill, ranging from their ability to develop successful curriculum to managing the classroom and teaching diverse learners effectively (see Table 3.1).

Table 3.1. Perceptions of Preparedness

	Comparison Group N = 420 (Percentage Responding "Well" or "Very Well")	Research Group N = 551 (Percentage Responding "Well" or "Very Well")
"How well do you think your teacher preparation prepared you to do this?"		
Teach the concepts, knowledge, and skills of your discipline(s) in ways that enable students to learn.	67	84**
Understand how different students are learning.	63	85**
Set challenging and appropriate expectations of learning and performance for students.	65	85**
Help all students achieve high academic standards.	55	76**
Develop curriculum that builds on students' experiences, interests, and abilities.	68	89**
Evaluate curriculum materials for their usefulness and appropriateness for your students.	58	79**
Create interdisciplinary curriculum.	56	82**
Use instructional strategies that promote active student learning.	78	91**
Relate classroom learning to the real world.	68	86**
Understand how students' social, emotional, physical, and cognitive development influence learning.	74	88**
Identify and address special learning needs and/or difficulties.	55	68**
Teach in ways that support new English language learners.	22	30**
Choose teaching strategies for different instructional purposes and to meet different student needs.	63	80**
Provide a rationale for your teaching decisions to students, parents, and colleagues.	62	79**

Table 3.1. Perceptions of Preparedness, *continued*

	Comparison Group N = 420 (Percentage Responding "Well" or "Very Well")	Research Group N = 551 (Percentage Responding "Well" or "Very Well")
Help students become self-motivated and self directed.	57	74**
Use technology in the classroom.	40	45
Develop a classroom environment that promotes social development and group responsibility.	70	86**
Develop students' questioning and discussion skills.	64	82**
Engage students in cooperative work as well as independent learning.	80	91**
Use effective verbal and nonverbal communication strategies to guide student learning and behavior.	74	79*
Teach students from a multi-cultural vantage point.	57	79**
Use questions to stimulate different kinds of student learning.	69	82**
Help students learn to think critically and solve problems.	62	85**
Encourage students to see, question, and interpret ideas from diverse perspectives.	54	77**
Use knowledge of learning, subject matter, curriculum, and student development to plan instruction.	70	86**
Understand how factors in the students' environment outside of school may influence their life and learning.	72	83**
Work with parents and families to better understand students and to support their learning.	45	63**
Use a variety of assessments (e.g., observation, portfolios, tests, performance tasks, anecdotal records) to determine student strengths, needs, and programs.	63	78**

	Comparison Group $N = 420$ (Percentage Responding "Well" or "Very Well")	Research Group $N = 551$ (Percentage Responding "Well" or "Very Well")
Give productive feedback to students to guide their learning.	66	78[**]
Help students learn how to assess their own learning.	42	64[**]
Evaluate the effects of your actions and modify plans accordingly.	63	81[**]
Conduct inquiry or research to inform your decisions.	47	73[**]
Resolve interpersonal conflict.	43	60[**]
Maintain discipline and an orderly, purposeful learning environment.	56	65[**]
Plan and solve problems with colleagues.	45	72[**]
Assume leadership responsibilities in your school.	52	68[**]
Overall, how well do you feel your program prepared you for teaching?	65	86[**]

Notes: *Z scores were calculated to evaluate the response differences between the two groups.*
*$p < .05$; **$p < .01$.*

Some dimensions of teaching stood out as particularly strong areas of preparation for the program group. As Table 3.1 shows, more than 90 percent of program graduates felt well prepared to use instructional strategies that promote active student learning and engage students in cooperative work as well as independent learning. These pedagogical strengths respond to the findings of recent research on how people learn, and they confront the age-old transmission teaching model that has been so inefficient and persistent.

A large majority of these programs' graduates felt well prepared on a number of dimensions where fewer than half of the comparison group did, including working with families and colleagues to solve problems and support students' learning, helping students to assess their own learning, and conducting research to inform teaching. These are all areas of teaching where the skills and dispositions of "adaptive experts" come into play to help solve problems and acquire new knowledge about how to proceed in improving learning and teaching.

Among six factors that emerged from factor analyses of these dimensions, graduates of these programs (and their principals) scored their preparation particularly highly in skills related to promoting student learning, understanding learners, teaching critical thinking, and developing curriculum. In these areas, both graduates and principals rated their preparation at 3.2 or higher on a 4-point scale, where 3 = "well prepared" and 4 = "very well prepared." (See Table 3.2 and Appendix B.) On all six factors, principals rated the program graduates' abilities, relative to other new hires, at "3" or above. All of the factor scores were significantly higher for the graduates than for the comparison group ($p < .01$).

Table 3.2. Graduates' Perceptions of Preparedness and Principals' Ratings of Competence (Factor Scores)

Factors	Comparison Group Mean Rating (S.D.) $N = 420$	Research Sample Mean Rating (S.D.) $N = 551$	Principals Mean Rating (S.D.) $N = 301$
1. *Promote student learning* (use effective instructional strategies and manage the classroom environment)	2.9 (.73)	3.3[**] (.61)	3.3[**] (.61)
2. *Understand learners* (understand different students, and help them meet high academic standards)	2.8 (.73)	3.2[**] (.62)	3.2[**] (.59)
3. *Teach critical thinking* (help students learn to question, discuss, think critically, and solve problems)	2.7 (.78)	3.2[**] (.71)	3.2[**] (.70)
4. *Develop curriculum* (use knowledge of content and learning to develop curriculum, plan, and evaluate materials)	2.8 (.82)	3.3[**] (.63)	3.2[**] (.70)
5. *Assess student learning* (determine student needs, adapt instructional plans, and help students self-assess)	2.5 (1.2)	2.9[**] (.74)	3.1[**] (.69)
6. *Develop professionalism* (work with parents and peers to solve problems, resolve conflicts, and assume leadership)	2.3 (.95)	2.8[**] (.84)	3.1[**] (.73)

Note: *T tests of factor score means;* [*] $p < .05$; [**] $p < .01$.

The only area where there was not a significant difference between the research group and the comparison group was in the use of technology in the classroom (where fewer than half of each group felt well prepared, 45 percent of study site graduates versus 40 percent of comparison teachers). There were substantial differentials among the study programs in this area, with a large majority of graduates of some programs feeling well prepared (Alverno, Trinity, and UVA) and others feeling less well prepared. This is an area where, prior to a recent major federal program to enhance technology training for teachers, teacher education programs in general lacked the technology infrastructure to prepare their candidates.

One other area where both groups as a whole felt less well prepared was for teaching English language learners (ELL), although the study site graduates were more likely to feel well prepared than others (and a strong majority felt adequately prepared). One program (UC Berkeley) stood out in this regard; more than 75 percent of its graduates felt well prepared and virtually all felt adequately prepared. Berkeley is not only located in a community with a large number of immigrant students; it is also in a state where teacher education policy has required attention to preparation for teaching English language learners since the early 1990s. California created special certificates for teaching culturally and linguistically diverse students (CLAD and B-CLAD credentials) based on coursework that most candidates in the UC Berkeley program pursued. The state has also required programs to incorporate training in these areas as a condition of accreditation.

Interestingly, in both of these areas, as in most others, the principals scored the program graduates even more highly than did the candidates themselves, underscoring the distinctiveness of their preparation in relation to other new teachers as perceived by supervisors who had the opportunity to see a wide range of teachers in action.

Feelings of Efficacy

In addition to asking how well prepared teachers felt, we also asked about their sense of efficacy—their belief that they can make a difference in students' lives and learning—and confidence about their ability to achieve teaching goals. We focused on this because teachers' sense of efficacy has been found to be a powerful predictor of teacher effectiveness, teacher commitment, and teacher behavior (for a review, see Tschannen-Moran, Woolfolk Hoy, and Hoy, 1998).

Teachers' sense of efficacy has been related to student achievement (Anderson, Greene, and Loewen, 1988; Armor and others, 1976; Ashton, 1985; Ashton and Webb, 1986; Berman and others, 1977; Gibson and

Dembo, 1984; Ross, 1992), student motivation (Midgley, Feldlaufer, and Eccles, 1989), and students' own sense of efficacy (Anderson, Greene, and Loewen, 1988). Furthermore, teachers' sense of efficacy appears to be related to particular teacher behaviors that affect student learning, notably teachers' willingness to try new instructional techniques (Allinder, 1994; Berman and others, 1977; Guskey, 1984; Rose and Medway, 1981; Smylie, 1988; Stein and Wang, 1988), teachers' affect toward students (Gibson and Dembo, 1984; Rose and Medway, 1981), and their persistence in trying to solve learning problems (Gibson and Dembo, 1984). Teachers' sense of personal teaching efficacy has been related to their level of planning and organization (Allinder, 1994) and to their practices—for example, using effective, hands-on science techniques (Enochs, Scharmann, and Riggs, 1995; Riggs and others, 1994).

Teacher efficacy has also been linked to enthusiasm for teaching (Allinder, 1994; Guskey, 1984) and commitment to teaching (Coladarci, 1992; Evans and Tribble, 1986). Perhaps not surprisingly, teachers' sense of their ability to influence student learning appears related to stress level (Parkay, Greenwood, Olejnik, and Proller, 1988) and to attrition from teaching (Glickman and Tamashiro, 1982). Several studies have found teachers' sense of efficacy related to feelings of preparedness for teaching (Darling-Hammond, Chung, and Frelow, 2002; Hall, Burley, Villeme, and Brockmeier, 1992; Raudenbush, Rowen, and Cheong, 1992). This fits with our findings (described later).

Our survey included two Likert-scale items similar to those originally used by a team of RAND researchers to evaluate teachers' sense of efficacy about what they can influence ("Most of a student's performance depends on the home environment, so teachers have little influence") and about what they can personally accomplish ("If I try hard, I can get through to almost all students"; see Armor and others, 1976). Items like these were strongly correlated with student achievement in the RAND study. Our study included additional efficacy items assessing teachers' confidence in their ability to accomplish certain teaching goals (handle discipline problems, teach all students to high levels, integrate technology) and their sense of certainty about how to help students learn.

We found that teachers from the study sites scored significantly higher ($p < .01$) on a factor measuring their sense of self-efficacy as well as one measuring locus of control—that is, their feeling that their influence on students' learning is stronger than that of peers or the home environment (Table 3.3). They were more confident that they could reach all students and less likely to feel uncertain about how to teach some of them. They were also less likely to blame students for failing "because they do not apply themselves" or to say that peers or the home environment have more effect on students than they do.

In contrast to most of the comparison teachers, who were more likely to say their ideas about teaching come from their own experience as K–12 students, the study site graduates were far more likely to say their

Table 3.3. Teachers' Sense of Self-Efficacy and Locus of Control

	Comparison Group Mean (S.D.)	Research Group Mean (S.D.)
Factor 1: Teacher self-efficacy	2.9 (.50)	3.0[**] (.50)
If I try hard, I can get though to almost all students.	3.1 (.77)	3.3[**] (.75)
I am confident of my ability to handle most discipline problems that may arise in my classroom.	3.3 (.69)	3.3 (.75)
I am confident of my ability to teach all students to high levels.	3.1 (.75)	3.1 (.80)
I am confident I am making a difference in the lives of my students.	3.4 (.66)	3.5 (.65)
A lot of my ideas about teaching and learning come from what I learned in my teacher preparation program.	2.5 (1.1)	3.1[**] (.92)
I am uncertain how to teach some of my students.[a]	2.0 (1.0)	1.9 (1.1)
Factor 2: Locus of control	2.0 (.64)	1.6[**] (.57)
Students fail because they do not apply themselves.[a]	2.2 (1.2)	1.5[**] (1.1)
My students' peers have more influence on their motivation and performance than I do.[a]	1.8 (1.0)	1.6[**] (.88)
A lot of my ideas about teaching come from my own experiences as a K–12 student.[a]	2.6 (1.1)	2.4 (1.1)
Most of a student's performance depends on the home environment, so teachers have little influence.[a]	1.3 (.93)	1.1[**] (.76)

Notes: *T tests of group means were calculated.*
[**] *p < .01.*
[a] *These items were reverse scored.*

ideas about teaching and learning came predominantly from their teacher preparation program.

Tschannen-Moran and colleagues (1998) use Bandura's model of efficacy development (1986) to explore how well-designed teacher preparation may influence teachers' self-efficacy. In addition to producing knowledge and skills that support effectiveness, teacher education supports *mastery experiences,* in which experience of success is supported through coaching. This in turn supports *positive emotional cues* and self-assurance rather than anxiety resulting in a sense of defeat. Student teaching allows prospective teachers to gain *vicarious experiences* in which they watch others teach successfully and debrief so that they can imagine themselves becoming equally competent. Finally, *verbal persuasion* through constructive feedback from supervisors, cooperating teachers, and peers supports teachers' beliefs that they can succeed in solving problems of practice. In subsequent chapters, we explore how the programs do these things.

Evidence of Practice

Of course, what teachers actually do with their preparation is more important than how well prepared or efficacious they feel. Having principals' perceptions of teachers' demonstrated abilities gave us some sense of what candidates may do in practice. We also asked the new teachers in the sample what they do in the classroom in several specific areas, and we observed graduates of each of the programs in action.

Teachers from the study sites did report practices differing significantly from those of the comparison group teachers. As Table 3.4 shows, they were much more likely to organize their teaching to promote students' ability to become independent learners (factor one) and to engage students in setting goals for their own learning, assessing their own work, completing portfolios or projects to show their learning, and revising their work for reevaluation. Research suggests that all of these practices are strongly related to student learning (for a review, see Bransford, Brown, and Cocking, 1999).

They were also significantly more likely to address students' learning needs, reflect on student learning, and adjust their teaching on the basis of students' progress (factor two). They were more likely to use research in making classroom decisions and to share ideas about teaching with other colleagues. Finally, they were somewhat more likely to have their students work in collaborative groups and as peer tutors (factor three), additional practices that have been found to increase student achievement (Johnson and Johnson, 1989; Slavin, 1990).

Table 3.4. Reports of Practices

	Comparison Group Mean (S.D.)	Research Group Mean (S.D.)
Factor 1: Promote independent learners	2.4 (.77)	2.6** (.87)
Students participate in setting goals for their own learning.	2.1 (1.0)	2.3 (1.1)
Students participate in assessing their own work.	2.3 (1.0)	2.4* (.98)
Students complete portfolios or projects to show their learning.	2.5 (1.2)	2.8** (1.1)
Students may revise their work for reevaluation.	2.7 (1.1)	2.8 (1.2)
Factor 2: Practice reflective teaching	2.9 (.60)	3.1** (.56)
I adjust my teaching to address different learning styles.	3.3 (.72)	3.4* (.66)
I adjust my teaching based on student progress.	3.4 (.67)	3.5* (.62)
I use research in making classroom decisions.	2.2 (1.0)	2.6** (1.0)
I share ideas about instructional approaches with other teachers.	3.1 (.85)	3.3** (.80)
Factor 3: Promote peer learning	2.6 (.70)	2.7* (.70)
Some of my students are tutors for other students.	2.3 (.96)	2.5* (.93)
Students work in cooperative groups.	2.9 (.73)	3.0 (.74)

Notes: * $p < .05$; ** $p < .0$.

When discussing their hiring preferences, principals often remarked on graduates' specific abilities:

> *As I look for teachers, I most immediately look for Alverno applicants. Integrating new teachers into the staff from Alverno is so much easier, because of their high ability to be self-reflective, their personally wide experiences with performance assessment at the college level, and their ability to apply critical research bases to their classroom experiences. They are highly collegial, unafraid to seek out all they need to know from mentors and staff around them. I'll take ten more teachers like the two I've had this year.*

> *MAT graduates* [from Trinity] *are self-assured, confident, and highly responsible. They continuously model a desire to improve the educational setting for their students. They are excellent mentors for other teachers. They appear knowledgeable beyond their years of "real life" experience.*

> [Trinity] *graduates have a knowledge of instructional practices and use a variety of teaching strategies that usually I find only with teachers who have four or five years of experience.*

> [UVA] *is producing teachers who are able to go into a leadership role. We can count on them and we know what we are getting.*

Many observations of graduates' practices are integrated into the following chapters. Here we offer one example of the practices of a first-year teacher recently graduated from UC Berkeley's Developmental Teacher Education Program (from Snyder, 2000) whose practice illustrates the understanding of children and curriculum that undergirds sophisticated teaching strategies that press for understanding while maintaining strong purpose in the classroom.

"Mary Gregg" teaches in a portable classroom at Wilson Elementary School in an urban California district. Wilson's 850 students, most of them language-minority, are the largest population of Title I–eligible students in the district. Mary's room, a smaller-than-usual portable with a low ceiling and loud air fans, holds thirty-two first graders (fourteen girls and eighteen boys); there is no teacher's aide. Of the twenty-five children of color, a majority are recent immigrants from southeast Asia with a smattering of African Americans and Latinos, and seven European Americans. The school is predominantly Latino, but most Spanish-speaking students are assigned to classrooms with bilingual teachers in order to receive some content instruction in their native language.

Despite the small size of the room, Mary fosters an active learning environment with her active group of students. She has plastered the walls from floor to ceiling with student work—math graphs, group experience stories, a student collage from *Bringing the Rain to Kapiti Plain.* The ceiling affords another layer of learning. Hanging down so that adults have to duck or wend their way through the room are student-constructed science mobiles and a variety of *What We Know* and *What We Want to Know* charts. In one corner, a reading area is set up with books and a carpet. When she realized the classroom had no cubbies in which students could place school materials, coats, lunches, and miscellaneous treasures,

Mary and her spouse built them on their own time and with materials paid for out of her own pocket.

On a February afternoon with the Bay Area fog beginning to lift, she eats lunch with two other first-grade teachers in a classroom within the main building. Eating messy Subway sandwiches, the three discuss an afternoon science activity that involves regrouping their classes to achieve some ethnic and language heterogeneity for this year's students.

The other two teachers, though not enamored with the prepackaged activity, have decided to use the materials pretty much as directed. The DTE graduate explains: "It doesn't make any sense to me. There is no active engagement, nothing particularly grabbing." She describes the activity she will use instead: a "sink or float" activity that teaches the same concepts and uses the same materials. Unlike the prepackaged lesson, Mary's redesign engages students in both recording data and generating and testing hypotheses on the basis of the data. The other teachers laugh and ask if she "woke up with this one." "No," she responds, "It was in the shower this time."

On the way back to the classroom, she explains that this packaged curriculum, like many others, dumbs down the content and "leaves out the kids entirely." "It isn't that I don't teach those ideas or the kids don't learn them. I try to make sure that they do. That's why I use my own stuff."

At 12:20, half of her class leaves the room to participate with a bilingual class in the science lesson while half the bilingual class comes to her. She groups the students in mixed-language and gender cohorts and introduces the science activity she has designed. The room is full of materials needed for the lesson. There are cups in large tote trays, two trays filled with salt water and two with regular tap water; small totes full of plastic bears and many kinds of tiles, quarters, rocks, and paper clips. The activity is to experiment with how many objects it takes to sink the cup in each type of water.

The thirty students conduct experiments, record on yellow stickies how many objects it takes to sink the cup, and then place the yellow stickies on a large piece of chart paper Mary has labeled in two columns, salt water and tap water. Before starting the activity, she reads the labels and asks students to do so. She has the students point out interesting language and spelling features. Two children excitedly point out, "That's the same weird spelling we saw this morning," referring to an earlier activity that introduced the vocabulary they will use. While organizing the groups, Mary gives directions for students to go to their assigned table and sit on their hands. She points out that they will be unable to put their hands in the water if they are sitting on them. This is one of many "management techniques" she uses to ensure students the opportunity to engage in the work.

Another example of her management strategies is a set of student-generated and signed rules, called a "Peace Treaty," which hangs from the ceiling:

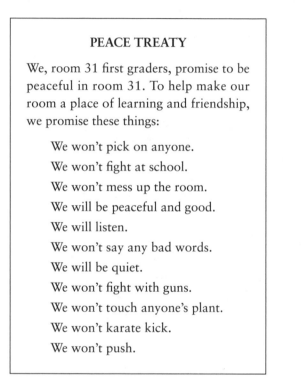

PEACE TREATY

We, room 31 first graders, promise to be peaceful in room 31. To help make our room a place of learning and friendship, we promise these things:

> We won't pick on anyone.
>
> We won't fight at school.
>
> We won't mess up the room.
>
> We will be peaceful and good.
>
> We will listen.
>
> We won't say any bad words.
>
> We will be quiet.
>
> We won't fight with guns.
>
> We won't touch anyone's plant.
>
> We won't karate kick.
>
> We won't push.

Mary chuckles about the Peace Treaty, "It worked for a day." Out of her hearing range, however, students praise and scold each other on their behavior as they refer to "our treaty."

Mary skillfully uses a range of other strategies throughout the day to keep her students working peacefully and purposefully: frequently praising those who are behaving, stopping and waiting until she has everyone's attention, questioning if all can hear, recording stars on the board when the group is "behaving" and erasing the stars to call their attention to the need to settle down, ending or extending an activity depending on behavior ("I have time for one more. Do I have a class ready for one more?"), and positively refocusing disruptive behavior. For example, she says to the class as several talk excitedly at once: "Lots of talking, which means lots of news out there, but I need you to share it with everyone." "This is so exciting because no one's ever published a book at the publishing center before. If you are excited to hear about it, sit on your stars." (Stars are marked on the group rug to help students locate a place to settle during group meeting times.)

Once into the science activity, management appears invisible. The adult observer, sensing a potentially treacherous activity with thirty-two first graders and only one adult, is ready to support the teacher. There is, of course, some splashing and throwing things into the water, but yellow stickies start to show up on the class chart. The adult observer sits down. The students are regulating themselves. As the lesson progresses, the teacher engages in on-the-spot logistical management decisions. For instance, everyone is supposed to get a chance to go to the table to choose objects to be placed in cups. After choosing whom the first person to go would be, Mary sets them to the task. Very quickly, it is the second person's turn and the students do not know how to choose who should get the next turn. At first she says "you choose," then foresees an it's-my-turn–no-it's-my-turn problem and redirects them with a counterclockwise motion to go around the table.

She brings the class together to discuss the recorded information. Students generate their own hypotheses and then, with teacher encouragement, match their hypotheses with the data. When the language becomes more abstract, she asks students to come to the front of the room and demonstrate their idea with the materials they all used. In California, this is one component of what is called "specially designed academic instruction in English" (SDAIE), a pedagogical reform focused on making content accessible to English language learners. Other SDAIE components visible in Mary's teaching are cooperative groups that enable communication, peer teaching, and development of group interaction skills; alternative assessments such as performance tests, projects, portfolios, and journals; hands-on and minds-on activities such as the development of products, simulations, and research projects; extensive use of visuals such as slides, posters, tapes, and realia (classroom aquariums, terrariums, field trips); inclusion of community members as conduits of language and culture; integration of first language and culture into class activities; and well-developed scaffolding techniques to accommodate multiple levels of language proficiency within a single classroom.

Workshops take place all over the state educating teachers in these techniques. "I learned it," Mary says, encapsulating in three words the essence of DTE's program design, "from watching kids."

In what follows, we describe how this program and the others we studied manage to develop teachers able to practice with such clarity, confidence, and competence from their first days in the classroom.

PART TWO

CONCEPTUALIZING KNOWLEDGE, SKILLS, AND PRACTICE

4

CONCEPTUALIZING THE KNOWLEDGE BASE FOR TEACHING

HISTORIAN ELLEN LAGEMAN ONCE QUIPPED that the history of American education in the twentieth century can be best explained by understanding that "E. L. Thorndike won and John Dewey lost." Her point was to contrast the effect on teaching of behavioral psychology, with its attempt to develop simple, unvarying laws for teachers to follow, with what Dewey (1929) had in mind in *The Sources of a Science of Education*, where he described knowledge of methods, students, and subjects that would empower teachers to make more intelligent, flexible, and adaptive decisions—knowledge that would make teaching more individually responsive rather than more formulaic.

Dewey's view reflects what the noted psychologist Robert Glaser (1990) outlines as the basic principles of modern learning theory. Glaser argues that twenty-first-century schools must shift from a selective mode ("characterized by minimal variation in the conditions for learning" in which "a narrow range of instructional options and a limited number of ways to succeed are available") to an adaptive mode in which "the educational environment can provide for a range of opportunities for success. Modes of teaching are adjusted to individuals—their backgrounds, talents, interests, and the nature of past performance" (pp. 16–17). In contrast to standardized teaching—appropriate only for the few students who learn in exactly the way and at the pace assumed by the teacher or curriculum program—adaptive teaching is focused on maximizing learning for each student. Such teaching, however, requires deep and sophisticated knowledge about learning, learners, and content.

Thorndike and other behavioral psychologists have illuminated much about learning and teaching and cannot be faulted for the misguided scientism that gripped schools for much of the last century. But, as Lageman noted, Dewey's interest in empowering teachers with knowledge for thoughtful, responsive teaching did not win out with policymakers. The confluence of behavioral learning theory and bureaucratic organizational theory in the early 1900s led to simultaneous efforts to deskill and control teaching by limiting both teachers' autonomy and their levels of education (Callahan, 1962; Tyack, 1974). The bureaucratic school sought to simplify and control teaching by creating curricular edicts at the top of the system and hiring teachers to march through a prescribed curriculum. In a book widely used for teacher training between 1907 and 1930, the need for "unquestioned obedience" was stressed as the "first rule of efficient service" for teachers (Bagley, 1910, p. 2). By 1911, when more than 70 percent of teachers were women, a study observed that their predominance "has been due in part to the changed character of the management of the public schools, to the specialization of labor within the school, to the narrowing of the intellectual range or versatility required of teachers, and to the willingness of women to work for less than men. [Almost] all of the graded school positions have been preempted by women; men still survive in public school work as 'managing' or executive officers" (Coffman, 1911, p. 82).

Limited training for teachers was seen as an advantage for the faithful implementation of newly designed "scientific" curricula: "Such teachers will almost invariably be in hearty sympathy with graded school work," Coffman notes. The less educated teachers were, the more they allowed and encouraged greater simplification and routinization of teaching tasks. Some schools of education resisted efforts to deskill teaching and teacher preparation, especially in the progressive educational movement, as with Bank Street College, Columbia University's Teachers College, the University of Wisconsin, and Wheelock College; but many normal schools (and later university-based programs) watered the teacher education curriculum down to a thin gruel of simple techniques to be used to implement a preset curriculum.

The notion of preparing teachers as knowers and thinkers was relatively rare for much of the twentieth century. Although some early leaders (like John Dewey, Ella Flagg Young, Lucy Sprague Mitchell, and Lucy Wheelock) saw teachers as intellectuals, pedagogical innovators, and "curriculum builders," teachers were viewed by scientific managers of the early 1900s as implementers of top-down mandates and techniques specified in curriculum packages designed by others. Teaching was seen as a series of distinct behaviors that could elicit or undermine student achievement. Policymakers typically sought knowledge as the basis for controlling teachers' actions, not for supporting sophisticated teaching decisions. Research knowledge was mostly used to design specifications for teaching—texts, curriculum packages, and teaching formulas—rather than as the basis for teacher education.

This trickle-down theory of knowledge envisioned that teachers could get what they needed to know from these tools and by following the teachers' manuals and procedures (five rules for a foolproof classroom management system; seven steps to a perfect lesson). However, process-product research that encouraged many attempts at creating behavioral prescriptions for teaching ultimately produced decidedly mixed results. As such research expanded during the 1970s, behaviors that appeared successful in some studies were found to have negative effects when used too much or in other contexts (Darling-Hammond, Wise, and Pease, 1983). In the aggregate, this research demonstrated that interactions are, as Lee Cronbach confessed, nearly infinite in number, and that context matters; the particular students and content being taught call for innumerable decisions about what to do, when, and how. Furthermore, behaviors that are easily prescribed proved much more effective at developing lower-level skills of recall and recognition than higher-order skills aimed at analysis, integration, and invention (Darling-Hammond, Wise, and Pease, 1983).

When various behavioral prescriptions have proved inadequate to the real complexities of teaching (whether these were the proverbial maxims "don't smile until Christmas," or "research-based" rules such as "maintain a brisk pace of instruction"), teachers were left to their own tacit knowledge—largely, how they themselves were taught. Even as knowledge about learning and teaching advanced in universities, it typically resided in departments where researchers, psychologists, and curriculum and evaluation "experts" were trained, rather than in teacher education programs. Teacher education has usually lived in other departments divided by a status differential that created a wide moat between those engaged in developing "knowledge" and those busy with "practice."

However, Dewey's conception of extensive teacher knowledge used to adapt teaching in support of successful learning clearly permeates the successful teacher education programs we studied. All have a clear vision of the teacher they are trying to develop and the research on which their view of practice is based; a coherent curriculum organized to instill the knowledge, skills, and dispositions the vision entails; and well-defined standards of practice that guide development and assessment of teacher candidates. The vision is one of teachers as knowledgeable, reflective decision makers, combining their understanding of how children learn and develop in social contexts with knowledge about subject matter and curriculum—what needs to be taught to achieve the purposes of education and meet the demands of the disciplines. To these understandings the programs add development of a range of teaching strategies and understanding of how to choose among them for differing goals, students, and circumstances. The programs work hard to ensure that this vision and these standards inform all their courses and clinical experiences in a seamless, integrated fashion.

How these programs conceptualize the knowledge base for teacher education involves a set of ideas about *what* teachers need to learn—the content of preparation—and *how* they need to learn it—the processes that allow teachers to develop useful knowledge that can be enacted in ways that respond to the complexity of the classroom. Moreover, the programs have created a *coherent* approach that integrates the tightly connected *what* and *how* of preparation throughout the coursework and clinical experiences candidates undertake.

The Content of Teacher Education

Central to any discussion of knowledge needed for teaching is a judgment about what teachers must be prepared to do. If teachers are viewed primarily as purveyors of information, perhaps they need little more than basic content knowledge and the ability to string together comprehensible lectures to do an adequate job. For this kind of teaching, it is easy to believe that reasonable communication skills and a liberal arts education could be sufficient preparation. But if teachers must ensure successful learning for students who learn in different ways and may encounter a variety of difficulties, then teachers need to be diagnosticians and planners who know a great deal about the learning process and have a repertoire of tools at their disposal. In this view, teaching requires a professional knowledge base that informs decisions about teaching in response to learners.

Similar conceptualizations of the professional knowledge needed for teaching have emerged in recent years from efforts of the professional community (INTASC, 1992; NBPTS, 1989) and the scholarly community (Shulman, 1987; Darling-Hammond and Bransford, 2005). These conceptualizations are consistent with each other and help to produce remarkable similarity in the programs we studied.

A practical conceptualization of professional teaching knowledge was initiated through the standards and assessments of the National Board for

Professional Teaching Standards. This independent organization, established in 1987 to set standards for advanced certification of highly accomplished veteran teachers, has served as the engine behind the standard-setting movement. During the early 1990s, the National Board's standards were integrated with the student learning standards developed by subject matter associations such as the National Councils of Teachers of English and Mathematics and were adapted for beginning teacher licensing by the Interstate New Teacher Assessment and Support Consortium (INTASC), a consortium of more than thirty states. The INTASC standards were in turn adopted by most states and incorporated into the standards of the National Council for the Accreditation of Teacher Education (NCATE). All the programs we studied used these standards in one way or another in articulating or justifying their conceptions of the teacher knowledge base.

In contrast to the recent "technicist" era of teacher training and evaluation—in which teaching was seen as implementing set routines and formulas for behavior, unresponsive to either clients or curriculum goals, these new standards conceptualize teaching as a complex activity that exists in reciprocal relationship with student learning. By reflecting new subject matter standards for students and the demands of learner diversity, as well as the expectation that teachers must collaborate with colleagues and parents to best meet students' needs, the standards define teaching as a collegial, professional activity that responds to considerations of subjects and students. By examining teaching in the light of learning, rather than by looking only at the implementation of specific teaching behaviors, the new standards put considerations of effectiveness at the center of practice.

The conceptualizations of knowledge in the programs we studied are consistent with these standards and with one another, and they stand in contrast to much traditional teacher education curriculum in several ways:

o They emphasize understanding *learners and learning* as central to making sound teaching decisions. Like the foundational importance of anatomy and physiology to the study of medicine, knowledge for teaching begins with deep understanding of human development and learning, how people develop and learn in distinctive social contexts, and how some develop and learn in exceptional ways. This foundation contravenes bureaucratic approaches emphasizing use of specific teaching techniques without reference to the learning process.

o They understand that the *subject matters*. Rather than the generic notions of teaching techniques that dominated teacher education for much of the 1970s and '80s (and still characterize many programs today), these programs begin with a conviction that subject matter provides the foundation for teaching. This means that teaching strategies must be learned in the context of specific content. They seek to ensure that candidates understand the central concepts and modes of inquiry of the subjects to be taught and develop the subject-specific pedagogical knowledge that enables teachers to represent the subject matter so that it will be accessible to learners.

o They unite the study of subject matter and children in the analysis and design of *curriculum*. When teachers are viewed merely as implementing prescriptions devised by others, curriculum is not considered part of their purview; however, these programs see curriculum as the place where learner and content meet. They recognize that if teachers are to enable important learning that adds up over time, they need to develop a "curricular vision" (Zumwalt, 1989) and the skills to select, organize, and design materials and activities enacting that vision.

o They see learners, subject matter, and curriculum as existing in a *sociocultural context* that influences what is valued and how learning occurs. Unlike the assumptions about individual, standardized learning processes that undergird teacher-proof curriculum, the centrality of context requires that teachers learn to understand and adapt their teaching to the content taught, the experiences of learners (their home, community, language, and cultural backgrounds), and the purposes for education held by society, local communities, and families.

o They seek to develop a *repertoire of teaching strategies* and an understanding of their purposes and potential uses for diverse goals and contexts. Rather than a simplistic battery of techniques based on the false assumption of unitary goals for teaching and standardized approaches to learning, they give teachers a strong theoretical understanding of what strategies may be useful for particular purposes and students. They also furnish teachers with practical tools that can help them enact their curricular vision and strategic intentions.

o They place extraordinary emphasis on the processes of *assessment and feedback* as essential to both student and teacher learning. Cognitive scientists now know that learning is intensely dependent on continuous feedback—and ongoing formative assessment is critical for informing teaching. Rather than conceptualizing assessment as the mechanical process used to assign grades, these programs teach teachers how to develop authentic means for constantly assessing learning and using it to inform their teaching and guide student learning. The programs themselves use numerous performance assessments to guide and inform their own teaching and candidates' learning.

o They seek to develop teachers' abilities as *reflective decision makers* who can carefully observe, inquire, diagnose, design, and evaluate learning and teaching so that it is continually revised to become more effective. The conceptualization of knowledge described earlier assumes that teachers must connect the child and the curriculum by weaving a fabric that incorporates the many curricular demands and modes of learning present in the classroom. This means that teachers must have tools to learn *from* practice by analyzing what and whom they are teaching, what is succeeding from minute to minute and day to day, and how to engage and sustain student learning.

o They see teaching as a *collaborative activity* conducted within a *professional community* that feeds ongoing teacher learning, problem solving, and the development of ever more sophisticated practice. In contrast to the image of the solitary teacher practicing behind closed doors based only on her own experiences and knowledge, these programs prepare teachers to learn from and contribute to one another as members of a professional community. The skills of collegial planning and the disposition to be responsible for the learning and practice of everyone in the community are both essential to a professional role.

There are many ways to display this conceptualization of teaching knowledge. One that closely tracks with the programs we studied is the National Academy of Education's depiction in its volume outlining a core curriculum for teacher education, *Preparing Teachers for a Changing World: What Teachers Should Learn and Be Able to Do* (Darling-Hammond and Bransford, 2005). This framework, represented in Figure 4.1, organizes the ideas described here into three general areas of knowledge, skills, and dispositions:

1. Knowledge of *learners* and how they learn and develop within social contexts

2. Conceptions of *curriculum* content and goals—understanding of the subject matter and skills to be taught in light of the social purposes of education

3. Understanding of *teaching* in light of the content and learners to be taught, as informed by assessment and supported by productive classroom environments

These interacting spheres of learners, content, and teaching are further framed by two important conditions for practice: first, teaching is a *profession,* which means that teachers must be prepared to make decisions in the best interests of their students using the best available knowledge to

Figure 4.1. Conceptualizing the Knowledge Base for Teaching

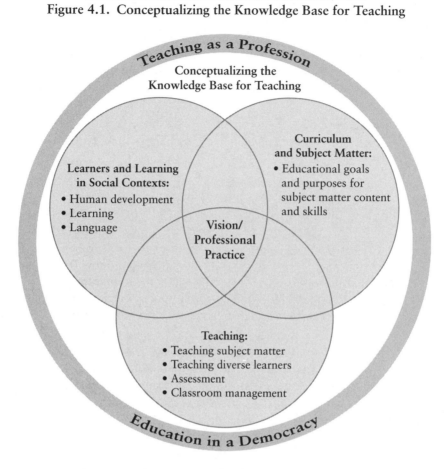

Source: *Darling-Hammond and Bransford, 2005, p. 11.*

do so; second, in the United States education must serve the purposes of a *democracy*. This means that schools assume the purpose of enabling young people to participate fully in political, civic, and economic life in our society. It also means that education—including teaching—is intended to support equitable access to social opportunities. These goals for education influence what teachers need to know and be able to do and what teacher education is expected to accomplish.

Later I discuss how the programs conceptualize the process of learning to teach so as to develop the kind of adaptive expertise that integrates these areas of understanding and allows them to be employed as knowledge-in-action (Schön, 1983). The forms of knowledge teachers need to practice are fluid and highly contextualized; teachers must be able, as Schön suggests, to reflect in action, framing problems and proposing and enacting alternative solutions after noting how their student's learning is progressing. If learning to think like a teacher is central to teacher knowledge, so is being able to act effectively on these insights. The capacity for enactment must be learned through action, with practical tools at one's employ, and through keen analysis. Thus a focus on *practice* in relation to theory is critical to developing useful teacher knowledge. All the programs have similar ways of approaching this problem of developing knowledge *in* practice as well as knowledge *for* practice (Cochran-Smith and Lytle, 1999).

Knowledge of Learners and Learning

As they seek to develop "pedagogical learner knowledge" (Grimmett and MacKinnon, 1992), all the programs emphasize the central importance of understanding diverse learners and the learning process. Just as medical educators believe physicians cannot properly apply the techniques of medicine without understanding how the human body works, teacher educators in these programs believe that without direct knowledge of how learning occurs teachers have no benchmarks by which to evaluate teaching ideas or materials, construct learning opportunities, or adapt their teaching when students do not respond to a particular approach. Ensuring that teachers understand who they are teaching and how they learn empowers teachers to organize their practice around the pursuit of learning rather than just covering the curriculum or getting through the book.

All the programs require coursework and field observations aimed at helping the prospective teachers understand children as learners who are growing and developing over time in multiple dimensions (cognitive, social, emotional, moral, and physical). All of them emphasize looking at individual learners with care and attentiveness, finding students' strengths as well as needs, and building on their interests and experiences. All include considerable attention to the needs of exceptional learners, while stressing that development occurs along several continua and every student learns distinctively.

The required courses in development and learning involve observation of children in classrooms, and often outside the classroom setting, for prospective teachers to gain experiential understanding of children as growing individuals. Prospective teachers are taught how to collect rigorous and detailed observations of children as evidence for making informed teaching decisions. Each program requires that candidates complete a child case study that requires intensive, nonjudgmental observation of a child over time to document how he or she learns and interacts with others in the contexts of family and community as well as classroom and school. Instructors indicate that they expect students to complete these courses having developed a willingness to understand children's learning needs and a set of abilities to synthesize and apply learning theory to practice—in diagnosing students' approaches to learning, observing their "zones of proximal development" for particular tasks, and designing appropriate tasks and experiences to move them forward in different areas of development.

Three of the elementary programs—Bank Street, UC Berkeley's DTE, and Wheelock—are particularly well known for their work to encourage developmentally appropriate teaching grounded in child development and learning theories. As a principal who hired several Bank Street graduates noted: "They bring a way of looking at kids that I feel is very unusual. There is very little negative language about children here and one never gets the sense that the inside of a child is ever attacked. This is a culture of looking at children's growth and strengths, a culture of collaboration and kindness. . . . A distinctive progressive pedagogy—a commitment to intellectually exciting content and to developing high levels of student competence—is part of the Bank Street ethos."

Bank Street's graduate program is built around a required three-course sequence:

1. Child Development
2. The Study of Normal and Exceptional Children Through Observation and Recording
3. Family, Child, and Teacher Interaction in Diverse and Inclusive Educational Settings

In conjunction, these courses focus on children, how they grow and learn, the influence of societal factors in their development, and how teachers and schools use knowledge of students and their strengths and needs to make decisions about curriculum, instruction, and assessment, as well as to communicate with families about their children's home and school lives. All three courses explicitly address concerns for diversity in learning and cultures, including exceptionalities generally treated only in special education courses elsewhere.

Like Bank Street, the DTE program emphasizes deep understanding of children as a guiding force in its conception of teaching through a four-course sequence on child development that extends over the two years of the program. The primary aim of the first-year core seminars is to give candidates understanding of how developmental theories address the learning process generally. Candidates observe children's behavior in the classroom, assess children's developmental levels, and on the basis of theory propose explanations for children's behavior and thinking. In the second year, the seminars focus on how the developmental process is realized as students learn traditional school subjects, thus introducing a curricular focus.

Wheelock's program requires an eight-credit human development course of every major in the college, and for education majors additional courses in the Assessment of Young Children and multicultural education. The emphases on development and social context are tightly integrated throughout, as is emphasis on families and communities in relation to classrooms and learning. For example, the syllabus for Children and Their Environments focuses on "an overview of the environmental and developmental issues relevant to understanding children and their lives" using an ecological model of human development. Course assignments are designed to help students understand children and families from a multicultural, multisocial, and multiethnic perspective. The course also includes a thirty-hour fieldwork component designed to help students sharpen their analytical skills through weekly observation assignments, much like those assigned in the other programs.

This commitment to understanding development and learning extends to the secondary teacher education programs as well. Trinity requires coursework in child and adolescent development beginning in the sophomore year with The Child in Society, which "explores the factors that shape a child's growth and development in America." Prospective teachers learn about the social influences on child development—issues related to cultural diversity and language acquisition; issues of affiliation, including gangs, in adolescent lives; the effects of substance abuse on development; and the effects of labels such as *gifted* and *learning-disabled* that are often attached to children at an early age. Candidates take the course Growing Up in America in their junior year. This course focuses on three developmental stages of childhood considered through multiple lenses: cognitive development, social and emotional development, learning variances, measuring intelligence, and issues of race and gender diversity. These topics are explored through the research literature, field observations, and experiences in school settings.

UVA and Southern Maine's ETEP both include a two-course sequence on development and exceptionalities focusing on basic knowledge of learning principles and human development as they occur generally and in distinctive patterns. The latter's assignment in the Life Span Development course to complete a case study of a child or adolescent is typical of the other programs. Candidates construct "a case study through observations and interviews with one child or adolescent and demonstrating applications of theoretical concepts or relevant research findings to the child/adolescent's current developmental status." In the case study, the candidate collects information about "the child in the family, the child in the school, the child as a learner, and the child in a developmental perspective." The case study includes formative assessments of learning along with interviews and observations and may result in proposals for teaching interventions that are tried out and reported upon. In the Exceptionalities course, as in other programs, candidates complete another case study of a child with a learning disability or other exceptional needs, in addition to learning about screening, modification of curriculum, adaptive technologies, and individual educational plans.

The goal of these efforts is to develop the capacity for strategic teaching. As a faculty member noted, "We want Wheelock teachers to be strategic thinkers and planners who can understand the subject to be taught, understand what a child knows, have a clear idea of what a child needs to know, figure out what a child doesn't know, and develop strategies to move a child from where she is to where she needs to be."

Of course, having a clear idea of what a child knows and needs to know and developing strategies to move a child "from where she is to where she needs to be" require not only an understanding of the child but also a deep appreciation of the subject matter under study and the capacity to select and design curriculum to connect the two.

Knowledge of Subject Matter and Pedagogy

Lee Shulman, who is generally credited with having first articulated the idea of pedagogical content knowledge, writes that teaching "begins with a teacher's understanding of what is to be learned and how it is to be taught" (1987, p. 7). How to develop what a teacher thinks is the "stuff" of learning and the nature of teaching is one of the greatest dilemmas of teacher education, especially since most teacher education programs begin where the candidate's many years of learning subject matter leave off. If, over fifteen or more years of elementary, secondary, and collegiate education, the teacher has come to think of history as lists of dates to be memorized and mathematics as the application of algorithms that do not make particular sense, then the teacher educator has an extraordinarily difficult task in planting a new sense of historical understanding or mathematical reasoning.

Shulman further notes that knowledge of subject matter must be even deeper if the task is to connect what is to be learned to the experiences of many kinds of learners. He notes that "in the face of student diversity, the teacher must have a flexible and multifaceted comprehension [of subject matter], adequate to impart alternative explanations of the same concepts or principles" (p. 9). In addition to flexible understanding of subject matter, Ball and Cohen (1999) suggest that content knowledge for teachers should incorporate a discipline's major ideas and modes of inquiry, their connections with day-to-day life, and the pedagogies most suited to teaching these subject-specific approaches to thinking, reasoning, and performing.

In the past, many teacher education programs largely ignored the challenges of subject matter by treating it not at all (or sometimes by teaching only a single generic methods course intended to give candidates a few general tools) or by assuming knowledge of content and layering a content methods course on top of whatever understandings of subject matter the candidates developed on their own.

By contrast, all of the programs we studied approach subject matter from a pedagogical perspective; likewise, they approach pedagogy from a disciplinary perspective. However, they do so in their own ways, in part because of differences in candidates' entry points to the study of teaching. As Grossman (1990) notes: "In fifth-year programs of teacher education, prospective teachers arrive with knowledge of their subject matter that is distinct from teaching; in four-year programs in which prospective teachers acquire disciplinary knowledge and pedagogical knowledge simultaneously, this distinction may not exist as clearly" (p. 12). Whereas graduate-level programs (in our study, Bank Street, UC Berkeley's DTE, and Southern Maine's ETEP) must find productive ways to revisit subject matter, possibilities for blending content and pedagogical study exist in undergraduate teacher education programs like Alverno and Wheelock. In five-year programs (Trinity and UVA), it is possible to blend content and pedagogical study and also to acquire a strong disciplinary major and include a full year of pedagogical study linked to student teaching. (I discuss these approaches briefly in what follows. Chapter Five further details *how* the programs go about constructing an understanding of subject matter that is integrated with an understanding of students and then made usable in the classroom.)

The graduate-level programs at Bank Street, Berkeley, and USM do not have direct control over the nature and depth of the disciplinary knowledge candidates bring with them from their undergraduate experiences.

In each case, they use an extensive battery of content-specific methods courses to develop subject matter understanding. At Bank Street and USM, candidates take separate courses in methods of teaching reading and language arts, mathematics, science, and social studies. At Berkeley, with its spiral curriculum, language arts and reading are each taught in separate courses and then in combination with social studies; mathematics and science are also taught in combination.

These courses are distinctive in several ways. In all cases, prospective teaching candidates are encouraged to think about the meaning and purposes of the disciplines and about what they contribute to student understanding and development, as well as how they are informed by development. In addition, the content pedagogical courses not only address methods for teaching a subject area, but they also highlight the disciplinary content that teachers need to understand for the particular group of students with whom they will be working, and they directly model the learning of the discipline.

Most of the courses simultaneously take both a subject- and a learner-centered focus, encouraging prospective teachers to think about developing multiple strategies for teaching the subject matter to diverse learners. (See Chapter Five for in-depth discussion of how these courses are taught.) Having candidates engage in the discipline through direct learning and inquiry of their own is a critical element of content pedagogical study in these programs. It is especially important in the graduate programs to confront conceptions of content that candidates bring with them; all the sites we studied used subject-specific methods courses to engage candidates directly in active learning in the disciplines through participation in hands-on science, manipulative-based mathematics instruction, writing to learn about writing, and so on.

The four-year programs we studied have the advantage of being relatively small colleges with a large proportion of students preparing to become teachers. Consequently, instructors in the liberal arts curriculum are often encouraged to think about how to present content so that it is generative for those who would teach. Although Alverno offers an elementary education major and Wheelock requires that students choose a disciplinary major, in both colleges elementary education candidates begin with a strong foundation in the disciplines they will teach, taking a required distribution of courses in the arts and humanities, natural sciences, mathematics, and social sciences. (See Appendix C for detailed program descriptions.) During the same years, they take courses in development and educational principles, drawing on the frameworks of the disciplines in these courses and on insights from their studies of learning and education in their disciplinary lessons. In addition, they later take subject-specific pedagogical courses that directly reengage the content to be taught while demonstrating and emulating the pedagogies to be learned.

The two five-year programs (Trinity and UVA) require prospective teachers to earn a bachelor's degree in a major field of study and a master's of teaching degree from the school of education. Both programs use the length and other structural possibilities of their five-year teacher education program to create a strategic bridge between disciplinary knowledge and pedagogical understanding. Students pursue their undergraduate liberal arts studies concurrently while exploring professional studies. All candidates must meet all of the requirements of the bachelor's degree, earning a disciplinary major plus a master's degree in education.

In both cases, secondary teachers earn a major in the field they will teach. These are not watered-down majors. UVA students who intend to teach mathematics must complete a major in mathematics that includes at least nine courses above the calculus sequence. Two of the nine courses must be graduate-level. All candidates must also complete at least three credits of computer science and three credits of educational computing.

At Virginia, elementary teachers choose a disciplinary major. Prospective elementary teachers at Trinity pursue a specially designed humanities major. Trinity's decision to intensify the focus on content knowledge at the undergraduate level was a response to university administrators' belief that the previous teacher education program overemphasized methods to the detriment of content knowledge, especially for elementary teachers. With the help of local teachers, the university planned the new humanities major with the goal of ensuring a firm foundation in a range of disciplines. The humanities major is made up of strands from the social sciences (history, government, economics, philosophy, and religion), science (geology, anthropology, archaeology, and environmental science), English (British and American literature), and mathematics (including calculus). The typical candidate also gains a major or a minor in a specific field within humanities.

Both programs begin the process of preparing teachers with an exceptionally strong liberal arts degree and an academic major, but their approaches to developing pedagogical skills then differ. UVA's program invests a great deal in content pedagogical coursework at the university, whereas Trinity uses school-based training in teaching methods conducted at its professional development schools. Both place candidates in fieldwork each year so that what they learn in the courses is applied in the context of work with children.

UVA has developed a number of thoughtful means for integrating disciplinary study with pedagogic thinking. As part of the reform that created the five-year program model, the Curry School of Education and the university liberal arts faculty worked to integrate disciplinary studies with professional courses in both schools. First, all of the subject-specific majors for teachers-in-training were formulated jointly by faculty in the academic department and the Curry School. In addition, a number of education courses are designed to merge teaching about subject matter and pedagogy; for example, in addition to courses in the English department, the UVA program in English education also offers subject-based pedagogical courses (Pedagogy of English Language Instruction; Teaching Composition; Literature for Adolescents). Finally, after UVA students complete their major, some pedagogical courses, and an intensive student teaching experience, they return to graduate-level courses in their academic field of concentration, honing their subject matter understanding after having seen the subject area from a teacher's perspective.

In a contrasting model, Trinity candidates undertake practica in the field starting in their freshman year, while also pursuing a disciplinary major. They receive discipline-specific pedagogical instruction from courses taught by mentor teachers in the PDS sites rather than through courses at the university. PDS mentors and Trinity faculty members cooperatively develop courses and seminar sessions that address a range of teaching and learning issues, such as multiple ways to approach the same teaching and learning problem or means for addressing different learning styles.

Although each teacher education program addresses development of subject-specific pedagogy somewhat differently, each offers prospective teachers opportunities to think pedagogically about the subject matter in school- and university-based contexts. University-based courses have the benefit of engaging prospective teachers in learning the subject matter with colleagues, placing them in the position of a learner who must make meaning of the subject matter. School-based opportunities, on the other hand, offer the opportunity to engage directly with children who are learning the subject matter. Assessment of learning is woven into this work through coursework and practice, thus connecting subject matter with information about students' needs and providing teachers with the grist they need for planning.

Only one program offers a specific course in classroom management, but they all teach candidates how to manage many kinds of learning and teaching, through effective means of organizing and presenting information, managing discussions, organizing cooperative learning strategies, and supporting individual and group inquiry. This occurs through a combination of university-based coursework and meticulously selected field placements, where candidates can see expert teaching using these strategies modeled and explained. In coursework and fieldwork, the programs teach candidates about how to work with children to develop and sustain engagement and productive behavior. Integration of learning about classroom management in courses and field assignments about child development on the one hand, where individual motivation, social dynamics, and strategies for working with children are taught, and in courses and field experiences examining teaching methods on the other hand, where strategies for organizing effective learning are taught, means that candidates can see their classroom work holistically. They learn how to create a purposeful and productive classroom, with strategies for supporting appropriate student behavior, rather than focusing first on student discipline and behavior in the absence of concerns for teaching and learning.

In addition, integration of knowledge about content and children is further encouraged as prospective teachers learn to develop a curricular vision that encompasses both *what* they are teaching and *whom* they are teaching, mindful of the greater goals for instruction held by their professional disciplines, states, districts, local communities, and schools, as well as themselves.

Knowledge of Contexts and Curriculum

In the technicist era of teacher education and in many truncated routes to teaching that have cropped up in recent years, courses in foundations of education have often been thought impractical and the study of curriculum unnecessary for teachers who are, in some views, implementers of curriculum designed by others. This perspective implicitly assumes that students, teaching, and curriculum can be fairly easily standardized; thus teachers do not themselves need to know how to construct or tailor learning opportunities. Furthermore, it assumes that the work of schools is largely context-free, so teachers do not need to understand diversity of communities, thought, and experience to be successful.

By contrast, because they conceptualize teaching as dependent on learning and the learning process as embedded in the linguistic, cultural, and other experiences of students, all of these programs engage candidates in studying the purposes and contexts of education and the design of curriculum. These studies are designed to help teachers understand the big picture guiding their efforts: to be clear and purposeful about what and how they teach, understand how content adds up to larger understanding beyond a single set of lessons, be able to plan and adapt curriculum with disciplinary goals and student needs in mind, and respond to students and families so as to promote equitable learning. Even more, these programs seek to help teachers understand how schools often reinforce unequal social status so that they are prepared to act as change agents, attending to questions of students' access to knowledge within and beyond the classroom.

CONTEXTS AND PURPOSES OF EDUCATION. Educational "foundations" courses typically examine educational issues from sociological, anthropological, historical, political, philosophical, and psychological perspectives, exploring debates on the purposes and aims of education; social and cultural contexts for learning; power relations within organizations and society; and accountability structures within schools for students, teachers, and administrators. Whether embedded within teaching seminars or courses on development or taught in separate courses such as Education in Inner Cities, Multicultural Teaching, or Schools and Community, these programs offer multiple opportunities for candidates to learn about the social, political, cultural, and economic factors that influence learning, teaching, and schooling. The goal is not only to have teachers better understand their students and the communities they teach in but also to develop a "philosophical perspective informed by . . . their personal and professional responsibilities to educate for democracy," as a Bank Street syllabus put it.

The content of these courses generally includes the structure of the U.S. educational system and history of reforms, the multiple purposes of education for intellectual development, vocational preparation, citizenship, and personal fulfillment (Goodlad, 1984) and how they have been and are pursued in various contexts, the historically unequal allocation of curriculum and resources by race and class, and strategies for securing more equitable education. A critical element is the study of language and culture and how to support learning for students who are not from the dominant group as well as how to construct classrooms that take advantage of the diverse experiences and knowledge students bring with them to school.

In addition, what gets taught in classrooms is informed not only by textbooks and state or local standards, but by broader social goals for education, and social policies that teachers need to understand. Should school tasks be designed to help students learn to love reading as well as to decode print? Should students learn to cooperate with one another as well master math facts? What learning opportunities should students with disabilities have access to? All the programs tackle such issues and many more. But they are not treated as abstract and "merely" philosophical. Considerations of why teach and who is taught, as well as the contexts for teaching and learning, are translated into practical understanding through guided school and classroom observations and through the development of curriculum that must take them into account.

One interesting strategy for helping candidates consider the practical implications of various philosophies is a Bank Street assignment that candidates make a series of school site visits to observe schools founded on particular teaching beliefs, from Waldorf education and Montessori education to back-to-the-basics strategies or open education. These observations are done in conjunction with coursework geared toward understanding the philosophical and social contexts of schools. Through visiting schools firsthand, students see philosophies in action and can compare a variety of educational ideologies that shape school organization and functions.

CURRICULUM DEVELOPMENT AND ASSESSMENT. The importance of engaging beginning teachers in curriculum development derives from a belief that, regardless of the textbook series, curriculum guide, or set of materials provided, the teacher must still be able to "draw connections to students' prior knowledge and experiences, choose appropriate starting places and sequences of activities, develop assignments and assessments to inform learning and guide future teaching, and construct scaffolding for different students depending on their needs" (Darling-Hammond and Bransford, 2005, p. 176). As the National Academy of Education's recent (2005) study of teacher education noted: "Curriculum guides, texts, and tests help the teacher respond to a subset of local and state expectations; however, by their very nature they cannot dictate a curriculum for a particular class. Because what is taught must connect to student readiness and interests as well as to community contexts, even topics that are routinely taught or presented in texts require curricular thinking and development. Subject matter teaching needs always to be infused with a developmental perspective and sensitivity to social contexts" (p. 176).

The capacity to plan instruction so that it meets the needs of students and the demands of content, so that it is purposeful and adds up to important, well-developed abilities for students, is not something most teachers know how to do intuitively or learn from unguided classroom experience. A study of experienced teachers without previous formal preparation found that among the things they felt they learned from the teacher education program they later entered were the abilities to engage in curriculum planning; set long-term goals and organize instruction in support of these goals; assess, reflect on, and improve their teaching; and make decisions grounded in useful theoretical frameworks about teaching and learning (Kunzman, 2002, 2003). Many of these experienced teachers spoke of their previous lack of curricular planning ability: "'I didn't have a big vision for where my class needed to go: What was my end result? Where did I want to be at the end of the semester, both in content and in skills? So I couldn't work cogently toward those goals'" (Kunzman, 2003, p. 246).

For these reasons, all seven programs require prospective teachers to evaluate curriculum materials and construct curriculum, usually in the form of one or more units of instruction on a particular topic that is either central to a specific discipline or embodies an important theme with strong interdisciplinary connections (and often both). Curriculum knowledge is forged at the intersection of subject matter knowledge, student readiness to learn, student interests, and community contexts. The teacher needs to consider where children are in their conceptual development, what motivates children at various stages, and what local resources are available for supporting curricular experiences. Candidates are often asked to evaluate resources for teaching specific concepts and find materials and examples that draw on experiences familiar to their students.

Central to the curriculum development enterprise is knowledge of assessment, which allows the teacher to monitor where students are, individually and collectively, in their understanding and development at the beginning of a teaching segment, so that the right entry points can be chosen and the right scaffolds for learning constructed; to identify what and how students are learning, so that teaching can be continuously adapted to students' emerging needs; to instantiate goals for learning in performance assessments that can guide both learning and teaching; and to provide careful feedback to students so they can strengthen their own performance and improve their work through revision. Some programs offer separate courses in assessment while others include it in curriculum or methods courses, but all provide their candidates with knowledge to select and design formative assessment tools as well as performance assessments and scoring rubrics, give thoughtful feedback, and plan curriculum and teaching from the results of student assessments.

Typically, as their own performance assessment, candidates plan a curriculum unit that must articulate a set of goals, describe and justify the selection of materials and activities to meet those goals, incorporate formative and summative assessments of student learning, and include plans to accommodate the needs of students with language and learning differences. Later, they teach the unit, collect evidence of student learning, reflect on what students learned, and often discuss what they would do differently in teaching the unit again to similar students.

The Process of Teacher Education

Although it is important to have well-chosen courses that include core knowledge for teaching, it is equally important to organize prospective teachers' experiences so they can *integrate* and *use* their knowledge skillfully in the classroom. This is probably the most difficult aspect of constructing a teacher education program. Teacher educators must worry not only about *what* to teach but *how,* so that knowledge for teaching actually shapes practice and enables teachers to become adaptive experts who can continue to learn.

The Importance of Coherence

One critical element in how these programs develop knowledge that transfers to practice is the extremely strong coherence each program has achieved. To a great extent, the experience of learning to teach in these programs is seamless. Unlike the critiques of many schools of education pointing to fragmentation among courses and between coursework and clinical work (see Feiman-Nemser, 1990; Goodlad, Soder, and Sirotnik, 1990; Howey and Zimpher, 1989; Zeichner and Gore, 1990), coursework is carefully sequenced based on a strong theory of learning to teach; courses are designed to intersect with each other and collectively complete a well-understood landscape of learning, and they are tightly interwoven with the advisement process and students' work in schools. Virtually all the closely interrelated courses involve classroom applications where observation or student teaching occurs. These classrooms are in turn selected because they model the kind of practice being discussed in courses and advisement. These program elements—along with a capstone project, generally a portfolio or major research project—are designed to connect theory and practice regularly.

One of our research protocols asked graduates about connections they perceived between what they did in their classrooms and what they learned in their preparation program. Contrary to conventional wisdom about "Mickey Mouse" teacher education coursework, the graduates regularly cited coursework as an important base for their practice, and almost every course was identified by someone. Graduates indicated that most of their courses:

○ Connected theory, practice, and field experiences

○ Were anchored in professional teaching standards

○ Modeled or demonstrated the practices they described

○ Infused concerns for learning and development within socio-cultural contexts

○ Required reflective papers, presentations, and demonstrations of teaching skills

○ Provided extensive feedback about candidates' analyses and performances, with suggestions for improvement and opportunities for revision

○ Required evidence as the basis for judgment

Our review of syllabi and assignments found that in almost every course, instructors asked students to relate what they were observing, describing, or writing to theory and to evidence about children, teaching, and learning from their fieldwork settings. The theoretical frameworks animating the courses and assignments were consistent across the program; core ideas were reiterated and built on throughout. Faculty worked together to create the program curriculum and understood what was being taught in other courses. These findings echo those of Howey and Zimpher (1989), who report that strong teacher education programs "have one or more frameworks grounded in theory and research as well as practice: frameworks that explicate, justify, and build consensus around such fundamental conceptions as the *role* of the teacher, the *nature* of teaching and learning, and the *mission* of the school in this democracy. . . . Programs embedded in such frameworks clearly establish priorities in terms of key dispositional attitudes and behaviors that are enabled and monitored in repeated structured experiences. . . . Conceptually coherent programs enable needed and *shared* faculty leadership by underscoring collective roles as well as individual course responsibilities" (p. 242).

The importance of program coherence was emphasized in a review of ninety studies that examined efforts to change entering student teachers' beliefs, understanding, and behaviors with respect to teaching, learning, and students. The authors concluded that:

> In the short-term interventions, which in all but one or two cases involved a single course, we saw little reported impact. In the studies of year-long programs, however, it was much more common for the researchers to report positive effects. Duration of intervention, as such, was not the main variable. More significant was what a given time

period enabled those in the program to do. In the short-term interventions there seemed a tendency for the other elements of the program to interfere with or even nullify the effects of the intervention. . . . The hidden curriculum in this case emanates from the type of structured fragmentation Gore and Zeichner (1991) refer to. Longer-term programs, on the other hand, were effective when the teacher educators maintained a consistent focus and message [Wideen, Mayer-Smith, and Moon, 1998, p. 151].

In addition to the influence of programmatic coherence, we found at least three critical aspects of these programs that appear to contribute to their powerful impact on candidates' abilities to practice:

1. Tight integration of theory and practice through continuous interweaving of clinical work with formal study
2. Use of pedagogies that build knowledge of practice *in* practice, including close observation and analysis of teaching and learning; case methods; and performance assessments and portfolios that document and support reflection on teaching
2. Ongoing opportunities for evaluation of teaching in response to student learning

Integrating Theory and Practice by Interweaving Coursework and Clinical Work

One perennial dilemma of teacher education is how to integrate theoretically based knowledge traditionally taught in university classrooms with the experience-based knowledge traditionally located in the practice of teachers and the realities of classrooms and schools. Older versions of teacher education often had students taking batches of coursework in isolation from practice and then adding a short dollop of student teaching to the end of the program, often in classrooms that did not model the practices previously described in abstraction. By contrast, all of these programs require students to spend extensive time in the field as observers and participants in the teaching process throughout the entire program, examining and applying the concepts and strategies they are simultaneously learning about in their courses.

Many teacher educators argue that novices who have some experience with teaching when they encounter coursework are more prepared to make sense of the ideas, theories, and concepts addressed in their academic work, and that student teachers see and understand both theory and practice differently if they are taking coursework concurrently with fieldwork. A growing body of research confirms this belief, finding that teachers-in-training who participate in fieldwork either before or alongside coursework are better able to understand theory, apply concepts they are learning in their coursework, and support student learning (Baumgartner, Koerner, and Rust, 2002; Denton, 1982; Denton, Morris, and Tooke, 1982; Henry, 1983; Ross, Hughes, and Hill, 1981; Sunal, 1980).

The sites we studied interweave coursework and clinical work throughout the entire program. At UVA, for example, field experiences and coursework at the university occur simultaneously throughout four years of study, overlapping and reinforcing one another and facilitating steady transfer of theory to practice and practice to theory. The program is designed so that prospective teachers engage in progressively more complex and intensive work with learners in combination with university course work aimed at developing a theoretical understanding of learning and learners. As second-year college students, the prospective teachers enroll in an introductory education course and spend twenty-five to thirty hours each semester in a field placement. They observe in both elementary and middle schools, focusing on school organization while taking the School in America course. During the junior year, the focus of field placement is on individual learners: While candidates take courses on development and learning, they are required to tutor individual children and complete child case studies. Working with students with special educational needs is emphasized in conjunction with a course on exceptional learners.

In their fourth year, field experiences focus on the classroom and instructional design. Candidates spend about two hours per week in the fall and two weeks in the spring in the classroom, observing, describing, and analyzing teaching and learning behaviors in connection with their coursework on teaching. They also develop and teach model lessons as well as a thematic unit of instruction while taking courses in teaching methods. Finally, in the fall of the fifth year students teach full-time as teacher associates, returning to the university for further study in the spring. Many students remarked that this integration of fieldwork and coursework throughout the five-year program was the "single biggest advantage of the BA/MT."

In similar fashion, the five-year program at Trinity involves candidates in fieldwork each year, with the additional benefit that much of this clinical work takes place in the university's professional development school settings where veteran teachers work closely with university faculty on development of the school's practice and the teacher education curriculum. An initial introduction to a Trinity PDS is part of a first-year course requirement. In the sophomore year, prospective teachers work in a PDS with a mentor for three hours weekly while taking education courses such as Child in Society. Like UVA students, candidates focus especially on the school perspective in the sophomore year, visiting and observing resource rooms, the library, counselor's office, administrative offices, and special programs as well as classrooms, and writing a school case study.

In their junior year, students' practicum focus is the *master teacher*. Assigned to a PDS other than where they did their sophomore practicum, students are to "become keen observers . . . and familiarize [themselves] with techniques and behaviors" of accomplished practitioners. How do veteran teachers begin a class lesson? How do they introduce new material? What management and discipline strategies do they employ? How do they move from one topic of study to another? How do they account for students' individual learning styles and needs? As with the sophomore practicum, students spend the initial part of the semester observing and then ease into more classroom-focused activity; finally they assume some teaching responsibility, under the guidance of their mentor. Students keep a journal recording observations and reflections on topics such as classroom organization, teacher and teaching style, discipline and management, attention to individual student needs, and classroom procedures.

The other side of the student-subject dialectic is pursued in the senior year, when the practicum focus is the *student*. The goal of senior-year inquiry is to learn to recognize and be sensitive to individual students' learning styles and needs and how they are addressed in the classroom. While assisting once again in a PDS classroom and taking related college courses, candidates complete a child case study. In three years of practica tightly connected to courses on teaching, students have observed a variety of lessons, developed their own lesson plans, constructed various student assessments, graded papers, assembled curricula, tutored individual and small groups of students, and conducted whole-class activities, all under the watchful eye of experienced mentors and faculty members.

In their fifth year, prospective teachers participate in a yearlong internship after completing summer courses in curriculum and teaching methods. Interns spend the fall under supervision of a mentor at a PDS school four days a week (increasing to five days in the spring semester). While teaching, they also take a course in school leadership, supervision, and evaluation, learning how to engage in clinical supervision with peers and critique their own practice. As the interns gradually assume more responsibility for classroom instruction, they are also encouraged to take on additional responsibilities within the school community. Virtually everything they study is observed and applied in the classroom, and through their own research inquiries they theorize issues and concerns they have seen unfolding in practice.

Bank Street students simultaneously engage in coursework on child development, teaching methods, and social foundations of education and field placement in classrooms with cooperating teachers. Because Bank Street faculty members serve as field supervisors and individual advisors as well as course instructors, they create especially close linkage between the college courses and advisement and the prospective teachers' experiences in the field, which they themselves oversee. As students read seminal works in educational theory, they are encouraged through classroom inquiry and observation to seek empirical evidence for how these theories operate within specific teaching contexts.

The one-year internship model at the University of Southern Maine and the two-year graduate program at UC Berkeley both have candidates in student teaching placements throughout the entire program while taking coursework. The undergraduate models at Alverno and Wheelock embed clinical assignments of various kinds in most courses over the years of undergraduate education, in addition to student teaching.

In addition to these clinical assignments and experiences, several programs have created such strong models of practice in the school environment that they serve as learning experiences in and of themselves. Both USM and Trinity conduct all of their training in professional development schools that are formal university-school partnerships, and Bank Street uses its School for Children and other public schools started or run by its graduates as laboratory schools for teacher training. All of the programs have close relationships with a number of schools where they are often engaged in school improvement or curriculum projects as well as student teaching. Intensifying these relationships, the practices of PDS schools are highly developed and closely compatible with the philosophies of the teacher education programs. In these settings, prospective teachers access strong and widely shared cultural norms and practices almost by osmosis.

In the Bank Street School for Children, for instance, a pre-K–8 independent school, located within the Bank Street College building, classes for prospective teachers are offered in the same rooms that children occupied in previous hours. This is also true of many courses offered in the PDSs connected to Trinity and USM. University courses conducted within school space allow prospective teachers to interact regularly with children and be surrounded by information about practice. Here prospective teachers are constantly exposed to artifacts of teacher's work and children's learning: lessons, assignments, and student work posted on walls, blackboards, and bulletin boards; books arrayed in classroom libraries; and the organization of desks, tables, learning centers, and classroom materials reflecting classroom management strategies. Knowledge about teaching pervades the environment in which the prospective teachers work and learn, surrounding them like the air they breathe. Embedding both academic and clinical learning within the children's learning environment creates additional links between theory and practice by developing common learning sites for both adults and children.

Pedagogies That Confront the Problems of Learning to Teach

It is not just the availability of classroom experience that enables teachers to apply what they are learning. Recent studies of teachers' learning suggest that when teachers study and reflect on their work and connect it to research and theory, they are better able to identify areas needing improvement, consider alternative strategies for the future, and solve problems of practice (Freese, 1999; Laboskey, 1992). All the programs share a number of pedagogies that facilitate this process: case methods, close analyses of learning and teaching, performance assessments, and portfolios. These approaches have emerged in response to the perennial problems of learning to teach: overcoming the apprenticeship of observation, supporting enactment, and managing the complexity of teaching—in particular, helping novices connect theory to practice.

Here I outline briefly the strategies these programs use for developing and assessing teaching, because they are an important aspect of how knowing is conceptualized. Indeed they constitute what Perkins has called "performances of understanding" (1998). In the next chapter, I describe in more detail how the strategies are used in the service of developing and demonstrating candidates' knowledge and skills.

CASE METHODS. All seven programs use case writing as a learning tool. In various combinations, student teachers are asked to develop case studies on pupils, aspects of schools and teaching, and families or communities by observing, interviewing, examining student work, and analyzing data they have collected.

Many professions, notably law, medicine, and business, help candidates bridge the gap between theory and practice and develop skills of reflection and close analysis by engaging them in reading and writing cases. Proponents of case methods argue that cases support systematic learning from particular contexts as well as from more generalized theory about teaching and learning (Colberg, Trimble, and Desberg, 1996). Shulman

(1992) suggests that cases provide "antidotes to the dangers of overgeneralization" (p. 3) and are powerful tools for professional learning because they require professionals in training to "move up and down, back and forth, between the memorable particularities of cases and the powerful generalizations and simplifications of principles and theories. Principles are powerful but cases are memorable. Only in the continued interaction between principles and cases can practitioners and their mentors avoid the inherent limitations of theory-without-practice or the equally serious restrictions of vivid practice without the mirror of principle" (Shulman, 1996, p. 201).

All of the programs require candidates at some point to develop at least one extensive written study of an individual learner from close observation and data collection about a student they teach or tutor, as well as theory and principles addressed in concurrent courses at the university. In the case study, the prospective teachers usually describe and interpret aspects of the student's development, home, and learning contexts and examine the student's learning progress. In addition, they may examine the impact of their own actions—and those of the school generally—on the student's learning and address how their knowledge of the student shapes how they conceptualize the job of teaching. In some programs, case studies of several kinds of learners—including English language learners and those with exceptional learning needs—are completed within different courses.

This intensive look at a single child is designed to instill the habit of looking closely at children to understand what they do and why. Many graduates reported that they came to understand their students afresh through this experience and that they developed a variety of methods for keeping track of children and of their own actions as a result of engaging in this initial process.

The programs also use case methods in other ways. Some focus on the family and community context, others on the school as an organization or on specific teaching and learning events within the classroom. Sometimes cases are a springboard for creating plans for future work—say, a yearlong plan for involving families or a plan for addressing certain teaching and learning issues within the classroom.

ANALYSES OF TEACHING AND LEARNING. Writing and reading case studies presents opportunities for candidates to analyze and reflect on examples of teaching and products of student learning. Such analysis can be a structured means for closely examining the process and outcomes of teaching and learning using real classroom artifacts—student work samples, videotapes of classroom practice, and curriculum materials. The use of these materials enables student teachers and teacher educators to jointly examine and analyze a "common text" (Ball and Cohen, 1999) to which all have access. Candidates examine texts produced by other teachers as well as their own materials: samples of work from learners in their class-rooms, lessons they were developing, videotapes of their teaching, and other records of their evolving practice as new teachers.

Analyses of learning are conducted through regular observation and evaluation of student work as well as the more ambitious case studies we have described. These efforts focus on numerous issues in the teaching and learning process, from challenges of student engagement, student understanding, and assessment to questions about the framing of subject matter concepts for students at particular developmental levels or with specific learning needs. A student teacher involved in a course on learning or development may examine student work samples to assess their degree of understanding and the misunderstandings or misconceptions that might be visible, and to propose steps to help the students develop their understanding further. Candidates might also analyze, compare, and contrast the work of particular students (English language learners and mainstream students; five-year-olds and seven-year-olds; students with special needs) to help them focus on the needs and strengths of different children as well as the challenges involved in each child's learning.

PERFORMANCE TASKS. Clinical experiences are an opportunity for practice, but a rather haphazard one that may not ensure either the occasion to encounter certain kinds of teaching problems or the impetus to develop and demonstrate particular skills. More structured performance tasks can be used to afford these opportunities and present another way to deal with the problem of enactment by enabling student teachers to engage in certain practices and analyze them, along with their effects. All of these teacher education programs develop specific performance tasks they require of students (such as planning and delivering a lesson, delivering a lecture, conducting a Socratic seminar, completing and teaching a curriculum unit) around which they organize coursework and practice opportunities.

Performance tasks are often structured as public exhibitions of knowledge and practice that are measured against shared, public criteria, with occasion for feedback. One of the most highly developed systems of performance assessment was created at Alverno College, using frequent exhibitions of performance, benchmarked against standards, as the foundation for much of its work. Virtually every assignment begins with reference to the criteria for the performance being developed and ends with a chance for candidates to evaluate their own work as well as to gain feedback from others to guide revision and improvement.

In addition to specific acts of teaching, students engage in performance tasks designed to evaluate planning skills, such as the development of lessons or units in light of key ideas about instructional design, and the design and use of formative and summative assessments of student learning. After teaching the lessons and units they have designed and implementing their assessments, candidates are encouraged to consider how to revise their teaching according to what they discover about student learning, reinforcing the view of teaching as responsive to learning rather than as implementing a set of routines.

TEACHING PORTFOLIOS. Most of the programs also use teaching portfolios, generally a collection of materials and artifacts from teachers' work, including such elements as statements about the teacher's educational philosophy; descriptions of the teacher's plans for classroom management; curriculum materials (such as unit and lesson plans, assignments, assessments, and daily logs); logs, journals, or reflections; research inquiries; videotapes and commentary about the teacher's own instruction; and samples of student work. Some include evaluations of the teachers' teaching by others through peer or supervisor observations, recommendations, or student evaluations. These elements are often accompanied by reflective commentary from the teacher about the process and outcomes of teaching.

Proponents suggest that teacher portfolios present opportunities for robust documentation of practice and for candidate reflection. As a tool for learning and reflection, portfolios can alleviate what Shulman referred to as "pedagogical amnesia"—a disease endemic to teaching at all levels. Characterized by the inability to record and recall the fruits of teaching experience, this is one symptom of the multidimensional complexity of teaching. So much happens so fast that it is a blur. Portfolios help make teaching stand still long enough to be examined, shared, and learned from. As an assessment tool, they foster a comprehensive look at how the various aspects of a teacher's practice—planning, instruction, assessment, curriculum design, and communication with peers and parents—come together.

Continuous Opportunities for Reflection on Learning and Teaching

Preparing teachers to learn from teaching throughout their careers requires a set of tools to develop the skills and practices of systematic, purposeful inquiry and critical reflection. Many teacher educators focus on developing these abilities by engaging student teachers in reflective activities, such as journals and logs about teaching practice, as well as in systematic research in their classrooms and schools (Gore and Zeichner, 1991; Price, 2001). By continually raising and answering questions about what students are learning and why, teachers can learn to deal with the complexity of practice and can overcome some of the limitations of their apprenticeship of observation.

LOGS, JOURNALS, AND REFLECTIVE ESSAYS. Most of the programs use a variety of tools to stimulate teachers' ongoing reflection, among them observation logs, reflective journals, and papers focused on specific teaching or learning situations. These are sometimes used to stimulate reflection on the readings and issues discussed in a specific class and make connections to related experiences outside of class. At other times they are tools for collecting observations in clinical settings about specific children, the learning of students individually or collectively, the cooperating teacher's practice, or the student teacher's own teaching attempts. Students sometimes use journals to record daily activities, reflections on readings, thoughts about practice observed, or their developing philosophies of education.

Key to the usefulness of these strategies is regular feedback from course instructors or supervisors, often raising additional questions for candidates to explore ("Why do you think Julian does this?" "What does your cooperating teacher say are her reasons for choosing this book?" "Why might students have had difficulty with this concept?"). Instructors refer candidates to readings that might be helpful in answering questions or shedding light on issues or suggest hypotheses that might be explored. These tools are used to develop the habit of inquiry, of always looking deeper, and of perpetually analyzing how activities in the classroom influence individual learners, the class as a whole, and the learning process.

RESEARCH INQUIRIES. All the programs require that teachers engage in inquiries or research about teaching. These range from modest investigations of specific problems of practice to more ambitious research studies that may serve as a capstone project. Advocates of practitioner research suggest such efforts help student teachers learn critical dispositions and skills that undergird reflective practice, including a commitment to search for answers to problems of practice and the skills of careful observation, data collection, and reasoned analysis (Zeichner and Liston, 1987).

The disposition toward reflective, inquiry-based and analytic thinking—what Cochran-Smith and Lytle (1999) term an "inquiry stance" toward teaching—is one element of developing adaptive expertise, or the ability to continue to learn productively by guiding one's own problem solving. Some research has found that classroom studies can promote systematic, intellectual, and practical critique of the assumptions and approaches being used in a classroom, leading the teacher-researcher not only to reframe questions but also to revise pedagogical approaches (Cochran-Smith and Lytle, 1993). We observed these outcomes in the work of the candidates and graduates we reviewed who were constantly looking for ways to analyze the success of their efforts and revamp and adapt their plans on the basis of this evidence.

AUTOBIOGRAPHY AND SELF-REFLECTION. All the programs emphasize the importance of prospective teachers understanding their own educational beliefs and values (including how they were formed and are reshaped) and their own learning strategies and cultural identities, as well as those of others. Understanding what their own implicit educational philosophies and values are, and sharing them with other candidates who hold other views, helps prospective teachers understand that there are many perspectives on education that need to be negotiated in any school or classroom. In addition, new teachers encounter many students who come from backgrounds and have experiences quite different from their own. If these new teachers can only imagine teaching students like themselves, then they will expect to teach much as they remember learning in their apprenticeship of observation.

Fostering greater self-awareness among preservice teachers potentially helps the new teacher understand the individual perspective on learning. By understanding their own individual needs, experiential backgrounds, and cultural contexts, and by learning of their colleagues' perspectives as well, prospective teachers can develop a sense of what the individual brings to a learning situation. This awareness of learners' experiences and perspectives informs the new teacher when designing instruction for students with diverse learning needs.

The programs are conscious about surfacing initial conceptions about teaching and helping prospective teachers reflect on their experiences, feeling that candidates must know themselves and their beliefs if they are to expand their visions, uncover potential biases, and effectively design and use multiple instructional tasks for others. This is often tackled through autobiography: having students reflect and write about their early school experiences, their family's attitudes toward and involvement with school, their road to literacy, how they felt in confronting an educational challenge, or other inroads to self-reflection. As a UVA instructor commented on an assignment to help her students gain a deeper understanding of what they believe and why, "The students develop a heightened awareness of the context which *they* bring to the classroom which they, in turn, can draw on to facilitate similar awareness in their students."

Quite often, this self-reflection focuses on the forging of an educational philosophy that can inform a practice consistent with a teacher's beliefs. In the Trinity program, students are asked to "confront their implicit education beliefs by examining their explicit teaching actions" in their fifth and final year of the program. They are first asked to express their own philosophy, stance, opinions, values, attitudes, convictions, goals, purposes, and beliefs about education. They are asked to "compare [their] stated educational platform with [their] platform in use." The students keep a log detailing teaching strategies, including assignments given to students, their relationship with students, and rationale for classroom decisions. A comparison of their logged record of actions and their stated beliefs is the basis for self-analysis. The written analysis of the differences and congruencies between stated beliefs and those in action helps the students understand their own theories of teaching and their own teaching practice. It also transforms practice as teachers come to see how their actions must change if they are to realize the values they hold dear.

Creating a Foundation for Learning Within a Professional Community

Finally, the programs conceptualize the knowledge base for teaching as unbounded, not finite, and as collegially developed, not individually acquired and owned. In contrast to the view of the lone teacher gaining a basket of knowledge for teaching that is complete and self-contained at the end of teacher education, these programs view teaching as inherently problematic, given the nonroutine needs of students and the ever-expanding nature of knowledge; they view professional teaching as inherently collective, something to be developed with colleagues who are partners in learning and problem solving.

All the programs view themselves as a starting point for the prospective teacher's learning and believe it is their role to create a foundation for the candidate's own lifelong learning. The faculty makes decisions about what and how to teach that are designed to help prospective teachers understand central features of the learning and teaching process and be able to inquire and reflect productively about their practice so as to learn and improve. They seek to develop teachers who can learn *from* teaching as well as learn *for* teaching. They view their primary responsibility as helping preservice teachers learn how to be reflective practitioners who can be proactive in their own professional learning.

We heard from many graduates how their teacher education program helped them develop skills that allow them to develop new teaching strategies and curriculum. As one mathematics teacher and UVA graduate noted, the program did not give him a "bag of tricks" but helped him understand "the big scheme of things." He commented, "The longer I've been out, the more I appreciate what Curry [School of Education] . . . did. Things that were started there are coming to fruition. The Curry School planted a lot of seeds."

Each of the teacher education programs also emphasize learning from collegial interaction, which is built into the core design of the programs in a variety of ways.

In many cases, field placements are designed so that more than one student teacher is assigned to the same school. Where colleges have PDS relationships, students are typically assigned in sizable cohorts to each school. These groupings create a built-in support network, offering the student teachers a friendly ear for discussing issues, planning, and instruction. The schools themselves are designed around teams of teachers planning and working together, creating a professional learning community for both veteran and novice teachers, and offering models of collaboration for prospective teachers to learn from.

In most of the programs, student teachers have the opportunity to observe one another teach and often to videotape and watch each other's lessons, offering comment and critique about practice as a means of improving their own as well as helping each other. The schools they teach in also value ongoing peer coaching and shared evaluation of how to improve curriculum and teaching. In a fifth-year course titled Leadership and Clinical Supervision, Trinity students actually implement a form of clinical supervision. Working in small teams, class members demonstrate teaching to one another, observe each other in a classroom setting, and develop record logs and supporting portfolio data designed around collegial supervision. Thus, early on, candidates are inculcated with the belief that peer assistance is a necessary part of developing as a professional.

Across programs, we saw that when novices participate in this kind of collegial work early in their professional lives they internalize the expectation that working together on improving teaching is the rule rather than the exception. They grow to value and invite feedback and seek opportunities to improve, rather than to fear sharing or analyzing practice. The demands of cooperative work as well as the benefits of collegial interaction become a norm for these prospective teachers.

This is reinforced by the collegial nature of the relationship between interns and mentors. Both view themselves as giving and taking within the relationship. We heard repeatedly how mentors or cooperating teachers saw their role as both to guide the student teacher or intern and to learn new ideas from them, "often based on the latest research." Every cooperating teacher we spoke to saw the relationship with the teaching candidate and with the university teacher education program as offering a powerful learning experience, because they had the opportunity to experience new strategies, have another pair of eyes in the classroom to notice things and raise questions, and reflect deeply on their teaching in order to explain their decisions to novices. Teaching candidates valued their mentors' wisdom and experience and saw themselves as partners in the process of developing the classroom environment and collectively solving problems of professional practice.

In most of the programs, university faculty also work closely with practicing teachers who serve as mentors or cooperating teachers, introducing another model of professional interaction for prospective teachers in the program. In the Trinity and USM PDS models, mentors and university faculty meet regularly to discuss planning, their students (both teaching candidates and children), successes, and issues of concern. In the Bank Street model of instruction and advisement, university supervisors work closely with cooperating teachers in planning the student teacher's experience and may periodically co-teach or do demonstration lessons in the classroom. Alverno faculty are involved in supporting curriculum reforms and teaching initiatives in a number of schools across the city. These school- and university-based faculty share strongly defined visions of teaching and work on classroom-level and school-level problems of practice together, demonstrating how members of a professional community collaborate to improve teaching.

In sum, these programs conceptualize the knowledge base for teaching as grounded in an understanding of learners and learning as they develop in social contexts, connected to subject matter by way of curriculum development and enacted through a range of teaching strategies chosen with reference to educational goals, the demands of the content, and the progress of students. The programs organize and convey this knowledge base through carefully designed and sequenced courses and clinical placements that are complementary and mutually reinforcing, and through pedagogies that connect theory to practice through use of cases, performance tasks, and in-depth analyses of learning and teaching. They emphasize the necessity of continuous adaptation and improvement of teaching through both individual reflection and collegial work in professional communities, which is developed and practiced in every aspect of the program from entry through graduation and beyond.

In the following chapters, I discuss in detail how the study sites actually carry out these intentions as they structure courses, assignments, placements, and the way they construct intersections among the individual elements of each program.

5

DEVELOPING AND ASSESSING TEACHING

CONSTRUCTING PERFORMANCES OF UNDERSTANDING

CONCEPTUALIZING KNOWLEDGE FOR TEACHING includes developing a view of what it means to "know" something and what it means to demonstrate understanding. A critical aspect of the programs we studied is that they have organized their curricula around "performances of understanding" (Perkins, 1998) that represent key elements of teaching knowledge and skill. These performances are both assignments and assessments—cases, performance tasks and exhibitions, portfolios, reflective tools such as autobiography, and action research—that require candidates to *use* their knowledge to produce teaching actions and analyses. They structure the learning process and create a strong bridge between theory and practice. Such strategies have become signature pedagogies that support the development of teacher reasoning in relation to knowledge about students, learning, development, and curriculum goals. These pedagogies of teacher education allow students to apply theoretical principles to problems in specific contexts, while appropriately complicating their effort to draw generalizations about practice.

The utility of these tools is that they press beyond knowledge to a deeper form of understanding-in-action that is grounded in performance. As cognitive psychologist David Perkins (1998) notes, although knowledge might be viewed as the ability to produce information on tap, understanding is "the ability to think and act flexibly with what one knows . . . a 'flexible performance capability' with emphasis on the flexibility" (p. 40). A performance view of understanding suggests that an individual can *use* knowledge and skills in the cause of accomplishing something that requires thought and judgment, "more like learning to improvise jazz or hold a good conversation . . . than learning the multiplication tables or the dates of the presidents" (p. 40). Perkins further argues that one can gauge understanding by asking someone to do something that "puts the understanding to work—explaining, solving a problem, building an argument, constructing a product" (p. 41). Not only does the act of engaging in such performances provide a window into the performer's current abilities and depth of understanding, it also advances understanding by creating a situation in which further learning can occur.

Indeed, a small but growing body of research suggests that engaging in performance assessments can help teachers understand more deeply the many variables that influence their work and its effectiveness. Teachers report that the act of writing a case or developing a portfolio in which they analyze various aspects and effects of their teaching enriches their ability to understand the complexities of classroom life and helps them better meet the needs of diverse students (Athanases, 1994; Bliss and Mazur, 1997; Bradley, 1994; Darling-Hammond and Hammerness, 2002; Hammerness, Darling-Hammond, and Shulman, 2002; Haynes, 1995; Ingvarson and Marrett, 1997; Roeser, 2002; Tracz and others, 1995).

The assessments used by these teacher education programs both evaluate what novice teachers have learned and organize learning, deliberately marrying knowledge and application, rather than assuming one automatically follows from the other. In this way, they also help to address the problem of moving from intellectual understanding to enactment in practice (Kennedy, 1999). As anyone who has taught realizes, it is one thing to know or intend something about teaching and quite another to act on it amid the many interchanges occurring among students and the teacher, while an array of curriculum goals compete with social and emotional goals and circumstances that vary with the child.

The multidimensionality, simultaneity, and unpredictability of teaching and learning (Jackson, 1974) require that teachers be able to engage in systematic disciplined learning from the contexts of teaching as well as from theory about teaching and learning. Without an understanding of how people grow, learn, and develop, of the influence of culture and context on learning, and of strategies for organizing instruction, it is difficult for untrained teachers to make intuitively good judgments about how to deal with the specific events in the classroom. At the same time, without appreciation for the intense, interactive realities of classroom life, and for the multidimensional problems and possibilities posed by individual learners, it is difficult for the theoretically knowledgeable to apply what they know in practice.

The problem of enactment, especially in light of current expectations for teaching, is not trivial. As Villegas (1997) notes:

> Because teaching must build upon and modify students' prior knowledge, responsive teachers select and use instructional materials that are relevant to students' experiences outside school [Hollins, 1989], design instructional activities that engage students in personally and culturally appropriate ways [Garibaldi, 1992; Irvine, 1990a], make use of pertinent examples or analogies drawn from the students' daily lives to introduce or clarify new concepts [Irvine, 1992], manage the classroom in ways that take into consideration differences in interaction styles [Tikunoff, 1985], and use a variety of evaluation strategies that maximize students' opportunities to display what they actually know in ways that are familiar to them [Moll, 1988; Ortiz and Maldonado-Colon, 1986; p. 265].

Assessment of such complex performances requires equally complex measures that are sensitive to the contexts shaping teaching: the nature of the content, instructional goals, students individually and collectively, and school and community norms and resources. Among other things, the assessment strategies used by these programs help teachers consider how teaching circumstances influence the appropriateness of teaching decisions. The extent to which context influences teaching—and determines which approaches are effective—is a factor only recently acknowledged in research on teaching, in teacher education, and in assessment of teaching. In contrast to earlier beliefs that teaching would be effective if teachers mastered a set of generic teaching behaviors appropriate to all settings and subjects, recent research has made it clear that all teaching and all learning are shaped by the contexts in which they occur—by the nature of the subject matter, the goals of instruction, the individual experiences, interests, and understandings of learners and teachers, and the settings within which teaching and learning take place.

Some research finds that effective teachers vary what they do across teaching situations; teachers who believe such adaptations are unnecessary are less effective (Doyle, 1979; Shavelson and Dempsey-Atwood, 1976; Stodolsky, 1984). Many studies of teacher characteristics have found that traits such as flexibility and adaptability are important determinants of teacher effectiveness (for a review, see Schalock, 1979), and that teachers who can plan flexibly and adjust their teaching in response to student cues are more effective (Zahorick, 1970; Peterson and Clark, 1978; Duchastel and Merrill, 1977; Melton, 1978). Teachers who learn to teach to decontextualized assessments that posit a set list of "correct" teaching behaviors consider a narrower range of teaching concerns (Hoover and O'Shea, 1987). Furthermore, they are much less likely to attend to issues of curriculum planning, content pedagogy, the relationship between teacher practices and student responses or outcomes, or teaching tasks that occur outside the observation context (Darling-Hammond and Sclan, 1992; French, Hodzkom, and Kuligowski, 1990). As Floden and Klinzing (1990) note: "Training teachers to follow a fixed set of prescriptions discourages teachers from adapting their instruction to the particular subjects and students they are teaching. Hence, the instructional effectiveness of teachers given such training is unlikely to be at a high level" (pp. 16–17).

Assessment Features

Assessments used across the study programs share four features that render them "performances of understanding"—that is, representative of the kinds of thinking and performance required for good teaching—and that appear to be important both for measuring teaching and enhancing candidates' ability to teach well (Darling-Hammond and Snyder, 2000).

A Focus on Performance

First, the assessments sample the actual knowledge, skills, and dispositions desired of teachers as they are used in teaching and learning contexts, rather than relying on more remote proxies. Although some contexts for assessment may be a step removed from daily classroom life, the tasks undertaken require the use and integration of knowledge and skills as they are employed in practice. Tasks represent the work of teaching (lesson plans, videotapes of teaching, and assessments of student learning) and analyses of teaching, learning, and curriculum materials. Such assessments seek to deal with the problem of enactment, the fact that talking or writing about teaching or recognizing answers to multiple-choice questions cannot fully predict a person's capacity to plan for, manage, or make sense of the complex realities of actual teaching.

The assessments, however, do not consist entirely of classroom observations. Many aspects of teaching are only indirectly visible during the classroom portion of a teacher's practice: among others, planning how to represent content and adapt lessons to the needs of particular learners; work with children, their families, and the community outside of classroom hours; analyze the special strengths and challenges students possess; and work with colleagues to plan instruction and to engage in problem solving. In these cases, classroom observations are more remote proxies for the actual knowledge, skills, and dispositions to be assessed. Therefore assessment tools such as interviews, teacher reflection and analysis, samples of feedback the teacher gave students or that others gave the teacher, and artifacts representing these aspects of practice may be more authentic in tapping teachers' understanding.

Integration of Knowledge and Skills in Practice

The programs' assessments require teachers to integrate multiple kinds of knowledge and skills as they are used in practice. One complaint encountered in preparation programs across the professions is that students experience fragmentation among courses that treat different subject matter and discontinuities in occasions for dealing with theory and practice. This leaves much of the assembling of a knowledge base to the student, with resulting gaps and problems of translation. Assessments that mirror teaching by seeking to integrate areas of knowledge used in combination can help forge these connections while better representing the tasks teachers must actually perform (Darling-Hammond, Wise, and Klein, 1999).

Multiple Measures

Multiple sources of evidence are collected over time and in differing contexts. Assessments include written analyses, observation data (from a supervisor's, cooperating teacher's, or principal's observations, for example), and performance samples such as videotapes, pupil work from the student teacher's classroom, and communications with families. In addition, because context does matter, the assessments give candidates an opportunity to show their abilities in varying settings with different students and lesson content. If teacher education is professional education rather than craft training, it should prepare candidates to take into account the needs of students and demands of subject matter and other context variables in making decisions. Learning to differentiate and analyze the factors represented in different settings for practice is what distinguishes preparation for professional practice from an apprenticeship model in which novices aim to copy the skills of a veteran practitioner, as though applicable in all contexts. Explicitly recognizing the importance of context helps candidates develop more finely tuned perceptual and analytic abilities to guide their decisions.

Opportunities for Practice

Assessment practices include multiple student opportunities for learning and practicing the desired outcomes, as well as for feedback and reflection. The assessments help develop competence, not just measure outcomes. Neither teaching nor learning is over at the end of the day. These programs believe that a core function of teacher education is to increase the ability of candidates to reflect on and learn *from* teaching. A teacher is not something one becomes but rather something one is constantly becoming. Assessments of the work of a teacher that include opportunities for learning from feedback can support development of a greater level of competence and measure a critical attribute of an effective teacher: the ability to learn from reflection on practice.

Every assessment tool is a means for organizing curriculum and instruction within or across courses as well as for assessing prospective teachers' developing abilities. No single tool represents the totality of teaching. Each, however, assesses essential aspects of teaching and could be said to reflect a different metaphor for teaching. Cases, for example, develop and assess teacher ability as observer and decision maker. Portfolios support the teacher as a continuous learner who reflects on practice. Exhibitions draw upon the performances of teaching and reflect the teacher as an artist. Research and inquiry develop teachers as social scientists and analysts. Used in combination, such tools allow novices to integrate various areas of learning and apply them in distinctive ways that together comprise the many dimensions of a professional teaching role (Darling-Hammond and Snyder, 2000).

Research on teacher development (Fuller, 1969; Katz, 1972) has suggested that beginning teachers may not be capable of advanced practice focused on the needs of students until they successfully move through concerns dealing with their own behavior and survival in the classroom. However, programs that use these assessments to scaffold opportunities for learning develop beginning professionals who are capable of much more sophisticated practice than previously believed. The caliber of the work generated by teacher candidates in programs where study is both rooted in practice and unremittingly analytic suggests that the concerns of beginning professionals can move more quickly from a focus on self to a focus on students if they have tools to help them train their sights on the effects of their actions and decisions (Hammerness, Darling-Hammond, and Bransford, 2005).

Case Methods

In the preface to their book *The Case for Education,* Joel Colberg, Kimberly Trimble, and Peter Desberg (1996) note that the growing interest in using case methods in teacher education can be explained with one word: context. Cases add context to theory. Whether they take the form of case reports (first-person narratives of personal experiences of teaching) or case studies (third-person analyses of situations or students), cases allow exploration of precepts, principles, theories, and perennial issues as they actually occur in the real world. Students may read and analyze cases, seeking the lessons and insights they offer; or they may write their own cases, developing an interpretation of events as they work through the process of representing their experience. These efforts can motivate learning and serve as instructional material for others (Shulman, 1992, p. 3). Typically, a case represents an instance of teaching and learning that poses a dilemma, offers carefully assembled evidence or data, and sometimes describes the outcomes of decisions in specific situations.

Cases may be developed from any number of perspectives. They may start with subject matter, probing teachers' understanding of curriculum and instruction by examining how teachers configure and analyze learning experiences aimed at mastery of specific concepts or skills (Shulman, 1992, 1996). They may develop a student perspective, assessing teachers' skills of observation and interpretation by examining how they evaluate student learning and development in terms of strengths, interests, and needs (Roeser, 2002). They may start from a cultural perspective, allowing teachers to inquire into students' lives and contexts to prepare teachers for the intellectually and emotionally demanding experiences that can arise in culturally diverse classrooms and communities (Kleinfeld, 1998).

With cases, teacher candidates read or construct context-specific narratives about students, teaching events, or teaching and learning environments; then they analyze and interpret those narratives in the light of other knowledge from research, theory, and experience. When teacher candidates construct cases themselves, as they do in the programs we studied, the process of writing the case helps them begin to understand the relationship between events they have experienced and larger principles or issues. We witnessed how drawing these connections is enhanced if there is tight linkage between theoretical readings and case writing, as well as an interactive process of review and commentary that pushes the writer to explore the deeper meanings of the case. When teachers systematically shared and analyzed their cases with one another, we also saw how they were able to profit from a range of specific examples illuminating both general principles and their application. At this point, the meaning of the narrative resides in the community, rather than the individual alone (Shulman, 1996). In this way, cases bridge the gap between personal situated knowledge and generalizable principles, as they do in law, business, medicine, and other professions.

The Child Case Study

Critical to development of a learner-centered view of teaching in all of the programs we studied is the practice of observing children to understand their learning and development. Every one of these programs engages its students in conducting child or adolescent case studies to help them link theories of development, learning, behavior, and motivation to specific children in their family, school, and community contexts. The goal of such case studies is to examine student learning and development with an eye toward identifying strengths, developmental progress, important influences, and needs. Collecting and analyzing data for the case study—from observations, interviews, records, and analyses of student work—helps teachers develop their skills of observation and documentation and their ability to analyze how children learn and can be supported in the process of development.

In this kind of case, the writer develops detailed examples of a child's thinking, learning, interactions, beliefs, concerns, and aspirations. In some instances, child case studies can be the basis for evaluating how better to work with a child who is having difficulty. Written versions of such studies codify what is done by teachers in action when they evaluate a student using multiple tools of evidence, or when they collectively consult about a student and pool their observations to figure out how better to support the child. As in medicine, these case conferences are built on careful, detailed observation and shared expertise aimed at powerful analysis of a situation.

Many of these strategies for understanding children were pioneered at Bank Street College in its earliest days. At the core of the Bank Street curriculum is a set of courses on child development aimed at understanding children from an experiential as well as theoretical perspective. The framework developed by the child development courses, taken at the start of the program, is further deepened in courses and fieldwork that follow, especially the Observation and Recording course, popularly known as O and R. This course, which houses the child case study, is constantly identified by students, graduates, and faculty as a trademark of a Bank Street education and a critical means for prospective teachers to learn how to look closely at children, see them as growing individuals, and find ways to foster their learning. The course stresses the interactions among knowledge of children, knowledge of one's own beliefs, and use of evidence and theory to make informed teaching decisions. The instructor of the course describes how it seeks to foster rigor in the use of evidence and theory to understanding children: "Observation and Recording or TE 502 is one of the courses specifically designed to help people get evidence from children. That is one of the ways we help students to be rigorous. They have to see child behaviors in relation to context. They learn about learning styles, about temperament, about special needs, and about subjects kids like. They learn about how kids think and how they make friends. The task of serious child study is to help students look for real evidence and to use theories that help them interpret what they see."

Students read texts on the observation and study of children while applying what they learn to their own child study. The main assignment for the course is an individual child study, for the purpose of "developing an increased awareness of the child's uniqueness, the relation of specific behavior to overall functioning, and the implications for learning." This document is developed over several months from a number of assignments, including short weekly written observations of the child at school, a paper that examines the child in the context of his peers or group, an age-level study designed to see the child in light of developmental theory, and observations and interpretations of the child as a learner and member of a learning community.

Each session is framed by essential questions designed to sharpen the *why* and *how* required for documentation and assessment. For example, questions that frame the first sessions are geared to learning and reflecting on issues of ethics, evidence, objectivity, and subjectivity: What is the meaning of objectivity? How should I select a child? Why did I select this child? What is needed in a record, and how might the child experience my observing and recording what he or she is doing? Class discussions usually center on these issues and on the evolving nature of children as learners. An outline describes how the course is designed to sharpen the teacher's knowledge of her personal biases and her skills for seeking evidence.

> Almost everyone "observes" children informally, but what we "see"
> and remember is influenced by what we are looking for, what we
> expect to see and what we think about the nature and capabilities of

children. Our observations of children are also influenced by our own values and feelings. In this course we will work toward sharpening awareness of our own cultural and personal assumptions when observing children. In this process we will work to develop greater sensitivity to ourselves as observers, to the language we use, and to the data we are choosing to attend to. The aim is to develop a personal style of observing and recording that is precise, vivid and nonjudgmental, one that will serve us well in our work with children and families [TE 502, Fall 1995].

Instructors review weekly observations and provide feedback. For example, on an early assignment instructors' comments might include questions related to the language the graduate student uses to describe a child or the clarity of contextual descriptions. Instructors also offer the eternal questions, "Why do you think that?" "How do you know?" "What is the evidence for this interpretation?" that often fill the margins of observation logs. Later in the semester, the questions are more specific to the child as a learner and call for a variety of recording techniques: a running record of a child's oral reading, observation of the child's use of language in different contexts, a collection of the student's work, recording of children's responses to on-demand performance of specific tasks, and children at play or in unstructured interaction with other children. Final requirements ask that students review all documentation, create categories of evidence, triangulate evidence to support their assumptions, make recommendations for teaching or further study, and use theoretical understandings to back up their recommendations. The final case studies can exceed one hundred pages of text—often with supporting appendices with observation records, transcripts of interviews, and student work samples—that describe the child's growth, development, and learning on the basis of close study and developmental theory.

Students often comment on the responsibility they feel after this experience to get to know their students well. As one graduate, a first-year teacher, put it: "O and R was very helpful in terms of a stance toward children. There was a huge amount of work, but it was worth it. One of the best things you can do is watch a child closely and try to understand why they're doing what they're doing."

Experienced graduates who are now cooperating teachers describe a variety of methods they have invented and adapted to keep track of children and of themselves. In fact, many of the observation, recording, and documentation processes examined in this course can be found in authentic assessments such as the Primary Language Record, descriptive reviews, and portfolios that are widely used by Bank Street teachers (Darling-Hammond, Ancess, and Falk, 1995; Freidus, 1995). "Lara Grant," another first-year teacher at Midtown West Elementary School, agreed that the course affected not only her practice but, because of the Bank Street influence schoolwide, that of her colleagues as well:

> O and R was very important because it showed me how to look at the children in my class and make nonjudgmental assessments of what's going on with them. . . . Individually, teachers have different methods of taking notes on children. Some teachers have separate little notebooks for each kid. A new method that one of the teachers brought in this year is doing it on stickers on a clipboard that you carry around to jot things down. Then you have a book with dividers with each kid's name and at the end, you pull off the stickers and put them next to the kids' names. When we send progress reports, they're all narratives describing what children can do.

A similar approach is used at Wheelock, where the required eight-credit core course on human growth and development also makes explicit connections between theory and practice by weaving together coursework and field experiences through a child case study. Students are asked to identify examples of concepts from their placements and directly relate their observations of a focus child selected for study to theories and research discussion in classes. This careful analysis is highly scaffolded through a sequenced set of observations guided by specific questions. For example, after reading about a number of theories of physical and cognitive growth in young children, and examining findings about motor development, students were asked to observe and record at least two behavioral events of a child and analyze them:

> The goal of your analysis is to construct an understanding of your focus child's physical abilities. As you analyze your focus child's behavior, think about what you have learned about theory and research on physical development. In analyzing the behavioral event records, use the information about theory and research on physical development discussed by Cole and Cole [1993, Chapters 5 and 6], as well as other course materials.
>
> Here are some questions to ask yourself as you begin your analysis:

- What do the child's locomotion and large muscle coordination show you about her or his perceptual-motor development? What does the child's behavior and vocalizations reveal about her or his awareness of body, time, space, and direction, and visual and auditory cues? How does the child's level of large muscle control influence her or his interaction with objects and with other people? [See Cole and Cole, 1993, pp. 183–184, 213]

- What do the child's fine hand movements and small muscle coordination show you about her or his perceptual-motor development?

- Does the child seem to be developing "normally" in the physical domain compared with other children of the same age and gender? If so, how do the child's physical abilities differ from what would be expected of a younger child, and of an older child?

- Do you think the child's level of perceptual-motor development is due to experience or maturation, or both?

As you answer these questions, consider why you answer them as you do. What behavioral evidence do you have to support your analysis of your focus child's physical abilities? What developmental research supports your analysis? You might also consider how the child's height and weight might relate to her or his perceptual-motor coordination. [Course syllabus]

The emphasis on helping prospective teachers become expert observers of children and their development is one of the principal reasons Wheelock teachers often believe their preparation is superior to that of their teaching colleagues. As one Wheelock graduate wrote: "Based on observing other teachers and working with these teachers and their knowledge and styles, I truly believe Wheelock College has given me the opportunity to develop an understanding and ability to teach children in a fashion that respects their backgrounds, abilities, and interests."

Other strategies used by programs for engaging in child study include assignments requiring close description of children's thinking and learning linked to readings on related topics. At UC Berkeley's DTE program, for example, students complete assignments throughout their four-seminar human development sequence that use clinical methods for assessing levels of cognitive development and samples of children's spoken and written language for assessing their language development. Like the entire four-course sequence, the first human development seminar is connected to the teaching methods courses and student teaching through overlapping assignments and experiences. As an example of how this works, here is the sequence of assignments for the first human development seminar:

Assignment One: Using Piagetian "clinical method," assess the cognitive-developmental level in different domains of knowledge of two or more of the children in your field placement. Write a report clearly describing what you did, why you did it, and what hypotheses you have formed about the cognitive-developmental level of children and about this type of cognitive assessment. The focus in this assignment is on assessing the cognitive level of the child related to schooling. The use of different domains of knowledge is crucial in that it helps the prospective teacher to understand that one cannot generalize a "general stage of development" across domains or subject matter and as such [it] cannot be used to label a child.

Assignment Two: Select two learning tasks from the curriculum in your classroom (e.g., school learning, not simply copies of Piagetian tasks) which your students will understand at different levels. Administer interviews based on these two tasks to three children in order to investigate the different levels at which tasks might be understood using Piaget's method and his theory of development as a basis for interpretation. The focus in this assignment is on assessing the difficulty of the tasks in terms of the level of operational reasoning required for mastery. Write a report including a clear description of the tasks, a summary of the interview procedures and each child's responses, [and] conclusions about each child's level of understanding and about the level of reasoning required for mastery.

Assignment Three: Collect and interpret at least five examples of developmentally interesting language data from children. In your write-up, include the "raw" data and address the following: (a) Could the child's use of English reflect some underlying hypothesis or qualitatively different knowledge that the child has about language? How so? (b) Could the child's use of language in this example be constrained in some way by cognitive and/or social factors? How so? (c) Could a teacher do anything to foster the child's development toward greater maturity regarding the aspect of language in question? How so?

The outcomes of this kind of concrete, guided assessment in the context of ongoing coursework can be seen in later work that DTE students do. In the third human development seminar, for example, which occurs during the fall semester of the second year of the program, we found the instructor leading students in a series of activities to complete their assignment to develop a task capturing an essential understanding in a non-number mathematical domain and then assess students' understanding of that domain. The final piece of the assignment, conducted with a child who "failed" the task, was to go back and rework the domain. The instructor's unspoken goal was to force assessment of knowledge rather than assessment based on observations like "the students were all involved" or "they all liked me." He first provided a handout from a third-grade activity sheet from a typically used text series requesting that students determine area by multiplying the length times the width. The dialogue that ensued illustrated how students were beginning to apply their understanding to practice:

INSTRUCTOR: How many students do you think could do this?

STUDENTS (TOGETHER): Not many.

INSTRUCTOR: Why? Who is going to be able to do what?

STUDENT 1: Filling things up will be easy. And they will conserve.

STUDENT 2: They will be in trouble, even when the directions tell them to multiply the perimeter to determine the area.

STUDENT 3: You could give them tiles and ask them to make different shapes to get at their readiness levels.

As their understanding deepens, DTE graduates use this knowledge of development and how to assess it to guide their instruction. In the classroom of Mary (Chapter Three), a first-year DTE graduate, we saw in-depth child study at work. When Mary met with a student support team consisting of three support personnel, the principal, and herself, she brought an impressive collection of documentation on a struggling student. The school's case history, begun in kindergarten, focused mostly on the child's tardies and absences. Mary brought with her the child's work. She focused the experienced team on the journal entries she had collected from the child in order to analyze how his writing had developed. She then took out a notebook with yellow stickies attached to each page. Each note was labeled with the child's initial and dated. Sample notes she took on one day (for several students) included:

"Easily discouraged but is starting to coordinate strategies."

"Uses pictures to decode."

"Using letter cues to unlock meaning. With practice he's going to be fluent."

"Just beginning to pick up on repetition."

Thumbing through, she got to the page for the child of focus and described with precision his progress in learning to read over time. She explained of her system, "I keep notes about each child on these [yellow stickies] and then transfer the notes onto a page I have for each student. These were a lifesaver at report card time. . . ."

Another first-year teacher explained: "The developmental psych background from DTE—moral, physical, cognitive, emotional, social—is incredibly valuable. Without it I would have no way to figure out what's going on—the multiple levels within each child. Without it, I would just give in and simplify the curriculum." She thought a while, looked around the room, and concluded, "I couldn't continue without those understandings."

When we observed a third-year DTE graduate in her classroom, we saw an even more sophisticated analysis shaping pedagogical decision making. This teacher had carefully structured a math lesson using manipulatives so that she could see how students were developing in their understanding of multiplication. After the session, she took the observer aside and explained what she had learned about their understandings and levels of development in this domain: "I just got a real understanding of what's happening cognitively. I don't use unifix cubes so they can do the worksheet. I ask them questions so we can find out what each kid is really understanding. [As a teacher] you also really have to know the content to know what's in between. It's not just that they got it right or got it wrong."

These abilities to examine and understand what children are thinking and learning, strikingly similar to those one would also see in a Bank Street or Wheelock or Alverno graduate's classroom, are the product not only of intense developmental study but of applying that study to the real conditions and concerns of children in classrooms, begun early on in these preservice programs. One way in which the work done in child studies becomes habitual is through reinforcement of these observational and diagnostic skills in other elements of the program. For example, student teachers explicitly apply these skills in their clinical placements. The Alverno Student Teacher Assessment Form rates student teachers in each field placement on a common set of skills, which include under "diagnosis" these expected behaviors, developed in child case study work:

○ Collects information through observation of classroom interaction

○ Uses questions to refine information

○ Weighs observations against varied frameworks of student development and behavior (e.g., learning style, cultural background, etc.)

○ Makes judgments about student learning needs

○ Integrates awareness of student needs into planning

Child study has long been a staple of progressive early childhood and elementary programs, but it is unusual at the secondary level. However, students at USM, Trinity, and UVA's five-year BA/MT programs engage in a similar exercise. At Trinity, for example, seniors focus their attention on the student. As part of their coursework tied to their practicum, they conduct a case study (or "case journal," as Trinity refers to it) of a single student, gathering data by "shadowing" the selected student for the semester, talking with the student's teacher, grading the student's work, and reviewing the student's official school records. This study aims to help candidates recognize and be sensitive to students' individual learning styles and needs.

A similar exercise at USM is only one of a number of case studies candidates complete. In addition to their large-scale case study of a child, they also develop child cases about specific teaching and learning questions. For example, student teachers conduct case studies of students with reading problems in which they use specific assessments to evaluate a child's reading strategies and readiness and try out protocols such as the Individual Reading Inventory. They also conduct a case study of a student with specific learning challenges in the Exceptionalities course, examining particular learning issues and strategies used in the classroom, along with the formal processes of identification, writing and implementing individualized education plans, and following up with assessments of progress.

Other Uses of Case Methods

Beyond the widely used child case study, several of the programs use other kinds of cases. For example, first-year students at Trinity construct *school-based case studies* in a course called School and Community. Using the framework of Sergiovanni's *Building Community in Schools,* students examine the culture of the school in which they are placed, and they explore questions of whether and how schools and classrooms become "purposeful" communities of learners. Reflective journals in response to guiding questions and daily observations are an important strategy for developing the case. This is the student's first introduction to journal writing, an important element of many of Trinity's education classes. For this particular course, students are required to submit, every other week, a two-page reflection on a topic assigned by the professor. In the practicum site, candidates are systematically introduced to the structure of the school as a whole, visiting the many offices and services available in the school—from the library and counselor's office to the nurse's office and special education programs—and are asked to notice aspects of these environments as well as of classrooms and attend to student and adult involvement. These guided observations, in conjunction with readings about school as organization, are used to build the case study of the school.

Students at the University of Southern Maine conduct a *community case study* during orientation to the program. Organized into small groups, the interns research various aspects of the community, put together a presentation, and then present a workshop for teachers new to the school system toward the end of orientation, just prior to the beginning of school.

At Wheelock, candidates develop a case about *out-of-school community organizations* students and their families experience. They research such a setting when assigned to a community-based field placement in one of their earliest courses, Children and the Environment. These placements—in after-school centers, hospitals, community centers, Big Brother or Big Sister programs—are specifically designed to place students in multicultural settings and challenge them to look at their assumptions about race and class. Candidates initially write responsive journals around guided observations. They are asked to analyze the social and physical environments of their field placement; observe children, individually and in groups; interview their supervisor; and write about the environment, children, and teacher in light of class discussion and readings. Candidates are asked to see the environment from the child's perspective. One typical assignment asks: "Look at the physical environment of the setting. Obtain an impression from your eye level, then get on your knees and look again as if you were looking from a child's eye level. What feels different? How does it feel different? What are the best and worst features of the environment and why? Consider the space, the color, the heat, the light, and any other variables that you think are important. How does the environment affect the children? How does it affect you?" (Course syllabus)

At the University of Virginia, cases are used both as texts for shared reading to deepen candidates' understanding of students and as opportunities to write about and analyze teaching experiences. In a Special Topics Seminar focused on issues of family and community contexts and of student physical and mental health, students read *cases of at-risk students* (sometimes developed by previous members of cohorts) to make real the discussions of homelessness, teen pregnancy, and family challenges they hear about and see in the literature and their placements. All students in this course present cases from their own field experiences. The set of cases used in the class "provide realistic exemplars of research-based principles of effective teaching" and "present realistic problems that defy simple solutions" (Course syllabus attachment on the "Rationale for Use of Cases").

In a seminar attached to a field practicum in which candidates tutor a child, candidates write a *case of teaching and learning* that shares many features of a child case study but focuses explicitly on analyzing the teaching and learning process. This case is conducted in the spring of the junior year. In addition to weekly tutoring sessions over eight weeks with a single child, they also observe the tutee at least three times in another setting and keep a journal with weekly notes on their work and the student's work, as well as the student's classroom interactions. The resulting case study describes the student's home and school environment, relationships with peers, and classroom behavior; it also carefully documents and analyzes the student's academic progress on the specific tasks undertaken in tutoring, the impact of the candidate's teaching actions and decisions, reflection on these teaching strategies and their effectiveness, and consideration of the student's influence on how the candidate now conceptualizes the job of teaching.

Candidates receive very detailed instructions about the necessary elements of a case study and how to prepare one, learning qualitative research skills as well as much about learning. The assignment requires students to ground their answers in the detailed data they collect in their weekly notes and gives specific directions about coding and interpreting data. In the final case analysis, student teachers describe the student, the specific teaching and learning interactions each week (including what they decided to do to achieve their teaching goals in terms of tasks attempted and how they sought to reinforce the student's efforts), the student's response to each attempt, and how they reshaped their strategies on the basis of these responses. They examine in detail what the student learned and was able to accomplish as a result of the exchanges, evaluating how they believe they were more and less successful. In closing, they are asked to reflect on the new puzzles that emerged for them in this experience: "Did you discover any new problems during your work with this student? What more would you like to know if you were continuing with this student?" This kind of case sets a framework for how to think about diagnosing learning and planning teaching, creating a reciprocal conception of teaching and learning.

Analysis of Learning and Teaching

In addition to structured case studies, the programs provide continuous opportunities for candidates to analyze and reflect on examples of teaching and products of student learning using artifacts and accounts of practice, such as student work samples, videotapes of classroom practice, and curriculum materials. Sometimes these are analyses of the work of expert veteran teachers, observed in person or on videotape demonstrating specific strategies or approaches that can be examined closely and discussed in depth. Sometimes analysis focuses on the candidates' own work and that of their peers. For example, an assignment at UVA asks candidates to conduct peer teaching sessions using the instructional models they have studied. They are videotaped, and then partners view the tapes together to discuss teaching strategies used for a particular instructional model and their effectiveness, producing a write-up of their observations and conclusions. In some other programs, candidates videotape their own teaching in the elementary or secondary classroom as a tool for close analysis of the teaching process with their supervisors or colleagues.

Close analysis of student work is used as a stimulant to think about what students have learned and what they understand or misunderstand, what the results of teaching have been, and what approaches may be needed next. In some contexts, candidates may compare what they learn from written work samples with what they learn from oral exchanges with the student in interviews, informal discussions, or close observation. Sometimes candidates analyze a common set of work samples as a class in order to focus in on specific things to recognize and address—the language development of an English language learner, for example, or the behavior of a student with special needs. What is important about the many ways in which candidates look at practice is that they use authentic samples of teaching, not generalized descriptions; review actual evidence of learning in relation to teaching; and examine deeply what teachers and students do in context, to figure out what the processes of teaching and learning entail in very specific terms.

Many of these analyses of teaching and learning are embedded not only in case studies but in performance tasks and research inquiries that candidates undertake.

Exhibitions of Performance

Case studies and other analyses of teaching and learning hone candidates' perceptions and insights; exhibitions of performance directly address the problem of enactment. Performance tasks and exhibitions allow teachers to demonstrate particular abilities, drawing on or closely simulating teaching contexts or events. Such performances can draw on tools such as observation or videotaped teaching, teaching plans and other artifacts, or even group activities that simulate what teachers do when solving problems of practice with colleagues. What differentiates an exhibition from an unguided observation of practice is that it formally displays and evaluates specific abilities in relation to standards of practice.

All the programs liberally embed exhibitions of performance into various courses and activities. Here we highlight as examples the extensive use of performance tasks and exhibitions at Southern Maine and Alverno, where the use of standards and assessments to guide development is a hallmark of the programs' educational philosophy.

Alverno College: A Curriculum of Exhibited Performance

Internationally known for its approach to performance assessment, the teacher education program at Alverno College uses continuous exhibitions of performance, benchmarked against standards of practice, as the overall foundation for its work. The tasks, designed to measure eight general education abilities (expected of all students in the college) and five advanced education abilities (specific to teacher education), require candidates to apply their knowledge and skills in realistic contexts. From their very first day at Alverno, when they make a videotape of themselves giving a short speech to their peers (a task repeated and reevaluated later) to a much later assessment in which a group is evaluated while collaboratively planning a lesson, students are constantly assessed in relation to these abilities.

Alverno's definition of abilities includes "a complex integration of knowledge, behaviors, skills, values, attitudes, and self-perceptions" (Diez, Rickard, and Lake, 1994, p. 9). The general education abilities at Alverno are *communication, analysis, problem solving, valuing in decision making* (the ability to understand the moral dimensions of decisions and to accept responsibility for the consequences of actions taken), *social interaction, global perspectives, effective citizenship*, and *aesthetic responsiveness*. Prospective teachers are also expected to develop the five professional education abilities that define the kind of teachers the program seeks to prepare:

1. *Conceptualization*—the ability to integrate content knowledge and understanding of education to plan and implement instruction

2. *Diagnosis*

3. *Coordination*—the ability to manage resources effectively to accomplish learning goals

4. Verbal, nonverbal, and media *communication*

5. *Integrative interaction*—the ability to act as a professional decision maker

A performance-based assessment system encompassing in-class and out-of-class assessments of students' work related to various levels of competence on these abilities is an essential aspect of teacher education at Alverno. The college premises its tight coupling of content, pedagogy, and assessment on the belief that learning occurs best when students have a good sense of why they are learning something, of the specific standards that they must meet to accomplish this, and a way of seeing what they have learned.

Instead of obtaining grades for various courses, students earn "validation" of their competence on particular levels of the abilities. The assessment system enables candidates and their teacher educators to know how well the candidates can apply knowledge and skills in realistic contexts. A number of students told us this approach was a key factor in their growth as teachers. As one explained: "With a graded system, I don't think that I would have been where I am now with the confidence and the strengths that I have. I've been able to demonstrate them not only on paper but through other means. It has made me a more well-rounded person and a better teacher. It has also given me direct feedback to where my strengths and weaknesses are and then I know what to focus on. . . . I work well in a cooperative atmosphere. It brought out my strengths and abilities. In a graded program . . . I would not have been as successful."

The Alverno abilities are assessed according to six developmental levels that outline increasingly complex knowledge, skills, and dispositions students must demonstrate, beginning with the ability to identify particular skills or behaviors; progressing through the ability to analyze, evaluate, and demonstrate those skills and behaviors; and ultimately facilitating their acquisition and use in group settings and interpersonal relationships. For example, some of the expectations for beginning teachers in the area of *conceptualization* are developing sensitivity to individual learners; making links between developmental theory and concrete individuals; planning instruction that recognizes the impact of differences (in culture, gender, learning preferences, and so on) on individuals and the group; and planning material to meet learners' current needs and lead to the next level of development (Alverno College Faculty, 1996).

When the college moved to the ability-based curriculum in the early 1970s, faculty redesigned all coursework, field experiences, and assessments to ensure systematic development of the knowledge, skills, dispositions, and attitudes implied by the abilities. All of the course syllabi at Alverno spell out the developmental levels of the specific abilities they address. In addition, syllabi describe the learning activities and assessments that help students develop the abilities and judge how well they have done so. These include essays, letters, position papers, case study analyses, observations of events, talks to simulated audiences, productions of videos and curriculum materials, simulated events such as parent-teacher conferences, and the like.

Students must pass a series of required external assessments to progress from one stage of the program to the next. For example, in a fifth-semester external assessment integrating learning from several courses, five or six students are asked to take on the role of a teacher group called by the district to review the district's mission statement. Candidates study background materials such as the district's philosophy, along with readings on such issues as curriculum integration and multicultural education. In preparation for the videotaped assessment, students review the criteria by which their performance will be assessed. Following the simulation and before receiving faculty feedback, they view the tape and complete a self-assessment response form.

Throughout the program, all assignments include a self-assessment component. This emphasis on self-assessment is designed to help students develop the habits of mind and skills to be reflective about their teaching. The specific criteria for evaluating class assignments are presented to students beforehand, and they always complete a self-assessment before receiving faculty feedback. For example, in the third integrated language arts methods course, candidates develop and use a rubric to assess actual intermediate-grade writing samples. They analyze student writing samples for strengths and areas of need and plan appropriate teaching strategies from their analysis. The students work in groups and collaborate on developing their teaching plans. Before beginning, students receive a list of specific criteria used to assess their performance. These include evidence that the candidate:

- Assesses the developmental level of the learner's performance and provides sufficient evidence to support the judgment
- Diagnoses areas requiring attention/instruction and presents an appropriate teaching plan
- Contributes to the group discussion of the process
- Evaluates own performance on all components of the task. (For additional work on self-assessment and its role in the education curriculum, see Alverno College Office of Research and Evaluation, 1995.)

Later, in an Integrated Reading Curriculum course, the students who had previously analyzed the writing of some of the pupils from their field placements discussed aspects of this writing (use of figurative language, paragraphing, varying sentence structure, and so on) that could be used as the basis for minilessons with their pupils, using assessment as a tool for learning.

Virtually every assignment and assessment begins with reference to the criteria for the performance being developed and ends with an opportunity for candidates to evaluate their own work. This practice creates a sense of internal standards and striving for improvement that carries over to the classroom in many ways. A student teacher reflected the widespread view: "They're always asking you how you could have done it differently, how you could have done it better, what are some changes you would have made. They always throw the ball in your court at Alverno. They are asking me to be just better and better, to constantly revise and reassess."

In addition to the high expectations for student performance on the part of the faculty, the explicitness of the criteria used to evaluate student performance seems to contribute to the impact of the program. One student told us she has begun to use this practice of stating explicit evaluation criteria in her own classroom: "Our teachers give us criteria before we do something. When we have a project or a visit to do, they give us criteria, what we have to do to successfully complete the task. I'm doing that in the classroom, letting my students know what is expected before they start on something. Then there is no fuzzy area. They know right away what is expected."

Another Alverno graduate explained how the practice of self-assessment carried over to how she treats her own pupils:

Alverno was always trying to get us to go a little bit deeper. And so, I think we ask that of our students. They always gave you a set of criteria. At the end of the paper, project, or speech, we were asked to reflect on whether or not we thought we met the criteria. You couldn't just hand in a paper and say "here it is." There was always a top sheet that you had to attach checking off the criteria that you used in your paper or speech with an assessment-type comment. The most important thing I've gotten from Alverno is the constant questioning: you question yourself, you question others, you seek information. You do all of these things to better yourself and your profession.

The end result, as indicated by the judgments of cooperating teachers, college supervisors, employing principals, and candidate assessments of their preparation, is graduates who are extraordinarily self-reflective and practically well prepared for sophisticated practice in the classroom. As one principal who seeks out Alverno graduates observed: "They constantly reflect on their instruction and they're very open to suggestions or to changing a lesson. They're very able to assess the actual lesson they've taught and in a fairly critical manner. They have the skills to do that That's not to say that other students are not able to pick it up. It's just that Alverno students seem to come with that knowledge. They've been forced to practice it on an ongoing basis so they have refined it."

University of Southern Maine: Linking Exhibitions for Teachers and Students

In a PDS context, the possibilities for reinforcing learning by mirroring practices that affect students and student teachers are heightened even further. At USM, where the experiences of ETEP interns are so tightly tied to their school placements, convergence of the university's and school districts' philosophies about teaching is a critical element in teachers' learning. For example, in both ETEP and the Gorham School District (a PDS site), there is a strong emphasis on student performance assessment and public critique of performance using predetermined criteria. These K–12 and teacher education assessment systems are intertwined and mutually reinforcing.

Student exhibitions in Gorham public schools occur regularly, and districtwide benchmark exhibitions happen each spring as all third, sixth, eighth, and eleventh graders publicly demonstrate their knowledge on a predetermined topic. A goal is to have each student's exhibition judged on districtwide rubrics assessing written and oral presentations; at least two adults from outside the school as well as teachers from within the school do the judging. In addition to teachers and parents, the panel members have included the superintendent or other administrators, professors from USM, other community members, and even outside researchers visiting the district. In the spring when we observed, all sixth graders did exhibitions on the topic Cause and Effect before a panel of adults serving as judges. The sixth graders selected a range of topics for their individual presentations: drugs, AIDS, deforestation in Maine, pollution, and others. Each student wrote an in-class essay relating the concept of causation to the selected topic. These essays became part of their portfolios. From the essay, they prepared a five-minute oral presentation and created a poster visually representing the topic. The exhibitions required a synthesis of knowledge and performance—thus evaluating knowledge and its application to real problems of concern.

In a similar fashion, interns in the ETEP-Gorham program conduct at least three formal public exhibitions of their knowledge: when they share their "short project" from orientation called All About Gorham with teachers new to the district in August; when they display their interdisciplinary units for teachers and administrators in April; and when they formally present their portfolios to a five-member committee of administrators, district teachers, and ETEP instructors in May. In addition, they present to their classmates in December the case study of a child from the first placement classroom and share with peers versions of other projects and studies (an action research study; a resource file containing lesson plan ideas, lists of resources, and bibliographies; and "coordinated journaling," a response journal in which interns link their experiences across classrooms and courses with their developing ideas about teaching and learning). Cooperating teachers and site coordinators read the journals and respond to interns' comments and observations. The journals are also shared in the home groups in seminar. There is thus a parallel between what is emphasized in the Gorham school district and what ETEP desires: students being able to demonstrate their knowledge, apply it in specific ways, and analyze and explain the appropriateness of their applications.

ETEP interns and veteran teachers also create their own scoring guides or rubrics for particular classroom projects, which they use to assess their work and that of others. Such performance assessment is routine with Gorham students and ETEP interns as they learn to assess and improve their own knowledge and practice. For example, in their Life Span Development course, ETEP students complete a case study of an individual child (as is common across the other programs) and also develop a performance assessment and rubric for evaluating performance according to one or several theories of development. They further refine their under-standings of performance assessment as it applies to their students and themselves through developing their interdisciplinary units, which are also publicly exhibited.

The ETEP faculty has developed a number of "shared assessments" connected to clinical experiences and linked across USM courses, making the interns' work focused, cohesive, and programmatic, rather than frag-mented, discrete, and disjointed. As one teacher educator explains, "We have worked hard to coordinate the assignments and assessments so that the literacy practica, for example, connect well with the action research study and the interdisciplinary unit."

All the programs engage students in developing curriculum units (see Chapter Seven for more in-depth discussion); USM has one of the more developed processes for public review and exhibition of these units. The ETEP interdisciplinary unit originates in the seminar that accompanies the second semester placement, and it is a major focus of that class dur-ing the spring. The criteria and unit assessment rubric reflect the program's focus on continuous improvement, feedback, and reflection. The five com-ponents that guide the unit construction and evaluation are infusion and explanation of local, state, and national standards; time line and assess-ment system; interdisciplinary lesson plans with documentation and evi-dence of student work; use of templates with explanations; and intern reflection and analysis (including an analysis of student work). Early in the spring semester, the interns bring their units in-progress to seminar for evaluation by both peers and coordinators. In a peer- and self-review process, they use feedback sheets that outline specific items of evidence for each criterion to assess the unit and receive peer and instructor sug-gestions for how to strengthen it.

The interns then begin teaching the unit in their classrooms. Each week during seminar, they share and discuss how it is going and continue to receive support and suggestions from seminar members. Toward the end of the semester, the interns present their final products to the seminar and turn in the units for evaluation. Once again, the notion of continuous improvement is honored. Interns can use the feedback from the assess-ment to change and amend the document and resubmit it. During one afternoon in April, the units from all of the ETEP-Gorham interns K–12 are put on display for review by faculty and administrators. As one instructor commented, "They are also models for Gorham teachers, who are now expected to create at least one such unit or project each year" by district policy.

With the interdisciplinary unit assignment, the interns do the work of being a teacher: deciding on specific learning goals; collecting, evaluating, and altering materials; developing and implementing lessons and embedded assessments; and continuously assessing student learning and making appropriate adjustments according to student needs. As one intern saw it, the unit was designed so "we could see how all the pieces go together." During interviews, many interns commented on the importance of creating the unit and the value of embedded assessments for understanding how students learn. Mirroring the utility of the feedback process they themselves experienced, one intern explained that the assessment process built into his unit convinced him that students could improve their work with teacher feedback: "It opened my eyes to see that [students] can see where they made errors and fix them."

In teacher education, as in elementary and secondary education, constant public practice and assessment through exhibitions of performance has multiple benefits. As Ted Sizer (1992) observes of exhibitions in his work with reforming secondary schools, these demonstrations can help make clear what students should be able to do and focus effort accordingly, help faculty "map backward" from their conception of desired learning to a curriculum that develops such learning, and form a basis for accountability to the student and the broader publics a program serves.

Portfolios

The benefits of exhibitions can be expanded when evidence of performance is assembled to allow a more integrated and holistic examination of abilities. With a portfolio, teachers select and reflect on artifacts of their practice collected over time and from multiple sources as evidence of their thinking, learning, and performance. Portfolios can include documents derived directly from teaching—copies of lesson or unit plans, syllabi, student handouts, assignments, tests, samples of student work (with or without teacher feedback) as well as photographs, videotapes, and audiotapes of classroom activities ranging from bulletin boards and displays to taped lessons, conferences with students, and the like (Darling-Hammond, Wise, and Klein, 1999). There may also be documents requiring additional work on the part of the teacher, such as teacher logs or journals, detailed description or analysis of lessons, student work, and reflection on the outcomes of teaching activities. Portfolio documents might be derived from others' evaluations: notes by an observer of teaching, peer or administrator recommendations, or student evaluations (Bird, 1990; Athanases, 1994; Haertel, 1991).

In these programs, portfolios help prospective teachers demonstrate and reflect on their learning, sometimes in relation to specific standards for teaching. In addition, the portfolios sometimes help new teachers learn to track student learning, much like the NBPTS assessments that ask candidates to include collections of the work of several students over many weeks of teaching. The candidates discuss this evidence of student learning in relation to their teaching, feedback they gave the student, and the student's responses to these teaching efforts. From reflection on a set of reciprocal teaching and learning interchanges, teacher and student learning is displayed in terms of mutual influence. Teachers consistently testify that the process of developing such a portfolio is a powerful occasion for their own learning (Athanases, 1994; Bradley, 1994; Haynes, 1995; Tracz, Sienty, and Mata, 1994).

Several programs use portfolios for aggregating and integrating learning experiences, and assessing candidates' readiness to assume the responsibilities of teaching. For example, the "goal and evidence" portfolio required at USM as a condition of graduation requires student teachers to organize their portfolios around a set of outcome standards for which each student teacher presents evidence from his or her teaching practice. At Alverno, a number of performance assessments are assembled for a portfolio interview assessment at the end of the preprofessional stage of the program, as a gateway to student teaching. Students create a portfolio by reviewing their work in all their courses to date. They collect examples of written work, lesson and unit plans, videotapes of their work with pupils, and instructional materials they have created, deciding what represents their strengths. The portfolio includes written analysis of a videotaped lesson, focusing on the five abilities. Student faculty advisors as well as teams of school-based educators from area schools review the portfolios. The principal and teacher assessors provide feedback on areas of strength and needed growth; they make a recommendation to Alverno about readiness for student teaching. Candidates use the input of school and college-based assessors to formulate specific goals for their student teaching experience.

Similarly, the professional portfolio at Trinity is combined with an exhibition of learning. The portfolio is meant to be a working professional profile. When we visited, typical elements included a sample unit or set of lesson plans, course syllabi, a written statement of the student's philosophy of education, the fifth-year research paper (described later), samples of student work, a videotape of the intern teaching, a resume, records of professional presentations (one entire group of interns, for example, had presented at the Texas Middle School Conference in the year we visited), publications (books or chapters published or in progress), and other artifacts (letters of commendation from their students' parents, mentors, principals).

Since we completed this study, the Trinity portfolio has become even more comprehensive, is electronic, and is evaluated according to six standards that are hallmarks of the program: (1) understanding of content knowledge, (2) planning for student learning, (3) engaging all students in learning, (4) creating and managing a classroom learning community, (5) demonstrating professional communication, and (6) developing as a professional educator. In addition to the elements described earlier, candidates present lessons and student work in every area in which they teach, describing why the content is important for students to learn, showing how learning activities meet these goals and how differences were accommodated, and analyzing student work samples to illustrate how these assessments helped the candidate better meet student needs. They also show how they create a classroom community, work with parents, and infuse technology in their teaching.

At the end of the year, each student presents his or her portfolio in a ceremony including Trinity Education Department faculty, PDS school mentors, and the other interns. Interns often present and demonstrate innovative techniques they have developed or adapted over the course of their years at Trinity. In this performance-based demonstration of teaching, interns explain to faculty and fellow students what they have been doing in their classrooms and why. They are required to communicate to peers the nature of their practice. We observed a group of high school interns, for example, displaying an interdisciplinary curriculum unit, describing how they developed and implemented it and analyzing the results reflectively and self-critically. Today, the portfolio is also formally assessed by school and university faculty using a detailed rubric that represents the standards.

The portfolio is one of three graduation options for Bank Street graduates, along with a directed essay or independent study (described later). The Bank Street portfolio process seeks explicitly to connect personal knowledge, classroom knowledge, and academic knowledge. As one student wrote in her portfolio reflection: "My current beliefs and practices concerning reading instruction are grounded in [my early learning]. However my [university] experiences have shaped and refocused these original ideas. As my classes, readings, and child work experiences each built upon themselves, and connected to each other, I learned a great deal about teaching and learning. I saw how the ideas and passions and beliefs that I had brought with me . . . could be applied within the specific context of reading instruction."

Portfolios constructed around a theme selected by the candidate make constant connections between personal and professional experiences, research and practice, and collective goals and individual children. In one entitled "The Importance of Creating a Caring Community in the Classroom," these perspectives are woven throughout a set of six studies: "Sam's Story" is on the author's own handicapped son and examines differences and universality of the human spirit. "The Classroom as a Community" explores the role of values in the classroom from a philosophical perspective. "Caribbean Day" reflects on a curriculum event used in the author's classroom as a means for celebrating diverse cultures while maintaining a spirit of inclusivity. "The Power of Books" examines how books can enable students to gain voice. "Building Community Through the Arts" looks at how two art projects enabled students to learn about other cultures while developing self-expression. "A Social Studies Curriculum" reflects on how to use a curriculum created by the author to achieve these goals. The portfolio lists as key theoretical influences Charney's *Teaching Children to Care*, Cuffaro's *Experimenting with the World*, Dewey's *Democracy and Education*, and Etzioni's *The Spirit of Community*.

Another recent graduate's "educational philosophy" portfolio was titled "The Teacher as Self-Esteem Builder." This graduate, an African American teacher who went on to run a program for at-risk adolescents, described how her interest in the topic began years earlier when she was an adult education tutor, "when I realized that my tutoring these people to read also involved helping them boost their self-esteem. Then, I discovered that this theme ran throughout my life, since early adolescence." The interrelationship of teaching, learning, and self-concept echoed in her life as a student and as a teacher in myriad ways. Through reflection and commentary about her work as represented in a series of artifacts—discussion of teaching events, student responses, analysis of multicultural literature and identity development, critique of teaching materials, and description of curriculum she created and evaluated—this teacher connected research to practice in several ways. "The process [of assembling the portfolio]," she noted, "helped me to realize that I can do research; I can write a book; I can run a program. It required me to think holistically."

In portfolio presentations ranging from "How Children Construct Meaning and Understanding of Their Experiences" to "Mathematical Transformation: A Professional Renaissance," we observed candidates reveal how their own thinking and teaching were transformed by the process of studying scholars, observing children, enacting their ideas in practice, and assessing themselves and the outcomes of their work.

Carrying higher stakes, the USM portfolio documenting practice over the course of the yearlong program is used to determine whether candidates are ready to complete the program and be certified to teach. A panel of university- and school-based faculty makes the final judgment about certification following a portfolio interview (much like a dissertation defense), in which the candidate presents and defends his or her work. The portfolio construction process is designed to foster continuous self-reflection and internalization of a set of standards for teaching. The standards for what beginning teachers should know and be able to do were developed by faculty drawing on the model licensing standards offered by INTASC (1992). The standards treat the knowledge, skills, and dispositions teachers are expected to have acquired in a number of areas:

- Knowledge of child and adolescent development and principles of learning
- Knowledge of subject matter and how to make it accessible to students while fostering independent inquiry
- Instructional planning based on knowledge of the learner, the subject matter, the community, the intended student outcomes, and the curriculum
- Uses of instructional strategies and technology to promote learning and independent inquiry
- Assessment for communicating feedback and promoting self-evaluation
- Respect for diversity and the ability to create instructional opportunities for diverse learners
- Well-articulated beliefs about teaching, learning, and education linked to demonstrable practices in support of those beliefs
- The ability to plan instruction that promotes the values and practices of citizenship
- The ability to work collaboratively to improve conditions of learning for students and adults
- Commitment to reflection and continuous professional development

○ Classroom management that supports individual responsibility and democratic community

Candidates assemble a body of evidence to demonstrate their competence across these areas, with artifacts such as their own statements of teaching philosophy, classroom lessons, student work. As candidates construct their portfolios, they write reflections that describe what each entry represents and why it is included, what the candidate learned from the experience about teaching and learning, and why it is important—that is, the personal meaning of the learning process. In addition, mentors or peers who are part of a portfolio team engage in critical conversation regarding the candidate's practice. The process concludes with a portfolio presentation to faculty and peers (Lyons, 1998).

In these presentations, candidates read the vision statement they have revised throughout the year, give examples of lessons and units they prepared during the internship, offer samples of student work, and reflect on what was learned by teaching them. They may present other pieces of work as well in discussing evidence of how they have met each standard. Members of the panel ask specific questions about the candidate's practice and evidence and, after hearing the responses, ask the candidate to leave the room so the committee can caucus frankly, discussing confirming and disconfirming evidence that affects its recommendation on certification. The committee includes the mentors and supervisors who worked with the candidate, often the school principal, and other faculty, so there is a great deal of knowledge of the candidate's track record throughout the year. Following the caucus, the candidate is invited back into the room for an in-depth debriefing of what the committee members considered and concluded about whether he or she is recommended for Maine's two-year provisional teaching certificate.

The process of construction, reflection, and feedback on the portfolio is as important for candidate learning as are the components of the portfolio itself. It is through this process of selecting and discussing artifacts of their practice that candidates internalize the standards, examine deeply what they are doing and what it means, and gain multiple perspectives on the meaning of events that extend their ability to learn from their experience. This notion is implicit in Shulman's early definition (1994) of a teaching portfolio as "the structured documentary history of a (carefully selected) set of coached or mentored accomplishments substantiated by samples of student work and fully realized only through reflective writing, deliberation, and serious conversation." How these processes contribute to the value of candidates' learning is illustrated by these comments from two USM teacher interns:

The portfolio process worked best when it helped me to reflect on what I can improve on and what I did well. I have found that when I am in the process of something I become convinced that I will remember it—including all the details. But I don't. . . . I have found that when I reflect and create my portfolio, I reinforce the event in my memory so that I am less likely to forget about it. The process of reflection imprints the event in a unique way. . . . What this points to is the need to create portfolios contemporaneously with the [teaching] process [Davis and Honan, 1998, p. 96].

Designing my portfolio helped me to clarify and articulate visually and in writing my teaching philosophy. It is the actual process that I value: collecting artifacts, organizing, reflecting, and receiving feedback at the portfolio evaluation. . . . By receiving positive feedback and constructive criticism, I concluded that my portfolio is a continuum of my learning as a teacher, i.e., it will *never* be done. Instead of my portfolio presentation being a final, pass/fail assessment, it was a learning experience in and of itself [p. 98].

Comments from students about the value of the portfolio process emerged from all of the programs where they were in use. The benefits for teacher learning of well-constructed portfolios appear to derive in part from:

○ Raising teaching decisions to consciousness and thus making them available for deeper consideration from many perspectives. The process of looking at and thinking about decisions changes consciousness about teaching and thus changes practice. Beginning teacher candidates who undergo such forms of assessment have to answer the question, "What am I aiming for as I learn to teach?"

○ Taking a long view of learning and of the development of performance. Because proficient performances must be developed over a long period of time with continuous practice and reflection, a cumulative record helps to scaffold and evaluate that process.

○ Supporting the learning process by providing benchmarks for good work, vehicles for self- and peer assessment, and opportunities for revision and refinement.

○ Connecting thinking and performance, which helps to bridge the traditional theory-practice divide by asking for evidence of performance along with a discussion of why decisions and actions were taken.

○ Furnishing multiple lenses and multiple sources of evidence, thus developing many facets of performance and allowing many pathways into learning.

○ Making teaching and learning more public, thereby facilitating development of shared norms and standards, as well as extending sharing of knowledge and experience.

These factors combine to enhance the candidates' abilities to integrate the knowledge, skills, and dispositions required of teaching and to provide tools for continuous development. As assessment tools, portfolios that are structured around standards of practice appear to bestow other benefits, among them the ability to examine a teacher's practice in light of a common set of expectations and benchmarks. By giving assessors access to teachers' thinking as well as to evidence of their behaviors and actions (through videotapes, lesson plans, assignments, and the like), portfolios permit examination of teacher deliberation and its outcomes for the teacher's actions and student learning. The long-range view that is encouraged and supported by portfolios helps assessors overcome some of the "limits of looking" (Stodolsky, 1984) that have plagued traditional observations of teaching. Assessors can examine a chain of events and thinking, analyze the quality of deliberation and the grounding of decisions, evaluate the quality and appropriateness of actions taken, and take into account evidence of student characteristics and learning that are the basis for gauging effectiveness. In short, assessors using portfolios can "see" teaching in progress and make it hold still long enough to understand its intentions and effects.

Action Research

Yet another way to promote deeper understanding of teaching is to embed systematic research about learning, teaching, and school contexts into the program of study. In action research or problem-based inquiries, teachers design and conduct investigations into concerns arising from their work with children and families. These inquiries may involve questions similar to those teachers explore with cases, but the method extends beyond personal reflection about the individual's experiences and observations to broader and more structured investigation involving collection of firsthand data as well as prior research about a problem. Teacher research advocate Marilyn Cochran-Smith suggests that "the ability to pose questions, to struggle with uncertainty and build evidence for reasoning . . . is an indispensable resource in the education of teachers" (1991, pp. 280–281). Pursuing immediate questions of practice helps teachers understand both the complexities of teaching and the effects of various solutions or resolutions of endemic problems.

In these programs, we did indeed observe how engaging in action research helped teachers learn to reason from evidence and connect professionwide knowledge to problems of practice in their schools or classrooms, while also developing the skills of observation and inquiry. At UC Berkeley, for example, work on the culminating master's projects begins in the first year of the two-year program. Midway into the first semester, students receive a copy of the previous year's topics and begin to consider what interests them. Every other week through their first year, students submit thoughts about possible topics by e-mail. The program coordinator reads and responds, usually with questions such as, "I wonder . . . ?" "How would you find out . . . ?" or "How can you ask that?" Judith Warren Little, a well-known researcher and professor, gives workshops on Practical Inquiry. Students learn how to conduct research, connect the problems they select to the broader research literature, design a study and collect empirical data during the second year, and complete their M.A. project in the fourth and final semester of the program. The research taps a range of topics of interest to individual students, for example:

- A Case Study of How the Use of Cantonese in a First-Grade Bilingual Classroom Serves Two Newcomers in Adapting to Academic Settings
- A Study of How Different Discussion Structures Affect the Rate of Student Engagement in Diverse Language Arts Classes
- Integrating Social Studies: A Comparison of Traditional and Constructivist Methodologies
- Math Recovery: Toward a Program for Individualized Math Intervention and Remediation

The master's degree program at Wheelock, which is completed by most of the teacher education students before or shortly after entering practice, requires all students to take a research course in an area of their choosing. In a research course focused on literacy development, for example, we followed a student completing research on a question derived from her classroom practice. Having taught for a year after her bachelor's degree and returning with developed interests, she wanted to know how kindergartners use visual representation as an early form of literacy to express their feelings. She collected data in her classroom, read widely in the field of early literacy development, met in a small cluster group of students with common interests, and produced a paper that she hoped to publish (a not-uncommon outcome of papers developed in several of these programs).

The capstone projects at Bank Street are also frequently of publishable quality. These independent studies, as they are called, can take numerous forms (a classic research study, development of original professional materials for classroom use, an educational policy study). Sometimes these documents reflect an educational innovation or program created by the student himself or herself. Independent studies are collected in the library for future use by Bank Street teachers. Among those we saw on display were "The Art of Homeless Children: A Lens for Understanding the Implications of Environment and Experience"; "The Development, Implementation, and Evaluation of a Whole Language Kindergarten"; and "A Learner's Guide: A Text on Logo for Graduate Students."

One independent study we reviewed, titled "Adaptive Learners, Adaptive Workers: Career Education for At-Risk Early Adolescents," evaluates a program developed by the author for at-risk youth in New York City. The 158-page document reviews research on early adolescent development and at-risk youth and describes the program design and rationale in detail, including its curriculum, scope and sequence of program activities, characteristics of participants, and evaluations by its own students and samples of their work. The study includes focus groups and interviews of students as well as questionnaires. The analysis treats differences between older and younger students, examines the evolution of students' metacognitive abilities, assesses the relation between students' understanding of their career potential and the needs of a democratic society, and develops recommendations for future program development. Like others of these studies, it is an example of practice-based scholarship that stimulates reflection while making a direct contribution to practice itself.

Many of the research projects completed at the University of Virginia also contribute to the broader profession and are published both at the university and in the ERIC bibliographic system. Students explore problems or questions of interest identified during their fall student teaching experience and design and complete their research in the spring Field Projects in Education course. Among the many dozens of projects available for other teachers to use and entered in ERIC when we visited were many studies of the effects of classroom instructional strategies ("The Effects of Peer Tutoring on Writing Improvement in a Combined Kindergarten-First Grade Class"; "Hypermedia Effects on Student Motivation and Knowledge Retention in History"), as well as studies of student perceptions and attitudes about learning and motivation when they experience differing instructional strategies in various content areas ("Attitudes of Remedial Readers in a Basal Reading Program vs. an Individualized Reading Program"; "Effects of Required Reading Time on Sixth Graders' Attitudes

Toward Reading"). In addition to these classroom concerns were a number of studies of school policies and practices ("Block Scheduling in 7th Grade Science and Social Studies Classrooms"; "Study of the Implementation and Effects of the School Community Approach") and studies of teacher and parent learning ("Effective Means of Instructing Teachers in Computer Technology"; "Teaching Parents Reading Strategies"), signaling a broad view of the educational process that leads many Curry students into leadership roles early in their careers.

The studies generally follow traditional research approaches, framing a question, reviewing the literature, generating hypotheses and a design to test them, conducting the study, and collecting and analyzing data. One study we reviewed examined how to use primary documents effectively in the history classroom. The candidate described how the study emerged from her experiences in student teaching: "I myself enjoy using primary documents because I believe they tell much more than secondary sources about the past and can be used to explore the past. Primary documents have the potential to engage the students in their thinking about history; yet simply reading them is not a sufficient way to explore. Through using documents in my teaching, I found that not using an instructional technique with the documents often left the students and the teacher frustrated and confused. Through this study I wanted to find a technique to use when utilizing primary documents in my classroom."

The teacher conducted a literature review about the use of primary documents in history and from this review chose a technique to use with her students: development of a guide for students to use as they read the documents. This strategy was used with one class and not with a second (the control), and she compared student survey results, pretest and posttest results on an assigned essay, systematic observation of on- and off-task behavior, and analysis of the question types students asked in each class to see how the strategy made a difference in their learning. Her study found some benefits of using the guide but raised other questions for her to pursue, leaving her to wonder about evaluating student knowledge over the long run and probing students' perceptions of their learning through an ongoing reflective process. This example illustrates how the research process helps strengthen the candidates' ability to ask further questions and develops an inquiry stance toward teaching.

The same kinds of outcomes were evident in the action research project required as a capstone activity of fifth-year MAT students at Trinity. The paper, which students lovingly refer to as "part of the Trinity indoctrination," is designed to encourage students to find their own answers to educational problems; for example, gender equity, teaching values, service learning, and assessment and standards were among the topics of papers we reviewed. This final writing assignment, says Trinity faculty member Tom Poetter, gives "people [the opportunity to] interact personally with the data and inform their own teaching." This, he says, is critical for helping students to develop a conception of the "big picture" of education and to "connect issues of everyday practice to wider [educational] issues." Students describe the paper as "establishing a basis for ongoing professional research and our own professional writing for the future."

These strategies often filter into graduates' own teaching. For example, we observed Maria Rodriguez, a fifth-year intern at San Antonio's International Studies Academy who was conducting social studies classes in which students were planning projects to be presented at a community "screening." It was April, near the end of Maria's intern year. The students' culminating activity for the semester was to present to a panel of educators and other adults their own research on a topic of particular interest. Maria helped the students with the research, worked with groups to organize their presentations, provided advice and counsel on data organizing and display strategies, and helped them anticipate the kind of questions they were likely to get. Having become a researcher herself, she was completely comfortable helping her students become researchers too.

It was clear that the students accepted Maria as their teacher, and she accepted that responsibility. Her PDS mentor was uncompromisingly enthusiastic, marveling at Maria's competence and confidence. Having interns in the PDS, the mentor said, "is like having double staffing" at our school. The Trinity interns were self-confident and professionally secure; they brought new knowledge and skills, modeling what they learned in their classes—a variety of teaching techniques, careful thoughtfulness about instructional strategies, and attention to the needs of individual learners. Using research to support decisions about instructional practices, remarked a Trinity intern, "is simply part of what we do."

Our observations across these programs are consistent with Shulman's suggestion (1996) that teacher research can help transform teaching from a private and hidden act into community property. Sharing and critiquing practice, along with research related to practice, are the cornerstones of professions. Such knowledge construction is not solely the domain of the outside expert; beginning teachers come with their own perspectives and concerns. When novices treat teaching as community property, problems, conjectures, analyses, and interpretations can be examined by colleagues. These inquiries, as we saw, can be preserved for future study and can be drawn on and built on by others.

Having prospective teachers engage in classroom inquiry from the start of their career helps prepare them as both consumers of research and producers of knowledge. As a tool for assessment, such research and inquiry can yield insights into a teacher's analytic ability and her capacity to frame a problem in a manner that allows it to be thoughtfully examined. Such studies can reveal a teacher's disposition and skills for responding to problems of practice with strategies that may lead to improvement, instead of personal coping mechanisms. As a tool for learning, action research gives them tools to make sense of their practice and helps them think analytically about the problems they confront.

6

CONSTRUCTING THE CLINICAL EXPERIENCE

THE GLUE FOR POWERFUL PREPARATION

ONE MAJOR CRITIQUE OF TEACHER EDUCATION, particularly in the years after normal schools were abandoned for university departments, was the apparent separation between theory and practice in many programs. In some places, teachers were taught to teach in lecture halls by instructors who had not themselves ever practiced what they were teaching, using texts that imparted psychological principles divorced from examples drawing on the real work of schools. Students' courses on subject matter topics were disconnected from courses on teaching methods, which were in turn disconnected from courses on foundations and psychology. Students completed this coursework before they began student teaching, which was typically a brief taste of practice—usually eight to twelve weeks—appended to the end of their senior year, with few connections to what had come before.

In the classrooms where they did their student teaching, many encountered entirely different ideas from those they had studied, because university and school-based faculty did little planning or teaching together. Sometimes, their cooperating teachers were selected with no regard for the quality or kind of practice they themselves engaged in, and often on the basis of seniority, favoritism, or parity, because it is their turn to have an extra pair of hands in the classroom.

The characteristics of the student teacher placement were also idiosyncratic in terms of what student teachers were asked or allowed to do (ranging from clerical work for most of the time to teaching alone with no assistance for the entire student teaching period) and what kind of support they had in learning to do it (ranging from careful goal-setting, co-planning, and mutual problem solving to almost no real assistance). Because they learned theory in isolation from practice and had a quick encounter with classroom practice divorced from theory, it is little wonder the problem of enactment has been severe for many beginning teachers. When new teachers who were trained in this way entered their own classrooms, they often could remember and apply little of what was learned by reading in isolation from practice. Thus they reverted largely to what they knew best: the way they themselves had been taught.

The traditional approach to clinical training caricatured here differs a great deal from that taken in many programs today and in all the programs we studied. First of all, they involve teachers in clinical work throughout the entire program. In all cases, prospective teachers participate in at least thirty weeks of mentored clinical practice under the direct supervision of one or more expert veteran teachers. Sometimes, as in the graduate programs offered at University of Southern Maine, Bank Street, and Wheelock, or in the fifth year at Trinity and University of Virginia, this is structured as a full academic year of student teaching or internship in the classroom of one or more cooperating teachers. In other cases, students rotate to several placements, spending nine to fifteen weeks in each one.

The placements are carefully selected to offer settings where particular kinds of practices can be observed and learned by working with expert teachers and with students having particular characteristics (various developmental levels, special needs students) in a range of community and school types). It is not just that candidates are placed in schools that serve diverse students; they are placed in schools that serve these students *well,* a more difficult situation to find. In fact these universities help to develop high-quality teaching in the schools where they place their student teachers, rather than hoping it might occur without cultivation or closing their eyes to poor practice where it is commonplace. They understand that it is impossible for novices to learn to teach well by imagining what good teaching might look like, or by positing the opposite of what student teachers see.

A major difference from the traditional caricature of student teaching is the care with which these settings for clinical learning are selected and relationships are developed. All the programs seek out and help to develop schools that have developed high-quality teaching for low-income students, recent immigrants, and students of color. In virtually all cases, individual teachers are selected as cooperating teachers or mentors not because they can offer a classroom in which novices can bungle about but because of their deep expertise and willingness to share it systematically with an entering colleague.

The programs often place novices with their own graduates who have learned a sophisticated practice and a way of thinking about teaching that are compatible with the program's university-based work. This enhances the coherence of the learning experience for novices and forges more powerful connections between the theoretical and the practical in both the university and the school. The divide is not the traditional one in which the university owns the theory and the school owns practice, but instead a more integrated set of experiences in which the school mentors rely on and impart theoretical understandings of practice while university instructors use and help develop practices that are theoretically rich but also eminently practical.

As we have described, the clinical experiences are also tightly tied to simultaneous coursework and seminars that pose tasks and problems to be explored in the clinical setting and that support analysis and further learning about practice. This combination of theoretical and practical study is a particularly important change from the traditional approach, which front-loads theory, does not enable applications, and therefore does not support grounded analysis of teaching and learning.

This integration helps to develop a new kind of teacher, one who is theoretically oriented in her own right: aware of learning principles that can be considered (and, when appropriate, used) to guide practice, as well as the many contingencies that intervene and must influence decisions. Graduates voice real appreciation for the connections between courses and their clinical experiences, supporting the view that there is nothing as practical as a good theory and nothing as theoretical as good practice. They feel empowered by their ability to reflect productively and by having a knowledge base they can use to inform their practice, in large part because they have seen it used that way by knowledgeable practitioners who work in schools that value and develop professionally informed practice.

Developing such schools is a novel element of the clinical work of these teacher education programs. Rather than leaving to chance the possibility of finding such intellectually rich sites for training, most of these programs undertake specific efforts to find and develop them. In some cases, as in the PDS initiatives launched by USM and Trinity, they take the form of special formal relationships with a small number of schools that work closely with the university on the mission of teacher training, as well as school reform and research. The PDS schools are an evolution of the concept of the laboratory school, created by many education schools earlier in the century. Bank Street College still maintains such a school in its School for Children, located in the same building as the college. Bank Street also places student teachers in other schools, some of which are essentially public school versions of the lab school, staffed almost entirely by Bank Street graduates.

In programs like Wheelock's and Alverno's, faculty work closely with teachers in a number of schools—some in institutional relationships similar to PDSs and others more classroom-based or tied to particular projects. Finally, in the more traditionally organized student teaching placements used by UVA's secondary programs and UC Berkeley, there are a number of strong school relationships as well as faculty relationships built over time that foster an intellectually rich environment for learning to teach.

Although not yet at the secondary level, UVA developed a PDS school relationship at one elementary school and had forged close relationships with several others. At the Jackson-Via Elementary school, all fourth-year elementary education majors took a yearlong course in Language Skills taught by university faculty members while school-based faculty demonstrated instructional strategies and candidates practiced the strategies with individuals and small groups of students in the school. Third-year elementary education students tutored Jackson-Via fourth graders in an after-school computer club, thus learning to tutor, study children, and teach with technology, while enhancing the school's technology capacity and helping expand the use of computers in instruction. The university faculty also offered professional development for school faculty in writing and science curriculum development.

In these relationships, the roles of university and school staff change from the norm in which university-based instructors teach courses at the university and then send students out to learn "techniques" from schoolteachers. In many cases, school- and university-based personnel co-plan the program as a whole along with courses within it, school-based teachers also work as co-instructors of university courses, some courses are taught in the schools by school-based and university-based faculty, some university faculty work in the field and are placed in the schools, and the university supports professional development for veteran teachers as well as novices. In many cases, school and university faculty and administrators are involved in school reform work together, with the goal being mutual renewal of the school and the university, rather than "missionary work" in which university folks see it as their crusade to go out and change the schools.

In what follows, I discuss some of the common features of clinical development across all the programs, including how novices are guided through their efforts to look at teaching and learn through practice and how they systematically assume graduated responsibility.

I then describe in detail three models of emerging school–university relationships that in many respects play the role the teaching hospital plays in medicine: the lab school, which is really an outgrowth of the teacher education program, as it exists in Bank Street College's School for Children and close public school partners; the PDS model developed by Trinity, which works closely with public schools that offer sites for shared learning for novices and veterans in collaboration with the teacher education program; and the PDS district model developed at the University of Southern Maine, which works with a set of districts collaborating around instructional policy and practice as well as teacher education.

Developing Teachers Through Guided Clinical Experience

Although student teaching is often a haphazard experience, it is carefully structured and managed in the programs we studied. Because it occurs concurrently with coursework, candidates are guided in their clinical work through assignments that shape what they notice and do in the classroom, as well as through specific tasks they are expected to undertake. Cooperating teachers are guided as well by the expectations outlined in the programs and by the kinds of evaluations or assessments they are asked to complete on candidates. The design of school-based experiences actually creates a clinical curriculum, providing an opportunity for graduated responsibility that is carefully scaffolded for prospective teachers. Finally, clinical experiences are shaped by the work the programs do with the cooperating teachers directly, through orientation, training, and ongoing interaction among university- and school-based faculties, something frequently missing in traditional programs that send student teachers out to relatively unknown settings without connections between the university and the school.

Many of the faculty at Alverno are closely involved with area schools in a variety of consulting projects. Faculty serve on school and district committees and lend consulting expertise in areas such as assessment, whole language instruction, integrated curriculum, and technology. Alverno does not have PDSs as they have been described in the literature, but it does have "professional development relationships" with a number of teacher teams and three partnership elementary schools in the Milwaukee Public Schools. At the time of our study, faculty involvement included projects to help a number of MPS schools incorporate performance assessment and portfolio assessment across the curriculum; incorporate technology into the classrooms of two local elementary schools; and provide consulting services, such as development of whole language programs in bilingual classrooms, in three partnership elementary schools. Teachers in the three partnership schools served as cooperating teachers in the program, advisory council members, and participants in the portfolio assessment that takes place for admission to student teaching.

These ongoing contacts with the schools give the faculty important information about which instructors should be cooperating teachers for field experience students and student teachers. Several principals we interviewed said that, unlike the other campuses they work with that request only a number of placements at particular grade levels, Alverno College requests specific teachers to work with particular student teachers. According to our principal informants, the care with which Alverno faculty select mentors for their students is characteristic of how they do everything. As one noted: "Alverno is one of the few universities that really handpick the cooperating teachers. They really know who they are. At some of the other universities they'll just say, 'I've got four student teachers. Will you take them?' And then it's at the principal's discretion to put them wherever they want. What [Alverno faculty] try to do, I think, is to really look at the cooperating teachers and match them with the most appropriate person. Every time they've called me they've identified the teachers that they want."

This kind of care in selecting placements, typical of all of the programs we studied, is a prelude to the important learning the programs expect candidates to do in these classrooms.

Learning to Look in Classrooms

One critical aspect of learning to teach is developing a cognitive map of the key elements of the classroom and school environment as they relate to the many things teachers must do (Darling-Hammond and Bransford, 2005). These programs help student teachers develop this map by guiding their observations and activities in the classroom. In addition to the in-depth studies of specific children and participation in teaching events described in Chapter Five, all of the programs ask novices to complete logs, journals, or other guided observations about elements of classroom organization and management, teacher behaviors and decisions, and school functions outside the classroom.

Alverno's weekly logs in the first of several clinical placements are an example of how these observations are often structured. Candidates are asked to examine and write about:

- Student body diversity and how cultural diversity is recognized at the school
- How the needs of students with exceptionalities are met at the school
- A map of the classroom layout and how learners use the space
- The teacher's daily schedule and how the teacher and learners use classroom time
- How students' developmental needs (concurrently under study) are met in the class
- How rapport and motivation are developed in the classroom (in relation to readings on those topics)
- How the teacher uses verbal and nonverbal communication strategies and with what outcomes
- How the classroom is managed with respect to setting up meaningful learning experiences and managing tasks and physical space

In addition to guided observations of this kind, candidates undertake activities like one that asks them to identify the student in their classroom who appears the least involved in learning; list student behaviors that prevented him or her from learning; consider what kept the student from becoming actively involved; the strategies the teacher used to try to involve the student and whether they were effective; and then investigate other strategies that might be productive for the student (ED 210 syllabus).

These logs reflect a particular developmental sequence for acquiring abilities over the four semesters of field experiences. As one of the faculty noted: "We give so much personal direction with our field placements. It's not that they go into a school and are on their own. Our fields are so developmental. We know what is developed in the first field, and what we can expect in the second, third, and fourth. So there is a real developmental framework that we can rely on to help guide the students."

In addition to the reflective logs, each field experience is coordinated with campus courses in the program. For example, when students are doing their first field experience, they are always enrolled in Principles of Instructional Design and a course on Educational Computing. All of the courses that are coordinated with field experiences require students to carry out some of the assignments in their field placements (see Appendix C).

Assignments of this sort, linked to readings and discussions in the college classroom, guide student teachers' attention to important elements of practice they need to construct—especially to elements that frequently elude the initial awareness of beginners—and help them see how these issues matter and can be addressed. By structuring conversation about these observations into courses that sit alongside clinical opportunities, candidates are able to learn about how such matters are handled in many classrooms, not just the one they themselves have experienced, and they can link individual instances to the literature so as to develop a principled understanding of issues like classroom management and student motivation.

Another example of this guided observation approach is seen in a practicum course at UVA, Curriculum, Management, and Conflict Resolution, which precedes the full year of student teaching. Candidates read and discuss classroom management models for secondary classrooms; observe, study, discuss, and write about communication patterns and conflicts in the classroom; construct a case study of a critical incident involving conflict in their field setting; study conflict resolution models; apply elements of what they have learned as relevant to their setting; and ultimately write about how their work in the field was influenced by what they learned about classroom management and conflict resolution. Again, this process is accompanied by readings and discussions with colleagues at both the university and school. By the end of this guided experience, candidates develop both theoretical and practical knowledge about how to create a strong, respectful classroom community they can build on when they enter their yearlong internship.

Assuming Graduated Responsibility

Each program has structured an approach to the clinical experience that allows candidates to gradually assume greater responsibility for independent teaching over time. The tasks of student teaching do not depend on the idiosyncratic views of cooperating teachers (some of whom might relegate the student teacher to watching or grading papers, while others might quickly leave the novice in charge without help or support); these programs have codified a set of expectations for the process of student teaching and what is to be learned at each stage, often moving from observing in schools and classrooms to working one-on-one with students in both a child study and a tutoring context to assisting on classroom tasks, co-planning and co-teaching with the cooperating teacher, and finally teaching one or more units of study independently.

At UVA, for example, students begin professional studies in their second year of college and have clinical experiences in the ensuing four years "with a gradual increase in the length, amount of responsibility, and degree of complexity involved in the field assignments" (program overview). These experiences are designed with a developmental trajectory for learning to teach in mind.

In the first of the four years of clinical work, candidates observe with a focus on the school as an organization, interviewing teachers, administrators, counselors, and others about their professional roles, spending time observing and assisting in various parts of the school (office, library, special education classrooms, lunchroom, nurse's office). Course assignments are tied to these experiences to guide students' observations and learning.

In the second of the four years, after candidates have been formally accepted into the teacher education program, the focus of the field experience is the understanding of individual learners. Candidates are assigned to tutor an individual child while they learn about learning and development, learn about tutoring, and complete a child case study. In the subsequent year, candidates focus on the classroom, observing and analyzing teaching and learning in their placement, developing and teaching model lessons, and developing and teaching a unit of instruction in the classroom. This occurs while they are taking courses in curriculum and instruction including subject-specific methods. The field experiences include about fifteen weeks of clinical work over the course of the year.

In the final year, candidates complete fifteen more weeks of clinical work in a full-time teaching associateship in the fall of their master's degree year, while they take a seminar in their content area and a seminar that treats a number of other student-related issues. Within this associateship, they co-plan and co-teach with their supervising teacher, gradually assuming increasing responsibility for the planning and teaching activities in the classroom. In the spring of that year they deepen their analytic skills by conducting an action research project on a topic they identified while they were student teaching, presenting their results to clinical and university faculty at the end of the semester. In this way they take on the professional responsibility of inquiry into problems of practice, developing a stance they are expected to maintain throughout their careers.

The specifics of the process of graduated responsibility differ from one campus to another, but all the programs have developed a theoretically grounded plan that guides candidates into teaching with a more complete set of experiences of teaching, learning, and schooling than they would otherwise acquire.

Preparing Clinical Placements

For clinical experiences of this sort to unfold as hoped, there must be extensive communication between the university and school faculties. Expert cooperating teachers or clinical instructors must be selected, and what is expected to occur in the clinical experience needs to be communicated. Many of the programs outline these expectations in handbooks or manuals given to participating schools and cooperating teachers describing what placements should include, along with examples of tasks and outlines of classroom-based assignments. A number of the programs have regular meetings with school-based faculty members to discuss the university-based curriculum, the clinical curriculum, and questions about mentoring and supervision. These include large group meetings for all the cooperating teachers to discuss plans, expectations, and approaches to mentoring, as well as individual meetings in which university supervisors meet one-on-one with a cooperating teacher and student teacher to plan the experience and then, later, to touch base about how it is unfolding and what adjustments or supports may be needed.

Some programs design preparation experiences for cooperating teachers, ranging from a two-day workshop before the start of school to a full semester course in supervision and mentoring offered for university credit. At least two of the programs offer syllabi and course readers from the university courses to the school-based faculty who want to enhance their own learning as well as understand what their student teachers are learning. The relationships created by programs with schools serving many student teachers and participating in a broader shared agenda for professional development and reform allow many opportunities for deeper conversation about educational goals and practices, as well as continuing opportunities for collegial learning on the part of school and university faculty.

School-University Partnerships

In what follows, I describe three models of school-university partnerships and how they shape the clinical experience for teachers-in-training and also the character of the entire teacher education program—transforming the content and delivery of courses; intersections between courses and clinical work; and understandings of university and school faculties about teaching, learning, and professional community.

In the first section, I describe Bank Street College's lab school, the attached School for Children, a private school that continues to function as an adjunct of the college and a site for demonstration of progressive, child-centered practice and a training ground for teachers. I also describe the partnerships more recently developed by Bank Street with public schools, often staffed almost entirely by principals and teachers trained at Bank Street. They are so closely connected to the college, through genealogy of staffing and ongoing coaching and professional development relationships, that they might be viewed almost as public lab schools.

The lab school model is unusual today; it was dropped by many schools of education in the 1970s or 1980s because of budget cutbacks and criticism of the fact that, as private schools, they often served an elite student body, largely the children of university professors. In some cases, lab schools lived on with no close connection to the school of education. For example, the University of Chicago lab school still exists even though the School of Education is closed. The lab school at the University of California, Los Angeles, continues to serve as a site for research, but few of the university's student teachers are placed there.

In the 1980s, the Holmes Group of education deans proposed a public school alternative to the lab school: the professional development school, defined as "a school for the development of novice professionals, for the continuing development of experienced professionals, and for the research and development of the teaching profession" (Holmes Group, 1986). Bank Street's more recent public school relationships might be viewed under this umbrella, though they have not adopted the terminology. Trinity, described in the second section, set out explicitly to enact the Holmes Group recommendations by creating a PDS model in which all of its candidates would be placed in reform-oriented partner schools that take on a major part of their preparation in close connection to the university.

USM's approach, described in the third section, also explicitly adopted a PDS model. This model has an additional element: the organization of the partnership with a set of local school districts that share a vision of teaching and commit to working with the university on teacher preparation, professional development, and school reform. PDS schools tied to the program are part of districts that have a formal relationship with the teacher education program.

Sometimes thought of as the analogue to a teaching hospital, PDSs are intended not only to support the learning of teachers who happen to be placed in such buildings, but also to strengthen the entire profession of teaching. Such schools advance knowledge by becoming places in which new practices are instantiated, and where practice-based and practice-sensitive research can be carried out collaboratively by teachers, teacher educators, and researchers (Darling-Hammond, 2005a).

Developing sites where state-of-the-art practice is possible has been one of many difficulties in constructing clinical experiences for prospective teachers. Quite often, if novices are to see and emulate high-quality practice, especially in schools serving the neediest students, it is necessary not simply to seek out individual cooperating teachers but also to develop the quality of the schools so that prospective teachers can learn productively and create settings where advances in knowledge and practice continue to occur. Thus PDSs aim to develop *school practice* as well as the *individual practice* of new teacher candidates. In this sense, they are a special case of school restructuring: as they simultaneously restructure school programs and teacher education programs, they redefine teaching and learning for all members of the profession and the school community.

Where the difficult work of creating these practices has been accomplished, there is growing evidence of positive consequences for teacher preparation, veteran teacher learning, teaching practice, and student learning. In terms of preparation, studies of highly developed PDSs suggest that teachers who graduate from such programs feel more knowledgeable and prepared to teach. In addition, PDS graduates are typically viewed by principals and supervisors as better prepared than other new teachers. Meanwhile, veteran teachers working in highly developed PDSs report changes in their own practice and improvement at the classroom and school levels as a result of the professional development, action research, and mentoring that are part of the PDS, and studies document gains in student achievement tied directly to curriculum and teaching interventions resulting from the professional development and curriculum work PDSs have undertaken with their university partners. (For a brief review of this research, see Darling-Hammond and Bransford, 2005, chapter 11.) In the programs we studied, these PDS partnerships were viewed as critical to the programs' success in developing stronger teaching and better prepared teachers.

The Lab School Model: Old and New

As noted earlier, Bank Street's famous School for Children might be considered a traditional lab school; it operates as a training ground and demonstration site in the same building as the college. In addition, Bank Street's extremely strong partnerships with several public schools have essentially created a new public school version of the lab school. Staffed largely by the college's graduates, these schools enact practices strongly influenced by the Bank Street philosophy. I describe both of these approaches in what follows.

The School for Children

Bank Street College has long maintained a School for Children as a central component of its work and a demonstration school for progressive educational principles, visited annually by thousands of educators from around the world. The school occupies several floors of the seven-story building that also houses the college and a day care center designed to include a substantial number of special needs students. It is an independent school staffed mostly by graduates from the various programs at the college. About eighty student teachers are placed in the school each year, and many more spend time observing children and studying their work. The day care center also serves as a site for placements. Many college courses are taught in the children's classrooms, and the school and college share the library. College faculty members have often been advisors or instructors to the School for Children teachers, just as these teachers now mentor student teachers. Some cooperating teachers are course assistants in graduate courses, some teach sections of curriculum courses, and many are guest speakers in courses.

Integration of schooling and teacher education is promoted by the use of physical space at the college. The School for Children and the day care center are in the same building; the library and the cafeteria are also shared spaces for children, their families, faculty, student teachers, school administrators from the leadership programs, teachers from the in-service programs, and the school's many visitors. In the library, it is as common to find graduate students asking a ten-year-old the titles of his favorite books as it is to find them checking out books for term papers. The attitude that children know things and have important things to teach teachers is evident in how these prospective teachers approach children.

At any moment of the day, one can see graduate students observing children and their work as they study teaching in their courses. For example, one night, graduate students taking Math for Teachers were working in small groups solving the same problem. After about fifteen minutes of this activity, the instructor, Barbara Dubitsky (who also directs the computer program and serves as an advisor in the preservice program), asked each group to demonstrate how they solved the problem. Eight different solutions were reported. After the groups presented their solutions, the class discussed the skills each group used in solving the problem and how they would teach students those skills. At the end of the class, three graduate students, on their way to get pizza before the next class, noticed some graphs on a wall and postponed their pizza run. They sat down on the floor to copy in detail the various types of hand-drawn graphs displaying the percentages of time each nine-year-old spent watching TV, eating, doing homework, listening to music, reading, doing sports, walking to school or riding the bus, arguing with siblings, and sleeping—in a day, a week, and a month. The graduate students finished copying down the graphs, and one of them exclaimed: "I would never have known that kids could think up all these different ways of doing graphs!" The other two nodded and smiled.

On another day, next to the elevators, we observed a group of graduate students connecting their observations of children of varying ages with the artwork (textured collages representing animals and people) displayed in the hallways. The labels next to the animal collages indicated they had been made by six- and seven-year-olds. Labels next to the collages of people indicated they were created by nine- and ten-year-old students. The graduate students took note of the artwork and the labels and questioned whether, if the two groups were put together, the younger children would be inspired to create people or the older ones might deal with animals. When the elevator came, graduate students left, still discussing issues of interage grouping raised in their child development course prior to observing the art displays.

In the cafeteria, we watched parents and children, graduate students, and faculty members having an early dinner. On the other side of a glass partition, the course Music and Movement for Teachers was under way. Diners smiled at the intriguing scene on the other side of the glass. They appeared to know why all those grownups were playing with a multicolored parachute and crawling though hoops to the fast-moving tune of a tarantella. Parents and teachers had seen their children in similar music and movement classes. Children knew that the teachers were learning to use the parachutes and other equipment to prepare them to teach music from all over the world. The instructor later explained that the tarantella was used to invent a spaghetti dance to accompany a cooking unit used by teachers of young children.

The work of the school and the college are closely interrelated. Rudy Jordan, dean of children's programs when we conducted the study, described the reciprocal collaboration:

> *A lot of the student teacher's work depends on the skills of the individual cooperating teacher, and where they are in their own development as a teacher. You also need many adults to work well with children, so the advantages are for both the children and for the teachers. I ask myself, To what extent do we need the student teachers to run our program and to what extent are we providing*

a service? The fact is that we are teacher educators. Furthermore,
the younger the children, the more we need additional adults to
run good programs. We need each other.

Most classrooms have one assistant or intern and at least one student teacher. Routine placement of student teachers and interns in virtually all classrooms allows the school to design instruction to take advantage of an intensified staffing model that includes a team of adults working together. Rather than a disruption to the one-person classroom, these differentiated staffing arrangements are the norm in a classroom organized to take advantage of the skills of multiple adults. In a classroom for three-year-olds, for example, we saw a teacher, an assistant, two student teachers, and an intern (a Bank Street student with prior teaching experience who receives a stipend during training and takes on greater responsibility). The directors of the upper and lower schools help teachers new to the school learn how to work with student teachers. Cooperating teachers in the upper school often use their weekly meeting time to discuss how to support their student teachers. The upper school director, Toby Weinburger, explained that the process of working with student teachers strengthens the practice of the cooperating teachers as well as of novices, something we heard from cooperating teachers in all the programs: "A benefit [of being a cooperating teacher] is that, as you are continually articulating what you do for the benefit of the student teacher, you are clarifying for yourself in a way that you can't do otherwise. You are evaluating their curriculum development and you are measuring your own and seeing how it can improve as well. So that is a big benefit for the cooperating teacher and for the children as well, and I think people see it."

Because of the unusual career paths of Bank Street teachers, most of whom are switching careers, student teachers bring a range of skills into the classroom as well: "I have had bank vice presidents, a guy who was a lawyer, another who had been in theater," noted Weinburger. "The richness of talent and the variety offer incredible opportunities to find the strengths of that person and integrate what they did into the classroom."

In recent years, greater collaboration concerning teacher education and school curriculum issues has emerged. Jordan described a two-way conversation in the formative stages about "what kinds of things the cooperating teachers see should be part of a teacher's preparation and, conversely, what the advisors see should be part of the children's education." Weinburger described recent efforts of the upper school faculty and faculty of the graduate school to work together on teaching reading to students having difficulty in the School for Children and on teaching teachers for reading. In reciprocal fashion, the teachers at the children's school were working with student teachers on how to teach reading in the upper grades, and teachers from the graduate school offered sessions with the cooperating teachers on assessing and instructing students with reading difficulties. After one such workshop, Weinburger noted: "It was just superb. Everybody felt really lifted. We now understand what [the graduate faculty] is teaching because we experienced it. Teachers had agreed to have another workshop in the spring, but after this they felt, 'Let's not wait until spring, because this is great.' It's a wonderful harmonic convergence of forces. . . ."

In another example, School for Children teacher Stan Brimberg, who works closely with candidates in the young adolescent program, developed a systematic set of tasks and learning experiences for inducting student teachers into his classroom. This work was soon incorporated into other classrooms and into the thinking of advisors about how to support student teachers. A project was under way during the year of this study in which faculty from the school and the college were beginning to work together to co-construct a "curriculum" for the student teaching experience, a measure of the importance placed on careful induction into teaching.

Of particular importance is the opportunity afforded by the School for Children for prospective teachers to spend significant time learning to teach in an environment that models teaching for understanding coupled with intense consideration of the learning approaches of different children. This sophisticated pedagogy is so unusual that it has rarely been experienced by many of the new teachers in their own lives as students, much less in the schools in which they may ultimately teach. Because it is virtually impossible to teach someone to practice in a manner they themselves have never experienced, these practicum opportunities are extremely valuable—and the teaching they require of cooperating teachers is itself quite challenging. As one cooperating teacher in an upper grades classroom explained:

> We are trying to prepare teachers who are interested in children and their development, not just in the content of the particular specialization that the teachers have. One thing that surprises my student teachers (particularly those from outside of Bank Street) is that emphasis on who the kids are, where they're coming from, what their particular needs are, how best to address those needs, not just to talk about what is the curriculum, what are we going to cover. And the amount of coordination that happens between colleagues here is also surprising to them. For example, this afternoon we were having a team meeting at which we talked about

particular students in terms of how they were doing, what had changed in their lives, any information we had about how well they were doing in certain areas or problems that they were having, emotional as well as academic. . . . With student teachers, I do a lot of explaining about what issues certain kids are trying to deal with, and I model for them. I let them see me and hear me talking to students when I'm having one of these conversations with students. I share with them the way I think about students and their needs. If they have an issue with a student, we have a discussion ahead of time about what might be the best way to approach the problem. I'm there with them to support them in that process so that they also get a chance to put that into practice.

Another upper school teacher emphasized how important guided experiential learning is to help teachers learn to understand teaching from the perspective of the students who are experiencing it:

Some student teachers already have an inclination toward this philosophy and may be relatively well-educated themselves. . . . But others may not have any notion of this philosophy and so everything in them—their intuition, their background, their inclinations, their own education—makes what they're seeing here counterintuitive. It's a real challenge to get them to appreciate the frameworks that guide our practice. When they should question "Why?" they say, "I want to bring in onomatopoeia," or "I'm very interested in Edith Hamilton's version of this," and I have to say, "I know you're interested in it, but that's not really what the lesson is about for the children."

It's not something you can explain only in words. They have to go in and start wrestling with it, teach a series of lessons, and for each painful bump they're more ready to admit that "There's something going on here with the children that maybe I hadn't thought about. . . . I guess what the lesson's really about is having them put together an idea for themselves." We are trying to teach our children to synthesize, make generalizations, find patterns, and react to things. For those student teachers who have not themselves learned those things, it's very difficult. In the end, what rescues us is experiential learning. New teachers need to teach and observe until they can understand ideas they could not admit before.

The power of practicing with expert teachers in a school where learning-centered and learner-centered practice is modeled was noted by many of the prospective and beginning teachers we interviewed. This statement by a graduate who had done an internship placement at the School for Children expressed the widely held view:

> *My first placement was at the School for Children with the six/ seven year olds. I found it an incredibly exciting place to be—the way the children were valued and the way education was approached. It's not just making sure that the children meet the city or state guidelines, it's about really preparing them for life and having them be workers within a community of learners. It's really looking at attitudes and values: acceptance of others, both their culture and their thinking. Simple things that people might take for granted, for example, sharing all the different ways kids can approach a math problem and how each is valid. It's exciting to see the kids say, "Gee, I didn't think of it that way, oh wow!" Or someone might say, "I really don't understand how you did it your way, but I see, OK, you worked it out." To see that exchange of ideas and the acceptance that you can be different and still have so much to share and bring to the group.*

We saw this approach to teaching—in which student thinking is elicited and built on in a collaborative setting—in Bank Street graduates' practice in schools across New York City.

Bank Street Partnership Schools

In addition to the School for Children, Bank Street has strong, multifaceted connections with a growing number of public schools in New York City. P.S. 234, an extraordinary school in lower Manhattan serving a multiracial, multilingual school of primarily low-income students, is staffed almost entirely of Bank Street graduates. Bank Street student teachers work in most of its classrooms throughout the year. Cooperating teacher Lena Hajar, who has supervised more than fifteen student teachers from various teacher education programs over her career, said of Bank Street candidates: "They're really good at interacting with kids—very caring, not patronizing, not condescending, not authoritarian or punitive. I also think they're very, very motivated. They're very committed to this kind of practice and to teaching."

An important reinforcement to this practice and sustaining it into the career, rather than being obliterated in the early "reality shock" of teaching, is the close connection between theory and practice made possible by these school-university connections that support an extended clinical experience linked closely to coursework. The college's relationship with P.S. 234 is so organically close that principal Ana Switzer remarks, "We're helping to define what is a Bank Street education as much as Bank Street shapes that." With most teachers having graduated from Bank Street and ten to twelve of its student teachers in classrooms at all times, it is not surprising that many of the trademark features of a Bank Street education are present and, Switzer argues, extended and strengthened in some ways, creating reciprocal influences:

> *The influence is two-way. When you've taken a course with some-body like Dorothy Cohen* [one of Bank Street's seminal thinkers and teachers], *she continues to live in your school through the other students you continue to work with, and you see her influence still impacting the school. At the same time, I actually think the work we've done here in mathematics has in some ways influenced the work at Bank Street. We were the people who brought Marilyn Burns* [a widely known mathematics teaching expert] *into the city, and she worked with our teachers and with my assistant principal, Lucy Mahon, who also teaches a course at Bank Street College. Laura Kates, another one of our faculty members, teaches reading at Bank Street, and carries with her the work we've done with people like Diane Snowball* [an Australian literacy expert]. *Then another Bank Street faculty member came and did some videos here with kids that he then used in his work, and that influenced his teaching. A number of our teachers do guest lectures in courses and I think that influences our practice. We also work with the Principals' Institute. There's so much back and forth.*

The P.S. 234 experience exemplifies many of the notions about synergistic practice and mutual renewal that undergird the concept of a professional development school. Switzer went on to describe how she and her teachers continue to rely on the Bank Street faculty for advice about improving practice: "I like having the advisors around. I feel that I can call on them, not just to talk about placements and their students, but about our school programs. I have called people up at the College when we are developing summer institutes. I also hope that if they notice something that I am not aware of that they will be able to talk to me about it. . . .

Also, many of my teachers who came from Bank Street enjoy having additional contact with their advisors when they return with new student teachers."

Similarly, Midtown West, an exceptionally successful, extremely diverse elementary school, reflects an intense professional development relationship that began when the school was founded with Bank Street support in the 1980s. Since its beginnings, the school has maintained a professional development liaison person who teaches at the Bank Street School for Children three days a week, does ongoing professional development for staff at Midtown West two days a week, and supports linkages between the school and the college, including placing interns and student teachers. When the school was started with the college, the original vision was that the college would support the school in helping to develop teachers and work with parents, and in return the college would learn about how the methods the teachers are being taught in their courses play out in this very diverse setting. Roberta Altman, Midtown West's professional development coordinator, is a Bank Street College employee paid for by school district number 2. Altman describes the close synergy between the school and college:

> *The connections play out in many ways. I have a foot in both worlds. I try to meet with the head teachers individually and in small groups, and we talk about what it is like to be a cooperating teacher, and what is working and what isn't. I teach graduate courses at the College and then I see some of the same students here during their supervision. Some of those students go on to become head teachers here, so there is a continuum of people in different stages of development. Many of the teachers continue to take courses at Bank Street after they have finished their degree, because they then become cooperating teachers and go back to the college. We have one teacher who got her degree at Bank Street who is now in the Reading Program and another in the Computer Leadership Program. . . .*

Mary Timson, principal at Midtown West, is a graduate from the Principal's Institute at Bank Street and would like to have Bank Street student teachers in every one of the school's thirteen classrooms—a goal she has nearly achieved. She sees preparation of future teachers as a benefit to practice in the school as well as part of the school's mission. Timson, like Ana Switzer at P.S. 234, has created a kind of school-based conference group to bring novice teachers together to discuss their practice. Mary explains:

When I was an intern in the Principal's Institute, I initiated a practice of meeting with all of the student teachers twice a month. I was placed in a large school and I wanted the student teachers to feel that they were all part of the school. I wanted to discuss with them what was happening in their classrooms, to share those experiences with each other and to rely on each other as a support system. When I came here, it is also something I wanted to establish. At our first meeting many of the student teachers had not spoken to each other. One day when I was very busy they ran the meeting themselves. One time I asked them to focus on classroom management techniques because that is really important. We have lots of children and very small classrooms. So we have to pay a lot of attention to that if we want to get creative work done.

In myriad ways, large and small, the schools and classrooms that are part of a Bank Street education demonstrate collaboration and in-depth learning. Walking the halls and observing other classrooms at Midtown West, one sees a culturally and linguistically diverse staff and student body at work on a variety of topics: raising animals, cultivating plants, writing books, researching scientific and historical ideas, making murals, and holding classroom meetings to solve problems, discuss ideas together, or decide what to study next. Decisions made by students and staff at these meetings often guide the direction of a community project, the study of an author, or a field trip to look at how people use the Hudson River. During meeting time, teachers often sit with notebooks on their laps, writing down children's questions or responses. Later on they use this information to design further curriculum experiences.

In places like Midtown West, with a strong Bank Street influence schoolwide, this foundation of shared experiences and knowledge has palpable effects on individual and collective practice, and on the overall success of the school as a place where diverse learners are successful. At the same time, the placement of student teachers at Midtown enhances the school's capacity to learn what Bank Street has to offer, since there is a strong coherence between the work students see in the classrooms they observe and the work they do in their college courses.

During the 1990s, several districts opened new small public schools where Bank Street graduates work and serve as cooperating teachers. These include the Manhattan New School, Brooklyn New School, Muscota New School, and Hostos Academy. Strong relationships can also be seen at other public schools where Bank Street has had long-term connections: P.S. 87 in upper Manhattan, P.S. 261 in Brooklyn, Central Park East II Elementary, and River East Elementary in East Harlem. All of these schools serve racially, ethnically, linguistically, and economically diverse student populations and are committed to a progressive educational approach that emphasizes experiential and project-based learning, interdisciplinary curriculum, and child-centered instruction. Dick Feldman, one of the advisors in the preservice program, spoke of the broad range of these relationships:

> *There is not just one way by which we influence, support, change, or assess what we see in classrooms. Working with cooperating teachers and schools is a very dynamic thing. It has to do with a lot of personal, trusting, and professional connections that take a long time to develop. But in the end, we are in schools to help the student teacher work well with the particular group of students and the cooperating teacher. In that sense, while we are there for the student teacher, the children, and the teacher, our first responsibility is the development of the student teacher and her or his responsibilities vis-à-vis the children in the school.*

Although selecting a school is important, selecting a good cooperating teacher is the highest priority of advisors. During a focus group where advisors shared their views about selecting placements, they were clear that their main concern was to get the best learning experience for their student teachers ("One year is a very short period and field experiences are lasting influences"; "I have to make sure they get a full understanding of everything that children experience in the school. I have to make sure they don't just stay with children during Math and Science periods but that they are there to greet children, to say good-bye at the end of the day, and to help them find their coats and bus passes"). Some spoke of themselves as guests in cooperating teachers' classrooms; others described how cooperating teachers with whom they had long relationships ask them about practices and how they participate in the work of these classrooms. Advisors who are also course instructors explained that their courses are informed by what they see in classrooms where they spend long periods of time observing their students.

We observed advisors, student teachers, and cooperating teachers at work during school visits and in advisory sessions after the school visits. The settings were several urban public elementary schools, a number of classrooms at the Bank Street School for Children, and new alternative schools such as the Museum School in Manhattan. In all cases, advisors were comfortable, welcomed, and involved. Their visits generally lasted almost half a day. For some of this time they observed and took notes of the setting and their students' activities. They worked directly with children, side by side with the student teacher. They also sat with the cooperating teacher, either observing the student teacher lead certain teaching activities or trying to understand more intimately the cooperating teacher's approaches.

Many principals appreciate this commitment as it ultimately translates into better-prepared teachers. Arthur Forresta, principal of P.S. 261 in Brooklyn, observed: "I find that the advisors treat placements with a lot of care. Here at the school we are in constant communication trying to find placements that offer students particular kinds of experiences they need. When I hire them I know that they have had good placements. I trust that their experiences in other places have been as carefully managed as the ones in my school."

Professional Development Schools: The Evolution of the Lab School

Stimulated by the Holmes Group's reports in the late 1980s, a number of colleges undertook a redesign of teacher education that focused both on creating a five-year program of preparation that could include a yearlong internship and on creating professional development school settings in which clinical work throughout the process of preparation could occur with expert guidance. These ideas were involved in reforms of preparation at Trinity and UVA. The PDS idea became central as well in the Southern Maine's new ETEP program at the graduate level.

The idea took an interesting twist in Wheelock College's efforts to work in urban communities. Although it placed student teachers more broadly, Wheelock worked to develop intensive collaborative partnerships with nine urban schools, four of which involved the school as a whole, rather like PDS partnerships. In these sites candidates participated in a yearlong practicum where there was co-development and co-teaching of courses and practicum seminars by school and university faculty, as well as opportunities for joint professional development for these faculties. Some of these sites then became focal points for professional development centers located in communities where candidates could take on an interprofessional perspective on the need and delivery of services to children and families. Training alongside other Wheelock students studying social work or child life, these prospective teachers were being prepared to transcend and challenge the roles and boundaries of their profession by coming to understand how an urban community functions, how to be a member of the community rather than an outsider, and how to work with other professionals in serving the community.

This communitywide perspective also informed Trinity's efforts in organizing Smart Schools for San Antonio's Future, a network involving school and community leaders partnering with the university to establish an arena in which schools could develop and implement school improvement projects that support the education, health, and welfare of children and families. City agencies were involved in the consortium, along with business and corporate sponsors, private nonprofit social service providers, and eighteen school districts. These participants co-constructed specific programs within local communities. For example, the YMCA was a partner in several of Trinity's PDS sites, providing after-school day care and instruction and connecting families to needed services.

By 1995–96, ninety-six San Antonio schools were members of the Smart Schools network. The "Smart Schools" image conveys they can take new information and adapt, incorporating new ideas that contribute to better educational programs. The network motto is, "What is now the exception must become the rule." The operating credo includes commitment to augmented teaching and learning for all students (mastery of multiple levels of skill and knowledge in the core curriculum and beyond), authentic assessment, interdisciplinary teaching, teamwork for students and teachers, and active involvement of students in their own education. In similar fashion, USM organized the Southern Maine Partnership, a consortium of local school districts involved in professional development and school reform around a similar set of ideas. In both cases, PDS partnerships grew out of these relationships.

Trinity's PDS Network

There were two elementary and three secondary schools in Trinity's PDS network when we conducted our study; together they ran clinical sites for all of Trinity's student teachers and fifth-year interns. (There are now six PDS sites, with some changes from the original group, including a private school that serves children who are learning-disabled.) The schools were located in the San Antonio School District and the Northeast School District (the latter a separate district within San Antonio city). All featured innovative program designs, active engagement of faculty in implementing reform and upgrading their own skills through continuous professional development, and structured support of novices. All served student bodies that are primarily low income and "minority," and all showed evidence of unusually high or improving achievement.

Hawthorne Elementary School, in the San Antonio Independent School District, serves a highly transient population of about five hundred students in grades K–5, most of them limited-English-speaking. Nearly all of the students (96 percent) qualify for free or reduced-price meals. Hawthorne became a Core Knowledge school in 1992 and organized much of its thematic, interdisciplinary curriculum around content-specific determination of what students should know and be able to do in such areas as history, geography, mathematics, science, language arts, and the fine arts. In this model, the entire school often works on a single theme (for instance, ancient Egypt), with each grade taking on progressively more complex subject matter. The school is a constant buzz of activity and a demonstration that children from economically disadvantaged backgrounds can thrive in an academically challenging environment.

Mark Twain Middle School is also located in the San Antonio Independent School District. More than 90 percent of Mark Twain's thousand-some sixth to eighth graders are Latino/Latina, about 25 percent are limited-English-proficient, and 92 percent qualify for free or reduced-price meals. Mark Twain was one of the first schools in Texas to adopt recommendations for middle school reform. Beginning in 1987, as part of Trinity's Alliance for Better Schools, Mark Twain faculty and administrators and Trinity faculty spent a year collaboratively developing a program to provide middle-level education consistent with research findings and create a laboratory for teachers-in-training interested in pursuing careers in middle grades education. Middle school principles shaping the program include collaborative learning, parent involvement, and academic teams— four core teachers and a reading teacher who design their own schedule to work with about 120 heterogeneously grouped students whom they share.

Located in the Northeast Independent School District, Jackson-Keller Elementary School was a founding member of Trinity's Alliance for Better Schools and a national pilot for the Carnegie Foundation for the Advancement of Teaching's Basic School, designed by Ernest Boyer. Trinity's faculty brokered and supported implementation of the Basic School design, grounded in four principles: the school as community, a curriculum with coherence, creating a climate for learning, and instilling in students commitment to character. Eighty-five percent of Jackson-Keller's five hundred students live at or below the federal poverty level. Jackson-Keller students are divided into five "family groups," each composed of students in kindergarten through fifth grade and their teachers. Students remain in the same family group as they progress to the next grade.

In this model, teachers in each family group cooperate with one another, and older and younger students learn together as they participate in activities and field trips throughout the school year. In addition to Trinity education students who come to Jackson-Keller to fulfill their practica and intern requirements, parents, retirees, members of the business community, and students from nearby Lee High School, another PDS, serve as mentors to the kindergarten through fifth graders.

Robert E. Lee High School, in the same district, is a large comprehensive high school. At the time of the study just over one-half of the school's twenty-two hundred students (56 percent) were Hispanic; 42 percent were Anglo and 2 percent African American. More than one-quarter of the ninth through twelfth graders (27 percent) qualified for free or reduced-price school meals. Forty-two percent were designated at-risk. Lee affords Trinity students a large high school teaching experience, but not a traditional one. When it became a PDS, the school was rethinking the way it organizes for teaching and learning, experimenting with new curricula, more intensive use of technology, and wider availability of resources for students; it has since engaged in a comprehensive redesign effort.

A stand-alone school that shares a campus with Lee, the International School of the Americas (ISA) is designed to foster connections among the United States, Mexico, and other countries in the Western Hemisphere. Enrollment is open to students from throughout the San Antonio area. Opened in 1994, with Trinity's support and encouragement, the school of four hundred offers a choice to those who want a nontraditional curriculum designed to "introduce students to international commerce and technology required to succeed in business in other countries." Emphasis is placed on mathematics and science. In this model, all students are expected to acquire a working knowledge of probability, statistics, and measurement and information systems. There is also a concentration in the areas of geography, politics, language, and culture. Ninth graders are required to develop conversational proficiency in a second language and a working knowledge of a third. All students participate in business internships and contribute to community projects. ISA's partners, in addition to Trinity, are Valero Energy and Southwestern Bell.

Clinical Work in the Trinity PDSs

Trinity students spend their field time, both as undergraduates and as fifth-year interns, in the classrooms of PDS master teachers, all of whom have been designated as mentors by the university. Mentors serve as guides, role models, collaborators, and coaches for Trinity students, modeling the kind of in- and out-of-classroom habits of professional practice Trinity hopes to inculcate in its teacher education students.

Appointed as Trinity adjunct faculty at a ceremony led by the university president, the sixty or so mentors refer to their role as "a celebration of teaching." Many mentors are themselves graduates of the Trinity teacher education program. Others are nominated by principals or nominate themselves for the mentor role.

Mentors receive no financial compensation for their additional duties, though they do receive support in the form of professional development opportunities. Why do they take on this extra work? Mentors point to the colleagueship, professional stimulation, and the opportunity to continue to learn. Participating in the Trinity program is "professionally enriching for me," says one. "It's what's kept me in teaching," says another. "It has made me feel like a valued professional," says a third. The benefit of the PDS work for the students and teachers in the schools is another incentive. In writing about the significant improvements that occurred at Hawthorne Elementary School with its engagement as a PDS and adoption of the core knowledge curriculum with the help of Trinity faculty, two teachers noted:

> The university faculty treated us like professionals. They asked *us* what *we* needed to do for our campus. They wanted to know what *we* thought. . . . It was one of the first times someone had asked our opinion. [They] challenged us, supported us, and made us feel that yes, we can do something. We can break the cycle. We can make a difference. It was a wonderful feeling to be trusted and respected and to have someone believe in us. Their support and encouragement empowered us to know that we could come up with a solution. . . . Just as it was a shot in the arm when they asked us what we wanted to do for Hawthorne, we were honored when Dr. Moore [director of Trinity's teacher education program] asked us to help Trinity create a fifth-year teacher education program. They wanted to know what we saw as the critical pieces necessary for becoming a master teacher. Trinity faculty asked Hawthorne teachers what ingredients were needed to ensure a teacher a successful start and therefore a successful future [Mentzer and Shaugnessy, 1996, pp. 15, 17].

The mentors' role is key to the Trinity curriculum, which includes no methods courses per se. There is nothing in the course catalog called "Teaching Elementary Mathematics" or "Social Studies for High School

Teachers." Instead, discipline-specific instruction is in the hands of mentors. In their role as clinical faculty, mentors teach classes that are conducted at the PDS. Classes might include, for example, study of multiple intelligences, examination of models of teaching, multicultural education, or specific pedagogy related to the reform efforts of a particular PDS (such as core knowledge at Hawthorne). The scope of the classes generally is developed cooperatively with Trinity faculty; the conduct of the classes is the province of the mentors.

Mentor teaching and demonstration takes place in less formal circumstances as well. A visitor walking into ISA, Robert E. Lee, or Mark Twain at lunchtime is likely to encounter a group of mentors and Trinity students chatting about the day's activities, planning lessons, and discussing students in their classes. On a visit to Jackson-Keller, practicum students can be found observing classes, working one-on-one with children having difficulty learning to read, tutoring small groups of students in math, and helping to organize the school's latest fundraising activity.

For the most part, Trinity students learn to teach by teaching under the watchful eye of the mentors; they begin with one-on-one tutoring, working up to partial and then nearly complete responsibility for their classes. In the fall, interns spend four days a week, from 8:00 A.M. to 3:00 P.M., in their assigned PDS. They also attend classes taught by the mentors an average of two evenings each week. In the spring, interns are at their assigned PDS five days a week and additionally take one evening course at Trinity. Regular cohort debriefings are also part of the program—opportunities for students to get together, discuss the activities in their schools and classrooms, and gain support, encouragement, and ideas from their colleagues.

In addition to classroom teaching responsibilities, interns are encouraged to become involved in other aspects of the life of the school, such as extracurricular activities. Involvement with their students' families is a given. The Trinity message is that the role of the teacher extends beyond the four walls of the classroom. Students are expected "to become involved in the entire school operation, including everything from governance to administrative duties" (Advanced Clinical Practice syllabus).

Mentors and Trinity faculty meet once a month at Trinity to reflect together on the month just ended, discuss mutual issues of concern regarding their Trinity students, and share successes. Mentors at each school also meet constantly with one another to hone their programs. One mentor at each school serves as PDS coordinator, assisting with the assignment of students to mentors and meeting with students and other mentors at the site.

In the Trinity model, university-based teacher education supervisors have been replaced by clinical faculty members, each of whom has a specific PDS assignment. All hold a doctorate and occupy tenure-track positions in the Department of Education. Placed in their positions on the basis of their commitment to work concurrently in university and in real school settings, these individuals spend half of their time in the university's professional development partner schools, where they provide counsel and assistance, advise student teachers, lead and organize professional development workshops for Trinity students and experienced teachers, write grants to raise money for school-based reform efforts, and sometimes work in classrooms. Their involvement in the PDS settings lends added credibility to the fieldwork component and allows the university members to offer synchronized professional development courses at the field sites for experienced staff and students. During the other half of their time, they teach courses at the university and conduct research, often on programs or teaching issues at the PDS. To attract and keep experienced faculty in the field-based program, the university counts publications stemming from research at the PDS sites toward gaining tenure.

The many benefits of the PDS model were summarized in an article coauthored by Laura Van Zandt, a clinical professor at Trinity, and Nancy Harlan, the principal of Mark Twain middle school, where Van Zandt works as the PDS liaison. In addition to offering preservice teachers in-depth experience in a developmentally appropriate urban middle school that exhibits strong practices, thereby increasing the pool of well-prepared urban middle school teachers, they highlighted other benefits for the university and the school:

> One obvious advantage for Trinity is having guaranteed, quality placements for middle level teacher education candidates each year. Unlike the student teaching model, mentor teachers play active roles in program development and work with university faculty to evaluate and improve practicum and internship experiences. This team effort occurs formally, through avenues such as the Forum and scheduled retreats, and informally on a daily basis, as university faculty interact in classrooms with administrators, mentors, interns, practicum (undergraduate) students, and young adolescents. . . . Empowering all involved, including the interns themselves, in continual evaluation and redesign of various program aspects is an essential key to program success. Another plus for Trinity faculty is the opportunity to conduct classroom research . . . within a developmentally responsive middle school. . . .

[An] advantage for the middle school comes directly from the university by way of various support services. These include access to business and foundation partners as well as the provision of resources and personnel to aid reform efforts. . . . In short, the success of the Trinity-Twain partnership attests to the fact that "two heads are better than one." The result over the past eight years has been a dramatic transformation not only in the quality of the educational experience but in the attitudes and actions of students and teachers at all levels [Van Zandt and Harlan, 1995, pp. 15–16].

University of Southern Maine's Partnership Model

One distinctive feature of the USM partnership approach is that it involves a group of districts engaged in long-term reform through the Southern Maine Partnership. SMP was launched in 1984, bringing together superintendents of several school districts with faculty from the university to discuss educational reforms aimed at improving curriculum and instruction and restructuring schools. Two years later, this collaborative work led Southern Maine educators to join John Goodlad's National Network for Educational Renewal. Shortly thereafter, they became active in the professional development schools network established by the National Center for Restructuring Education, Schools, and Teaching (NCREST) at Teachers College, Columbia University. Interest in reform was spurred by the network of educators established by the SMP (Lieberman and Grolnick, 1996). The partnership was repeatedly cited by study participants as significant to the intertwined work of school reform and teacher education reform that we observed in our fieldwork.

Because of the high degree of collaboration already under way among districts, schools, and the university around multiple school improvement agendas, the new teacher education design created by the Extended Teacher Education Program was able to employ a variety of blended organizational roles, arrangements, and distributions of responsibility and resources. ETEP was unique among the programs we studied in serving cohorts of students admitted both to a master's program and to one of the five PDS district sites. (There are now a number of other districts and schools involved in the PDS collaboratives, and some shifts in involvement.) The first site established in ETEP, Wells-Ogunquit (which now includes Kennebunk schools), is located about thirty-five miles south of Portland and, at the time of the study, placed interns in two high schools, one junior high school, and three elementary schools. The Yarmouth site, a suburban district twelve miles north of Portland, also offered both elementary and secondary preparation. Fryeburg, about fifty miles west of Portland, involved schools from two public school districts as well as Fryeburg Academy, a private school high-school-age students attend by means of publicly paid tuition since there is no public high school in the community. A fourth site, Portland, offered secondary preparation only, through two high schools and one middle school. Gorham is the fifth site, offering K–8 and 7–12. Located ten miles west of Portland, it is also the home of the main campus of the University of Southern Maine.

Each site admits a cohort of fifteen to twenty students who progress through the internship as a group. A university teacher educator and a teacher employed by the district share major responsibility for co-directing each site's program. These key roles are called university site coordinator and school site coordinator. The role of coordinator includes administrative and teaching responsibilities: managing and allocating the site budget, coordinating calendars and courses within and across sites; admitting, placing, mentoring, observing, and evaluating interns; and leading the yearlong, weekly internship seminar. The program is overseen by the director of the Department of Teacher Education, but the details of daily management are handled by the site coordinators in the five sites and through regular meetings of all site coordinators and other teacher education faculty.

Most courses for interns are offered onsite, held in local school buildings to permit an authentic setting. Course instructors include both university and school-based teachers and administrators. A course leader (university or school staff member) is designated to help coordinate the design and content of each course and facilitate communication among the instructors across the five ETEP school district sites. In some cases, university faculty members and school district teachers and administrators coteach a course.

The strong dose of classroom and school life is a benefit of the PDS model that places interns in a school for a full year. Both Trinity and USM interns are immediately incorporated into the classroom life that becomes their first placement. As one of the ETEP site coordinators pointed out: "The first two weeks [of school], there are no [university] classes. The interns' only job is to be there every day all day long, doing, helping, observing, connecting with kids, that kind of thing. We don't have seminar; there aren't any courses going on. They just have an opportunity to settle in."

Teacher education courses, where possible, are arranged to enhance the immersion. Over time, coursework and classroom experience have been increasingly integrated, and courses are scheduled to minimize taking time away from working directly in classrooms. In fact, in interviews the ETEP-Gorham coordinators repeatedly stressed the importance of basing program courses on the interns' work in classrooms, which in turn is determined by, as one put it, "what first-year teachers should be expected to be able to do."

The attempt to link course content directly to daily practice also means that theory and practice are juxtaposed almost daily. One side effect of the school-university collaboration is to embed the program in the practices of each particular district and to bring ETEP practices to the table as well. Thus we saw interns in Gorham learn how to use the district's performance assessment and portfolios as ongoing assessment tools, how to plan curriculum using the district's template, and how to reflect on their practice using evidence from their work and that of their students. The practices spread into the university. We interviewed a USM faculty member not involved in the ETEP program who was using the Gorham planning template to organize a course she teaches on assessment in the master's program. Meanwhile, rubrics and portfolios are used for performance assessment of ETEP interns in the other sites as well as in Gorham.

Integration of the school and university programs was supported by several perspectives held by USM and school-based educators. First, in our fieldwork it was obvious that practitioner knowledge is valued. The site coordinators shared much of the responsibility for the internship and the seminar, maintaining contact several times a week with each intern. Local teachers are also involved in ETEP by interviewing possible interns, recommending them for admission, mentoring them, and serving along with district administrators as members of the portfolio committees that make certification recommendations. The university site coordinator noted that "in this assessment process, we're banking on diverse points of view and different sources of evidence, and the system has to be built that way."

Further, teachers often served as ETEP course instructors, fully sharing course responsibility. As one principal stressed, "This arrangement does not mean that teachers teach practice and professors teach theory." Teachers' involvement in ETEP is commonly seen as enhancing their own professional development. A principal observed: "When teachers serve as instructors for interns' courses, their own teaching improves. Others learn from them, and they learn from others." A teacher, commenting on her role as an ETEP instructor, reported: "It's a nice professional development opportunity for people in Gorham, but it's also very beneficial for the [interns], because they get to see what happens in the classroom and to hear from people who know the pitfalls. It's not just the theory. It's also a lot of the practical, day to day: "here's what [the theory] says should happen, and here's what it looks like."

We also saw that knowledge brought into the schools from the university was valued. One principal, admitting that his school was behind others in using portfolios, said that ETEP interns are "models for portfolio development." Another principal reported that interns bring in new skills and experiences that existing staff do not have. In considering how local educators view the university, this principal commented: "Both parties have an interest in getting better . . . because no matter what we [in schools] do that we think is good, we always have a long way to go to get better at it, and universities can be a great help in that—their access to research and information, the kinds of studies they want and need to do, all those things can really help school systems."

Third, the ETEP interns themselves are seen as valued members of the school district, not a drain on resources. As one cooperating teacher said:

> *The benefit that I have seen is that it gives the teacher a partner to talk about their work with. You don't always have that, even if you say you want to team with so-and-so who's next door, you never have the time. [With an intern,] someone's in the room watching you teach. So, for the practicing teacher, the benefits of team teaching, the collaboration, the conversations are wonderful. Also it keeps the practicing teachers current on research, and the interns help the practicing teachers learn about the new documents that are out there such as the new state learning goals or the social studies standards.*

As another cooperating teacher noted: "I know that we need to teach people how to teach—that's a mission that I have. But I also do it because I learn from them. Five years ago, I took the first [intern]. I hadn't been in [college] in thirty years, for goodness' sake. Anyway, when I took the first one, I realized there's a source of knowledge for me right there because they were getting knowledge . . . and coming right into my classroom."

Yet another cooperating teacher captured the views of many when she joked, "Interns are another warm body. But they come with a brain, too!" Cooperating teachers see benefits for their students as well. As one teacher said, "An intern supplies an extra facet to the classroom. I would never have tried a poetry unit, but our intern did, and it was wonderful for the children. You learn, but the kids learn, too." She went on: "What I also think is very important is that [the interns'] whole process is modeled after what we expect kids to do here. . . . So when I can say, "Hey, kids,

Ms. Jones's big portfolio presentation is next week, we've got to make a card for her," they know what we're talking about. They know she has to stand up and go through this whole thing, just as they do in their conferences, just as they have to do for their unit project."

The high degree of trust among partners is evidenced by the many ways in which the district and the university share responsibility: the university coordinator's membership in the district's leadership team, teachers' voting rights in ETEP program meetings, and joint determination of the direction of the teacher education program.

Clearly, a key to dramatically successful preparation of teachers is finding ever more effective ways of connecting the knowledge of the university with the knowledge of the school. The more tightly integrated the learning experiences of novices, veteran teachers, and university faculty can become, the more powerful the influence on each other's practices and capacity for constant improvement.

PART THREE

BRINGING IT ALL TOGETHER

7

THE DOUBLE HELIX
OF TEACHING

MANAGING THE DIALECTIC BETWEEN
STUDENTS AND SUBJECTS

PERHAPS ONE OF THE GREATEST CHALLENGES IN TEACHING is creating intersections between the concerns of children and those of content. Continuously interweaving the demands of the subject matter with the needs of the students so as to shape the curriculum toward the child and the child's interests toward the curriculum is rather like sculpting a double helix of teaching and learning. As Deborah Ball asks: "How do I create experiences for my students that connect with what they now know and care about but that also transcend their present? How do I value their interests and also connect them to ideas and traditions growing out of centuries of mathematical exploration and invention?" (1993, p. 378).

Ball's questions capture the tension experienced by teachers everywhere as they strive to connect the subject matter they teach to the interests, experiences, and understandings of their students without losing sight of broader curriculum goals. In their effort to prepare teachers for powerful teaching, programs must wrestle with how to maintain a healthy dialectic between the complementary and sometimes competing goals of teaching toward a common set of curriculum goals and teaching in ways that attend to students' uncommon starting points and pathways.

If they are to succeed, teachers must become *learner*-centered and *learning*-centered, being clear both about what the nature of the subject matter is (why it is important and what is to be learned) and about how the particular learners they are teaching come to that content (what they know and need to know, how they learn, and what they care about) and then connecting the two. John Dewey ([1902] 1956) observed in *The Child and the Curriculum* that this is part of the ongoing, generative negotiation that must always occur in teaching: "We realize that the child and the curriculum are simply two limits that define a single process. Just as two points define a straight line, so the present standpoint of the child and the facts and truths of studies define instruction. It is continuous reconstruction, moving from the child's present experience out into that represented by the organized bodies of truth that we call studies" (p. 11).

As Ball indicates, maintaining both the rigor of the curriculum and its relevance to the learner is not an either-or decision; nor does a simple balance exist. With respect to teaching mathematics, she reminds us that "figuring out powerful and effective ways to represent particular ideas implies, in balanced measure, serious attention to both the mathematics and the children" (Ball, 1993, p. 378). The goal is to bring the students to the subject in a way that allows them to understand it deeply and make it part of their own experience without watering down the content or neglecting the fundamental concepts and modes of inquiry that characterize the discipline. That well-prepared novice teachers *can* do this is suggested by a vignette of this first-year teacher who recently graduated from Bank Street College:

---------- o ----------

On a spring morning just before the last week of school, when many teachers are just biding time, "Jean Jahr's" classroom of twenty-eight second- and third-grade students is intently engaged in a mathematical investigation. Jean teaches at P.S. 234, a New York City public elementary school launched by a Bank Street graduate and staffed by Bank Street-trained teachers. The multiracial, multilingual class of students is working in small groups on a single problem. Some children use calculators; others do not. Some draw clusters of numbers; others develop a graphic display for their problem. As they finish, everyone takes a solution with him or her and sits on the carpeted meeting area facing the board.

Jean begins by reading the problem with the group: "The problem: In September each person in class 113 brought one ream (1 package) of Xerox paper. There are 500 sheets of paper in one ream. There are 28 children in class 113. How many pieces of paper were there altogether?"

She opens the discussion with an invitation: "Let's talk about how different people solved the problem, and why you decided to solve it that way." Over the next twenty minutes, students show, draw, and discuss seven different strategies they have used to solve the problem. Jean questions them to draw out details about their solution strategies and frequently recaps what students say. With patience and careful choice of words, she helps each member of the group understand the thought processes of the others.

As the session nears its end, she asks if everyone understands the several solutions. Three children from one group seem in doubt and raise their hands. Jean asks one of the girls to come up and show "her way." Teacher and children observe patiently, obviously pondering the girls' thought process. Suddenly, Jean's face lights up as she sees what they have done. Her response clarifies their work: "That's how you did it! I was wondering if you had used tens groupings, but you had a totally different pattern. You started as if there were 30 children and then you subtracted the 1,000 sheets that would have been brought by the additional two children from the total number. You rounded to a highest number and then you subtracted. Wow. I get it. Let me see if I can show it to the others."

The young girl is pleased when the teacher shows the group "her" system. Once everyone seems clear, Jean asks, "Does anyone remember where this problem came from?" A girl raises her hand and says: "That was my problem a long time ago." "You're right," her teacher responds. "You asked that problem during the first week of school when all of you were asked to each bring a ream of paper for the year. You saw all those reams of paper stacked up in front of the room, and you wanted to know how many sheets of paper we had. I told you that we would find out some day but that at that point in the year it was hard to figure it out because you had to learn a lot about grouping, and adding large numbers. But now you all can do it and in many different ways." Another child recaps by noting, "That means that we used 14,000 sheets of paper this year." Jean exclaims, "You got it!!" The problem stays on the board for the day, along with the students' multiple solutions.

Elsewhere throughout the room, children's work is displayed on walls, bulletin boards, and shelves, along with teacher-made charts listing information related to work that is under way. Near the book collections and writing materials, for example, three charts pose guiding questions to help students meet the expected writing standards for content, mechanics, and personal goals as a writer. The *content standards* ask:

○ Does the beginning tell what my piece is about?

○ Does the order in which I wrote it make sense?

○ Did I use examples and details to create a picture in the reader's mind?

○ Does my story make sense?

The chart on *standards for mechanics* asks:

- ○ Have I checked for correct spelling?
- ○ Have I used upper- and lowercase letters in the right places?

The chart on *being a writer in a community of writers* asks:

- ○ Am I willing to share my writing?
- ○ Do I listen to others, share, and give helpful feedback?
- ○ Am I willing to revise my work?
- ○ Can I say why I selected this piece for publication and what I like best about it?

These artifacts representing disciplinary standards and ways of working as a writer reflect some of Jean's curriculum goals. Behind the scenes, she has also developed a sophisticated system of documenting students' work, developmental stages and progress, learning needs, and interests. This occurs through informal and formal assessments of reading and writing, for example, as well as records of books read, samples of writing, and Jean's notes taken daily about what she sees and hears individual students doing and saying about their interests, experiences at home, and learning at school. It is clear in watching Jean at work that she cares equally about the quality of her students' work and their experiences as learners in her democratically managed classroom. Her students feel connected to the curriculum as she skillfully builds their learning tasks to capitalize on their readiness and stimulate their engagement.

○

In this example, we see evidence of shared discourse grounded in clear disciplinary standards for work in mathematics and English language arts, a community of learners able to work effectively together on problems and their solutions, and sophisticated pedagogy for teaching important concepts in ways that make them accessible to diverse learners. This practice is typical not only of Bank Street graduates but also of many graduates of the other programs we studied. That this is a function of consistent teaching in the teacher education program is suggested by a comment from a veteran principal and district leader in New York City, who noted how reliably Bank Street graduates can be counted on to develop sophisticated curriculum strategies that link to big ideas in the field and to students' lives and interests: "I have sought out Bank Street graduates in all my positions in the last ten years. . . . I hire them for their high level of professionalism and for their willingness to engage in serious conversations about children, their needs, and their potential. For me, it is important that they are able to balance the development of serious curriculum while paying attention to the needs of students in a diverse population."

Just as classroom teachers do, so must teacher educators decide how they will connect the teacher education curriculum to their candidates' experiences, and how they will help *their* students create a productive nexus between teaching the curriculum and teaching the child.

In the programs we studied, we noted at least three things that appeared to enhance the ability of candidates to do this well:

1. *Creating a new "apprenticeship of observation"* that models how subject matter can be taught in ways that are accessible and responsive to students

2. *Examining student thinking and learning in the disciplines* to help teachers perceive what students understand about the content they are learning

3. *Helping candidates develop a curricular perspective on learning* and the ability to plan curriculum in response to the demands of the disciplines and the learning of students

Next I describe some of the powerful and creative strategies programs used to do these things, including how they organized specific learning experiences to help candidates integrate their learning about subject matter and students and enact productive practices in their own classrooms.

Creating a New Apprenticeship of Observation

Giving prospective teachers an education that successfully integrates pursuit of content knowledge and development of learner-centered teaching is not easy. Among the obstacles a program must overcome are the deep-rooted conceptions prospective teachers bring about children and subject matter—and the relationship between the two—that they have developed through years of their own apprenticeship of observation. In her *Making of a Teacher*, Grossman (1990) demonstrates that, without close examination of what it means to teach, even teachers with strong content knowledge may possess only vague notions of the purposes of subject matter teaching and what students might need to learn this material. The untrained teachers she studied often relied uncritically on the methods they experienced themselves in their years as students and ignored the learning of their students.

To overcome the strong tendency to fall back on old, familiar, and often ineffective methods, Ball and Cohen (1999) argue that prospective teachers have to experience subject matter "in ways quite different from those they learned as students." They identify four areas teacher education programs must address to overcome the apprenticeship of observation: (1) development of subject matter knowledge that emphasizes the reasoning and "meanings and connections" specific to each field, (2) understanding of children as capable of thinking and reasoning and as people who come to school with a host of knowledge, (3) knowledge about cultural differences and the historical and societal forces that shape them, and (4) a firm grasp of both learning and pedagogy. The challenge for teacher educators is to do justice to each component as they try to weave together a comprehensive experience that will help candidates create strong bridges between children and content knowledge.

In the study sites, this is accomplished in substantial part by creating experiences that engage prospective teachers in the kind of learning eventually envisioned for their students, including teaching subject matter as teachers are expected to teach it themselves—in other words, by creating a new and strongly experienced apprenticeship of observation. This "hidden curriculum" is, as Bank Street's Barbara Biber explained, quite deliberate: "We have assumed for many years that, beyond the structured curriculum that is provided, the students internalize the pervasive qualities of the learning environment we try to create for them, that the qualitative characteristics of their own teaching styles will reflect, later, the qualities of their own personal experience in learning to become teachers" (1973, p. 3).

It has long been accepted that teachers generally teach in the way they were taught; in the case of subject matter teaching, the long apprenticeship of observation in K–12 and higher education typically means that teachers have experienced many years of transmission methods where they saw teachers lecturing to relatively passive students in a whole-class configuration. To overcome this powerfully entrenched experience, these programs not only "talk the talk"—supporting more learning-centered and personalized teaching—but they also "walk the walk" (adopting these methods and attitudes in their work with student teachers).

The adage of practicing what one preaches extends through all aspects of the programs, from advising to courses to assessment. In all cases, we heard about dual goals for practices used by instructors and supervisors: to benefit the candidates directly and to have them see and experience practices they might use with their own students. Many faculty also consciously make their teaching decisions transparent, explaining to their classes why they make a particular choice such as turning the discussion in a particular direction, selecting a specific reading, following a line of questioning with one student, grouping students for an activity in a special way, or leaving a question unresolved.

Modeling Teaching Strategies

We heard from candidates in all the programs about settings in which they were taught as they learned to teach. For example, Trinity's teacher education faculty strongly believes that as university instructors they must be the kind of teacher they want their students to become. Thus teaching strategies that are part of the intended repertoire of Trinity graduates are demonstrated and modeled through the daily practice of the university faculty. The mentors who work in the Trinity-PDS partnership schools also provide models of these teaching strategies and the collaborative professional relationships Trinity hopes to instill in candidates.

At Alverno, we heard similar discussions of learning to teach through experiencing a more powerful pedagogy, where faculty and students commented especially on the three-course literacy sequence integrating the teaching of writing, reading, speaking, listening, and children's literature. The faculty expressed a concern that Alverno students, most of them educated in urban schools where integrative language practices are not commonly found, could not become competent at teaching more holistically—with emphasis on teaching writing and literature as well as higher-order reading skills—if they had never experienced this kind of teaching. One strategy is to overcome limitations of students' prior socialization by creating more concentrated periods of time in the program to work with students. As instructors Maggie Sneed and Kathy Henn-Reinke reported: "Very few of our students have been taught throughout their K–12 experience in what would be considered a learner-centered classroom. So, to help them see there is a better way of doing it, we figured we needed them for a longer period of time. The old sequence was that they might have had reading here, language arts methods there. It was just kind of a smattering of things. This way, it's very sequential. We know what happens the semester before, so we can build on that. We keep trying to build on those experiences."

A number of faculty told us how important it was to model the kind of student-centered and interactive teaching they hoped to develop in their graduates: "We want to model how you want to work with your students. You want to take from your students and find out what they want to know and how they learn, and go from there." Another said:

"My practice should be consistent with the philosophy that I want them to have. So my classroom has to be inviting. I have to be tuned into students who are not understanding, and I have to find a way to bring them in and address a variety of learning perspectives. I have to put learning at the center."

The structure of many of the methods courses integrates content across disciplines. Most of the classes we observed were dominated by a high degree of student-student interaction and actively involved students in the activity at hand. In our interviews with students, cooperating teachers, principals, and graduates there was ongoing reference to the fact that Alverno faculty not only practice what they preach, they also preach what they practice, making explicit their decisions and reasoning about the pedagogy they model.

Students at Wheelock made similar comments about their courses. Most noted the explicit links between their study of content and pedagogy and that fact that, in their college courses, "most of the teaching is what we call good teaching." As one student remarked, "I like the way in which many of the professors model their classes after the teaching styles that are used in the elementary classroom." Another deemed herself fortunate to witness good teaching as a student at Wheelock. She explained that she did not experience the disconnection of many education students elsewhere: "My friends at other places complain that their teachers only lecture." At Wheelock, she and her colleagues experienced lectures, but they also spent time in group projects, field placements, seminars, hands-on design and construction of materials and lessons, critical oral and written dialogue, independent and collaborative research, and applications of theory to practice. She had multiple opportunities to experience team teaching and came to understand the benefits of team planning and collegial work.

A student we interviewed commented on the time and effort her instructors put into their teaching and how hard she had to work to reach their expectations, especially in liberal arts courses emphasizing critical thinking and clear written expression. Although initially ill-prepared for this kind of scholarship and reflection and daunted by the quantity of written work required in her Wheelock courses, she explained that her professors (who brought this new content to her in ways that enabled her to stretch, try, revise, and incorporate new ideas and skills) became role models for her: "I want to challenge and engage children the same way my professors have challenged and engaged me." In short, this student learned to *teach* in the Wheelock Way by *being taught* in the Wheelock Way.

Modeling the Process of "Thinking Like a Teacher"

In Bank Street's program, the belief that teachers must have opportunities to learn as they will someday be expected to teach develops a strong and distinctive practice, visible the moment one enters any classroom touched by Bank Street training. This robust practice, as we saw in Jean Jahr's classroom, engages students in active learning around central concepts and modes of inquiry in the disciplines that are skillfully connected to students' experiences and thinking. In their training at Bank Street, candidates find that virtually all of the courses not only connect concrete problems of practice with theoretical ideas and ongoing fieldwork but also foster habits of mind that raise questions about students' interests and readiness as well as subject matter and its purposes.

Almost all courses are taught in a workshop fashion. Each features plenty of curriculum resources, opportunities for working individually and in groups, opportunities for enacting methods (painting, counting, reading and writing books, feeding snails, growing butterflies, harvesting beans), and seeing them in action in classrooms where children are working. Seeing teaching practices and student responses in action stimulates important inquiries about what is being learned, how this relates to teaching, and how different students approach learning.

In a course such as Mathematics for Teachers in Diverse and Inclusive Educational Settings, the substance of the class is mathematics, engaging the students in mathematical discourse and learning as a means of helping them understand both the subject matter and the pedagogy of the subject matter. The pedagogy of the course models the pedagogy of mathematics that the prospective teachers can apply to their own practice. Prospective teachers leave the program with a repertoire of instructional methods as well as a way of thinking about the subject matter that allows them to identify multiple strategies for learning the content so they can best meet the needs of their individual students. Candidates apply what they learn in such courses through student teaching and practicum assignments, which generally occur simultaneously with the methods courses rather than sometime in the distant future.

Graduates often mentioned the course as critical to their current practice. Many saw it as an opportunity to understand deeply the logic behind mathematical concepts, equations, and formulas they had not really understood well in their own schooling. Some experienced it as a key course for understanding patterns in music, science, and the world at large. For still others, the workshop format allowed them to try all kinds of materials experimentally. Students often stayed after class in the math resource room to roll dice, for example, getting a better grasp of probability before teaching it. Paul Scantini, a forty-two-year-old candidate completing his training at the college after changing careers, explained the learning process he and his classmates experienced in the course:

> What happens here—it certainly happened in math—is that we did the math in math class, we didn't just talk about it. Every week when we came in, we did problems like the kids would do problems, and we tried to make sense of it. We worked on some number stations activities and pattern stations activities, and that was important for me because there was this real piece of work. We had to do an activity and write about it mathematically, and that's what we're asking the kids to do. I like math, but for the people who were math-phobic, this was an especially wonderful experience for them. They went through this process of understanding. . . . For me, the course was about beginning to understand and learn about learning styles. It sets my wheels turning about how in my nine- and ten-year-old classroom I can provide this variety of experience.

Some students and graduates mentioned the course as a way of learning about different perspectives by experiencing how everyone solved problems differently. As one student observed: "I thought the Math for Teachers course was great because it's so hands-on. I really couldn't believe it when they talked about how does everyone add 20 plus 22, and everyone had a different way of figuring it out. It was just amazing to me. I mean you hear a lot about learning styles and you hear a lot about 'Everybody has their own method and there's no one right way,' but you kind of think to add two numbers there's one right way. But really everyone has a different way, and that was pretty amazing."

In discussing assignments, students and graduates mentioned how they had learned to understand mathematics more deeply, be responsive to learning styles and developmental capabilities of students, create or secure resources that would help students understand concepts, and work with the new national standards in mathematics.

Similarly, UVA's courses in mathematics and English pedagogy were described as offering prospective teachers both models of pedagogy and of ways of thinking about pedagogy. Like candidates in the other programs, these students experience the course material in ways similar to how they will be teaching it themselves. In addition, students are encouraged to reflect on why they are teaching what they are teaching and what choices may be available to them while they encounter a range of techniques and strategies.

In the mathematics methods classes, students use graphing calculators to solve problems, regularly engage in mathematical discussions of problems, and are asked to describe problem-solving strategies used in a variety of instances. In the English methods courses, students engage in book discussions, the writing process, and critical reviews of selected literature. These courses are not how-to sessions; they aim to develop a way of thinking that empowers graduates first to consider their students and then to apply strategies, techniques, and methods of reflective inquiry they have observed. The course instructors carefully gauge the progress of these candidates and design instruction appropriate for the needs of the students in the class, thus modeling responsiveness to students as well as particular teaching strategies.

For example, from the first day in each of Joe Garofalo's courses, Teaching in Secondary Mathematics and Seminar in Mathematics Teaching, students reflect on the nature of mathematics, what it means to teach mathematics, why it is taught, and how it should be taught. Another explicit goal of Garofalo's courses is to introduce students to new thinking and reforms in mathematics education. Finally, the activities in these courses are explicitly designed to develop multiple pedagogical techniques and strategies.

Garofalo's style is infectious, the modeling deliberate. He starts nearly every class with a mathematical problem for everyone to try. He believes that one effective way to encourage students to think about mathematics is for them to do it. His course problems are challenging and thought-provoking and offer opportunities for students to discuss their approaches and understandings and to reflect on their feelings and beliefs about the subject or a particular topic. "Have you ever been lost in a math class?" he asks a group of prospective teachers. "How did it feel? What did you want the instructor to do?" Garofalo intentionally exposes students to many resources, ideas, techniques, and models of instruction. Of fifteen class sessions in his Teaching Secondary Mathematics course, more than a third focus explicitly on particular teaching strategies, including those grounded in technology using new software and graphing calculators. For these sessions, students work in small groups to develop their presentations and then teach excerpts of these lessons to their classmates and the instructor. Peers and Garofalo critique the presentations.

Garofalo's Teaching Mathematics course does not offer predigested recipes for teaching mathematical topics such as computing area, solving linear equations, or taking a derivative. Instead, he stresses the development of multiple strategies and the ability to match them to student needs. The focus is on both the instructional technique and the learner. Garofalo's final exam illustrates his explicit efforts to connect these ideas, when he asks students to:

○ *List three different heuristic strategies which you believe would be helpful to teach students taking algebra and explain how and where you would teach these strategies in an algebra course;*

○ *List three different control strategies which are important in problem solving and tell how and when you would teach them to students in an algebra course; and*

○ *Discuss why or how teaching heuristics without addressing aspects of control is less than adequate.*

In addition to Garofalo's demonstrations of such strategies, the fact that candidates have observed him reason through teaching problems in this way throughout the semester enables them to "think like a teacher" about these sophisticated aspects of mathematics pedagogy and to consider choices they can make in relation to their students' needs.

Examining Students' Thinking in the Disciplines

Prospective teachers' apprenticeship of observation is also expanded by observing and assessing students who are engaged in learning content. A constant refrain of these programs is the importance of deeply understanding children in order to make decisions about teaching. A DTE faculty member's comment underscores this priority: "Traditional disciplines do not correspond to children's construction of knowledge. But good teachers do not analyze content and impose it on the child. They analyze the child and fit the subject to the child's developing understanding." DTE, like the other programs, aims to "mesh the developmental needs of children with the cognitive demands of the curriculum." Both sides of the balance are fully examined.

To make teaching decisions that are responsive to the needs of students, teachers must know how to find out what those needs are. Teachers must assess student abilities, learning styles, and developmental levels, both general and subject-specific. They must become, in a sense, researchers about their own students, skilled in ferreting out students' thinking and reasoning as well as experiences that may serve as building blocks for learning, and able to interpret what they learn so as to translate it into curriculum and teaching decisions.

Studying Student Thinking and Learning

The programs help teachers develop a number of skills for this kind of inquiry. Candidates study how students learn and what they know and understand by listening to them, observing them, examining their work, investigating how language, culture, and other aspects of experience affect their learning, and discovering what interests or approaches each brings that might offer entrée into the subject matter. The process never ends. Teaching, according to these programs, should be a perpetual cycle of monitoring the effects of teaching practices on students' learning, reflecting on what has been learned and why, and building this understanding into subsequent teaching decisions.

At UC Berkeley, during the first year of the four-course sequence on human development, the faculty focuses on using a developmental lens to understand the general learning process. Students conduct experiments at their placement sites exploring the theories learned in class. For example, the first assignment asks students to use Piaget's clinical method to assess the cognitive development levels of two children in differing domains of knowledge and then form a hypothesis about this type of assessment. A later assignment for this same course asks students to collect language data from children and interpret them along with the theories presented in class. Students then hypothesize about constraints on the children's language use and consider possible ways to foster their language development.

In the second year, attention to learning in specific subject areas comes to the foreground as developmental issues and concerns are linked to content areas. In a second year course, Advanced Development and Education: Mathematics and Science, students focus on a developmental analysis of elementary school math and science curricula. At this point, the program explicitly revisits and builds on the mathematics and science teaching methods course the students took during their first semester in DTE. The assignments emphasize identifying and remediating common problems in mathematics and adopting hands-on, minds-on science curriculum.

The assignment sequence permits insight into how the program scaffolds candidates' increasing ability to integrate understandings of content, pedagogy, and development. Beginning with discussion of what students at varying developmental stages typically understand about mathematics and what they may have difficulty with, candidates review curriculum for a span of three grade levels and consider how to sequence topics to help students develop their mathematical thinking. Then they hone in on a specific knowledge domain and consider learning sequences within it.

Eventually they construct and teach a curriculum unit and then assess student learning and reasoning with Piagetian-like tasks, using the assessments to figure out how to remediate one or more students who did not fully grasp the content they taught.

Assignment One (a): Using clinical interviewing skills, interview your cooperating teacher about mathematical concepts that children have difficulty learning each year and what children learn easily each year. Include what the teacher does that seems to work.

Assignment One (b): Review the mathematics curriculum for three grades with the grade you are teaching in the middle. Then, for the number knowledge strand, do your own ordering of topics by picking a concept to be taught in your grade and breaking it into subtopics that can be ordered from least to most difficult. To begin with, include at least six steps in your hierarchy. Give a brief concrete example of what you mean for each step.

Assignment Two: Pick a second mathematics topic (e.g., a domain other than number) for the same grade. Do the same type of learning hierarchy for this topic with an example for each step. Link the concepts between the two domains in content and/or cognitive-developmental requirements. We will call this a horizontal linkage between knowledge domains. Indicate milestones in cognitive development for the identified strand(s).

Assignment Three: Use one or both of the ordering of topics produced in assignment two to construct a mini-math curriculum complete with teaching methods. Choose two Piagetian-type tasks you feel will tap the key cognitive concepts required to master the material. (Students are encouraged to invent their own Piagetian-type tasks so that they construct the connections between development and "content." The purpose is not to label the child, but rather to understand the child's reasoning about key concepts.)

Assignment Four: Use the mini-math curriculum from assignment three with a small group or a whole class. Target three or four children for closer study including at least one child experiencing difficulty. For the entire group taught, collect the results of your lessons to obtain initial and final math performance lev-

els. In addition, for the in-depth students: (a) administer Piaget-
ian-type tasks to assess the extent of their understanding of the
targeted concepts; and (b) attempt to remediate with one or
more of the children by finding a level within the curriculum
where they are truly proficient and then move them forward.
Give careful thought to the factors limiting the success of your
teaching program.

As these assignments suggest, DTE students experience pedagogical approaches as part of their methods courses and also delve deeply into questions of cognition, learning, and teaching through inquiry that places them
in the role of scientist, as well as pedagogue. While examining children,
they also examine subject matter and conceptions of content. They discuss underlying philosophies behind reform efforts, examine and reflect
on student work, and begin to engage in conversation about national
issues and state and local frameworks.

The two approaches—focus on general learning and subject-specific
learning—complement one another. Aware that faculty's strengths lie in
child development and learning, the program resourcefully taps into well-
established networks of professional teachers for work on subject-specific
methods. Students learn about teaching mathematics and science in several courses they take at Berkeley's Lawrence Hall of Science, a learning
environment that elicits active engagement of students, mirroring what
DTE hopes students will establish in their own classrooms. Experiencing
teaching that is similar to how candidates hope to teach is a crucial part
of the DTE experience, but the addition of knowledge about student
thinking and reasoning renders the learning from these demonstrations
much more profound. As one of their instructors noted, DTE candidates'
earlier work on learning allows them to go more deeply into the nuances
of content-specific pedagogy when they encounter it. A Lawrence Hall
presenter, asked to compare the DTE student workshops he does to his
decades of workshops with experienced teachers, replied: "They [DTE
students] are open. They latch onto the 'I know that will work' just like
experienced teachers, but they can step back into their students' heads better. When I work with them I am not just presenting activities, I am
exploring pedagogy and content."

Pedagogical content knowledge and methodology in the language arts
are addressed in conjunction with the Bay Area Writing Project, where
students take a ten-week course. Like the science pedagogy they learn at
Lawrence Hall, the DTE students participate as writers in the writing
process, just as their students will, and they learn methods they can use

to engage their students as writers. By reflecting on their own and each other's responses to the writing process, they also acquire a grounded theoretical base on the nature of writing and learning to write, one that considers the student writer's perspective. As Grossman (1990) notes, this student learning focus within the study of content-specific pedagogy is critically important: "Knowledge of student understanding differs from more general knowledge of learners in its focus on specific content; the emphasis is not on how students learn in general, but, for instance, how students develop fluency in written expression" (p. 105).

Developing Tools for Assessing and Developing Learning

If candidates are to understand student learning and use it to organize their teaching, they need to know both how students generally learn concepts and skills in particular domains and how individual students are progressing in their learning. This requires a range of tools for assessing learning. The programs engage candidates in using existing tools and developing their own. For example, a typical assignment at Alverno, used in the third integrated language arts methods course, asks students to develop a rubric for assessing the writing of middle-grades children on the basis of a writing sample. In small groups, candidates use the rubric they have created to assess the developmental level of the learners' performance. They must present evidence to support their judgment, diagnose areas requiring attention or further instruction, and create an appropriate teaching plan, linking their analysis of learning to their pedagogical proposals.

Students at USM undertake similar inquiries. For example, assignments in the content methods classes (math, science, social studies) include assessing work produced by children and developing lessons and units based on students' needs and the content standards promulgated by various national organizations (for example, National Council of Teachers of Mathematics, or NCTM; National Council for the Teaching of English, or NCTE). In USM's literacy course, as with the UC Berkeley mathematics and science methods course described earlier, students closely examine children's learning and development within a content area. The syllabus includes topics and activities for practica—ten classroom experiences the interns are to try with children, some of which can be combined with the case study of a child assignment in a class called Life Span Development. Interns try various reading assessments with their students, including an Early Literacy Assessment that helps them to assess a child's reading readiness. In a course we observed, the instructor, Susan Sedenka, a classroom teacher and member of the school-based ETEP faculty, demonstrated this assessment with a five-year-old and then went on to discuss how to use an Individual Reading Inventory in doing case studies of students with reading problems. She encouraged the interns to try it out with a student or two in their classrooms and to reflect on what they learned.

In a later conversation about "semantic webbing," the class began to analyze how teachers can help young children develop vocabulary through categorization of words. Sedenka described how teachers can ask children to name five words associated with another word or concept, such as Halloween. "This approach to vocabulary building is more than brainstorming, however," she warned. She explained that many teachers end the lesson after generating a list of words; however, another level of learning is achieved if students are encouraged to sort the words into categories, or "mental file drawers," as she described the process. To demonstrate this process, Sedenka had the interns construct a web of words. Using the web, she then demonstrated a classification process by using prompts such as, "Which of these words seem to go together? Why?" and "What are some things that scare you?" She later explains that this process demonstrates how children can begin to develop conceptual categories and justify the appropriateness of these categories. "In this way," she elaborates, "students are building on what they already know and attaching meaning to new words."

After a minilesson on free writing, Sedenka illustrated writing conferencing techniques, emphasizing the importance of using phrases such as "I wish I knew more about . . . ," "Here's what I like about . . . ," and "I wonder if . . ." to stimulate student thinking about their writing. By using such prompts, she explained, the teacher can encourage students to develop a plan for rewriting, understanding that it is essential to the writing process. The interns learned how to listen to what students tell them as a guide for figuring out how to teach them. They then spent some class time doing their own free writing, about scary stories or about their draft vision statements or another assignment they might have. They later formed pairs and small groups for peer conferences on the writing just completed. As in other programs, USM courses thus model the pedagogies teacher educators hope their students will use in the classroom.

In similar fashion, candidates in Bank Street courses such as The Teaching of Reading, Writing and Language Arts and Teaching Reading and Writing in the Content Areas engage in the kinds of activities they will use in their own classrooms and examine student responses to those activities. They keep reading logs, examine methodologies and how students respond to them, and learn about assessment. A first-year teacher told us how Teaching Reading and Writing in the Content Areas included strategies for teaching English as a Second Language that now help her in her multilingual classroom. She found she must constantly assess whether children's difficulties arise from not knowing concepts in math or other subject areas or from not comprehending the English language in the texts. Using strategies she had learned for observing and assessing students, the teacher discovered that her children did better academically when they read the math problems or the science directions in the group rather than alone; in addition to the help they received in the process of working in a group, hearing them allowed her to assess if they needed more help in the subject or in understanding the language of the problem or its related instructions.

Attention to children's thinking and responses is a critical element of this kind of curricular learning. We traced this in the cluster of courses on literacy development. After a series of courses, a current student ready to enter the job market told us how confident he felt about teaching children how to read, an area that many beginning teachers find especially anxiety-provoking.

> *Teaching of reading was about working with kids. I have all my stuff here—the logs and everything. I know that if someone said to me, "Can you tutor my six-year-old in reading?" I could really teach that child. I know how to do the early assessment for reading and see their interests and how to read with them and to them. I reviewed all my stuff in cueing and decoding from one course. Since I worked with one child extensively, the cooperating teacher told the child that she would help me become a reading teacher. So, Anna, the child, took it upon herself to tell me how she had figured out things. I learned so much from her. Sometimes she would tell me that she remembered what a word looked like, while other times she sounded words out, and other times she had memorized the pictures. It was great.*

Asking questions regarding student learning and figuring out why students respond as they do is a frequent routine. For example, an evening session in Madeleine Ray's course The Uses of Language began with an introductory segment asking students for reports from the field. Students reported on humanities teaching issues that arose in their classrooms that week. In contrast to the usual reports of novice teachers, which focus on the teacher and what she did or how she felt, these comments typically focused on evidence of student learning and on how students appeared to respond to their teaching efforts. One student discussed a writing assignment that did not go as he had hoped. He had had good success with the reading of Greek myths with his eighth-grade students, but he found it difficult to get students to write their personal reactions to characters they played or read about. Another student suggested that it might have been hard for students that age to be so personal. Maybe if he asked them to write as reporters it would have been easier. "Yes," noted Ray, "writing in the third person creates a little distance. Why don't you try that?" "I think I will," the student replied. "My advisor was there when it happened, and she also suggested that I not hit them so head-on with the personal reflection."

Ray engaged the group in discussing the importance of reflecting on practice in sharpening one's craft, and of being sensitive to different interpretations of material. To illustrate, the group was asked to do portrayals of a scene from "Cinderella." The group commented on how each individual developed the scene. Ray suggested the same thing would happen with their teaching. They might all be teaching *Of Mice and Men* but each would differ, according to their students' backgrounds, prior knowledge, and experiences, as well as their own style as teachers. This conversation led to a discussion of how to figure out what entry points might help children succeed with various tasks, a foundation for developing a successful curriculum.

Developing a Curricular Perspective

Central to all the programs' approaches to connecting content and children is a pervasive curricular perspective on teaching. Whereas some schools of education have reserved courses in curriculum design for advanced master's or doctoral students who plan to become specialists at textbook companies or in central offices, these programs see development of curriculum as intrinsic to the process of learning to teach. Built into each program are assignments and activities that gradually introduce student teachers to writing and implementing their own lessons and units. As is true of everything else the programs do, these curriculum efforts are never created in a vacuum. They reflect what candidates know about how the content is learned, about development of the children to be taught, and about the sociocultural environment in which the work will take place.

Developing the Habits of Curricular Thinking

As prospective teachers learn to evaluate, select, and organize important subject matter concepts and materials, they also spend considerable time figuring out how to bring them to students in ways that will provoke deep learning. Subject matter teaching is always infused with a developmental perspective and sensitivity to social contexts. Because what is taught must connect to student readiness and interests as well as to community contexts, candidates learn that even topics routinely taught or presented in texts require curricular development.

For example, Alverno's *Handbook for Education Students* (1995) articulates well the nature of curricular thinking at every step of the planning, implementing, and assessing process, beginning with consideration of the *outcomes* intended—Why teach this material? What are students expected to learn? How do these outcomes relate to students' individual lives, other curriculum areas, or the broader world?—and continuing with consideration of *students,* their characteristics, needs, and strengths (including special needs of individuals); *methods* that are likely to work most effectively to accomplish the outcomes with this group of children; and *resources* (people and places as well as books and artifacts) that can be used to teach this material. As candidates consider how they will *implement* their plans, they are asked to consider what concepts they will focus on, how they will present material and motivate students, what role they will take and what role the students will take, what choices the students will have, and how they will provide assistance for the students' learning process, including opportunities to apply and practice the skills or concepts.

As candidates consider *assessment,* they are asked to figure out what evidence they will use to determine if students have met the outcomes, how students will engage in self-assessment, and how they will provide feedback to students. They are also asked to clarify how they will know if they have successfully met the outcomes they set for themselves in teaching the lesson or unit and how they will use what they have learned to inform their own teaching in terms of both next steps for students (including those who may need additional assistance) and their own professional development goals. Assessment starts the cycle of planning all over again. As the *Handbook* notes, "Your use of assessment as a teacher will assist you to stand back and look at the experience of a lesson or an interaction, but it also provides direction for the next experience. And so, assessing also brings you as a teacher back to planning" (1995, p. 39).

In addition to thinking through the many considerations that must be brought to bear to create connections between the child and the curriculum, teachers who aspire to ensure learning, rather than merely "get through the book," must understand how children are likely to learn particular skills and concepts in a domain. As UC Berkeley's Kroll and Black (1993) note, curriculum developers historically "have attempted to introduce changes in educational practices by constructing developmentally appropriate curriculum for teachers [to use] rather than by providing teachers with the theoretical knowledge necessary to understand the inadequacies of existing curricula and to construct or implement viable alternatives for themselves" (p. 418). If teachers are to "acquire expertise as curriculum developers, not merely as curriculum managers," they need to learn to "analyze how knowledge is acquired in all domains, along with the specific steps in knowledge acquisition within domains of knowledge encountered in schools" (p. 432).

In the previous section, we saw how students in Berkeley's DTE program develop this kind of knowledge of domain-specific learning progressions in mathematics. To take this thinking still further: the fourth development course at Berkeley is organized so that the class can develop an entire pre-K–6 developmental literacy curriculum. Starting with the curriculum created by the previous year's cohort, students in this class work together to integrate their reading and learning about literacy development, multicultural education, and special education into a coherent seven-year program, bringing concerns for their own students and materials suited to their own communities into the mix. At the end of the course, candidates produce a document presenting the curriculum and its theoretical foundations to an audience of teachers, having learned a great deal about how to think in curricular terms and work collegially.

Importantly, in this case these elementary teachers have conceptualized the process of literacy development from kindergarten through sixth grade, achieving a sense of the whole and assembling a repertoire of materials and strategies to help their students progress along this continuum. They are not limited in their vision to what they think an average fourth grader should be doing at that grade level but can place students in their actual development anywhere along the continuum and think productively about where the students have been and where they are heading in their journey toward literacy.

In like fashion, Bank Street teachers are prepared as curriculum builders rather than mere implementers of texts or programs as they use their knowledge of children, families, learning, and subject matter to design learning experiences in virtually every field they study. John Dewey's concepts of "experience," "child and curriculum," and "school and society" are central to how Bank Street's curriculum courses are conceptualized and taught. In Deweyan fashion, the social studies are used as a major focus for constructing participatory learning processes organized around motivating inquiries that connect students' experiences to the disciplines. For example, in a social studies curriculum course for prospective teachers of adolescents, students create their own elaborate interdisciplinary curriculum units that help them learn to conduct a "dialogue between the disciplines." For example, a social studies unit on the Harlem Renaissance weaves together study of historical, economic, political, and geographic conditions to understand what influenced the lives and artistic expressions of individuals in that time period. Field trips to research such a unit might include the Schomburg Center for Research in Black Culture and the Studio Museum in Harlem.

While reviewing these units in small and large groups, instructors and peers invariably raise questions such as "Why is this an important study?" "Why and what would children of a particular age learn through these experiences?" "What resources do my students and families bring to this study?" "Who in the school's community can contribute?" "How can we integrate other subjects into this study?" "How does it relate to the present, and do we have a role to play?" This type of probing helps students realize that their curriculum decisions should attend to core concepts in the discipline and aim for developmentally, socially, and academically important outcomes for their students. Sample curriculum studies are kept for reference so that students learn from others' work.

For teachers of younger children, Early Childhood Curriculum helps candidates learn to place the learners at the center of integrated curriculum that weaves literacy and numeracy into studies of the social world, helping them grasp historical, geographic, economic, political, and environmental issues in the present and the past. As the course description notes, "This course assists students in setting a framework for planning and developing curriculum based on the principles of growth and development, areas of knowledge, and one's values. Emphasis is given to the opportunities offered by curriculum areas and materials, with the area of social studies being viewed as the core of an integrated curriculum. The course interweaves theory and practice as students plan, develop, and reflect on curriculum experiences from nursery through third grade."

Assignments ask students to evaluate educational ideas from the perspectives of purpose, subject matter, and experience and always include development of curriculum units and presentations. These must take into account a developmental perspective, understanding of concepts, and identification of resources to carry out the study. Instructors in this course include cooperating teachers from the Bank Street School for Children as well as graduate faculty. Public and private school teachers are invited to discuss their curriculum development strategies. Class discussions, small group work, and videotapes treat central topics such as the study of families, neighborhoods, markets, the city, immigration, the Hudson River, Old Manhattan, and New York today. Helping children understand the community in which they live has been part of Bank Street curriculum thinking since its founder wrote the first edition of *Young Geographers* in 1931, which was updated by current faculty in 1991.

Anne Marie Mott, coordinator of the Lower School of the School for Children, feels that one of the biggest challenges in teaching this course is broadening the narrow, event-bound conception of social studies that graduate students often bring with them from their own childhood experiences in school. Few have previously experienced social studies as a process that prepares individuals to understand their environments, live productively in groups, and develop systems that support democratic living. Nor have many explored linkages among curricular areas or developed an understanding of how to assemble ideas to reach a larger goal.

The experience is an epiphany for many students. One current student, who was making a transition from a management career, noted of the curriculum course: "Curriculum was very worthwhile, because I'd never seen this holistic way where you integrate math and everything else into social studies, and you can teach everything in a connected way. I'd never known that. This was an eye-opening experience for me. Having to devise a curriculum really helped me think out every little process. I liked this course a lot, and then I did a new curriculum for my directed essay. Now I can think in terms of the big picture."

Developing Curriculum Materials and Designs

In addition to developing the ability to think in terms of the big picture and connect students' needs and interests to disciplinary concepts and the development of critical skills, the work the programs do around curriculum design is practically useful. For many novices who have had inadequate clinical training, one of the great stresses of beginning teaching, aside from classroom management, is the need to develop curriculum and teaching materials. New teachers often flail around, trying to figure out what to teach and how to find or make materials. If they have textbooks available, they may become slaves to marching through the book, assigning the questions at the end of each chapter, because they do not have knowledge or means to assemble supplementary texts, activities, assignments, and assessments that lead elegantly to powerful learning for children. These programs, by contrast, launch beginners with a substantial body of well-designed curriculum equipment that they are prepared to adapt and use for their students.

At Bank Street, for example, almost all content methods courses include curriculum design activities that yield real-world and text-based curricular materials. For example, in addition to the literacy, mathematics, and social studies methods courses discussed earlier, candidates have three course choices on science for teachers, taught at the college or a science center at Harriman State Park, about twenty-five miles outside New York City. These are frequently cited by graduates as having helped them learn to build curriculum and develop hands-on teaching techniques. Two other courses, Art Workshop for Teachers and Music and Movement, are often cited by graduates as places where they learned to teach for multiple intelligences and developed a larger curriculum and assessment repertoire. The combined results of prospective teachers' experiences in content pedagogical courses is an appreciation of critical constructs within the disciplines and of strategies that can cut across disciplines to bring the coherence for their own students that they experienced in their apprenticeship of observation at Bank Street. As a first-year teacher who came into teaching from a career in public relations noted of the Early Childhood Curriculum: "The curriculum class I took was very important to me because it really showed me how to integrate curriculum. A lot of what I brought into my classroom came directly from that class. It came from being shown slides and videos and being talked to about curriculum and being able to do it ourselves, including going out into the community, observing, and figuring out how to recreate experiences in the block area, in the dramatic play area, through art, through writing. That really all came together for me in the curriculum class."

In all of these courses, curriculum units from former students were kept and offered as models, often over the years in a curriculum library, thus offering candidates the fruits of their colleagues' work as well as their own when they went out into the field.

We heard similar reactions to the interdisciplinary curriculum unit students develop at USM and Trinity. Like Bank Street students, ETEP and Trinity interns use the unit to learn to teach purposefully and reflectively: to decide on specific learning goals; collect, evaluate, and alter materials; develop and implement lessons and embedded assessments; and continuously assess learning and make appropriate adjustments according to student needs.

Construction of curriculum at Southern Maine has become a collegial enterprise. Through assignments in their content area methods classes, students begin to develop curriculum units that reflect the subject matter standards in their fields, published by professional organizations such as NCTM and NCTE. They combine these aspirations for learning with what they have learned from classroom observations, readings, and assessment of children's work. These smaller curriculum development tasks may ultimately be used in a major project to implement a large interdisciplinary unit that is the focus of their spring seminar. Known to students as "the Big Kahuna," this project inspired a district requirement in Gorham, one of the PDSs, for all district teachers to create and implement such a unit each year. Both cooperating teachers and student teachers use the Gorham planning template and the Gorham outcomes (described in Chapter Three) to structure their unit development. This resonance contributes to a powerful learning situation in which student teachers, cooperating teachers, university faculty, and other teachers in the district can collaborate, speak a common language, and learn from each other as they consider how to achieve important learning goals for their students. It also creates a shared bank of materials that can be used, adapted, and further refined from year to year.

At Trinity University, prospective teachers take two courses on curriculum development in the summer between their fourth and fifth year of the program. The timing for taking these courses is deliberate, giving the prospective teachers an opportunity to study curriculum design immediately prior to beginning their teaching internship in schools.

In the curriculum course, students study the history and key issues and debates in the development of public school curriculum in the United States. They explore contemporary learning theory research, multiple intelligences, and issues surrounding performance-based assessment, and they design an educational program for students with varying learning styles. A research project, culminating in an oral presentation, is required of each student, as is development of an interdisciplinary curriculum unit.

A related course, Teaching Inquiry and Practice, is designed to give students more in-depth understanding of teaching models and styles. The elementary version of this course, for example, focuses on "describ[ing] the optimal methods of classroom organization which provide the support structure for learning; develop[ing] a reading program for students with a variety of learning styles, incorporating phonics, structural analysis, whole word teaching, and the whole language approach; describ[ing] optimal classroom grouping methods, both heterogeneous and homogeneous; and develop[ing] methods that regular education and special education teachers can use to work together to design the best programs for all students."

This work on lesson design, classroom grouping strategies, classroom management and student motivation, and strategies for working with special education students and teachers is applied to prospective teachers' own curriculum and program designs. In addition to designing an educational program for students with differing learning styles, candidates must develop an interdisciplinary curriculum unit and complete a research project on a curricular issue. In the full-year internship that follows, they have the opportunity to test their designs, reflect on their successes, and fine-tune their curriculum in response to student learning from day to day.

The end result of these experiences is a strong understanding of learning and teaching for understanding, exposure to an array of methods, and a sense of how to organize these methods into curriculum that adds up to powerful learning. Principals see Trinity graduates as quite able to integrate their strong knowledge of content with strategies for reaching learners. Said one: "Graduates have a knowledge of instructional practices and use a variety of teaching strategies that usually I find only with teachers who have four or five years of experience." And another: "MAT [master of arts in teaching] graduates have a good understanding about the scope and sequence of what is to be taught. This does not mean they are linear in their teaching. It does mean that they are more experienced and are better able to build connections in learning."

As at Trinity, the length and sequence of the five-year program helps UVA develop curricular thinking that interweaves the perspectives of student and content matter. The ability to take subject matter courses during the entire program, including advanced courses in the disciplinary major, while engaging in classroom teaching experience helps forge relationships between subject matter and teaching in the students' minds. The link between the B.A. English program and the MAT English education program illustrates how the connection works. As in all subject-specific majors, the English major for teachers-in-training was formulated jointly by faculty in the academic department and the Curry School. A secondary teacher of English must take at least thirty-two credits in upper-division English courses, including:

- An eight-credit history of English survey course
- Six credits in literature written before 1800
- One course each in Shakespeare, American literature (pre-1900), twentieth-century American literature, the novel, poetry, and history of the English language
- Three courses offered in the school of education: pedagogy of English language instruction, teaching composition, and literature for adolescents

Faculty from the English department in the College of Arts and Sciences and the Curry School coadvise students. The strongest bridge connecting the English department and the English education program is formed by the UVA Writers Workshop, which serves both as a teacher-training forum for English education students and a source of jobs and internships for English students in the Master's in Fine Arts program. Students and faculty in both programs gain an appreciation of one another, and English Department faculty come to respect Curry School faculty as they witness the enhanced pedagogical skills in their students.

In Margo Figgins's Teaching English course, offered during the spring of the fourth year, these experiences come together as students discuss multiple strategies, techniques, and approaches to teaching English so as to help them develop a curricular vision and a "defensible pedagogy." Among the course objectives are:

- To consider how your own school/learning experiences (a part of the context in which you teach) inform your educational beliefs and classroom practice

- To develop a more conscious use of varied instructional methods, beyond your own particular learning preferences

- To generate strategies for "reading" one's students and their worlds in order to create a classroom culture that validates both

- To design a series of sequential lesson plans that successfully join learning objectives, instructional procedures, and assessment and to demonstrate the use of feedback for purposes of revising instructional plans

In addition to using the study of autobiography to explore the notion that "curriculum is autobiography," the class requires students to revise a language unit they prepared in an earlier course and design another unit including daily plans for the first week of school (focused on community building and setting the stage for the unit to follow) plus three weeks of instruction to follow that week. The assignment notes that "if your plans for the first five days are effective, they will have produced for you a profile of the membership in each class detailed enough to inform your instructional choices as you begin to invent further instructional units geared specifically toward those students."

Candidates are asked to focus this unit on the most challenging material they expect to teach to a heterogeneous group of students "with a wide range of ability levels and varying degrees of resistance to being in school . . . [a group] that schools traditionally overlook through their privileging of the college-bound student" (EDIS 5460 course syllabus). The unit begins with the candidate's definition of literacy to guide all of the other goals, rationale, and specific plans. Candidates are told that "activities should involve students in a variety of language arts activities including language study, writing in a variety of discourse modes, drama, oral communication, small group work, and individualized study." Organizational designs should involve students in experiential learning, "placing students at the center of the action"; integrate the study of literature, writing, and language; extend the primary subject matter through other texts, such as film, visual art, newspapers, and student-created texts; and incorporate cooperative learning.

As students revise one unit in response to feedback and design, try out, and revise another, they also see and learn from each other's work, carrying into their first year of teaching a well-planned start to the year. In addition to these curriculum activities aimed for and piloted in the secondary school classroom, the course also engages candidates in writing and analyzing primary texts themselves, placing them in the role of teacher, student, and analyst to fine-tune their curriculum sensibilities further.

For example, in one evening session toward the end of the semester, a student led the class in analyzing a piece of political rhetoric, establishing a careful map of the semantic environment using an instructional technique called a "ladder of abstraction." The thirteen students in the class discussed the perspective of the writer, the audience, and the purpose of the statement. The quality of discourse was very high; the students were deeply engaged. Figgins's skill as a teacher was evident. She reminded the students that the purpose of analyzing this piece of political rhetoric was "so that you can think about how you'll approach similar tasks with your students." She emphasized the importance of audience (the learners) and drew out from the students ways in which a particular exercise could be undertaken with their own classes. Thus the course consciously exposed students to inquiry and reflection toward a goal of constructing curriculum that connects disciplinary goals with student experiences.

Much more than a didactic demonstration of pedagogical techniques is on display in English education classes at UVA. Both Figgins and her colleague Joe Strezpek, who was teaching the seminar that runs concurrently with student teaching in the fall of the fifth year, press students on their rationales, asking why they suggest and take certain approaches or interpretations. Indeed, in addition to modeling multiple techniques and matching these techniques with individual learner needs, much of the work in the secondary English and mathematics teacher education program at UVA is based on the assumption that it is important for the students to develop a roadmap and rationale for constructing the bigger curriculum picture for their students.

Maria Morelli, a UVA graduate and second-year teacher at Charlottesville High School, reflected on the impact these and other exercises had on her image of herself as a teacher and as a professional. She credited Figgins and the UVA program with helping her see herself for the first time as a writer *and* as a teacher who could construct analogous experiences for her students. Her exposure to many techniques for responding to student writing at the same time she was thinking about her own perspective helped her to think about how to connect the goals of the writing process to student experiences. In this way, teachers learn not only to bring their students to the subject matter but also to bring their subject matter to the students (Bruner, 1960/1977). When teachers are able skillfully to bring students to their subject matter, the results can be electric. When we visited the classrooms of University of Virginia graduates from the English and mathematics programs, we saw the sparks.

_____ o _____

Inside Fluvanna High School, nestled in the rolling green hills of rural Virginia, one room is buzzing with busy ninth graders working on strategies for finding the area of polygons without using a formula. Some students are counting square units inside rectangles that they have superimposed on the figures, while others are estimating the number of units inside the odd leftover pieces. The twenty students are working at tables in groups of four. Though the atmosphere seems relaxed, everyone is engaged—counting, drawing, writing, and reflecting. Amid this din, it takes a moment to locate the teacher.

After ample time to explore and count, the voice of "Bill Daly," the math teacher, is heard: "What is area anyway? What is a formula? What is the difference between perimeter, area, and volume?" The heterogeneous group of students, drawn from a school population that is 70 percent white and nearly 30 percent African American, look up. "Anyone care to conjecture about a formula for finding the area of a rectangle?" Daly waits with an air of expectation that suggests everyone must, of course, be thinking about these questions. Many respond.

Bill is in his fifth year of teaching after graduating from the BA/MT program at the University of Virginia. He is a man who clearly loves his job. In the span of ninety minutes, Bill displays a virtual clinic of instructional strategies, all seamlessly woven together: small-group work, whole-class discussion, models on the overhead, piles of manipulative materials, sample problems that he makes up on the spot to check student understanding, puzzling workbook problems, and adaptations of textbook exercises for skill development. The list goes on and on and seems dizzying to the observer. Yet curiously, the students do not seem confused; no one seems overwhelmed. Skillfully, all the activities are connected to what has been learned before and what is to come next.

Leaning over the shoulder of one student (which enables him to write so that everyone at the table can see), Bill says, "See, you could divide it up into seven little pieces. Or, you could think of one large rectangle and take out this little piece. Or, you could think of it as a square and three-quarters of another square. Or, you could try breaking it up into other shapes. . . . Or . . ." Eyes and minds are glued to the paper. With a deft hand and a soft word, Bill gets these students thinking about the relationship between parallelograms and rectangles. "What if" seems to begin nearly every sentence he says to the clumps of adolescent bodies, book bags, and backpacks.

Bill circulates unhurriedly among the groups, visiting in a friendly yet purposeful way at each table, inviting—indeed, imploring through his eyes and body language—the participation of all learners. Explaining his philosophy, he states, "Kids learn in a variety of ways, so I vary my instructional strategies. I want to see the students be active and engaged." His questions, his expressions, his tone of voice make engagement all but impossible. How does he know he is succeeding? How does he know the students are learning? "I look closely at their faces, their body language, as well as their work," he replies. "I also listen carefully to their conversations around the tables. When they are still talking about the problem after they're done, I know they are engaged and learning."

Near the end of class, he turns to the entire class and asks, with an expectant look, "Why do we care about area?" As the students shout out answers, he listens, grins, and probes the students' thinking more. "Yes, area is all around us," he says, "in buildings, calculating surfaces on a tin can, also pricing is often done by area." By asking the "big scheme" questions, exploring the reasons mathematics is the way it is, Bill is practicing what he learned and observed in his math methods courses at UVA. Such explorations, he hopes, will lead students to love mathematics the way he does.

In his teaching, Bill Daly shows he is a master at engaging his students in mathematics using multiple techniques and strategies. When asked how he can find so many ways to teach so many kinds of students, some of whom love mathematics and some of whom do not, he replies that he reads about and tries various approaches in order to understand them better. Each time he reads the NCTM standards (something he does each summer), he says he finds new ideas or approaches. Daly is also a frequent workshop participant and attends as many professional conferences as he can.

Daly credits the teacher education program at Curry with giving him skills that now enable him to develop new strategies for dealing with students who have distinctive learning needs. The secondary mathematics education program at UVA did not, he says, give him a set of recipes or a "bag of tricks." Rather, he credits Joe Garofalo and his field experiences with showing him "the big scheme of things." Through these experiences in the program, Bill "learned so much about my subject, ways to teach, where to go" that he now can expand his strategies by knowing "where to look."

Initially, Bill said, he was disappointed that he did not have a complete set of lesson plans to teach certain common mathematics topics. This is not an unusual reaction for a beginning teacher. But now, he says, "The longer I've been out, the more I appreciate what Curry and Joe Garofalo did. Things that were started there are coming to fruition. The Curry School planted a lot of seeds." Garofalo is in many ways a curriculum pioneer. In addition to designing and developing mathematics lessons that are made available on Virginia's Public Education Network (PEN), Garofalo also engages his students in graphing-calculator activities in his courses. Experiences of this kind showed Daly how to acquire new skills and how to grow as a professional.

Daly's appreciation for the program at the Curry School is shared by other graduates. Gretchen Merritt, teaching at William Monroe High School in Greene County, Virginia, is a five-year veteran teacher and a graduate of the UVA BA/MT secondary math education program. She comments: "Somebody who comes out of the Curry School is going to be able to walk into a classroom prepared for almost anything. They'll be knowledgeable in the subject area, knowledgeable in a variety of strategies of teaching methods, of classroom procedures and discipline."

Meanwhile, many miles away, "Selena Cozart" is sitting at a teacher's desk on the side of Room 223 in the west wing of Albemarle High. It is a school of eighteen hundred students who reside in Albemarle County, which surrounds Charlottesville, Virginia. Albemarle's student population is 80 percent white, 10 percent African American, and 10 percent "other," mainly Asian Americans and a few Hispanic students. The school is located just outside the city limits, but it is fair to characterize the students as coming from a mix of suburban and urban homes.

Selena, who is in her third year of teaching, is one of a relatively few African American teachers in this district. She is clearly comfortable in this place and in her work and well liked by her students. This is a college-preparatory class of approximately twenty-five students who are predominantly white, along with a few students of African American descent. Most of the students in this required English class are in the ninth grade. Selena is working with students who are making group presentations on novels they have read. Works include *Annie John, Far from the Bamboo Grove,* and *Somewhere in the Darkness.* Each group has read a different novel; their assignment is to share the central ideas with their classmates. In turn, classmates who are listening are asked to write a paragraph summarizing the plot of the unfamiliar novel. Selena listens to the presentations intently, careful not to interrupt or offer her own viewpoint. She communicates respect for student work through an expression of grace and caring on her face and the way she positions her body. The students have her full, undivided attention.

After the third group has made its presentation in a talk-show format, Johnson steps forward and her teaching style comes alive. Immediately, one feels Selena has a clear sense of purpose for her work with these youngsters as well as deep respect for each of them. Encouraging her charges to write their paragraphs, she manages several other tasks at once: collecting books, checking make-up work, and coaching students in their writing by quickly reading drafts and making focused comments. She undertakes these tasks with equanimity and good humor, matched with a firm expectation about getting the job done. This is a class in which students clearly are expected to learn about novels, their structure, content, and multiple meanings.

Students seem comfortable speaking up in class, and the mutual respect between teacher and students is evident. Selena insists that there be no interruptions when students are talking. Indeed, the environment has a feeling of safety, in which all opinions and comments are accorded equal respect.

At dismissal time, when several students get up to leave before she releases them, she gives a low laugh and holds her arms apart in a kind of benediction. They sit down without making a sound. She then makes another gesture that signals they can leave. This is all done without words, yet the class parameters and the mutual respect between learners and teacher are clear. Johnson explains that she has worked hard to create a "sense of community" in her classroom. She seems certain of her role and the structure within the classroom that will help her achieve her purpose. Permeating this culture and structure is a sense that this classroom is a warm, safe, and caring place.

Johnson's interactions with the students and their obvious respect for her reveal a practitioner who is learner-centered. She is in tune with her students and thinks carefully about the needs of each individual. She stresses the importance of classes with clear goals but also champions the importance of structured choices, so that students can control their learning. For example, though all must meet a common objective, she allows students to choose groups and partners (unless they show they cannot handle such an option responsibly) and she gives them options on paper topics, stressing that there are multiple ways to reach a stated goal. Selena worries about her "problem children . . . and . . . kids not motivated by grades." She talks about individuals and focuses on them as learners.

Johnson is also subject-centered and focused on her students' learning of literature and communication. Her personal passion for the material she teaches is palpable and infectious. She is enthralled by language. "I love language," she declares, indicating she hopes to help her students share her passion. She works hard to communicate her knowledge and love of literature so that her students will learn to appreciate and revisit it later in their lives.

Selena is a reflective teacher who practices the discipline of inquiry about her practice every day. While teaching students at Albemarle High School, she thinks about who she is, how she was taught, and how she wants and needs to teach these particular students and why. She questions her own practice, identifying and testing assumptions about students, methods, curriculum, and assessment: "I reflect on what I teach, how I teach . . . not just in a practical sense, but why we do what we do." She explains that she finds herself questioning the rationale of the canon, not for the sake of opposition but rather because she wants to understand it better. "Why is it," she asks, "that certain books have particular value?"

Selena is also quick to acknowledge that students need more than passion for a subject or genre. They need skills. She is unwavering in her commitment to help her students gain sufficient skills to write well and communicate clearly. Johnson is clear with her students about the need for these skills in the real world and seems certain of her purpose. She focuses on grammar, spelling, reading, and speaking, but not without reference to an overarching purpose—the purpose of literacy—and a hint of her love of language. Invoking a belief in the importance of basic skills and the responsibility of teachers to teach them, Selena states, "I do drill on grammar [but] we talk about what the purpose is of those drills." She also expects her students to spell correctly—spelling matters in the real world, she tells her students—and she teaches them how to correct and check their work using dictionaries, spell-checkers, and peer and adult tutors. Her teaching exhibits the influence of a clear and strong philosophical perspective combined with an array of instructional strategies to achieve her purpose.

8

EDUCATING FOR EQUITY

DURING THE SPRING OF 1996, the Oakland Unified School District experienced a teacher's strike that, perhaps least among its effects, interrupted the student teaching experiences of candidates from the University of California at Berkeley. Two student teachers assigned to a school in Oakland for their final field experience did not let the closing of schools stand in the way of their work with students. In the midst of the strike, "Jennifer Anderson" and "Samantha Miller" joined with Melrose neighborhood children to design an eight-by-twenty-foot mural depicting an illustrated map of Oakland surrounded on all sides by self-portraits of the children.

Meeting at a community center after school hours during the five-week strike, they constructed a paper prototype of the mural design. Children chose what to include; their mural map celebrates widely recognized Oakland spots, such as the zoo and the downtown, as well as lesser-known Melrose neighborhood landmarks such as the local burrito truck and, of course, the school. When schools reopened, the work continued at the school site. Fortified with donations of materials from local businesses, the 110 participating children completed their work. The mural map's rainbow of colors, illustrating the area from the Bay to the hills, brightens the formerly drab playground. At recess, students crowd around the wall pointing out their favorite spots and reveling in their own and others' self-portraits. After school and into the evening, the mural gathers a crowd of community spectators marveling at the talent of the neighborhood youth and discussing elements of their community and the school's place in it.

The mural stands as an example of the commitment of students and teachers to let nothing interfere with their education—a central commitment of Berkeley's DTE program as well as the other programs we studied. Such moral commitment, which professions hold at the core of their identity, is one key element of an equity pedagogy. The other essential ingredient is the set of knowledge and skills needed to engender learning for all students.

In earlier chapters, we looked closely at the work of Jean Jahr in New York City, Mary Gregg in Oakland, and Maria Rodriguez in San Antonio, who demonstrate that it is possible for new teachers to successfully teach diverse students from low-income communities. These teachers exhibit serious commitment to the individual and collective welfare of their students and also command a sophisticated battery of skills to meet their students' needs, grounded in knowledge of learning, development, cultural contexts, and effective teaching methods. These abilities are developed quite deliberately through the elements of each program's design that focus on enabling teachers to teach all students well. In this chapter, I describe how these programs organize themselves to enable their graduates to educate for equity and describe what these teachers are able to do as a result.

Learning to Teach for Social Justice

Explicit preparation for teaching diverse learners represents an important advance in the field of teacher education. For some time, research on teaching in urban schools has suggested that, as a result of some teachers' limited skills and the belief that their students are not capable of learning to a high level, many low-income and minority students receive a steady diet of low-level material coupled with unstimulating, rote-oriented teaching (Anyon, 1981; Cooper and Sherk, 1989; Darling-Hammond, 2001). Other research has suggested that many teachers hold particularly low expectations of African American and Latino students, treat them more harshly than other students, and discourage their achievement (Irvine, 1990b; Carter and Goodwin, 1994). Cultural differences between teachers and students also influence many teachers' decisions about the type of community in which they prefer to teach, with a majority of teacher education students avoiding urban schools where students' backgrounds are most divergent from their own (Zeichner, 1992; Ladson-Billings, 1999).

A number of teacher education programs have begun to address the dilemma of preparing a predominantly white and female teaching force to work effectively with increasingly diverse student populations in settings dissimilar from those in which the teachers lived and went to school (Ladson-Billings, 1999). These efforts include:

1. Carefully selected field placements in urban schools and other culturally diverse settings linked to consciously guided discussions and readings

2. An ecological view of human development that includes concrete tools for learning about students' lives and contexts and for turning that information into teaching knowledge

3. Integrated study of multicultural concerns and classroom strategies throughout the program, not isolated in a single course

4. Commitment to social action

5. Willingness to struggle with issues of race and class

Program efforts also, of course, include development of teaching strategies and skills that can be successful with a wide range of learners, because without such skills any belief that "all children can learn" soon devolves into little more than rhetoric. In what follows, I discuss each of these building blocks for what James Banks (2001) calls an "equity pedagogy."

Carefully Guided Field Placements

Several things seem to separate the efforts of programs that succeed at enabling their teachers to teach diverse learners effectively from those that result only in lip service to equity concerns. First, although many programs include field placements serving culturally diverse students and those with special learning needs, few explicitly manage what students learn from these experiences. As I noted in Chapter Six, these programs are extremely proactive in designing and managing clinical experiences to meet their goals. Here I discuss the specific elements that support learning to teach for equity in learning and for social justice, using as examples initiatives in Oakland, Milwaukee, Boston, San Antonio, and New York launched by the programs we studied.

Field placements offer prospective teachers an opportunity to challenge their apprenticeship of observation and obtain an informed experience of teaching students from diverse cultural backgrounds (Zeichner, 1992). But if student teachers do not witness high-quality teaching and success on the part of students of color, such placement may merely reaffirm beliefs that these students cannot learn or that the status quo cannot be changed. Novices may see practices and possibilities through the narrow lens of their prior personal experience and prejudices and draw stereotypic conclusions shaped by assumptions of which they are unaware. The same is true of placements serving students with particular learning needs, such as English language learners or special education students.

The success of field placements in developing knowledge for productive practice depends on the expertise of cooperating teachers or other professionals at the site, their capacity to explain what they are doing and why, and the extent to which novices' perceptions can be elicited, analyzed, and extended. Guidance and facilitation through coursework, readings, and supervision are needed to enable new teachers to build an informed understanding of their experiences, so that they do not revert to preconceived notions based on students' race, ethnicity, social class, or language (Ladson-Billings, 1999).

UC Berkeley

UC Berkeley's strategies for supporting this learning are similar to those in several other programs. The program deliberately merges school-based classroom studies with university coursework, field experiences, and construction of materials enabling students to enact their intentions. In the fourth semester of the two-year program, students are in classrooms two full days weekly for twelve weeks. In this last of five placements, the program clusters students in a small number of urban schools with a high density of students whose first language is not English. The fifth placement has several foci:

- A "school project" requirement (such as the Melrose Mural) as a process for a structured study of the school as an organization
- Work with individual children, especially English language learners, to align with the Teaching Linguistic and Cultural Minority Students course also taken in this semester
- Attention to the school's role within a community and the teacher's role within the school

Since we completed this study, this fifth field experience has further deepened the work with ELL pupils. Now, pairs of DTE students both assist regular classroom teachers with English language development in the classroom and design and operate after-school "English language development clubs" of their own for small groups of students. The after-school component—where there is no master teacher, and candidates are guided by a collaborative supervision model featuring peer observation and self-evaluation—gives candidates an opportunity to take on a more independent role in anticipation of having their own classroom the following year, while they are also coming to know ELL students more comprehensively in and outside traditional school classrooms.

The Teaching Linguistic and Cultural Minority Students course offers experience-based opportunities for students to construct practical answers to the questions they began asking more than a year previously in the Education in Inner Cities course—specifically, What can a teacher do about issues of race, class, and first and second language development in classrooms, schools, communities, and the educational "system"?

Meanwhile, students complete the fourth seminar in the human development sequence, which focuses on developmental analysis of reading and language arts curricula. The assignment demands that students outline and explicate a complete K–6 curriculum in reading and writing, including provision for students who are linguistically diverse and those who have special educational needs. Students produce a document describing and explaining the curriculum for an audience of teachers. The starting point for this assignment is the previous cohort's curriculum. Thus the product of this assignment actually becomes the initial text for the following year's class. This work is supported by state requirements that programs focus on teaching candidates to learn to teach "culturally and linguistically diverse" students—requirements that California put in place long before other states considered the issue of student diversity as a necessary context for developing teaching competence.

Alverno

In Wisconsin, the state leverages coursework and fieldwork experiences to engage issues of teaching for diversity by requiring all newly certified teachers to complete a minimum of fifty documented hours of direct involvement with adult and pupil members of a group whose background the student does not share, including at least one of a designated set of ethnic minority groups. In addition to the documented field experience, students are required to fulfill seven points in the human relations code by studying topics such as the psychological and social implications of the forces of discrimination, especially racism and sexism, and their broader impact on relationships among members of various groups in American society.

Alverno welcomes this emphasis and takes it further. In the student handbook, discussion of the concept of diversity reveals a proactive view of teaching for diversity: "The view of diversity your faculty wants you to develop goes beyond having background knowledge of cultures to developing a proactive stance, which includes looking at the role that culture plays in society and its institutions, such as schools. It means working actively to negate stereotypes and taking actions that move toward the full inclusion of all learners. You will do this by reviewing literature for bias, by examining your own teaching performance for actions that neglect one group or individual, and by planning for the infusion of diversity throughout the curriculum" (Alverno College Faculty, 1995, p. 27).

At least two of Alverno's four field experiences and one of the two nine-week student teaching placements are in the Milwaukee public schools. These experiences are carefully managed. All placements are made with teachers who have successfully completed a preparation course for cooperating teachers that is offered three times per year. In each field experience, students complete weekly reflective logs in which they are asked to make observations and draw relationships between what they see and do in the classroom and the various theoretical frameworks they learn about in other courses in the program. These preplanned and sequenced logs are submitted weekly to faculty for review and comment. Among the guiding questions used in the third log of the first field experience is, "How is cultural diversity recognized at this school?" The log continues: "Reflect upon your personal experience as well as your experience in ED116 [human relations workshop]. In your opinion, does this school appropriately meet the diverse cultural needs of this school population?" (Alverno College Faculty, 1992, p. 3.7)

This structuring of students' time in the field contrasts with the norm in many programs where students and their cooperating teachers are left to make decisions about the use of teacher education student time being based at most on a set of very general guidelines. One student commented about how Alverno's policy of requiring all students to complete several field experiences in the Milwaukee public schools helped her overcome the stereotypes she brought to the program about city schools and what could be learned in school by city students:

> *I grew up in a suburb and heard all these horror stories about what it would be like teaching for MPS—that there are all these terrible schools and the children aren't learning and that you have to take a crummy car and all these terrible things. And now I have been in a number of city schools and have not seen these things in any school. I've seen children learning. I've seen teachers actively engaged and a lot of really good things going on. And now I take that back to my friends and relatives and say "No, you're only*

pointing out one side of the picture. Did you know that this is hap-
pening and that is happening?" I am in a school now that teaches
toward reform and I would like to be part of that.

The reflective logs help students understand what they are seeing; they represent a particular developmental sequence in acquiring abilities over the four semesters of field experiences, and they intersect with coursework the students are taking, where multicultural and diversity concerns are addressed through pursuit of the professional education abilities. As a consequence of these efforts, Milwaukee principals noted their pleasure with the number of student teachers of color who worked at their school as part of their training at Alverno and with the general ability of all the Alverno students they worked with to "be involved with folks of differ-ent ethnic backgrounds or different cultures from themselves." One prin-cipal described how Alverno student teachers were more willing than students from other institutions to go out into the community with their cooperating teachers to make home visits and that they seemed to be bet-ter prepared than students from other institutions to interact with parents and to involve them in the school program.

Wheelock

At Wheelock, at least one of the two major practica takes place in a multi-cultural setting and at least one must include special needs children. As part of the Children and Environment course and associated field place-ment, students are challenged to look at their assumptions about race and class. Students check in with their instructor once a week and write re-sponse journals that allow the instructor to surface perceptions and ad-dress them through individual questions, discussion, and reading as well as through group conversations. In one assignment, students are asked to observe and analyze a child learning English as a second language and a child's growing awareness of race. For example, one journal assignment for the first semester asks: "Children are aware of racial differences at a very early age. Observe and record behavioral events which illustrate your focus child's (or any child's) awareness of race. Think about develop-mental theories and research about children's awareness of race (see Cole and Cole, 1993, Chapter 10, and other readings). Analyze each behav-ioral event record for what it shows you about the child's understanding of race. Also, analyze the ways in which your placement site responds to children's awareness of race, and develops in all children a respect for racial differences" (course syllabus).

In their journal entries, students are asked to relate their observations to developmental theories and research and then evaluate the appropriateness of classroom practices in relation to child development. For example: "Analyze the ways in which your placement site meets this child's needs and develops in all children respect for language differences . . ." (course syllabus).

A unique feature of Wheelock's field placements, particularly in the first year, is that prospective teachers are placed in nonschool settings: hospitals, community centers, after-school programs, and Big Sister programs. The director of field placements takes great care in selecting settings that address the student teacher's needs and stretch his or her experience base, challenge preconceptions, and expand understanding of children, families, and communities. For some, this may mean placement with children much older than those they have worked with before. For others, it may mean working in a community youth center; and for still others, it may mean a first experience in a multicultural environment. This early immersion in an unfamiliar and personally challenging setting with children had a powerful impact on many candidates cohort group. As one young woman put it: "There's more to teaching than I ever anticipated. I learned in Children and the Environment how all aspects affect a child's life. That raised a lot of issues I never thought about before."

One graduate, "Angela Johnson," noted that this field placement marked the first time she had been in a predominantly nonwhite environment: "In the beginning, I had fear about going into the neighborhood. Now I know and appreciate the strength of the community. I'm very proud of all of us. If you're going to work with children, you need to know their neighborhood. You can't be a teacher halfway."

Later, when Angela entered the classroom, she chose to teach in an urban elementary school. By the middle of her first year of teaching, Angela had created a kindergarten class that reflected her commitment to "create a culture that supports each student" and demonstrated her knowledge of her children as members of families and communities. Worktables were distributed throughout the room for small-group and individual projects. She designated learning areas for block building, listening to tapes, reading big books, writing, dress-up, arts, computers, and science and animals. There was a large carpeted area for morning meeting and large-group instruction. Along the top of the wall was a streamer with the letters of the alphabet. Posters were hung throughout the room with sayings such as "This room is your room" and "Treating children equally is not teaching each child the same; it is giving each child what he or she needs" and "Children have great expectations and so should we."

Angela began each day on the carpet with a calendar activity and guessing game. The children would sit quietly in a circle as she introduced the activities for the day. She often used student-created objects as the basis for discussion and would carefully balance students' selections with teacher direction for assignment to the learning areas. She called on children by saying something special about them. For example, she would say, "This person has a sister named Josie" or "This person has a brother in the school" or "This person just had a birthday."

Throughout the day, Angela maintained her enthusiasm about both the children and the subject matter she taught. She planned for large-group, small-group, and individual work. She demonstrated numbers by having the children count off quantities of food. She taught science by having children observe the classroom pets. She rarely seemed ruffled, kept a watchful eye on each student, and took time to interact with each child in the class individually. She made it a special point to acknowledge children's achievements ("I was so surprised that Teddy would make a book. He usually learns through play. I made sure to celebrate his book with him and his family. I didn't want to overlook his accomplishment.").

Angela frequently involved parents and community members as resources for her classroom. She had parents come in and read with children and share their special knowledge. One afternoon, she invited a parent who was a carpenter to show the children how he built a puppet theater for them. The children sat rapt as Molly's father measured and cut the wood, planned his next steps, and talked out loud about what he was doing. Angela was delighted with several outcomes of this experience: "This was important for the class and for Molly. The class got to see how math is used in everyday life on the job, and Molly got to see how important her dad is. She tends to be very shy, but she spoke out confidently about what he was doing. She saw that she can make a contribution and that she can be a leader."

Angela credited her preparation at Wheelock for giving her the knowledge and confidence to construct the kind of classroom she believed in: one she referred to as learner-centered, family-focused, and community-based.

Trinity

This kind of practice is also sought in Trinity's PDSs, all of them urban schools that serve a high proportion of students of color and linguistic minority students. The PDS settings create a rich set of possibilities for guided observation and practice over all five years of the program. First, the PDSs are sites where Trinity undergraduates and interns can see students of color being taught well and can talk to teachers about what they are doing and how it succeeds. (Evaluations of the PDS schools have found increases in student achievement as an outcome of PDS work. See Center for Educational Leadership, 1995; Schubnell, 1996; Van Zandt and Harlan, 1995.) In addition to their classroom work, Trinity interns also attend classes taught by mentors after school in their assigned PDS. Classes include topics such as the study of multiple intelligences, examination of models of teaching, multicultural education, and pedagogies associated with the specific efforts of the PDS (for example, a Basic School or Core Knowledge curriculum).

Furthermore, the elementary PDSs all work in partnership with the YMCA, which is a member of Trinity's Alliance for Better Schools. The YMCA provides sports activities, family weekend experiences, child care, and after-school tutoring, among other things. Each school's partnership takes its own form. At Hawthorne Elementary, for example, the YMCA and Trinity's education department coordinate the efforts of corporations, neighborhood businesses, human service agencies, religious organizations, and families in support of the school and its students. The YMCA has a full-time onsite coordinator for the program, whose elements include mentoring, outdoor education, youth fitness, and introduction to city and community resources such as the Children's Museum, airport, planetarium, theater, symphony, and circus.

The partnership aims to develop a program model in which the school serves as the focus of the community, responding to the community's needs and its expectations. It is an effort to meet many of the challenges children from low-income households often confront (gangs, drugs, violence, unemployment, and a high dropout rate) and to stop problems before they actually begin. Funding is provided by Chapter 1 of the Elementary and Secondary Education Act and the Drug Free Schools and Communities fund. Student teachers have the opportunity to participate in these programs and the community outreach they provide, as well as in PDS classrooms.

From these settings, interns develop an expectation that the role and responsibility of the teacher is broad and comprehensive. To be successful in their classrooms, Trinity-prepared teachers believe they must be active in the communities in which they work; they must engage with students' families; and they must remain active in their profession by continuing to read, write, research, and present. "The program," said one Trinity intern, "helped me to think of myself as a leader in a school and to think that being very active in the lives of my students was right and proper." Another explained, "We have a moral contract to be change agents."

As these experiences suggest, teacher education programs that connect schools and communities can improve prospective teachers' knowledge of their students and families within the community context. This may enable prospective teachers to view the community as a part of their students' lives and as a positive resource, rather than as a hindrance to their students' learning. It may also enable teachers to see their students whole, and to understand much more about the experiences students bring to school, so that they can be incorporated into the curriculum and inform teaching decisions. Awareness of student learning in varied contexts may enable teachers to view students as people with multiple strengths and competencies.

Connections to families and communities may also increase teachers' sense of their own efficacy. Beginning teachers' responses to surveys indicate that many locate student difficulties in achievement and learning as a consequence of their lives outside of school, which they see as beyond the purview of teachers (Darling-Hammond, Chung, and Frelow, 2002). To counter this dominant view, teacher education programs need to help prospective teachers develop their knowledge about students' lives outside of school and about the capacity of families and communities to support formal and informal education. As I noted in Chapter Three, the graduates of these programs were much more efficacious than most novices and were significantly less likely than a random sample of beginning teachers to believe that "most of a student's performance depends on the home environment, so teachers have little influence" or that "my students' peers have more influences on their motivation and performance than I do."

An Ecological Perspective on Child Development

Most of the programs take a sociocultural approach to child development that consciously looks beyond the traditional paradigm that views children as proceeding largely on their own through a sequence of stages in isolation from contextual factors that might influence their development. At Wheelock, for example, the syllabus for Children and Their Environments explains that the goal for the course is to provide students with "an overview of the environmental and developmental issues relevant to understanding children and their lives" using an ecological model of human development. The ecological perspective prepares prospective teachers to consider factors affecting a child's development that influence how she or he encounters and progresses through school. This expanded concept of human development allows teachers to broaden and make problematic their notions about social contexts and how these contexts interact with students' backgrounds, characteristics, and needs.

In this course, assignments and the thirty-hour practicum are designed to help students understand children and families from a multicultural, multisocial, and multiethnic perspective. For ten weeks, pairs of students spend three hours weekly in a field setting as participant observers; they must prepare weekly journal entries in response to instructor-chosen prompts. These prompts ask students, for example, to observe and write about the social and physical environment of their placement and the environment surrounding the placement, as well as writing about their interactions with children and families. Here is a typical assignment: "What have you learned about the life of the children in your placement? What family interaction do you see? If none, discuss why you don't see family interaction. What effects do either of these have on the children? What systems in the ecological model do these questions refer to and how do you know?" (course syllabus)

A parallel perspective at Trinity includes an ecological approach to The Child in Society, a sophomore-year class that "explores the factors that shape a child's growth and development in America," introducing students to a range of individuals whose professional lives are devoted to issues many Trinity students confront as they move from the sheltered university environment to the very real world of urban schools. The course explores issues of gangs, substance abuse, medically fragile students, gifted and talented students, limited-English-proficient learners, students with emotional and other learning disabilities, and cultural diversity. This course is followed by one in the junior year that focuses on child development in ways that highlight concerns of race, ethnicity, and gender, and by a senior-year practicum in which prospective teachers are required to view schooling from the standpoint of a student whom they study to understand his or her in-school and out-of-school experiences. Similarly, at the University of Southern Maine students conduct child case studies in two courses, Life Span Development and Exceptionality, the latter focusing on a special needs child.

The child study assignment (described more fully in Chapter Five) is shared across all seven programs. It accomplishes multiple purposes for candidates: development of close observation abilities, understanding of how to find and interpret evidence about learning, and a capacity to understand the perspectives of others, especially students whose experiences are quite different from their own, and to use this knowledge in developing effective pedagogy. Learning to reach out to students—including those who are difficult to know—requires boundary crossing, the ability to elicit knowledge of others and understand it when it is offered. As Lisa Delpit (1995) notes, "we all interpret behaviors, information, and situations through our own cultural lenses; these lenses operate involuntarily, below the level of conscious awareness, making it seem that our own view is simply 'the way it is'" (p. 151). Teachers must develop awareness of their perspectives and how they can be enlarged to avoid a "communicentric bias" (Gordon, 1990) that limits understanding of areas of study as well as of those who are taught.

Developing the ability to see beyond one's own perspective—to put oneself in the shoes of the learner and understand the meaning of that experience in terms of learning—is perhaps the most important role of teacher preparation. One of the great flaws of the "bright person myth" of teaching is that it presumes anyone can teach what he or she knows to anyone else. However, people who have never studied teaching or learning often have a difficult time understanding how to convey material that they themselves learned effortlessly and almost subconsciously. If others do not learn merely by being told, the intuitive teacher often becomes frustrated and powerless to proceed. This frequently leads to anger directed at the learner for not validating the unskilled teacher's efforts. Furthermore, individuals who have had no powerful teacher education intervention often maintain a single cognitive and cultural perspective that makes it difficult for them to understand the experiences, perceptions, and knowledge bases that influence learning among students who are different from themselves. The capacity to understand another is not innate. It is developed through study, reflection, guided experience, and inquiry.

This kind of understanding is critical to develop if teachers are to move beyond stereotyping and to acquire skills of inquiry for coming to understand future students. If knowledge about issues of cultural diversity is pursued as a kind of static content, it may encourage teachers to define their students by categories of race, language, ethnicity, and socioeconomic status rather than as individuals whose life experiences are influenced variously by these factors and many others. In an effort to enhance knowledge of cultural diversity, teacher education programs could inadvertently solidify negative or simplistic attitudes about particular cultural groups (Delpit, 1995). This danger is exacerbated if a deficit model poses the framework for understanding environmental influences on student learning, instead of an asset-based approach that encourages prospective teachers to appreciate and build on students' strengths and capabilities (Delpit, 1995; Ladson-Billings, 1999).

Balancing prospective teachers' content knowledge of cultural diversity with process knowledge about how to come to know their students well includes helping teachers learn methods they can use to develop relevant understanding of the diverse students they will teach once they enter the profession. As Ball and Cohen (1999, p. 10) explain: "Practice cannot be wholly equipped by some well-considered body of knowledge. Teaching occurs in particulars—particular students interacting with particular teachers over particular ideas in particular circumstances." Teachers need "pedagogical learner knowledge" (Grimmett and MacKinnon, 1992)—that is, knowledge of individual students and of students within a community—if they are to adapt their teaching to the real contexts in which learning must occur. The child case is one strategy that helps prepare teachers to develop knowledge of their students' diversity within the context of communities and neighborhoods.

An Integrated Approach to Multicultural Study

One significant benefit of the ecological approach is that theories and issues of multiculturalism are integrated into virtually all of the coursework. This counters the more common practice in teacher education programs of offering a single elective class on multiculturalism or diversity, which can sometimes marginalize the subject matter and reduce opportunities for application. As Ladson-Billings (1999) notes, the effectiveness of one course in changing the attitudes or teaching practices of prospective teachers toward diverse students is significantly limited.

At Alverno, skills associated with understanding and addressing children as individuals and as members of social groups are woven throughout the curriculum. They are infused in the professional education abilities and appear in the child case study and many other assignments. For example, here are some of the expectations for beginning teachers with regard to the ability of conceptualization:

o Developing sensitivity to learners as individuals within the group as a whole

o Making links between developmental theory and concrete individuals in order to use appropriate depth of subject matter

o Recognizing the impact of differences (in culture, gender, learning preferences, and so on) to plan instruction that meets the needs of individuals and the group

○ Planning material to meet learners' current needs and lead to the next level of development (for instance, preparing developmentally appropriate activities, relating subject matter to previous work) (Alverno College Faculty, 1994, p. 1.11)

The comments of the students we interviewed in two focus groups clearly confirmed the program's stated emphasis on a learner-centered approach sensitive to diversity and inclusion. Students noted that all of the courses and fieldwork in the program focused on getting to know students well and then modifying the classroom program to fit student needs and learning styles. This comment was typical: "At Alverno, they've taught us how to look at students, assess their needs and make the material fit with the students, rather than asking students [to] fit with the material."

Graduates felt they had the tools to get to know their pupils as whole people and then construct learning activities for their classrooms based on what they learned: "I feel very confident in my ability to look at children as a whole. I do a lot with kids outside of school so that I get the big picture. I spend every Saturday with a group of students. Just . . . watching them, what they do in their free time, tells me what kind of learners they are. I feel like I really know my students."

Similarly, the process of developing this kind of understanding starts early in the undergraduate years in UVA's five-year program. English education candidates are strongly advised to take at least one course in linguistics, women's studies, African American literature, or other literature from nondominant cultures, in addition to the required thirty-two credits in upper division English courses. This gives them a sense of how language is developed in context as well as a knowledge base about literatures from distinctive cultural experiences. Through field experiences combined with structured reflection, graduates have multiple opportunities to work with diverse learners in different settings.

Margo Figgins, who was the instructor for secondary English methods when we conducted our study, illustrated in her courses how to extend the process of thinking multiculturally and from multiple perspectives. She regularly injected consideration of matters of race and class into her instruction. She included these issues because she observed that most English teachers are educated in the "traditions of the dominant culture." She says, "They expect to be taught as they have been taught and to learn how to teach in the same way. And they can only imagine teaching students like themselves." Figgins understood that these new teachers will encounter many students who come from backgrounds and have experiences quite different from their own. They need to learn how to read their students so that they are able to instruct in ways that are meaningful to and respectful of all their students.

Evidence of Figgins's efforts to surface issues of race and class can be found in the books she asked her students to read, which explore issues of race, class, and multiculturalism from multiple perspectives. They include Freire and Macedo's *Literacy: Reading the Word and the World*; Kutz and Roskelly's *Unquiet Pedagogy: Transforming Practice in English Classrooms*; Deborah Stern's *Teaching English So It Matters*; and Mike Rose's *Living on the Boundary.*

One activity we observed Figgins using to surface candidates' own perspectives was development of a list of "What's worth knowing?" as a teacher of English. She encouraged students, as part of the assignment, to list what "you think you need and/or want to know at this point in your preparation in order to create a classroom in which both you and your students experience success." Students were asked to bring these lists to class to share. In their questions, students queried how to develop a diverse and vital community in their classrooms. Two students, for example, asked: "What is the best way of determining what is relevant to my students, especially if their backgrounds are different from mine or unfamiliar to me?" and "How can I make space for humanness in my classroom?" Another asked, "How can I be a 'subversive,' questioning, inquiry-focused teacher and still cover the required curriculum?" At the end of a discussion about community and the tension between accepting the "dominant discourse" and appreciating individual views, one student summarized the conversation's major theme in this way: "We can't survive as a community if we don't understand multiple viewpoints."

Figgins explicitly uses critical pedagogy as a model for preparing new teachers. She sees "teaching as a political and critical act . . . one that is not neutral," and she seeks, through the design of her class experiences, to develop teachers who are also critical pedagogues. One objective from her syllabus illustrates this perspective: "To become more aware of one's learning and teaching preferences in order to develop a more conscious use of varied instructional methods which result in students' cultural production (as opposed to reproduction)." By modeling instructional practices that allow prospective teachers to engage in authentic dialogue and interrogate the relationships among literature, language, and literacy, she encourages her students to determine for themselves what, why, and how they want to learn. They then carry these practices over into their own classrooms. Figgins also makes explicit the role that power plays in determining the extent to which teachers can act on their understanding. As a result, students are led to consider the politics of schooling and the implications of developing a "liberating pedagogy" in a contemporary education system.

English teacher Maria Morelli, who graduated two years earlier from UVA's program and went on to teach in an urban high school in Charlottesville (see Chapter Seven) credited the teacher education program with "training [me] to take a reflective stance." She, like other graduates, described her belief that education should work toward social change and voiced her appreciation for the fact that the Curry School helped make her more aware of the implications of race and class for education and the world. A former superintendent of the Charlottesville schools observed that UVA graduates "know who we have in our schools. They are particularly well-prepared to work with the urban child."

Commitment to Social Action

The view that education is a social force and that teachers are moral change agents is also evident throughout the programs we studied. Concerns for social justice and educational equity are found in foundations courses but also in those on methods of teaching and child development and the advisement process. As an instructor in Bank Street's Child Development course explained, "I look at issues of a period and their relevance to teaching and educational policy. Right now we can't think about adolescents and teaching them without considering AIDS, diversity, violence, extreme wealth, drugs, and poverty." This press to make courses relevant to the contemporary contexts of American and urban life is seen across the campuses, where issues of diversity, equity, multiculturalism, poverty, language differences, school funding, and reform are evident in assignments, reading, and discussions.

In all these programs, students are repeatedly asked to think about the consequences for students' individual and social development of teaching decisions, means of organizing the classroom, and choices of curriculum materials. Questions concern how these connect to children's family, community, and cultural roots, how teaching decisions support or undermine equity, and how they contribute to a participatory society in the classroom and beyond. Student teaching placements are typically well-developed sites for democratic practice in which antiracist and egalitarian norms are pursued.

In the Bank Street College course Family, Child, and Teacher Interaction in Diverse and Multicultural Settings, for example, we observed students conducting simulations of teacher-family conferences, preparing progress reports on children, researching and reporting to one another about stressful social conditions (poverty, homelessness, parental work stress, substance abuse, violence) and their effect on children and families, and learning about services available to children and families in the metropolitan area. A first-year teacher noted: "In the Family, Child, Teacher courses we talked about students who come from a different culture than the teacher or a different culture than the school. Since I'm working with a primarily Dominican population, which is different from my own culture, this is very important."

Candidates role-played teacher-family conferences so they could learn to create constructive rather than adversarial relationships on behalf of the students. Assignments were carefully constructed to enable students to gain information about specific problems and services as well as to develop skills in working with families and children with particular needs. An educational autobiography was the occasion for students to reflect on their own family's attitudes toward and involvement with school and to raise questions and issues they would like to work on throughout the term.

An analysis of the school setting engaged students in critical examination of the patterns of interaction at their own school site between differing families and parts of the school organization. The analysis focused especially on families in the minority in that school community and on students with special needs. Students created a yearlong plan for involving families in their work: initial introductions, home visits, curriculum meetings, parent-family conferences, individual reports, plans for general communication with families, and involvement of families in the classroom. The work done in this course extends teachers' ability to support students in their development and learning by understanding them in context and marshaling the resources of families and communities on their behalf.

Student experiences in courses such as Family, Child, and Teacher Interaction are extended in courses on the social context of education. Depending on their area of concentration, students must take one or two of the four courses that focus on social foundations: Foundations of Modern Education, Principles and Problems of Elementary and Early Childhood Education, Issues in Adolescence, and Anthropology in Education. Each course helps prospective teachers develop their own philosophical perspectives informed by knowledge of the events, theories, and practices that have shaped education in this country and by their personal and professional responsibilities to educate for democracy.

Harriett Cuffaro, a long-time faculty member and Dewey scholar (1995) who was teaching Principles and Problems in Elementary and

Early Childhood Education, described the aims of the course as those common to many in foundations: "To develop an awareness of the history of early childhood and elementary education in the United States; to deepen students' understanding of the social, political, and economic forces which influence their work and the lives of children; to deepen their understanding of the relations among educational theory, developmental theory, and educational practice in a variety of settings; to strengthen their competence in achieving an informed and critical approach to teaching." Rather than merely discussing which influences shape schools and education, however, students connect their readings directly to practice. Their own biographies and school experiences are augmented by visits to schools founded on particular philosophies; these school visits are the basis for research about educational policies and practices as well as presentations to their peers.

The course focuses on historical trends in views of education; equity issues, including racism, classism, and sexism; and multiculturalism defined broadly to include not only racial and ethnic cultures but also defining factors such as geographic locale, family norms and roles, and one's identification as a member of a teaching culture. Questions are always raised from a personal and philosophical perspective with a view toward influences on practice. So, for example, when students read George Counts's *Dare the Schools Build a New Social Order?* (1932) they work through questions of "What's the dare? What's the challenge? How do you feel about accepting it? And why do you feel that way?" Throughout, a set of recurring questions arise:

- Who determines the aims of education?
- Who defines and articulates the problems of education?
- Who is responsible for the "solution" of these problems?
- What principles may guide action?

These experiences encourage prospective teachers to reflect about the meaning of their work for their students and for society. The college culture also models engagement in the larger issues of democratic participation and children's welfare. In June 1996, one of the observations for this study took place aboard one of the three buses taking Bank Street faculty, families, and students to Washington, D.C., to the Stand for Children March. At the march, the group stayed together and individuals took turns carrying the Bank Street banner.

Like Bank Street, Wheelock faculty, administrators, trustees, and alumni were well represented at the march. Though neighboring colleges had responses ranging from disinterest to sporadic support, at Wheelock the Stand for Children campaign captured the attention of the entire campus. Banners and posters were displayed from windows in classroom and administration buildings and from dormitories. Seminars and symposia were held, and the college arranged for buses to transport students and faculty to the march, funded in part by alumni and trustees. The role of faculty in the campaign was central to its success at Wheelock.

These commitments are not transitory. As Wheelock's graduate catalogue states: "Emphasis is placed on a commitment to equity in a multiracial and multicultural society, in working partnership with families, enabling all children to participate fully in the learning environment, and collaboration with community agencies" (Wheelock College, 1995). A faculty member long committed to social causes describes the distinctiveness of the Wheelock faculty this way: "I was once considered odd. Now I'm part of a faculty committed to social idealism. We really believe that teaching can change the world—child by child. I am no longer the only person in a setting who is committed to developing a fully inclusive, multicultural, and just society."

This emphasis is reflected in virtually all courses. Required courses on teaching and learning emphasize frameworks for understanding children from a social and cultural perspective, just as the many courses explicitly focused on multiculturalism, inclusion, and communities do. In courses like Multicultural Children's Literature or Curriculum Design for Inclusive Elementary Education Programs, students learn about resources that can be used to reach learners of diverse cultural backgrounds and learning styles. These courses are complemented by the work students do in Multicultural Teaching and Learning Styles, where they are asked to deal with issues of identity and culture from an autobiographical perspective. For instance, graduate student Angela was asked to describe in a reflective essay what she considered to be major influences that shaped her own cultural identity.

Because of these continuous academic and field experiences, Angela and the students who entered Wheelock with her underwent some powerful changes by the end of their preparation. They discovered that a desire to work with children was a necessary, but not sufficient, condition for success: "I used to think that teachers only have to love children. Now I see a teacher as a moral and physical presence who knows children inside and outside of the classroom and values where they come from and what they know before they ever get to school."

Wheelock students learned that their own experience of school was not enough to power their careers as teachers. As one explained, "I always had successful school experiences as a student. I've always loved children. Now I know that much more goes into teaching." They learned that they had to understand and value the diversity of student backgrounds and the integrity of cultures other than their own: "This is not about political correctness. It's about being sensitive. It's about understanding children in a variety of ways. It's about being a teacher who can and should teach all children."

Willingness to Struggle with Issues of Race, Class, Gender, and Social Inequality

Learning to consider the experiences and perspectives of those who have been the victims of discrimination is not easy for members of a majority group who have not encountered similar trials. An important aspect of the effort to educate for equity is the necessary, always difficult struggle to help all members of the teaching and teacher education community confront and deal with the deep social and psychological influences of the -isms that affect society and schools and must inevitably affect teachers and students as well (Darling-Hammond, French, and Garcia-Lopez, 2002; Delpit, 1995; Nieto, 1999).

At Berkeley, DTE faculty consciously work with their students each year to engage these issues as they arise in the course of day-to-day practice, as well as in the planned and safer territory of courses. They have become aware that dealing with issues of race, ethnicity, and culture is not an option or an add-on, but a necessary part of the core: "It became clear ten years ago that we would have two foci: development, which we had always had, and culture. Multiculturalism had to come because the students are in the schools all the time. The program was initiated in theory, primarily Piaget; then multicultural-cultural issues arose from the constructivist, developmental practice we were asking of our students. The issue now is to integrate the two in a significant theoretical way."

The faculty are also increasingly convinced that this work cannot be limited to formal discussions of readings in classrooms. It must be experientially confronted in field placements and ongoing discussion of daily teaching and learning issues. Like all educators who allow race, class, language, and other cultural issues to surface authentically, this creates tensions that must be surfaced and worked through to enable participants to reach new levels of awareness, and ultimately greater comfort and competence in working with students different from themselves. A similar process is needed to support teachers' work toward social justice in their classrooms and their schools. In a supervisor's meeting, an African American woman supervisor commented on a lesson she observed: "The student needed help on being firm and direct and not being afraid of her actions being [viewed as] racist." The coordinator responded, "It is as if our students need somebody of color to authorize them, to give them their power of judgment. It bears a conversation, probably in supervisory group. [In the past], we almost ignored race, but now when we have vowed not to ignore it anymore, we're almost stepping back. . . . The [student teachers] sometimes seem to be scared of the kids, scared of their own racism, scared of cultural differences."

The timing of the supervisory meeting where these comments were exchanged added to their intensity. Immediately following the meeting, the total cohort met to try, phoenixlike, to raise a discussion of race and class issues from the ashes of the previous session's difficult attempt. Following her own inquiry on the earlier discussion, the coordinator e-mailed her thoughts and plans to the students.

> *Two weeks ago in 390 we tried, with little success, to discuss* Life on the Color Line *[by Gregory Williams]. Everyone left the room with a great deal of frustration and with many questions about what went wrong. It was a dramatic illustration of how overpoweringly difficult it is, even for articulate, well-intentioned people, to discuss race in a group setting.*
>
> *There are two issues here which we must address: (1) the content of the discussion; (2) the format of the discussion. Both are important.*
>
> *The first will be the focus of 390 this Tuesday. It is my impression that we have all given a lot of thought to the experience and that many substantive personal conversations have resulted. We would like to build on these to meaningfully address the very relevant pedagogical issues raised by Williams.*
>
> *At the beginning of class you will have a few minutes to note (in writing) a critical incident from the book which most affected you and to think of an event (or a silence) in your own background which you have thought about since reading the book. We will then have discussions in pairs, followed by foursomes. Supervisors and I will all participate.*
>
> *The second issue will be addressed by repeating the topic in a different format. You may use journals and/or your supervisory groups for more detailed comparison of the two sessions. . . .*
>
> *I look forward to working together with you to keep developing our collective potential. Till Tuesday.*

In the second attempt at discussing "race in a group setting," the program coordinator led students through the process she had outlined in advance to help students relate their reading of *Life on the Color Line* to their own lives and to their chosen career. The weather outside was hot. The room, windowless, was small and close. Quickly, heat and intensity brought sweat. Following individual, small-group, and whole-group processing, several students wondered, with more than a trace of annoyance, why not everyone was participating. The group labored in response and the result seemed less a coherent conversation at times than a series of individuals speaking across each other from deep out of their own experiences with the issues of race.

COORDINATOR: I don't agree with the notion that it is too early to raise these issues—that we have not bonded yet. It is always going to be hard. We cannot blame folks for their assumptions. We have to get them out. Many of us have grown up thinking the police are benevolent or at least benign. But many of us grew up knowing that was false in our experience.

STUDENT 1 (TO HER PEERS): Did you not read the same book? We are trying to be deep and multicultural and we can't even have a discussion. You guys have a choice to discuss. People of color don't have a choice. We live with it twenty-four hours a day.

STUDENT 2: It made me feel pity, anger, and guilt. The whole thing made me feel guilty and wonder if I can ever work with children of color? How do I find them? Where are they? How do I take them with me? It is scary, sad, and depressing.

STUDENT 1: When we feel discriminated against, how do we respond? When and why are we capable of responding? We have to take a look at our surroundings every time we enter a room. Think about how the kids feel.

STUDENT 3: I feel like I cannot function in this society with the values I have. So, what do we tell our students? The world ain't safe for them and it ain't gonna change in my lifetime?

STUDENT 4: Should we teach as we wish the world was or as the world is? It is every African American parent's dilemma. What's the ultimate goal? What are we preparing kids for?

COORDINATOR: Truth—and you will be chipping away at it all your life.

STUDENT 1: Try not to intellectualize so much. Let it hit you in the heart, not in the head. Forget the theory for a while. Genuineness will always come across. Have a heart for the kids. Feel the pain.

This emotional session ended with the sharing of tears and hugs as participants reaffirmed their commitment to one another and to the struggle for a better world. Although this discussion did not resolve racism or instantly create new pedagogies for the teachers, its intensity and candor marked a significant moment in the evolving understandings of all the participants. This kind of racially heterogeneous conversation begins the process of helping students to talk with, rather than talk across, each other about deeply felt issues of race. Though difficult and almost always initially uncomfortable, such conversations are needed to move people beyond a natural response of feeling comfortable with their in-group and fearing their out-groups. If teachers are to be responsive to all the students they will ultimately teach, teacher educators must structure opportunities for prospective teachers to feel safe enough to open up the conversations that can eventually lead to authentic practice.

At Bank Street, foundations courses are a prime site for raising questions that students must struggle with. There is willingness to confront uncomfortable social issues, even if answers are not readily available. Cuffaro illustrated this with an example from a recent class discussion of issues of inclusion and multiculturalism:

> Last week one of the things we were talking about was heterosexism. I raised the question, "In early childhood a lot of people are dealing with family; since we are talking about inclusion, what do you do about gay and lesbian-headed families?" We talked about the fact that it is a difficult topic, more than any other topic we had discussed. There is a strong religious foundation for the critics, and I made the statement that this was one of the -isms, in contrast to sexism and racism, that doesn't necessarily have an economic base, other than people getting fired in some situations. As I said to the students in the class, "We raise more questions than we have answers for, but the questions are important. I don't have the answers for a lot of questions, but to me it is imperative to ask the questions."
>
> Students frequently cite these courses as having helped them develop a broad understanding of schooling and shape a personal philosophy that really informs their work. As one student observed:
>
> I took a foundations course that really taught me about being a critical thinker. That had not been part of my educational experience before. I was very traditional. Even college was about, "Let me figure out what this or that teacher wants and what I will need

to give back to them at exam time to get a good grade." I was
good at that. So this whole thing about having strong opinions,
about reflecting in a deeper way about the philosophical questions,
about what I want to teach and why and how will it be meaning-
ful for me, is new, and I learned it through Social Foundations.

Although foundations courses are not generally thought of as practical, many Bank Street teachers found these classes directly influenced their practice and helped them succeed in New York City schools. "Lara Grant," a beginning public school teacher, explained: "The Foundations class was very helpful to me for the kind of children that I'm encountering in this school. There are a lot of children in this school from homeless shelters who have a lot of emotional and behavioral needs. In this class, we studied a lot about children from these types of environments and the effect that it has on them, the types of education they respond best to, what they need, and what helps them. And the class helped me to come to a whole new understanding of how to deal with them."

In this program and others, willingness to ask difficult questions created a stance toward inquiry and a commitment to struggle for answers. Once readiness was fostered, the programs did not assume candidates' strong beliefs would be enough to help them find their way to effective practice. They understood the need to integrate an understanding of these complex issues with a strong set of skills for reaching students and teaching them well.

Skills for Teaching Diverse Learners Well

We saw the results of having acquired the skills needed to teach diverse learners well when we visited Lara in her kindergarten and first-grade classroom in one of the most economically disadvantaged parts of New York City. Lara's twenty-six children were involved in mathematical problem solving using multistep word problems often considered suitable for much older children. They were also engaged in reading children's literature (some were reading and others were being read to) and studies about the authors of their favorite books. Lara's ability to construct this environment was, she believed, a function of her understanding of the children; her commitment to an equitable, high-quality education for them; and the knowledge of curriculum she acquired at Bank Street College. She commented, for example:

I do a lot of word problems with them in math—the kind of stuff
I learned in [my Bank Street] *math class—using math manipula-*

tives and problem solving. I see the kids can do it, so I know it's developmentally appropriate. . . . I think a lot of people underestimate what five- and six-year-olds can do. I think that a lot of people have buried in their mind that when a child is in kindergarten they're just learning "in, under, on, in front of, behind," numbers 1 to 10, letters A to Z. I've had a lot of parents who have switched their kids in from other schools who have said to me, "He wasn't doing this in his last class. . . . You're doing addition with kindergartners? I can't believe that." But they really get it, and with the word problems it's amazing to see the strategies they come up with to solve problems. They're really learning to use the math materials to solve the problems and to show their thinking. Now I'm trying to get them to understand why and how they know it, so that they can start examining themselves as problem solvers.

Lara's enthusiasm and commitment to democratic practice on behalf of students who suffered many of the most severe injustices life has to offer were clearly made effective because they were supported by her well-developed knowledge and skill.

Bank Street students, like those from other programs, invariably noted that this kind of teaching is complex work requiring intensive preparation and ongoing professional development. Although many have had other successful professional careers—in fact, most of the college's preservice teachers enter from other careers (Crow, Levine, and Nager, 1990)—few considered entering teaching on an emergency license, even though this is a common practice in New York and many other cities. "Michelle," an African American teacher now leading a state-funded program for at-risk students, described how when she switched from a career in journalism, she was amazed to find out that she could have entered teaching without any background or training. Instead, she decided to make the financial sacrifice to attend Bank Street to give herself the best preparation she could find. She described poignantly the inadvertent disservice to children she had since witnessed at the hands of unprepared teachers who had committed to teach for two years in the city after a brief summer training:

After I graduated from Bank Street, I taught a special education group at a high school in Harlem. That was fun. However, I was also asked to coteach a social studies class with two new teachers. It was a madhouse for many reasons. One, because these were two teachers who not only were new and not only were they

*white—which didn't have to be an issue but it was because of the
way they responded to the kids—[but also they] were untrained. It
was sad for them because they were trying, but I don't know how
much they really truly were committed. It was like they maybe
wanted to come to Harlem and do this thing, but really . . . what
came out was . . . when they got angry they would say things they
shouldn't have. And you saw that they were not only antichild but
anti the whole community, because it was such a different community. And it was unfortunate. In retrospect, it really wasn't fair
to them; they truly needed support. And as time progressed, I realized what was really going on in the school, and it was really sad
to me that Harlem and the school and the kids were actually being
made to suffer from this.*

This example illustrates one of the frequently unacknowledged harms
from lack of adequate preparation: in addition to, and perhaps as a function of, their own insufficient teaching skills, those who have had little
preparation often become antagonistic to their charges, as the teachers
blame the children and their families for their own lack of success. In contrast, the programs we studied produce poised and confident teachers who
perceive themselves and are perceived by others as successful and innovative teachers, and who produce high levels of student success.

The difference in what children experienced in the Harlem school just
described and this Milwaukee school is stark, as another vignette shows.

At 8:30 A.M., following a half-hour informal period where students
read some of the numerous trade books that are scattered throughout the
room and a spirited group recitation of the school creed, which emphasizes pride in self and school and academic success, "Berthina Johnson"
gathered her twenty-six first graders on the floor in front of the calendar.
Adams School is located in one of the poorest neighborhoods of Milwaukee. About 93 percent of the 746 pupils in the school qualify for the
free breakfast and lunch program, and the school has a mobility rate of
34 percent, which means that this many students do not spend the whole
academic year at Adams. All twenty-six of Berthina's pupils (thirteen girls,
thirteen boys) were African American, like their teacher and nearly all of
the school's students, and for several of the six- and seven-year-old pupils
first grade at Adams was their first formal school experience.

Berthina, now in her early thirties, had graduated from Alverno College four years earlier with a degree in elementary education, after a brief
career in the insurance industry. She was beginning her fifth year of teaching first grade at Adams. The walls of her bright and cheery classroom

were covered with colorful materials related to the alphabet, numbers, colors, shapes, days of the week, and basic vocabulary words. Almost every inch of space on the walls was used to review and reinforce concepts and words found in the students' everyday world. The desks were set up in two large groups facing each other in a way that encouraged social interaction. Several learning centers were scattered throughout the classroom.

One of Berthina's major goals for her first graders this year was to encourage them to become more independent and responsible for their actions over the course of the year. Throughout the morning, she constantly reminded her pupils that they were first graders and not kindergartners, so they must do things such as speak in complete sentences and take responsibility for their own behavior. Throughout the morning, she repeatedly posed questions to the class as a reminder of things discussed beforehand and invited a choral response from the class. To the question, "How can we become good readers?" the class answered in unison, "By reading good books!" These choral response strategies resonate with the familiar call-and-response rituals many of the students are familiar with from church and other family and community settings. Throughout the morning, the pupils were focused intently on the activity at hand, and the class buzzed with talk about the things they were working on in their group activities and during an interlude of choice time at the several learning centers.

This Wednesday morning, Berthina used the calendar time block in her schedule, a period of about one-half hour, to review and reinforce with her pupils basic ideas such as the date, the meaning of "yesterday," "today," "tomorrow," and "weekend," and basic math concepts such as place value and counting forward and backward. The pace was very quick and the expectations were high for student success. Berthina posed one question after another and asked for a response either from an individual child or the whole group. If a child or the group did not answer a question correctly ("How many 1's are in the number 15?" "What is tomorrow's date?"), she kept encouraging the children until they were able to figure it out.

The class moved almost immediately after finishing the calendar lesson to an activity involving the short *a* sound. The pupils cut out and colored a cap with the letters *ap* marked on it and slipped in sheets of paper with consonants and consonant blends and read the words together as a class and in pairs. Berthina encouraged the children to take their materials home that night and read the words to someone else. The rest of the morning, before a break for lunch at 11:30, was spent working on penmanship skills and on math problems involving place value and simple addition. For the addition problem, the pupils were asked to draw a picture to show how they solved the problem. Two pupils were then asked to draw their pictures on the board and explain to the rest of the class what they had done. They solved the problem using differing strategies, something that drew favorable comments from Berthina. During the half hour when students were free to choose to work at any of the various learning centers in the room, several students sat at computers working on math games and reading skills; others read, drew, or listened to tapes while following along in a trade book.

Throughout all of the academic tasks, Berthina was attentive to individual children and their needs and was quickly on top of potentially disruptive situations before they got out of hand. Two boys complained of feeling ill and required individual consultations about whether they wanted to stay in school or go home (both decided to stay), and a girl complained about her eye hurting. Another young boy, who was crying because he could not find his pencil, also required a few minutes of hugging and support. Several parents come into the room during the morning and spoke with Berthina about various matters. Each time she warmly welcomed them into the room and spent a few minutes talking with them. In her responses to her pupils throughout the morning, she revealed knowledge of all of the special circumstances involved with contacting the children's homes. In one case she planned to contact an older brother to pick up an ill child. In others Berthina referred to a child's grandmother, uncle, mother, or father. She seemed to know, in each case, who would need to be contacted.

Berthina had carried what she learned at Alverno into this urban first-grade classroom, adapting it to address the needs of her students and the circumstances of her work. She was comfortable integrating skills work into a rich curriculum that yielded meaningful, thought-provoking work. Her room was filled with trade books that the children read daily and learning centers that posed a variety of activities for students to pursue in several subject areas. She also took time regularly to teach particular phonics skills she knew would be helpful to her children's development of reading competence. Although she made time to teach specific skills and concepts, she always attempted to have the children use them in relation to events and circumstances in their everyday lives. For example, instead of just having the children fill out worksheets about the days of the week and basic number facts, she kept asking them to talk about these things in relation to what they had done or would be doing as a class and as individuals.

Delpit (1995) argues that those teachers who are most skillful at educating black and poor children do not allow themselves to be placed in the "skills" or "process" boxes many educators fight about, but understand the need for both approaches. We saw this with all the Alverno graduates we visited in the Milwaukee public schools. Consistent with the focus of her preparation at Alverno, Berthina focused first and foremost on what she perceived to be in the best interests of her pupils. Her classroom transcended the simplistic "process" and "skill" categories and incorporated elements of both approaches within the context of warm and caring relationships between the teacher and each of her students. Along with the warmth and affection evident between Berthina and her students, there was also a clear effort on her part to push her students to do their best work and to achieve at a high level. For example, a number of the students responded to her questions with phrases instead of complete sentences. Berthina was then persistent, pushing in a friendly and supportive way for a response in a complete sentence and would stick with it until the student did so.

Also consistent with the focus of the Alverno program on preparing teachers who will be leaders in educational reform, Berthina was a member of the school district's assessment team and was involved in piloting the use of portfolios to assess the work of her pupils. Finally, like many of the other graduates from the Alverno teacher education program, she remained involved with the program after her graduation by mentoring field students and by talking about her teaching to Alverno students on campus. Her experience reflected the widely held view among principals and teachers in Milwaukee public schools that Alverno graduates have been influential change agents in urban schools. As one observed: "If you were to go into the Milwaukee public schools, almost anything that you saw that excited you probably was started by an Alverno grad."

Comments of this kind about the graduates of all seven programs suggest that they have succeeded to a substantial extent in their quest to prepare their graduates to teach for social justice.

9

PREPARING TEACHERS
TO REACH ALL STUDENTS

AT FIRST GLANCE AROUND THE FOURTH AND FIFTH GRADE CLASS-
ROOM, the scene seems commonplace: students are seated at individual
desks with detached chairs; the room is lined with instructional materials; and a teacher, Jane Kopp, a graduate of the University of Southern
Maine's Extended Teacher Education Program, is standing by her desk
holding an open book. A student named Beth is at the front of the room,
quietly talking about a book and occasionally referring to a diorama she
has made to illustrate it. The other twenty-five or so students are attentive and quiet. Seated at a table at the back of the room, we strain to hear
what Beth is saying.

When she concludes her report, our first impression of "typical" begins
to change. Without prompting, several students immediately raise their
hands. Beth calls on Jeff, seated at the back of the room. Smiling, he asks,
"On a scale of one to ten, how would you rate this book?" Beth quickly
replies, "Ten." Jeff immediately comes back, "Why?" A few students
groan. (We later learn that the "one-to-ten-and-why" is Jeff's stock question during their monthly "book talks.") Another student asks Beth to
give more detail about the plot, and she does. Referring to a half-size sheet
of paper that includes a rubric for evaluating such presentations, another
suggests that more eye contact with the audience would help. This is when
we notice that, in addition to asking questions, the children are also scoring the presentations using criteria printed on the half sheet of paper. Still
another student comments that Beth was not loud enough to be heard at
the back of the room. As she listens to these comments from her classmates, Beth seems at ease and unembarrassed.

A second adult, seated in a student-sized chair across the room, gently
asks her what she specifically liked about the book. This is Peter Black-

stone, a special education teacher whose five students are part of this class of twenty-five. Later, we learn that Beth is one of them. Blackstone praises her for her diorama. Several students quickly point out that the visual is really a "triorama," not a diorama. At this point, Jane cautions the students about talking out of turn. Beth's presentation ends with the students applauding.

A third adult, who has been seated at a child's desk across the room, stands and reminds the students to be sure to turn in their rubrics. This is Tom Taylor, an intern from the ETEP program, who will work with these teachers and students all day, everyday, until the December holiday break. Tom collects the scoring guides as students hold them in raised hands.

The children and teachers then move into predetermined groups for an hour of mathematics instruction. Peter Blackstone stays in the classroom with about half of the children to work on one topic. Jane Kopp and Tom Taylor work with two separate groups of children on different content in a vacant room across the hall. In these small groups, the teachers use interactive strategies that encourage each child to participate. Jane is seated at a table with eight children conducting a question-and-answer discussion about fractions, using a textbook. The conversation is lively, and the children seem enthusiastic about the content, firing back responses and asking additional questions, which Kopp sometimes responds to and sometimes turns back to the group, asking them to respond.

Taylor is working at another table with three boys, also on fractions. These three, he later explains, are working at a different level of knowledge of fractions from the other students in the class. He has developed an activity where two of the students compete with each other while the third keeps score. These roles rotate during the hour. The intern has created a set of cards, each displaying two fractions, such as 9/16 and 3/5. As he holds up a card, the students competing must say which fraction is larger. The third student decides who is correct, and that student keeps the card. After going through twenty or so cards in this manner, the one with the most cards "wins" and competes with the student who kept score in the previous round.

Perhaps two or three times in each round, all three students are stumped and need to do some calculations to figure out the answer. In these situations, Tom patiently queries the students about their approaches to finding the answer, having each one demonstrate his strategy, and poses questions that elicit from them alternative ways of determining the correct answer. Among the strategies the students offer are "estimation" and "converting the fractions to common denominators." With Tom's prompting, they compare the strategies, describing how estimation gives them clues to the correct answer faster while finding common denominators demonstrates the correct answer but can take more time. It is clear that Tom has already learned a great deal about individualizing instruction to meet the needs of unique learners in the few weeks he has been in this student teaching placement.

Teaching Diverse Learners to High Standards: A Comprehensive Approach

In this brief morning we observe a number of elements of classrooms and teaching strategies that research finds important in reaching a range of learners. One feature is an emphasis on student performance assessment that is evaluated by scoring rubrics (in this case, in writing and oral presentation) used across classrooms over many years. This approach demystifies the notion of competency and makes it accessible to all students by giving them many opportunities to develop products, get feedback, internalize the standards, and steadily revise their work to become increasingly proficient. This is particularly important for special needs learners, who benefit from explicitness and multiple opportunities to practice in a nonthreatening environment.

Second, the ongoing formative assessment around these common standards—as well as the Gorham outcomes or "habits of mind," as some refer to them—emphasize growth and mastery through collaboration rather than competition, anticipating that students can take multiple pathways to attain common expectations. The Gorham outcomes state that students are expected to be self-directed learners, collaborative workers, complex thinkers, quality producers, and community contributors. Other classroom materials emphasize the importance of recognizing learners' multiple intelligences (Gardner, 1983). Teachers are diagnostic in pinpointing students' strengths on which they can build, as well as their needs, so that they can individualize effectively and help all students engage in challenging work without watering down the curriculum.

On each student's desk is taped a set of goals toward which the student has agreed to work during the school year. These goals, set during parent-teacher-student conferences held at the beginning of the year and often led by students, are structured around the five Gorham outcomes enumerated in the preceding paragraph. Teachers' work with parents, through regular conferences, family involvement in the classroom, and parents' participation in evaluating exhibitions, creates reinforcement for the work students are doing in the classroom. Throughout the year, in their individual portfolios students accumulate evidence bearing on the goals along with other examples of their work. This strategy allows all students to experience growth toward individually appropriate goals as well as common expectations. The portfolio process encourages a clear focus on standards and goals, revision and development of higher-quality work, and motivation born of a sense of developing competence. This approach is much more supportive of progress for students who may struggle to learn than is a one-shot, all-or-nothing test that ends instruction with a grade on a discrete event—often indicating what it is students have done wrong without giving them an opportunity to try again and learn how to do it right.

A third feature of this classroom is its inclusiveness and continuity. The multigrade, multiage, and multiability group of fourth and fifth graders, which includes regular program and special needs children, "loops" with the same teachers for two years, giving them time to get to know each child (and their family members and situations) well. Kopp described the importance of a safe, secure, and encouraging environment, especially for such an inclusive class: "A student [needs to] feel safe to try new things, to venture into unknown subjects, and to hazard answers." She stresses that to teach children how to learn and pursue their ideas "requires a cooperative venture among the classroom, the entire school community, and the larger community."

Finally, there is sophisticated teaching that includes regular diagnosis of learning needs, along with individualization and adaptation of the curriculum to meet student needs. At times, every child in this classroom is expected to do the same work. For example, about once a month each child does a book talk similar to the ones we observed. At other times, the children are grouped and regrouped for instruction and assignments responding to their needs, as with the mathematics lessons we observed. Also important is the explicit teaching of and coaching in reasoning strategies for learning and studying, as when Tom worked with students on their strategies for adding fractions—to deepen their understanding rather than resorting to rote learning, which leaves special needs students further behind as they cannot make sense of what they are learning or transfer it to new problems.

Later we learn that, as part of its training, ETEP seeks out such classrooms for its interns, so they have an experience of working with special needs children with skilled mentors available, both regular educators and special educators. Many of these, like Jane Kopp, are ETEP graduates. As a result of this training, ETEP teachers are not just comfortable with but eager to work in inclusive classroom settings with students who create more diversity and with colleagues who support this work. This stands in contrast to many teachers' experiences elsewhere, who feel dramatically underprepared to work with special needs students and seek to avoid such students, or find themselves pushing the students out of class through disciplinary referrals or transfers to remedial programs.

USM builds the capacity of its partner districts to offer good education to special needs students (and to become sites where classrooms that serve as good models for training are more widely available) by supporting the learning of veteran teachers and administrators. This occurs through widespread professional development offered by way of the Southern Maine Partnership and through coursework in ETEP that interns bring into the classrooms in which they student-teach, creating access to greater knowledge for the teachers with whom they work.

As part of their work at USM, all interns complete a case study of a special needs child for a course titled Life Span Development and Exceptionality. The focus for the course is on children with learning disabilities, behavior and emotional disorders, and mental retardation. Topics include "collaborative teaming, screening, referral, modification of curriculum, adaptive technologies, individual educational plans, behavior management techniques, and state and federal legislation regarding exceptional children" (EXE 540 Exceptionality syllabus, p. 1). At the end of the semester, all of the students present their case studies in an exhibition. This gives them all access to grounded understanding of the learning needs manifested by a range of children with disabilities, as well as the one they have deeply studied themselves.

They are also asked to reflect on their readings in their response or dialogue journal, which is used across all the various program components. This is a means for them to connect what they are studying to their experiences in their placements, where inclusion of special needs children with "push in" support from special educators gives the interns firsthand experience with quite diverse needs. In addition to the case study, interns participate in microteaching, disability awareness activities, skits and simulations, and debate on topics such as inclusion.

Because of his case study assignment in the fall semester, we learned that Tom Taylor felt he had developed heightened awareness of special needs students and of multiple intelligences. This awareness was reflected in his comments about the activities he planned and carried out. It also helped him develop special empathy for the special needs students he taught. At one point in his portfolio exhibition at the end of the ETEP year, he recounted a story of a special needs student who was reluctant to talk in class but was drawn out when, at his suggestion, her deskmate read her comments to the class. As Tom remarked, "Her smile lit up the whole room. It made her day. And it made mine."

Whereas many beginning teachers are stymied and frustrated by the exceptional needs children they encounter and find they do not know how to teach, Tom and his colleagues have developed keen diagnostic insights that help them see what is needed, and a repertoire of teaching strategies allowing them to create opportunities for students who learn differently.

Learning to Teach so That All Students Can Learn

As schools educate more students who were earlier excluded from school altogether or segregated in "special" classes, teachers increasingly need knowledge about learning differences that is typically reserved to a very few. In 1999, for example, 13 percent of students participated in special education, and half of them spent 80 percent or more of their time in general education settings, a sharp increase from only a decade earlier (NCES, 2002). As more and more of these students are included in regular education classrooms, expected to meet the same standards as other students, teachers need a much more diagnostic approach to assessing learners' needs and a much wider repertoire of teaching strategies to address them. In addition to students with identified learning disabilities or handicapping conditions, there is a full continuum of perceptual and expressive abilities that create distinctive learning profiles for all students, most of whom can be better taught by teachers who are sensitive to how they learn. Finally, there are many students whose learning is affected by home and community conditions that require support and often intervention from teachers—conditions ranging from poor health, vision, or hearing coupled with inadequate health care to violence, abuse, homelessness, death of a loved one, and divorce.

Inclusion policies coupled with tough-edged standards-based reforms predict ever greater stresses for many students in most states and districts. The 10–20 percent of students who have learning disabilities are disproportionately represented among students having difficulty passing the growing batteries of required standardized tests, as are the many students who experience other challenges in their lives. Special needs students are also disproportionately represented among those who are retained in grade or not graduated (Figlio and Getzler, 2002; Heubert and Hauser, 1999).

These students are present in virtually all classrooms, but few teachers have had preparation to teach them effectively. Not only are regular education teachers often underprepared to teach the range of students in their classrooms but, tragically, many communities assign to special education classrooms inexperienced and unlicensed individuals with little or no training or background in teaching. Unlike other professions that expect their most skilled practitioners to take on the toughest cases, in the educational pecking order quite often the least skilled practitioners are disproportionately assigned to teach those who most need sophisticated, diagnostic practice.

A number of states now require all teachers to have some familiarity with the needs of exceptional learners and to know about other issues affecting students' lives. However, relatively few require serious preparation to meet those needs. Instruction is often limited to legal requirements under laws governing special education or reporting of child abuse. Sometimes categories of health or learning problems are reviewed. Rarely do programs present concrete skills and strategies for addressing these issues in the context of actual practice.

The programs we studied went well beyond the requirements of most of their states, which is why their graduates felt better prepared than most. Among the random sample of beginning teachers whom we surveyed for this study, only 55 percent reported feeling well prepared to "identify and address special learning needs and difficulties" among their students. Among the graduates of these seven programs, 68 percent felt well prepared and 92 percent felt adequately or better prepared to identify and meet special learning needs. Eighty-five percent felt well prepared to "understand how different students are learning" and 76 percent felt well prepared to "help all students achieve high academic standards."

This is one way in which quality of teacher education matters most: if the goal is to teach all children to high standards, the need for differential teaching strategies carefully chosen for their appropriateness to specific needs becomes critical. This is what distinguishes a professional teacher from a craftsperson who has a single set of techniques, or an assembly line worker who mindlessly plows through the book, so to speak, without regarding to learning. Lacking the knowledge to understand what many children require and how to meet those needs, teachers are doomed merely to cover the curriculum while the students fall further and further behind. Teaching diverse learners well is less a specific set of techniques for students with particular labels than it is a stance toward figuring out what all kinds of students need, where they are in their learning, and responding to their needs in a diagnostic fashion. Jane Kopp drew these distinctions in her own experience as a teacher, attributing her ability to attend to each child's learning to her ETEP training:

> *Because I substituted for ten years* [before I entered teaching], *I would have come in using textbooks and would have read off the*

questions at the bottom of the page. I still fight wanting things to be orderly, "Sit down and do your pencil and paper work," and I feel I still have a tremendous amount to learn in terms of hands-on instruction, but I have gotten better. . . . I learned through ETEP how to put out there what we're aiming for in terms of learning . . . of saying "Where am I now, where are the gaps, what do I need to know?" I wouldn't have known any of that without the program.

Given the critical need to increase teachers' skill in teaching students with special needs, programs that do a particularly good job of preparing all teachers for this twenty-first-century mission make an especially important contribution to the knowledge base about how to educate teachers for the real demands of schools and students today.

Combining Practice with Research and Theory

All of the programs we studied include specific courses and field experiences that address issues of teaching exceptional learners more thoroughly and methodically than what has been the norm at many other institutions. In most cases, these experiences combine acquisition of content knowledge about specific student needs, including family and community challenges as well as learning disabilities and handicapping conditions, with practical work supporting learning about diagnosis and teaching strategies in inclusive classrooms. Particularly important is the fact that this preparation goes beyond didactic instruction focused on taxonomies of laws and disabilities, to applied work in classrooms that helps candidates develop curriculum and teaching strategies. The work is cumulative over time, embedded in many learning contexts (not just a single course), and holistic in its orientation—looking at all students as distinctive. The goals of this work are for candidates to develop the ability to:

- o Evaluate school and classroom environments and understand the elements needed to serve a range of student needs
- o Assess and diagnose individual students' contexts, strengths, and learning needs
- o Tailor curriculum and teaching to address these strengths and needs
- o Teach explicit strategies to allow students to become successful learners
- o Involve families and colleagues in helping support student success

As noted earlier, in addition to attention to the diversity of learning styles and family contexts for all students, each program has coursework linked to practicum work that includes case studies of exceptional learners (like the one Tom Taylor completed in the ETEP program) and that additionally explores teaching strategies for students who learn differently. The embeddedness of this pedagogical work in settings where candidates have responsibility for designing teaching for diverse students is critical. For example, at UC Berkeley students take Assessment and Education of Exceptional Pupils in Regular Classes while they are in one of their final placements, which is in a high-needs inner-city school. The course helps them understand characteristics of special needs children and strategies to work effectively with those children while they are taking major responsibility for planning for an inclusive classroom. Students take a similar course at Alverno College in the second phase of the program (semesters four through six) that includes a field experience. In addition, at Alverno as in the other programs, candidates are continuously coached in how to look at students as individuals, seeking out strengths on which to build instruction as well as needs to be addressed. As one Alverno faculty member noted: "We really focus on child-centeredness: that they look at the child as an individual and look at what that child has as far as strengths—knowing about children's backgrounds and knowing how they can support them as learners, rather than writing them off because they don't have something. [We try to prepare] teachers who look at what [pupils] do have and work with them."

Particularly interesting in tracking a long-term comprehensive learning process are the four-year sequences at UVA and Trinity, where students experience a gradual, guided approach to understanding the needs of exceptional learners from school, classroom, and individual student perspectives. At UVA, for example, when teacher education students focus on school organization in the sophomore year, they visit and observe in regular and special education classrooms, and they interview counselors and teachers. During the junior year, when they focus on individual learners, students serve as tutors while they take the courses Learning and Development and The Exceptional Individual. Particular emphasis is placed on working with students with special educational needs. Later, when they take teaching methods courses, students learn about strategies for a range of learners and can link what they are learning to their earlier coursework on development and their personal experiences with exceptional students. Employers note how well prepared Curry students are for dealing with the needs of diverse students, including those identified with special educational needs.

Among the programs we studied, graduates of Trinity University felt best prepared in this area: fully 87 percent of candidates felt "well" or "very well" prepared to "identify and address special learning needs and/or difficulties" compared to only 55 percent of the national sample. Virtually all (97 percent) felt at least adequately prepared. Extensive work regarding special needs learners is consciously integrated into classes in each of four years of preparation, in both courses and practicum experiences. In the sophomore year, The Child in Society course deals not only with students with physical, emotional, and learning disabilities but also with medically fragile students and those involved with gangs, substance abuse, and other risk factors. In the junior year, Growing Up in America treats child development from many vantage points and includes work on children with learning differences. In the senior year, while in student teaching, candidates are asked to attend to issues associated with diversity in learning. A course that summer asks students to design a reading program for pupils with a variety of learning styles and to "discuss appropriate ways of including students with a variety of exceptionalities into regular classrooms so that their learning, social, and personal needs will be met" and "develop methods that regular education and special education teachers can use to work together to design the best programs for all students" (Syllabus ED 392, Teaching Inquiry and Practice). In the fifth year, when candidates are earning their MAT, they take Pedagogics alongside the Clinical Practice seminar and placement that explicitly includes clinical practice in special education.

At Wheelock College (runner up to Trinity in graduates' perceptions of strong preparation to teach special needs students), issues of inclusion also pervade nearly all courses and are the subject of specific coursework and practicum experiences. Wheelock's expanded concept of human development includes not only the traditional notions of stages and supported child development but also attention to family and community, understanding of cultural identity and privilege, and advocacy for full inclusion of diverse learners.

Of the two major practica, at least one setting must include special needs children. The first practicum is actually part of any integrated core, consisting of three courses that students take concurrently: Curriculum Development for Inclusive Early Childhood (or Elementary) Settings, a seminar, and the three-hundred-hour practicum in either a birth-to-five-year setting or a K–3 setting. Both this three-hundred-hour practicum and another 150-hour practicum are paired with courses in Inclusive Curriculum. The syllabus for Curriculum Design for Inclusive Elementary Education explains that the course is designed to "provide the opportunity for students to develop and evaluate inclusive environments for students. This course emphasizes meeting the needs of all children through an integrated approach to planning, implementing, and assessing instruction in all areas; developing Individual Education Plans; and promoting collaboration among families, school, and communities. Service delivery systems and transitions between programs are reviewed in relation to curriculum."

One important aspect of linkages between courses and practica experiences is the opportunity for students to raise pressing questions as they occur and to be guided as they explore the answers. We saw an example of this when we followed a Wheelock student, Angela, though her teacher education experience. As part of the practicum and seminar, she kept a reflective journal that her supervisor read and commented on. These interactions helped Angela clarify her thinking and come up with appropriate responses to difficult situations. She particularly remembered a problem she had with thinking about how to discipline children. In her journal, she had written:

> *Every Thursday, I have been given the opportunity to spend the morning in another kindergarten classroom. This has given me the opportunity to see the difference in class structure, teaching styles, as well as discipline. Though I look at every child as having special needs, this kindergarten class has a range of students with noticeable special needs including Down's Syndrome, autism, and severe behavior problems. Even though I can in no way compare this classroom to my own, the discipline taken in the other classroom is really different. My first day here I witnessed a child being dragged out of a class for hitting a boy in the face and making his nose bleed. I sat there in shock over how the behavior was treated. I do not want to make a false judgment because I have not been in the class long enough to do so. What I wonder about is why this one class has so many issues to deal with, while mine has minor issues. I would think that instead of putting all these special needs children in one classroom, they would be shared among the classes. That would make more of a balance.*

Angela's supervisor responded with thoughtful comments in the margins designed to provoke reflection and motivation for future learning: "You are expanding your knowledge and definition of inclusive classroom. How would you have dealt with the situation?"

The supervisor also asked for more detail: "What percentage of the class represents children with special needs? Did you ask the teacher what she was trying to accomplish? Did you talk about this to your practicing teacher? Are you aware of how the school groups children in classes?"

This quality of back-and-forth interaction between Angela and her supervisor continued for the duration of the practicum, as was true throughout all of her field experiences. Angela credits these conversations with helping her become aware of schoolwide issues of grouping students for instruction, developing understanding of the need for better-integrated heterogeneous classrooms and more supports for teaching in such classrooms, and ultimately developing the teaching skills to successfully manage such a classroom effectively.

To foster school environments in which the needs of special learners are better addressed, Wheelock made this the focus of its work with several partner schools, among them public schools in Boston and two private institutions, the Walker Home and School and the Germaine Lawrence School, which have developed and implemented special needs inclusion models. Candidates placed in these schools pursued joint elementary education and special education certification, taking extremely rigorous coursework tied to a yearlong full-time clinical internship in the schools.

Within these school partnerships, Wheelock faculty worked with professionals and preprofessionals as they sought to transform their schools into places where children with a range of special needs "can be educated in progressive, humane, and sound ways alongside children whose development has been more placid" (personal correspondence with Mario Borunda, May 24, 1994). The school- and university-based faculties designed curriculum together, taught side by side in college seminars and school classrooms, and linked theory and practice continuously. Additionally, Wheelock began linking partnership schools with each other, connecting the faculties of private schools designed to serve special needs youth with faculties in public schools, attempting to build a wider community of learners who could work together to learn to meet children's educational, social, and psychological needs.

Analyzing and Understanding Student Needs

A key cornerstone of practice that responds to students' needs is the skill of incisive observation and diagnosis. We saw well-developed examples of this in Bank Street's many strategies for helping teachers understand their students through observation and recording of behavior. All three courses in the sequence Child Development; The Study of Normal and Exceptional Children Through Observation and Recording; and Family, Child, and Teacher Interaction in Diverse and Inclusive Settings explicitly address concerns for diversity in learning, including exceptionalities generally treated only in special education courses elsewhere.

Observation and Recording must be taken while working with children, either during the year of advisement or when teaching. Family, Child, and Teacher Interaction must be taken while working with children and families. When we asked instructors what they expect from their students, they described attitudes as well as skills, including reflectivity, the ability to synthesize and apply concepts and theories, and willingness to take children's feelings and thinking seriously. The emphasis on this last one should not be mistaken as an ideology that children always know what they need. Instead, careful observation of children is a basis for understanding what children are experiencing, to diagnose how they learn and what will help them progress.

During one of our visits, students entered a session of the Child Development course focusing on older children and adolescents, having just read a highly technical article from a medical journal on "the learning disorders of adolescence." Rather than launching into a discussion of the article, instructor Joe Kleinman began the class by having the students undertake a series of tasks to help them experience what these "out-of-sync" children might be experiencing. First, the students were asked to take dictation with their nondominant hand. "Keep up," Joe admonished them as he read at a conversational rate. "Neatness counts." Some students laughed; others stopped and scratched their heads in bewilderment. Beginning a second task, Joe announced, "Now, I'm going to show you a list of words for thirty seconds. Take a look at it." When the thirty seconds were up, Kleinman removed the list and instructed students to write down as many as they can remember. "You can't work with your partner on this one," Joe instructed. After students scored their work, he asked, "How was it?" Students responded of the first task: "I couldn't keep up"; "It was pretty awful—physically uncomfortable and frustrating"; "I just gave up and skipped words."

"I heard laughter," Joe noted, as he pointed out how some kids might become the class clown rather than dealing with the psychological discomfort they felt. "Did you wonder how you compared to others?" he asked, leading into a discussion of his students' feelings of competence, and how they thought their students might feel when they cannot fulfill adults' expectations.

Joe then moved on to the question of how students compensated. One mentioned memorizing words; another created a sentence from some of the words to try to make it more meaningful; a third tried to memorize the words in alphabetical order to bring some structure to the task; a fourth, who used to make up songs as a child, created a litany. These examples were the basis of a discussion of coping and compensation strategies that students might use to make difficult learning more accessible to them. Students drew relationships between emotional and cognitive development and performance. Kleinman noted the anxiety raised by failure, and the frequent example of a child who opted to become bad rather than be labeled stupid.

Ready to engage the article now, students could discuss from firsthand experience as well as their reading how difficulty in writing and remembering—the basis for many learning difficulties that become apparent in late childhood and early adolescence—may translate into school failure and demoralization unless they are addressed by compensatory teaching and learning strategies. Kleinman emphasized some of the key ideas from the dense and complex reading, especially the behavioral clues of learning disabilities that often emerge in the transition from elementary to middle school: restlessness and difficulty concentrating while sitting still for a long period of time; problems with organization and planning; difficulty in paying attention, recalling information, sequencing ideas, and synthesizing information from multiple sources.

Students then broke out in groups of three or four to discuss a case study of a student. Joe reminded them that "we are not therapists" and that they should try to understand the case, look for strengths, and design interventions. After a half hour, Joe went to the board to record the groups' ideas about how to help Ramona, the case study student. He used three focusing ideas that are similar to those heard at the start of discussions in many other Bank Street classes:

1. What's going on here, and why?
2. What is the source of the school failure?
3. How can we intervene?

In the discussion that followed, we learned that Ramona's strengths included her physical and musical abilities as well as social skills. Her difficulties included organizing things, synthesizing information, and memorizing certain kinds of material. Her move into middle school was accompanied by attitude changes, growing rebelliousness, and severe test anxiety. The discussion of interventions included, at Joe's gentle insistence, as much emphasis on strengths as it did on needs as a basis for instruction. When students began to debate whether to allow Ramona to draw cartoons or paint a mural rather than write an essay, Joe intervened to remind them to ask the question, "What is the goal? There are several goals, including mastery of material and the development of writing skills. How would you be able to move Ramona into developing her skills in writing?" The discussion focused on how to use Ramona's strengths to help her develop these skills. At the end of class, Joe urged the students to "take this question to your conference groups" to explore it further. The learning continued there.

But does this kind of thinking continue in the practice of graduates? Our observations suggested that it does. For example, when we visited new teacher "Marilyn Morroca's" kindergarten and first-grade classroom in P.S. 234, we found her reading to the children gathered before her on the classroom rug. After reading a page, she showed the students the picture of a flower it included, asking with a big smile, "How many letters does the word *chrysanthemum* have?" After they counted together, Marilyn pulled out name tags she had prepared with the children's names on them. She asked each child, one by one, to come up to a large piece of newsprint on an easel to her right and post the tag above the number that denoted the number of letters in his or her name. The title at the top of the chart read: "How Many Letters in Our Names?" The tags gradually stacked up to create bar graphs depicting the number of children in the class with names that had a given number of letters. We noted that Marilyn watched carefully as students posted their tags, and she occasionally made notes about how they tackled this task and what kinds of assistance some of them needed to be successful.

After they completed this task, Marilyn asked, "Does anyone's name have the same number of letters as the word *chrysanthemum*?" This puzzle occupied a few minutes of checking and counting, after which the children agreed that no one had a first name that was thirteen letters long. Marilyn then asked if they could put two names together to make a name with as many letters as *chrysanthemum*. She used small colored blocks to illustrate a combination of letters that equaled thirteen. A student suggested another combination. Once they realized that there is more than one way to combine numbers to equal thirteen, Marilyn sent them back to their tables to work together on "making a chrysanthemum"—that is, a combination of names that will produce the number of letters in that word. A quiet hum filled the room as the children worked in pairs and small groups combining names, adding and subtracting letters and numbers, and explaining their solutions to one another. Again, Marilyn watched and listened carefully, making notes about students' mathematical efforts, their knowledge of letters and numbers, and their discourse with one another. For those who finished early, Marilyn had another problem to extend their learning. Some who finished their own work continued helping other students who were still at work.

When we talked to Marilyn after her chrysanthemum lesson, she spoke in great detail about the learning strengths and progress of individual children, about how the lesson was designed to address them, and about the learning puzzles she was working on. One student, for example, could write fluently but was not yet motivated to take care with her work or to improve on it. Another could produce only a single word at a time and had just been diagnosed with an auditory perceptual disability. Marilyn was interviewing the first child to find out what might change her approach to her writing; she was also developing new strategies for the second student that relied more on visual recognition of words than on aural decoding. She knew a great deal about the learning approaches and needs of each student and chose activities carefully to maximize their ability to build on strengths while addressing shortcomings.

Connecting to the Home and School Communities

The emphasis on understanding children as individuals as well as students is reinforced in many Bank Street courses, as is the expectation that teachers will take proactive steps to discover and meet their needs. In the Child Development courses, for example, assignments are carefully constructed to enable students to gain information about specific problems and services as well as develop skills in working with families and children with particular needs. Analysis of the school setting includes a focus on school-family interactions and on students with special needs. Candidates are asked to "critically examine the patterns of interaction between family and school as well as expectations, attitudes and policies which encourage or inhibit family-school collaboration. What works well? What would you change, and how, in order to improve family-school collaboration? In what ways does your school support families with children who have special needs?" (Syllabus for TE 501, Family, Child, and Teacher Interaction).

In addition to extensive reading about students with learning differences from an educational perspective, candidates read about special needs from a family perspective (Featherstone's *A Difference in the Family,* 1980; Seligman and Darling's *Ordinary Families, Special Children,* 1989). In discussion, they consider some of the commonalities shared by families with special needs children and how teachers can use this knowledge to help families work with and advocate for their children. They also learn about how to use parent-teacher conferencing to gain information about the child and his or her strengths and ways of behaving and learning, and to create a collaborative partnership with parents. Using a guide, they role-play conferences and conduct them in their clinical placement.

Finally, students develop a case study that tracks their own advocacy efforts on behalf of a child with special needs (diagnosed or not) in their classroom. They describe their own work in the classroom with the child; collaboration with the family and other professionals on behalf of the child; curriculum modifications and other interventions involving the child and the family; and outcomes of their teaching and advocacy efforts, and those of the parents, on behalf of the child.

The range of needs examined through readings, discussion, and student-led research includes not only special educational needs but those associated with students who are homeless or in foster care; in families dealing with substance abuse, violence, or child abuse; and in families with medical concerns for the child or other family members. Candidates research and report on issues, contact child and family service agencies, and figure out how to support children in their classrooms with an eye toward ensuring that they can fully engage with the curriculum and interact with their peers, rather than being isolated or excused from high expectations because of the challenges they face.

Helping Students Develop Strategies to Guide Their Learning

One thing graduates of Bank Street and many of the other programs noted was how important it was for them to have knowledge about strategies for teaching special learners so as to be able to continue to hold high standards for them and help them meet these standards, rather than watering down the curriculum. In addition to required courses, many graduates frequently mentioned as particularly helpful electives from the special education program, such as Designing and Managing Classroom Environments for Children and Youth with Special Needs, and Language Development, Diversity, and Disorders: Impact on Reading and Literacy Development. These courses enabled them to make good on the commitment to serve children's needs that they developed at Bank Street. They felt they had developed tools to allow them to go beyond good intentions to effective teaching for more of their students. One fourth and fifth grade teacher expressed how important it was to her to take Learning Disabilities and Reading Problems as her final elective after she began her first year of teaching:

> The course was really helpful. I took it with a few of my students in mind. I have three kids who can't comprehend beyond the most

literal meaning and I have one kid who is reading at first or second grade reading level. And I have another student with expressive language problems. I have all these kids with very distinct and very important needs that I didn't feel well equipped to handle, so I wanted to get smarter. The course helped me realize that there are different factors for a problem: if someone is having trouble with expressive language, what could it be? And how can you help? So it was helpful to me in my practice.

Carolyn Gear, principal of P.S. 37 in the Bronx, observed that she found Bank Street graduates "very, very well prepared" to work in her multilingual school, organized around the multiple intelligences work of Howard Gardner, which serves a high proportion of special education students. The school's emphasis on diverse approaches to learning was stimulated by a culturally and educationally diverse population that is more than 70 percent Latino, about 15 percent African American, and the rest "other," which includes nine special education classrooms. Having recently hired three Bank Street graduates to work with this special needs population, Gear declared, "They're excellent!" and illustrated with a description of one new teacher she hired the previous year: "In terms of her knowledge base, in terms of curriculum, the kinds of approaches she uses and activities she provides for children and how she handles the class . . . in terms of how she teaches children to reason and respond to situations, she is excellent. She teaches them problem solving and logical thinking."

Gear's point about the importance of teaching children reasoning skills and problem solving confirms what researchers, and good teachers, have learned about successful teaching for students with learning disabilities. In contrast to earlier beliefs that special needs students require highly repetitive, rote activities if they are to learn, research demonstrates they benefit most from strategic instruction that helps them learn approaches to accessing information, attacking problems, and producing high-quality work. This includes helping students develop some of their own strategies for organizing and retaining information (task analysis, webbing, outlining), tackling texts, writing, and approaching various tasks and problems. It also includes strategies for enhancing metacognition—students' ability to evaluate what they know and what they don't know and to reflect on and guide their own learning (Darling-Hammond and Bransford, 2005, Chapter 7).

This kind of strategy instruction is central to the classroom we visited at the start of this chapter. As we rejoin the class, we can observe how Jane Kopp; her intern, Tom Taylor; and her special education colleague, Peter

Blackstone, organize their instruction to help their students master strategies for independent learning.

○

After lunch, the class members, organized as small groups, take turns visiting the library to begin research for a new unit on regions of the United States. Blackstone and Taylor accompany the groups while Kopp stays in the room, working one-on-one with students who are engaged in a number of assignments—completing journal entries, organizing their groups for the upcoming research, or reviewing the assessment criteria shown on the rubrics that will guide how groups should work on this unit.

The clarity of the goals and careful organization for the assignment allow the special needs students to undertake this challenging work alongside their classmates. A skillful blend of independent work and guided group work—often heterogeneously organized to allow students to learn from each other, sometimes in skill-alike groups to ensure that students work on particular tasks at their level of immediate need, supports students in a sophisticated learning process that combines inquiry learning with attention to specific skills. In this and other assignments, the teachers give explicit instructions about how to do the work they ask of students: how to use resources, how to organize and synthesize material, and how to assemble ideas into well-developed products, including research papers, visual artifacts, and exhibitions. Open-ended projects challenge "high-ability" students to stretch and explore; meanwhile, the painstaking scaffolding also allows the special needs students to succeed at the same work.

Later, we see another example of this careful scaffolding when Kopp and Blackstone introduce the science textbook to the class, explicitly teaching them how to use the book as a resource before continuing their work on the unit on regions of the United States. An excerpt of the discussion illustrates the kind of practice they model for Taylor, who both observes and records aspects of classroom practice in his response journal for ETEP and participates in classroom teaching and tutoring.

KOPP: How would you go about finding information in this book? (The class talks about the index and the glossary, as the teachers alternate asking questions of the children. They point out the bold print, the major sections of the book, and how each chapter contains headings.)

KOPP: What else is helpful in this textbook?

MIKE: It tells you where to look up things.

KOPP: OK, and how else is it different that helps you?

JENNY: It has summaries to help.

KOPP: Right. It tells you the *what* and the *so what,* so if you only have the *what* and you don't have the *so what,* you need to go back and look some more.

BLACKSTONE: Look at page 136. (pause) Turn back a few pages. The chapter is Chapter 3 and the unit is Unit 6, and they tell you, when you finish this section, there's the list of "What I need to know."

KOPP: Mr. Blackstone, is it enough to just read about this list? When I finish reading, I should be able to. . . .

RONNIE: No, it means you really have to be able to *do* what's there, not just read it.

Connecting this exercise to the unit on regions of the United States, Kopp points out:

KOPP: We have lots of different kinds of weather in the regions [of the United States]. We're going to study that. What do we need to be experts on before we could set up a weather lab to determine our own weather? (pause) Remember the video. Maybe you want to refer to your notes on the video. (pause) Let's not make that an option. Everyone, get out your notebooks. Good, Sally [a special needs child] has hers out. [At this comment, Sally looks at Kopp with a smile.]

JOANNIE: Air pressure.

KOPP: Good . . . what else do you need to know about?

AUSTIN: Humidity.

JENNY: Condensation.

KOPP: We're focusing on what we need to know that makes up weather. (As they continue naming elements of weather, Blackstone writes them on the board.) OK, you are already divided into groups. I think the fairest way to do this is just randomly. You guys are number one and you'll talk about temperature, you guys are number two and you'll study precipitation. (She continues around the room, assigning other groups clouds, air pressure, humidity, and wind.) After recess, some of you will go to the library and begin looking for information. What did the librarian tell you last year about how to get started on a topic? (Several children mention the card catalogue and taking notes from headings in books.) Well, you are all headed in the right direction. You also need to ask yourselves some questions. Jenny, how will you get started? (Jenny mumbles a response.) Jenny, I don't think anyone heard you. Just belt it out.

Jenny's response doesn't satisfy Kopp that all the students understand what they are to do, so she instructs the students to write down the topic assigned to their group. Then she encourages them to think about and write down questions they have about the topics. The three teachers go to small groups of students as they begin talking among themselves about their questions.

KOPP: (getting the students' attention) At the end of this, you are going to teach what you have learned to the rest of the class.

BLACKSTONE: So learners will become teachers.

KOPP: That's right. You need to know it well enough to teach it to the rest of the class. So that's what you are heading toward. Think about that as you go along with this work.

As these students prepare their research so that they can teach what they learn, they are engaged in the kind of deep, metacognitive process that will help them organize and retain what they know. In this classroom, because of the preparation their teachers have received, all students will get the scaffolding and supports they need to do this complex work successfully.

Reforms that aim to increase educational "press" and challenge for all students rest substantially on preparing teachers to work effectively with those who have traditionally been allowed to fail—not because they were unable to learn but because their teachers were not equipped to teach them. It seems clear that, given the critical need to increase teachers' skill in teaching all students well, programs that do a particularly good job of preparing all teachers for this twenty-first-century mission make an especially important contribution to our growing knowledge about how to educate teachers for the real demands of schools and students today.

PART FOUR

ISSUES OF CONTEXT AND CHANGE

TRANSFORMING
TEACHER EDUCATION

INSTITUTIONAL CHALLENGES

DEBATES ABOUT QUALITY HAVE BEEN PART of the teacher education landscape for more than a century. Historically, public dissatisfaction with schools has been coupled with dissatisfaction with schools of education as well. At the same time, there is evidence that, even with its flaws, teacher education makes a difference for teachers' effectiveness (see Chapter Two), and that reforms undertaken over the past two decades have strengthened how well schools of education prepare people for the increasingly difficult work of teaching. In contrast to previous reports of teachers' negative views of teacher education, since 1990 several surveys of beginning teachers who completed teacher education have found that the great majority—more than 80 percent—felt they were well prepared for nearly all of the challenges of their work (Gray and others, 1993; Howey and Zimpher, 1989; Kentucky Institute for Education Research, 1997; California State University, 2002a, 2002b). Veteran teachers and principals who work with current teacher preparation programs, particularly five-year programs and those that feature professional development schools, also perceive their young colleagues as much better prepared than they were some years earlier (Andrew, 1990; Andrew and Schwab, 1995; Baker, 1993; Darling-Hammond, 1994; NCES, 1996, tables 73 and 75). The programs described in this volume are cases in point.

To be sure, the programs we studied do not view their efforts as perfect or complete. All of them engage in ongoing efforts to improve the quality of preparation they provide and are the first to point out their own shortcomings and challenges. They worry about finding time to take candidates even more deeply into studies about learning and teaching and to help them confront difficult issues of practice: how to work with students who do not learn easily or are not able to engage with school, including those who are handicapped by homelessness, abuse and neglect, and lack of health care; how to teach the growing number of students who have immigrated from dozens of other countries with distinctive language backgrounds and with widely varying levels of previous formal education; and how to infuse technology into their teaching, often in schools that do not support its use.

They worry about keeping their courses current, incorporating growing knowledge bases about learning and teaching, and fighting the centrifugal forces of fragmentation that threaten every program as times and personnel change. They worry about how to furnish strong clinical placements in urban schools that are increasingly underresourced and that often hire teachers without strong knowledge and skills, thus making it more difficult to develop self-perpetuating models of strong practice. Where programs have created strong PDSs, they worry about how to maintain solid relationships between the university and the schools in the face of changing staff and in many cases dwindling dollars, including frequent shifts of superintendents and policies.

These worries have stimulated ongoing improvement in all seven programs. For example, after ETEP was launched, USM discontinued undergraduate majors in teacher education and required all of its undergraduates interested in teaching to major in a disciplinary field while pursuing a credential. Finding that this model did not allow adequate time for clinical work, the university is now expanding the undergraduate models to four and a half years to allow a full-year internship for all teacher education students.

For all these worries, programs like the ones documented here demonstrate that it is possible to prepare teachers so they are ready to enter teaching armed with knowledge and skills enabling them to serve diverse students well and learn continuously from their practice. There are common elements in how they accomplish this:

○ *Coherence,* based on a common, clear vision of good teaching grounded in an understanding of learning, that permeates all coursework and clinical experiences
○ *A strong core curriculum,* taught in the context of practice, grounded in knowledge of child and adolescent development, learning in social and cultural contexts, curriculum, assessment, and subject matter pedagogy

○ *Extensive, connected clinical experiences* that are carefully chosen to support the ideas and practices presented in simultaneous, closely inter-woven coursework

○ *An inquiry approach* that connects theory and practice, including regular use of case methods, analyses of teaching and learning, and teacher research, applying learning to real problems of practice and developing teachers as reflective practitioners

○ *School-university partnerships* that develop common knowledge and shared beliefs among school- and university-based faculty and allow candidates to learn to teach in professional communities modeling state-of-the-art practice for diverse learners and collegial learning for adults

○ *Assessment based on professional standards* that evaluates teaching through demonstrations of critical skills and abilities using performance assessments and portfolios that support the development of "adaptive expertise"

Unlike many teachers who enter the profession with enthusiasm and good intentions but insufficient knowledge and skill, the graduates of these programs (and their employers) find they can succeed where many beginners flounder, and they can make a difference for children where others strive mainly for survival. Documenting what these programs do, however, is only a small contribution to the goal of helping these practices become widespread. There are many issues, pragmatic and political, that must be confronted if pervasive reforms of teacher education are to make this kind of preparation the norm rather than the exception.

What institutional supports allowed these programs to develop the kinds of practices described in this book? How does the policy context matter? What changes are needed in how organizations and governments behave if we are to ensure that all teachers are given access to the knowledge and skills they need to become effective? This chapter and the final one take up these issues, beginning with a review of the problems that undergird the current unevenness of teacher education, and then outline an agenda for the transformation of teacher education.

The Nature of the Problem

If teaching is a low-status occupation in the United States, teacher education is an even lower-status enterprise within most universities. Ever since normal schools for teachers were incorporated into universities during the 1950s, many schools and departments of education have tried to lift their prestige within the institution by distancing themselves from the world of schools and practice, seeking to adopt the ivory tower norms of departments of arts and sciences rather than embracing the training responsibilities expected of professional schools. The incentive systems of universities favor research and inward-looking faculty service over the intensive and time-consuming work with prospective teachers and schools demanded by professional training. Some of the same dynamics occur in schools of law and medicine, where clinical instructors typically have subordinate status and are not likely to be tenured. However, these pressures are exacerbated in schools of education, which are lower in the academic pecking order and have limited access to resources both within and outside the institution.

Institutional Investments and the University Context

Historically, teacher education programs have been funded well below the level of other departments and professional programs on most college campuses (Ebmeier, Twombly, and Teeter, 1991; Howard, Hitz, and Baker, 1998), and teacher educators on average have received lower salaries than other education faculty, who in turn have earned significantly lower salaries than other university faculty (NCES, 1997a). These funding issues have affected the number and quality of faculty recruited, the ratio of instructors to students, class sizes and the load of courses and other responsibilities carried by instructors (and hence the attention they can offer students and the extent to which they can be involved in research and instructional innovations), the quality of supervision and clinical placements that can be offered, the availability of technology to support instruction, and opportunities for launching such initiatives as professional development schools.

Many of those who have found themselves teaching teachers—faculty in English or mathematics, for example—have not thought of themselves as "teacher educators," and most have had little preparation for the task of educating teachers. They have taught their courses as they would to any college student, leaving it to the prospective teachers to integrate subject matter and pedagogical studies. Many faculty in schools of education have not thought of themselves as teacher educators, either. Instead, they are specialists in subjects like sociology, psychology, or reading. They have not always felt a mandate to figure out how what they know should apply to teaching or to coordinate their work with that of other faculty who work with prospective teachers (Darling-Hammond and Ball, 1998).

The relationship between clinical work and the work in the academy has often been attenuated by organizational barriers within the university and between the university and schools. Unlike other developed professions, teacher education exists in a more highly politicized regulatory environment in which standards for accreditation and licensing are substantially governed by political bodies rather than by the profession itself. As a consequence, the key levers for change are more complex and difficult to manage.

These issues undergird many of the criticisms that have dogged teacher education programs for the fifty years since they became part of colleges and universities. The critiques have included, at a minimum:

○ *Inadequate time.* The confines of a four-year undergraduate degree make it hard to learn subject matter, child development, learning theory, and effective teaching strategies. Elementary preparation has been considered weak in subject matter; secondary preparation, in knowledge of learning and learners.

○ *Fragmentation.* Elements of teacher learning are disconnected from each other. Coursework is separate from practice teaching, professional skills are segmented into separate courses, and faculties in the arts and sciences are insulated from education professors. Would-be teachers are left to their own devices to put it all together.

○ *Uninspired teaching methods.* For prospective teachers to learn active, hands-on and minds-on teaching, they must experience it for themselves. But traditional lecture and recitation still dominates in much of higher education, where large classes are common and many faculty members do not practice what they preach. Haphazard student teaching placements often model these same ineffective methods, rather than demonstrating how to teach extraordinarily well.

○ *Superficial curriculum.* Once-over-lightly describes the curriculum. Traditional programs focus on a few teaching methods and a smattering of educational psychology. Candidates do not learn deeply about how to understand and handle real problems of practice.

○ *Traditional views of schooling.* Because of pressure to prepare candidates for schools as they are and placements in schools that do not represent leading-edge practice, most prospective teachers learn outmoded teaching techniques and prepare for chalkboards and textbooks instead of computers and CD-ROMs (NCTAF, 1996).

These conditions have undermined the quality of many teacher education programs, while lack of enforcement of quality standards in many states removes much leverage for change. Universities are not easily changed; as one pundit quipped, one reason professors spend so much time trying to change K–12 schools is that they know they cannot change their own organizations. Reformers on the inside typically need some pressure from the outside of the organization to leverage change.

Weak Standards

A critical element in transforming other professions has been the role of accreditation, which is the vehicle used to require universities to incorporate new knowledge into courses in engineering, law, and psychology; to adopt structural reforms such as the teaching hospital in medicine; and to ensure adequate resources for teaching, research, and clinical supervision. However, only five states require national accreditation of education schools, and few state agencies have the resources or capacity to evaluate programs and enforce high standards through their program approval processes. Candidates are licensed if they graduate from a state-approved program, and virtually all programs, regardless of their quality, are state-approved. Even with the advent of teacher testing since the early 1980s, few states have adopted performance assessments that evaluate whether candidates can actually teach. The basic skills and subject matter tests that predominate do not measure the quality of preparation and afford little incentive for programs to improve. Thus existing quality control systems exert little productive pressure on the quality of teacher education.

Market Incentives That Undermine Quality

A major reason many candidates do not get access to adequate preparation is that they cannot afford the tuition, or the opportunity costs of being without employment for a period of time. Furthermore, these costs are harder to bear when a recruit is entering a profession that does not promise a large salary later to compensate for loans taken earlier. Whereas many countries fully subsidize an extensive program of teacher education for all candidates, the amount of preparation secured by teachers in the United States is left mostly to what they can individually afford and what programs are willing and able to offer given the resources of their institution. The increasing availability of short-term routes into teaching, and the combined absence of effective standards of program quality and subsidies for training, can make it difficult for a school of education to increase its expectations of candidates, since the marketplace of programs in states that have deregulated teaching is driven by cost and brevity rather than quality and effectiveness. Some states seek to create subsidies for preparation and incentives for improved program quality, but others treat teachers as low-skilled factory workers and teacher education as a cost to be avoided, lowering standards in the face of shortages rather than increasing the incentives to enter teaching or the supports to teach well.

As a consequence of all of these factors, teachers' knowledge and skills in the United States are tremendously uneven. Whereas many new teachers who attend redesigned programs are better prepared for teaching than ever, others—particularly those who teach low-income children in high-minority schools—have little or no training for their work. In like fashion, when Flexner and Pritchett (1910) published their landmark report on the state of medical education in the United States, medical education suffered from dramatically uneven duration and quality; medical practice suffered from doctors' differential access to knowledge, as well as an enormous divide between research in the new sciences of medicine and the state of practice. In the medical schools that emerged in the preceding decades, coursework was frequently divorced from clinical work, and curriculum was often fragmented, superficial, and didactic—the same kind of complaint that has dogged colleges of education since they took up the charge of educating teachers in the latter half of the twentieth century.

Eventual widespread reform of medical education occurred as the profession set standards for medical training and infused them into the standards for accrediting professional programs and licensing and certifying medical candidates, who had to graduate from a professionally accredited program to sit for licensing and board certification examinations. This same process, with some variations, was later followed for law, engineering, nursing, psychology, accounting, architecture, and other occupations that became professions in the twentieth century.

A similar set of strategies for preparation—simultaneously strengthening and connecting theoretical and clinical training—was embedded in the goals of the Holmes Group (1986), the Carnegie Task Force on Teaching as a Profession (1986), and the National Network for Education Renewal (Goodlad, 1990, 1994), among other efforts at teacher education reform. These initiatives stimulated important reforms in many preparation programs, including some of those we studied. However, the improvements have not reached all programs, and the policy contexts within which teacher education operates often work against productive reforms rather than for them.

Ensuring that all teachers receive strong and effective teacher education requires expanding access to programs and achieving greater clarity about how to enhance quality across the enterprise. It entails greater sophistication about how to approach organizational change as *institutional development* instead of a series of single innovations that cannot survive (Fullan, 1993). It also demands greater engagement with the policy community that exerts strong influence on teacher education programs' goals and strategies and on the context in which they operate. In what follows, I describe the institutional issues I believe must be tackled if all teachers are to have access to the knowledge they need to succeed with all children. In Chapter Eleven, I discuss the policy issues.

The Pragmatics of Improving Preparation: Strategies for Institutional Change

There have been many attempts to create new models of teacher education, and although some have succeeded in individual institutions none have become institutionalized on a large scale as hoped. In his analysis of the federally sponsored Teacher Corps and Trainers of Teacher Trainers programs that existed in the 1960s and 1970s, Michael Fullan (1993) identified five reasons for the failure of these and other initiatives to transform preparation:

1. The policies were based on vague conceptions of the desired change and the change process. "Having an ideology is not the same as having conceptions and ideas of what should be done and how it should be done," Fullan notes (p. 109).
2. The initiatives focused on individuals rather than institutions.
3. They were nonsystemic, giving little thought to changes in interinstitutional relationships, for example, between schools and universities.
4. They ignored the knowledge and skill base required if teachers are to teach a variety of students effectively and transform the conditions in schools that influence what teachers can do.
5. To the extent that they worked on change, most of the effort was directed at school systems, not at universities (pp. 109–110).

These insights suggest the importance of a systemic, institutional perspective on change that includes both universities and schools, a perspective that clarifies the goals for knowledge and skill development, and a strategy for implementing a change process within a community focused on these goals. Each institution we studied, in its own way, developed such a perspective and created a context within which teacher education could be supported and could succeed. Accomplishing this required:

○ Creating a culture that values teacher education as a centrally important enterprise, not a marginal activity

○ Developing a community for preparing teachers, within and beyond the university, including strong partnerships with schools

○ Designing institutional incentives that support high-quality preparation

○ Investing resources in ways that pay off for long-term goals

How did the programs pursue these goals? And what lessons does this suggest for the wider struggle to transform teacher preparation?

Supporting Teacher Education: Can Universities Prepare Teachers Well?

Interestingly, when our research team set out to conduct this study, the initial recommendations we received from scholars and teacher educators across the country identifying high-quality teacher education programs of long standing disproportionately referred to a set of unique, independent institutions of teacher education, in many ways the descendents of normal schools. Alverno, Bank Street, and Wheelock Colleges were among them, as were Teachers College at Columbia University and Pacific Oaks College in California. These places in which teacher education is a major focus of the college's mission inherently have a culture that appreciates the importance of teacher education. Many of the things that are possible in these colleges—for example, faculty who have themselves been expert teachers in schools and who are deeply involved in classrooms as well as research on practice—are possible because the colleges were designed from the beginning to support teaching and the preparation of teachers.

But in other kinds of institutions, such a culture is not a given. Building a teaching culture was a function of the organizational mission at Alverno, a Catholic women's college initially founded as a normal school for teachers by an order of nuns that has a social justice mission in which education is a central element. The strong collaborative approach that enabled a highly coherent program was also largely a function of the college's religious and organizational missions, which value creation of community and engagement in community service. Alverno's ability-based curriculum was designed by faculty leaders during the early 1970s as an enlightened response to the "competency-based teacher education" reforms that were then popular. Incorporation of these concepts and associated performance assessments into the whole of the college's curriculum was made possible by the holistic approach to education embraced by this small college with strong norms and core educational values.

Other institutions, however, have had to surmount different traditions and histories to institute a culture that supports teacher education. This is not unique to the United States. In France, for example, a major reform in 1989 took teacher education out of traditional university departments and created new University Institutes for the Preparation of Teachers, regional organizations that sponsor two-year graduate-level programs and connect them to schools, rather like a new approach to the normal school.

Our research suggests it is possible (if not easy) to create a context for high-quality teacher education within even the most resistant institution: the research university. In the unusual case of UC Berkeley, reforms of preparation started in the early 1980s, shortly after a governance body recommended doing away with the teacher education program because it was viewed as low-quality. At that time, UCB's program was a one-year postbaccalaureate credential program like all others in California since the state eliminated undergraduate teacher education and set a maximum cap of one year on graduate-level programs. The Developmental Teacher Education program was formed by a small group of tenured developmental psychology faculty who took up the challenge and who were interested in giving a developmental perspective more weight in teacher education. With support cultivated from university leaders, they created a two-year program that was granted "experimental status" by the state and brought in other tenure-line faculty to teach most of its courses, giving the program the status needed to access the many other university resources that were needed to run a top-quality enterprise.

In the other three research universities we studied, where teacher education was also viewed as a marginal activity, we found that creation of a culture in support of teacher education was stimulated both by outside reform initiatives, such as those that proliferated in the late 1980s (the Holmes Group of education deans and the Carnegie Task Force on Teaching as a Profession), and the commitment of top leadership in the university, which dovetailed with the efforts of forward-looking faculty within schools of education. Three of the programs we studied launched major reforms in the 1980s as a function of these influences.

Trinity University and the University of Virginia both took advantage of the Holmes Group's recommendations (1986), which urged research universities to create five-year programs of teacher education. UVA's Curry School of Education was in fact a founding member of the Holmes Group and began redesigning its teacher education program in 1984 with the arrival of a new dean who had a national reputation as a teacher educator, who joined the school with an agenda to elevate the status of teacher education. Trinity's efforts began a few years later when it convened the

Brackenridge Forum to design its new approach to teacher education, partly in response to broader reforms launched in Texas. Both were supported by university presidents, provosts, and deans committed to the importance of high-quality teacher education as part of the university's obligation to society and its commitment to community. This internal support, coupled with external calls for reform, gave them an opportunity to seek far-reaching, fundamental reforms of the enterprise, rather than merely incremental change. By virtue of constructing an entirely new model of teacher education, they were able to reach out to the faculties of arts and sciences as well as local schools, and thus redefine the role of teacher education within the university and upgrade its status while improving quality.

The University of Southern Maine also created its new graduate-level program during this period of time, drawing on the Holmes Group's proposal for creation of professional development schools. The new USM teacher education program also grew out of the work of the Southern Maine Partnership, one of the original sites in John Goodlad's National Network for Educational Renewal—growing from informal "dine and discuss" meetings about educational issues among university faculty and six local school superintendents to a consortium of twenty-five districts that collaborated on everything from educational meetings and conferences to school quality reviews that sent teams of faculty across sites to assess and provide feedback to each other's schools.

In 1989, the dean of the college and the university president urged the creation of a graduate-level professional preparation program to replace the bachelor's degree in education. This program drew on the Southern Maine Partnership for relationships with five districts that provided its fifteen original PDS sites and for the clinical capacity to sustain a three-stage program, including a minor in education for undergraduates who begin at USM, the graduate-level credential training provided by ETEP, and the two-year master's degree in education that many ETEP graduates complete after they enter teaching. The program's success became self-sustaining as faculty and local educators came to believe what they had jointly created was superior to the previous undergraduate program, which suffered from the front loading, fragmentation, and other design flaws of most such programs.

Wheelock was also stimulated to create professional development schools through its participation in the National Network for Educational Renewal, and it responded to a Massachusetts State Task Force on Teacher Preparation by creating a multidisciplinary liberal arts major and redesigning its teacher education programs.

Across these institutions, the improved reputations of the much stronger programs created through these reforms helped to sustain the climate of support for teacher education in the institutions at large. These experiences argue for continuing investment in the kind of cross-institutional professional leadership represented by the Holmes Group, the National Network for Educational Renewal, and other initiatives that have helped schools of education mobilize around a vision for reform and serve as models and referents for one another. The history of these programs also argues for pursuit of fundamental rather than incremental reforms of programs, so that they can reach out to new constituencies—in the arts and sciences and in the schools—who can help to shape the new model and thus buy into it. Such fundamental changes are more likely to overcome the weak reputation of teacher education programs, and to generate more powerful outcomes so that their benefits will garner the ongoing support needed to weather the vicissitudes of budget and personnel changes.

Tweaking traditional programs that are still organized around the fragmented and front-loaded designs adopted in the 1950s is unlikely to result in the political capital or the educational momentum to allow them to become powerful exemplars of what is possible in preparing teachers for the challenges they now face.

Developing a Community for Preparing Teachers

To learn to teach diverse learners for deep understanding, teachers must negotiate a web of interactions that sit between general propositions about learning, development, and teaching and the situated realities of subject matter, students, and classrooms. Studies suggest that changes in teaching practice and student achievement occur when teachers participate in sustained, collaborative learning grounded in the curriculum they teach and emphasizing examination of teaching methods and student work (Brown, Smith, and Stein, 1995; Cohen and Hill, 2000; Wiley and Yoon, 1995). Without an opportunity for genuine praxis, abstract theoretical ideas seem inadequate to the complexities and idiosyncrasies of students; meanwhile, the outcomes of classroom efforts seem random and unpredictable.

The efforts of these programs to develop "whole teachers" in programs that are designed to help candidates create a coherent, powerful practice with a strong theoretical base require many changes in the traditional management of teacher education programs. As Barbara Biber and Charlotte Windsor (1967) argued in describing Bank Street's approach to integrating advisement, clinical work, and coursework:

Of critical importance is the assumption that teaching competence and style is tied not only to the information a teacher gets in training, but also very crucially to the mode in which that teacher experiences and internalizes the information and through which he [or she] transmutes it into continuous professional growth. This assumption leads to a model of learning which engages the student teacher in concurrent mastery of theory and responsible apprentice-training; activates feeling as well as thinking; and regards personal maturity as relevant to professional competence.

Teacher education [is] the task of moving the student from having learned deeply to readiness (and skill) to teach wisely. . . . This means, in essence, that a program of teacher education must provide a situation in which the student can experience a change in his own psychological stance, a shift in position from the role of the student, partly dependent and not fully responsible, to the role of the teacher in which he is the one to nurture, demand, judge, and appreciate. . . . Any teacher's capacity for teaching excellence at the classroom level depends upon the degree to which he has internalized a coherent rationale which regards teaching as an ever-changing process, involving not only a thorough grounding in substantive content and the psychology of learning and growth, but also a constant dynamic of actions, observation, analysis, and new hypotheses for further action. The theoretical basis for this dynamic rests upon a recognition of learning intimately related to the total process of development in child and adult, and the conviction that intellectual mastery cannot be divorced from affective experience if the goal is to facilitate personal and professional competence [pp. 4–6].

A critically important feature of the programs we studied is that they enable teachers to learn *about* practice *in* practice (Ball and Cohen, 1999), in settings that deliberately construct integrated studies of content, learning, and teaching, and create strong connections between theory and practice. In contrast to the eight-or-ten-week dollop of student teaching added to the end of traditional programs, candidates in each of these programs spend at least thirty weeks in classrooms while also engaged in coursework about teaching and learning. In addition, they study content in the disciplines while they are studying pedagogy.

As this discussion suggests, schools of education alone cannot prepare teachers well. It is critically important to develop a community for preparing teachers, within and beyond the university. This is important for political and substantive reasons, but doing so is much easier said than done.

In the programs we studied, we saw how faculty members in universities were able to create strong connections between the study of the disciplines and the study of education. They used strategies ranging from thematic studies across the college at Wheelock and a common ability-based curriculum at Alverno to planned intersections of coursework and advisement in the arts and sciences and education in five-year programs at Trinity and UVA and integrated content pedagogical courses at Bank Street and Berkeley.

We also saw how these programs were able to create partnerships with schools that did much more than offer placements for student teachers: engaging in mutual reforms that created common purpose and improved the quality of education in both settings. To unify the work of schools and universities, they needed to develop relational trust and a sense of shared turf, blurring the lines between the two organizations and working to integrate the kinds of knowledge each contributes to teachers' expertise.

Building Connections to the Field

The relationships described here were often built on the shoulders of other connections, such as USM's work in the Southern Maine Partnership, Trinity's creation of the Smart Schools Alliance, and Alverno's efforts on curriculum reform throughout Milwaukee Public Schools. In addition, as programs were more and more successful in training effective teachers who felt well prepared, they were able to rely on their own graduates as the building blocks of a growing community of educators who could help prepare the next generation. Wheelock's efforts to create interprofessional communities of practice were built on the ten PDS partnerships it had already developed. In the case of some large, long-standing institutions such as Bank Street, graduates had founded or become principals in schools that maintained strong professional development relationships with the college and staffed them with a large number of Bank Street graduates, thus creating a community of practice for both reform of schooling and ongoing preparation of educators.

As we described, many of these programs joined with local school districts to create PDSs where clinical preparation of novices can be more purposefully structured. Like teaching hospitals in medicine, these schools aim to furnish a site for state-of-the-art practice that is also organized to support the training of new professionals, extend the professional development of veteran teachers, and sponsor collaborative research and inquiry. In the most highly developed sites, programs are jointly planned and taught by university-based and school-based faculty. Cohorts of beginning teachers get a richer, more coherent learning experience when they are organized in teams to study and practice with these faculty and with one another. Senior teachers report deepening their knowledge through serving as mentors, adjunct faculty, co-researchers, and teacher leaders. Thus the schools help create the "rub between theory and practice" (Miller and Silvernail, 2005) that teachers need in order to learn, while creating more professional roles for teachers and building knowledge in ways that are more useful for both practice and ongoing theory building (Darling-Hammond, 2005a).

Dean Corrigan, one of the founders of the Holmes Group, predicted that "PDS will bring about a new type of school and college. The PDS is like a fishnet. If you pull one part of the web, you will change the rest, because the web is part of the system" (Watkins, 1990, p. A20). This deep-level change has clearly not occurred in every college that launched professional development schools (Teitel, 1992; Darling-Hammond, 2005a). However, intensive change did occur at USM and Trinity Universities, and pervasive, important influences of partner schools on teacher education practice were also obvious at Bank Street and Wheelock. Like the PDS initiatives Teitel (1992) studied, these substantially changed the experience of student teachers, giving them more models of practice and a schoolwide perspective, increasing interdependence and mutual support among student teachers and veteran teachers, creating a professional community, and changing how school and university faculty think about teaching and teacher education.

We were able to see the benefits of professional development school models in several contrasting contexts (described in detail in Chapter Six) and examine how these new organizational forms were created and sustained by both college and school commitments of personnel and funds. The success of these efforts seemed to depend at least in part on having a shared educational focus and mission, a functioning shared governance model in which PDS work was the responsibility of more than one liaison from the college and the school, and ongoing strategies to support time and staff for these efforts (to be discussed more fully under "Staffing Teacher Education"). In these cases, there were also schools offering strong instruction to diverse learners that were sufficiently engaged in reform to be useful sites for student teacher learning. The availability of such schools was a function of university faculty who were willing and able to work with individual schools, and networks of schools, on a continuing improvement agenda. Where partnership school efforts remained on the margin of the teacher education programs, these issues of developing a common agenda and staffing collaborative work had not yet been worked out.

Integrating the Work of Universities and Schools

Integrating the work of universities and schools is not an easy undertaking. As Ann Lieberman observed, most collaborative arrangements between schools and universities are "little projects that do little things—maybe even important things—but they are not part of the institutional fabric" (Watkins, 1990, p. A1). Professional development schools are a particularly intrusive way to create school-university collaboration. As Goodlad (1990) noted in propounding creation of PDSs, "the tasks and problems line up like a long string of boxcars on a railway track waiting for the little engine that could, with the bettors lining up to say it can't" (p. 282). Among the questions that must be resolved are: Who owns the knowledge? How can such initiatives be staffed and managed so that they intrude into the core of each organization rather than existing only on the margin through the work of individuals? How can long-term funding be achieved?

Fullan (1993, pp. 121–123) describes a related initiative among four school districts and two large universities in Toronto, which initiated a new field-based teacher education program linked to induction, mentoring, professional development, and school restructuring. There a common focus on collaborative learning guided the content of preparation, professional development, and school improvement. This afforded a concrete, shared focus for the initial work of the consortium. In addition, each partner committed to a six-year renewable term of participation and invested $20,000 annually to generate a base budget that helped to staff and support the work. This initiative, like those we studied, suggests that serious partnership requires an institutionally grounded model of educational change that differs from most transitory project-oriented efforts of the past.

For both parties, it means sharing costs and decisions they are accustomed to making on their own. At USM, for example, the partnership was strengthened as the university moved the teacher education program from a "soft money" funding model (in which it was treated like the university's continuing education programs in a pay-as-you-go fashion) to a stronger foundation as part of the regular university base budget system. To manage and teach in the program, each university coordinator receives one-half of a normal semester load. The school coordinator receives at least one-half of her or his salary from the school district. In return, the school district receives a stipend of $17,000 yearly (as of 2005) to help defray these costs. The university pays $600 to each mentor teacher; additional costs of the partnership are covered by the district, as part of its contribution to shared funding.

Perhaps even more important is the sharing of decision making and knowledge production. ETEP interns are admitted to the program by both the school site and the university. The school coordinators are considered members of the Department of Teacher Education and have voting rights there. Many teacher education faculty serve on school-site committees, and the university site coordinator for at least one site has served as a member of the district's leadership team. A new Compact with Portland Public Schools is focused on the continuum of teacher development—preservice, induction, and ongoing professional development—and is led by a steering committee of twelve people, four each from the teachers association, the district leadership, and the College of Education. Discussing the strength of these relationships, the Gorham superintendent commented, "They [USM faculty] are a tremendous resource for us. They have been so supportive of our work. I sometimes feel that they're part of our organization and we're part of theirs."

At both USM and Trinity, many courses were offered at school sites, often by school practitioners, and their content was co-determined by school and university faculty, with differences of perspective sometimes requiring negotiation. Even the faculties at Bank Street College and its School for Children described having to work hard to share their differing perspectives on teaching, learning, and preparation, sometimes finding they had a need for more communication even though they resided in the same building. In each site there were ongoing negotiations between the roles of the school and the university.

We saw some of the issues involved in these negotiations highlighted at USM, as school- and university-based faculty sought to balance coursework and classroom experiences—and give appropriate attention to the knowledge that could be derived from each—in their tightly integrated one-year program. As with the other programs we studied, ETEP interns are involved in simultaneous coursework and clinical work throughout the year, although their program is more condensed and intensive than those of longer duration. The immersion approach to candidates' training begins with their participation in classroom life at the beginning of the school year when there are no university classes. Courses are added a few weeks later and are scheduled after school hours, to minimize taking time away from working directly in classrooms. As course content is linked to teaching, theory and practice are juxtaposed almost daily. On the one hand, this greatly enhances the likelihood of integration between theoretical work and practical classroom experience. On the other hand, it can lead to questions about the value of knowledge that does not derive directly from practice or find immediate, practical applications, and it can create pressure that makes it difficult to maintain sustained, thoughtful attention to coursework. As one professor commented:

> Not all the knowledge that we have about teaching is in any one given place. The work that's done by researchers, by people working on language development, the work of Vygotsky, for example—all of this work has been critical in terms of expanding our knowledge. Gardner's work came from working with people who had severe injuries to the brain. [Knowledge] doesn't only come out of the schools. So you've got to have a bigger catch. You've got to have a bigger place to say what counts as knowledge.

The same issues arose at Trinity University, where concerns were raised that locating methods courses primarily in the schools limited the kind of knowledge and insights candidates could gain access to. Indeed, after our research was completed these courses were redesigned in collaboration with university faculty to tap broader professionwide knowledge. In this case and others, faculties have rolled up their sleeves to work through ways of integrating the wisdom of practice with the more wide-ranging lessons offered by research, to attain a stronger amalgamation of the two than is possible when they exist in parallel play.

Across programs, we saw how organizing courses and clinical studies around case studies, analyses of learning and teaching, action research, and performance assessments not only helped teaching candidates integrate theory and practice but also strengthened the shared norms and knowledge for the broader community of educators involved in their preparation. Where these activities were planted in university and school work so as to involve professors, supervisors, cooperating teachers, and other members of the school community, they created another set of substantive bridges among the sites where perspectives on practice were being built.

We observed that when the work in both places is connected by a common educational vision among the educators involved, a strong community of practice can emerge in support of teacher education. This suggests that the *content* of the shared work—the tools that allow members of the teacher education community to reflect on practice *in* practice together—is at least as important as the governance arrangements that often absorb the attention of those who are seeking to design new relationships.

Designing Institutional Incentives
for High-Quality Preparation

Historically, teacher education has been a low-status enterprise in higher education, and there have been few incentives for faculty to spend time developing and implementing good programs. On many campuses, faculty are penalized in the reward structure for such work by having to spend time on tasks that do not count toward promotion and tenure (Goodlad, 1990). Yet it was clear to us that teacher education is a high priority for a number of faculty members in these institutions, and that these faculty undertake a lot of work related to teacher education. In addition to their teaching load, they spend time in departmental meetings continuing the development of the program, planning and integrating courses and field experiences, administering and evaluating the various assessments such as performance tasks and portfolios that are placed at specific points throughout the programs, and serving on interdepartmental committees that treat cross-cutting issues. Many work directly in the schools and serve on committees with school faculty who are involved in curriculum development and management of field placements. Functions such as field placements that have traditionally been marginal and assigned to staff to protect the time of faculty who are busy with more "important" things are, and must be, in the laps of faculty if the program is to be tightly integrated and coherent.

To find success in these programs, faculty members must want to work as part of a team and participate in ongoing refinement of the program vision. They must be comfortable constructing their course plans and syllabi in collaboration with others and fitting what they do into a grand plan that takes into account both other courses and the connected work that will be done in the field. They must be interested in regularly sharing materials with each other and working together as a group. These are not the traditional norms of higher education. Accomplishing this kind of work depends on leadership that provides expectations, time, and supports for developing collegial norms and a focus on ongoing improvement; selecting and supporting faculty who value teaching and teacher education; configuring staffing so that the time-intensive functions of teacher education can be well and competently handled; and redefining the ground rules for tenure and promotion so that the service and scholarship of teaching and teacher education is recognized.

Incentives and Norms for Collegial Work in Support of Teacher Education

In the programs we studied, leaders supported time and incentives for collaboration around teacher education and gave visibility and continuing reinforcement to improvement efforts. For example, at Alverno College an institute program that supports faculty development and the ongoing renewal of the teacher education program is mounted three times each year: in August for three or four days, in January for three or four days, and in May for a week or two. At these times, all faculty in the college get together and study some aspect of teaching. Recent institute topics included critical thinking, group discussions, integrated curriculum, and gender equity issues.

Bank Street maintains two organizational structures to support curriculum development at the faculty level: the curriculum committee and program curriculum reviews. The curriculum committee includes faculty members from the several programs. This group comes together to propose and help design needed courses. Criteria for courses include the infusion of developmental perspectives, grounding in relevant research, and balance of theory and practice. In curriculum reviews, instructors are encouraged to present their courses to colleagues at monthly faculty meetings. This process allows instructors to share their craft, connect their work to what is happening in other courses, and guard against redundancy or exclusion of important information. It also helps ensure that faculty are up-to-date on courses so they can advise their students with knowledge of the course content and assignments.

The coherence of the Bank Street experience rests in part on the means by which faculty organize curriculum together; in part on the relationship between teaching, supervising, and fieldwork; and in part on how students are encouraged to integrate their learning through projects of various kinds. The learning process is under close observation by the faculty. As we conducted our research, faculty members were studying the developmental, social, and cultural concerns of career changers and older students, who had come to make up the majority of students at the college (Crow, Levine, and Nager, 1990). In another study, faculty were learning about the commitments and concerns of teachers of African American descent who were in the in-service program (Toppin and Levine, 1992).

Similarly, faculty at other colleges were involved in ongoing, collaborative inquiry into student learning in relation to the program's teaching and assessment practices. For example, as new procedures were introduced into an interview-based self-assessment at Alverno, the department and the college's Office of Research and Evaluation analyzed student performance to ask questions about how students took up self-assessment activities and how they understood the curriculum's advanced outcomes (Alverno College Office of Research and Evaluation, 1995). At Trinity, a study of program outcomes had just been conducted as part of ongoing faculty efforts to review and revise the program (Van Zandt, 1996). These processes were aided by college leadership through support of faculty time and consideration of such initiatives as valuable service and scholarship.

Promotion, Tenure, and Scholarship

In several of these programs, almost all the time of faculty is devoted to teaching and the teacher education program and to consulting work in local schools. Indeed, at USM and Trinity, many of the tenure-line faculty responsible for teacher education spend at least half of their time onsite in the PDS schools for which they are responsible as liaisons, along with school personnel. There they teach courses and conduct seminars, advise and supervise student teachers, and often work with veteran teachers as well on developing teaching and conducting research. Much of the research and writing done by faculty focuses on their teaching and their teacher education program. There is a strong emphasis on the scholarship of teaching and developing a scholarly attitude toward teaching, which has been to varying degrees legitimized in each institution, including the research universities.

In the Trinity model, university-based teacher education supervisors have been replaced by clinical faculty members, all of whom hold doctorates and occupy tenure-track positions in the Department of Education. Placed in their positions on the basis of their commitment to working concurrently in university and school settings, these individuals have split professional personalities. Each spends half of his or her time (on average, half of each workday four days a week) in one of the university's professional development partner schools. The other half of their time is occupied by the typical pursuits of university faculty: teaching, research, and writing. Because these university faculty spend such concentrated hours in the schools, they come to know these institutions well and be accepted as part of them. Principals and faculty know and welcome them. Other faculty at Trinity follow the traditional model; they too benefit from having some of their colleagues working in reforming schools. Noted one of the clinical faculty members, "[Our PDS work] brings added professional perspectives to

[Trinity] faculty. It's the kind of professional engagement that keeps [university] faculty rejuvenated and in touch with the real world of school."

At Trinity, reconceptualization of scholarship was confronted head-on when these clinical faculty positions were designed. At the time of our research, two of four clinical faculty members were tenured; the others had been recently hired. The Education Department faculty, with the blessing of the university president, who has final authority in tenure and promotion decisions, defined education research so as to enable clinical faculty to use publications resulting from studies conducted in the PDSs in which they work to be counted toward tenure and salary advancement. In its Position Statement on Scholarship, the department declared: "Professional development schools serve as effective laboratories for the scholarly endeavors of the clinical faculty from the Department of Education. The scholarly work has the potential of improving teaching and learning in the professional development schools, and at the same time strengthening public education throughout our community and beyond. We believe this form of scholarship is an integral part of offering high-quality professional preparation programs at Trinity University."

The president of the university took a personal interest in making sure that conditions for their scholarly production and review would allow teacher education clinical faculty to succeed on the university's terms. He made it clear he was willing personally to intervene to ensure that research on practice and research derived from work in PDSs, including work coauthored with school-based faculty, would be given appropriate recognition as scholarly work. Since the years of our study, at least one of the junior-level clinical faculty members has been promoted to associate professor.

Similarly, the University of Southern Maine adopted the conception of scholarship outlined in Boyer's *Scholarship Reconsidered* (1990), including the scholarship of teaching, integration, discovery, and application. Consideration of integrative and applied scholarship, as well as scholarship on teaching, broadens what is viewed as important inquiry beyond the constraints of conventional "discovery-oriented" research. In addition, it encourages public reflection on teaching. This enables teacher education faculty to engage fully in the demands of their work and make contributions to knowledge without undermining their opportunities for tenure and promotion. For example, one of the USM faculty who was a site coordinator when we conducted our study has since been promoted to full professor largely on the strength of his scholarship of teaching. This approach to scholarship, embraced by the American Association of Higher Education, extends beyond teacher education and is often endorsed in the arts and sciences, where faculty in anthropology, for instance, have gained recognition for their work in museums, and faculty in environmental sciences for their work related to enhancement of habitats.

Staffing Teacher Education

The distinctive expectations of faculty in many of these programs also require new approaches to staffing the programs and hiring instructors. In most of the programs (Alverno, Bank Street, USM, and Wheelock), many faculty who teach courses also serve as advisors to candidates, meet with them and review their work regularly, and supervise student teaching as part of their load. The responsibility of supervising typically includes teaching the weekly seminars in which students analyze and discuss their school experiences. This practice helps to integrate, for the individual candidate and for the program as a whole, the usually fragmented worlds of advisement, course taking, and clinical work. Bank Street faculty have written extensively about this "guidance approach" (Biber and Windsor, 1967) and about the importance of carefully selecting the advisor as teacher-counselor-supervisor for each student on the basis of a match between student needs and advisor skills. The advisor stays with the student throughout his or her entire program, coming to know him or her equally as a student within courses, a practicing teacher-in-training, and an advisee.

This structure for advisement and supervision differs significantly from the norm in many universities where supervisors are often short-term graduate students, adjuncts, or retired teachers rather than faculty members, where there is little continuity in the function and sometimes little warrant for the expertise of the supervisor, and where faculty members who teach courses rarely see their students (or the results of their work as teacher educators) in the field. This normally fragmented structure contributes to the traditional disconnect among courses, between coursework and fieldwork, and ultimately between theory and practice. In most universities, asking tenure-line faculty members to take on this kind of task would be viewed as impossible, given their responsibilities for research as well as their poor preparation for these kinds of tasks.

Related issues arise with selecting faculty to work in these programs, particularly since all of them have as a goal that faculty will be able to model the kind of teaching they would like candidates to undertake in their own classrooms. For example, consistent with the importance of teaching and teacher education in the culture of Alverno College, the faculty pay a great deal of attention to potential faculty members' teaching backgrounds in K–12 schools and their current capability to work effectively with teacher education students in a way that is consistent with the philosophy of the Alverno program. As program director Mary Diez noted: "We look for people who have preferably had recent experience in K–12 schools and solid experience. People who have been successful as teachers themselves. We are looking for people who are wanting to teach and focus their research on improving their teaching."

This description of an exercise given to two finalists for a faculty position at Alverno illustrates the careful attention faculty pay to hiring people who not only prioritize teaching but can also coach novices in line with the program's philosophy:

> When we hired X, we had [the two finalists] view a tape of a recent student teacher, and then we videotaped them giving feedback to that person. The first candidate sat down with the student and said, "Well, you should have done this, you should have done that." X sat down with the person and said, "Tell me what you were thinking as you designed the lesson and carried it out" and just drew from the student every point the other woman gave her. The other woman talked as if she believed in constructivism, but when you saw her interacting with the student, it was telling. We hired the second candidate.

At USM, all of the teacher education faculty, including the current and former dean, have had K–12 teaching experience. The same is true at Wheelock, which draws its faculty from among the ranks of experienced K–12 teachers. It does not seek to hire recent Ph.D.s, no matter how impressive, if they do not bring with them a distinguished teaching history. A large proportion of Wheelock faculty have a history of engagement in the civil rights movements of the last decades. Wheelock faculty consistently referred to their work as a "calling" or "vocation" or "mission." Such a view of teaching goes beyond technical views of professionalism; it is a form of professional commitment that is linked to principled social action.

This faculty must not only be good teachers and scholars of teaching, committed to a greater agenda, but also collaborative in their practice, since teaching rarely occurs in private. Team planning and team teaching are the norm, in both liberal arts and professional courses. Faculty plan together, teach together, and assess students together. They are in the habit of asking for and receiving feedback and critique from their peers and holding their teaching practice up to close examination and scrutiny. As one faculty member states, "Here you can't get by with being 'good enough.' The goal is to be excellent and you judge yourself harshly if you fall short of that goal." Evaluation of teaching performance occurs frequently and is taken seriously by administration and faculty. The core of the institution is devoted to the improvement of teaching. The dean of the Graduate Division described the entire institution when he said, "What distinguishes us is our common purpose, our belief that we are here to do the best for children, families, and communities. What holds us together is our single focus, the preparation of professionals who will fulfill the college's mission. Our beliefs run deep. They are not only what we teach in classes. They are what we live in the life of the college."

In research universities like UVA and UC Berkeley, it is not imaginable that all or most of the key faculty involved in teacher education could be tenured faculty who also serve as supervisors and advisors. Other solutions have emerged in these programs, unique to their institutional settings but sometimes more dependent on the commitments of individual professors, deans, or presidents. It is worth noting that, although they have developed strong university-based programs of preparation, these institutions created relatively weaker connections to schools with respect to long-term relationships and broader reforms of practice than the programs that had developed nontraditional roles for faculty and different incentive structures for their work.

The Curry School at UVA has worked under the guidance of two consecutive deans of long tenure to recruit a number of serious scholars of teaching and teacher education to its tenured faculty. Among the one hundred faculty in the school of education, a noteworthy subgroup are known nationally and internationally for their research on teaching and teacher education. They have been directly involved in designing the program and teaching selected courses, although management of some courses and most advisement and supervision is in the hands of nontenured instructors and staff. Continuation of a high-quality model like that developed by UVA depends on the steady commitment of leaders to hiring and supporting such faculty and keeping them engaged in the intellectual guidance of the program, while ensuring that nontenure-line instructors are also top-flight and integrally involved with faculty in building a coherent program.

At UC Berkeley, a unique quality of the DTE program is the direct involvement of research faculty as course instructors for the core seminar sequence of the program. A small cadre of ladder faculty decided to take on the design and leadership of a new program and teaching of the developmental sequence, which they did for twenty years. These faculty were hired for their research expertise measured in the traditional manner (publications in refereed research journals), something that does not always correlate with the knowledge, skills, or disposition to be a strong teacher educator. Yet they chose to take on the often-unrewarded and always time- and labor-intensive teacher education courses and, by their own admission, taught themselves to become teacher educators, recruiting other faculty to their cause.

Teaching methods courses are often taught by nonladder faculty with conceptual and pragmatic ties to the Graduate School of Education. Increasingly, a key criterion for instructors in these courses is recent classroom experience. In addition, math and science courses have tapped into the rich resources of the Lawrence Hall of Science. For instance, the math methods course for elementary teachers, offered in coordination with the core seminars, was taught by the director of mathematics education at the hall, who was also the coordinator of the nationally recognized Equals Project. A secondary mathematics education program, begun later, was headed by a nationally known professor and researcher in mathematics education.

Supervisors are selected in part from among doctoral students and partly from other corners of the extended professional community (employees of the Hall of Science, DTE graduates on leave from teaching), all with elementary school teaching experience. The DTE coordinator who led the supervisory team when we were doing our research received her doctorate from Berkeley after teaching for nineteen years in elementary and middle schools in Oakland. Before being appointed as program coordinator, she served five years as a supervisor for DTE. The coordinator oversees weekly two-hour meetings of supervisors. Grounded by discussion of individual student teachers, the sessions are a rich source of supervisory professional development and program improvement. In addition, the coordinator "asks to be invited in to observe the other supervisors' observations of their student teachers." In this way, she can support the supervisors as well as get to know cooperating teachers better, which helps her select and match placements with firsthand knowledge of teachers' practices. In addition, during supervisory team meetings as supervisors report on their observations and conversations with student teachers, her notes as often as not focus on the cooperating teacher's role, behaviors, and classroom comments, as well as on student teacher behavior.

For a substantial period of time, this model has been made to work within the context of the University of California at Berkeley. It began as an attempt to create an appropriate teacher education program for a prestigious research institution and was sustained in part through a valuable line of research. It has influenced, as the university mission mandates, other teacher education programs through impact on state policy. For instance, multiple placements and some background in human development are now state requirements. The program also influences other teacher education through the education its supervisors receive. An exemplary teacher education program at a nearby college, whose core faculty received their graduate education and their introduction into teacher education at Berkeley, is referred to in the area as "daughter of DTE." An instructor/supervisor in our study was later hired by Trinity University in San Antonio, another exemplary program documented in this book.

However, the process has been difficult. One founding member recollected that in the beginning "working with the CTC [state credentialing agency] was easier than working with the GSE [Graduation School of Education] at Berkeley." The basic tensions between the demands of a research orientation and those of a professional preparation orientation remain. For instance, discussing institutional support for the program, the coordinator noted, "We would get more resources if I wrote grants and published more about the program. It is so difficult to balance doing it and writing about it . . . a career buster because of the time and labor involved." For a period of time, DTE found research faculty with the ability, inclination, talent, and time to meld those two orientations, but some of the core faculty members have since left the program. A worry persists that DTE may end up a conceptually sound program with good students but headed for demise because of eroding support from ladder faculty. A question frequently posed and not yet answerable is whether construction of a high-quality teacher education program at a prestigious research institution reflects a sort of Camelot in higher education—a magical place at a serendipitous moment in time—or if it is ultimately sustainable.

Investing Resources Purposefully and Well

Clearly, the programs we studied have made important investments in the quality of teacher education and they have done so differently, rethinking how to organize and staff the enterprise to make it more productive and powerful in achieving its goals. Interestingly, research universities increased their investment in teacher education during the 1990s, when efforts were underway on the part of the Holmes Group and others to elevate the status and quality of preparation programs in these institutions, and by the end of the 1990s expenditures on teacher education in these institutions surpassed investment in teacher education at other kinds of universities (Howard, Hitz, and Baker, 1998). In some cases, programs were able to develop shared investment strategies with local school systems, developing partnerships to enhance the quality of teaching by addressing preparation, recruitment, induction, and ongoing professional development.

In addition to the PDS partnerships already described, schools pursued investment strategies that changed the way they conduct teacher education. One example is the technology infusion strategy of the University of Virginia, which was cited by NCATE and the U.S. Congressional Office of Technology as a model and, among the programs we studied, produced teachers who felt among the most skilled in using technology in their teaching. In what follows, I describe this process at UVA as a case of an innovative investment strategy with long-term consequences for program quality and outcomes. I then turn to broader discussion of the programs' policies and practices for selecting teachers, which is perhaps the most important and typically overlooked element of strategic decision making about investment: Whom should programs of teacher education invest in to achieve the goals of high-quality career teachers for schools?

Infusing Technology in Teacher Education: A Case of Strategic Investment

Between 1985 and 1995, and about a decade before most other education schools did so, the Curry School of Education became one of the first programs in the nation to fully integrate technology in the training of teachers. One important aspect of this process was the strategic vision that brought together resources and technology applications for conducting university business, enhancing faculty and student productivity, supporting the teaching process for faculty and student teachers, and helping local schools improve how they use technology with students by way of the assistance of student teachers (Mergendoller, Johnston, Rockman, and Willis, 1994).

This process was led by a dean who made education technology a priority and used internal and external funding to create an infrastructure of computer labs, electronic classrooms, and desktop computing throughout the school; involved library staff in teaching technology-based research skills; and used technology throughout the school to accomplish functional tasks ranging from e-mail to database searches.

UVA pursued strategies that have since become conventional for incorporating technology, such as creating computer classes for students, encouraging methods faculty to include technology use in their courses, and seeking student teaching placements in schools that incorporate technology. But it did several things that are particularly noteworthy as investment strategies that added to the success of the process and may be instructive for other reform initiatives.

First, part of the institutionalization of the reform was bringing it from the margin into the core of the program. Rather than relying only on peripheral staff, a tenured faculty member with expertise in technology was given long-term release from other duties to work with faculty on infusing technology into their teaching and work lives and to develop a research agenda around uses of technology in teaching. Within a few years, 100 percent of faculty had adopted some uses of technology, with 20 percent of them finding a research focus and another 20 percent making it a central element of their pedagogical repertoire in teaching. An Instructional Resources Center, run primarily by graduate assistants and undergraduates in the instructional technology program, was developed to support hardware and software needs, and a cross-departmental educational technology committee was created to advise on investments, thus drawing in faculty from across the school. In addition, technology use was infused into teacher education coursework throughout the program, not in a balkanized course setting, with candidates getting assignments and support for its use in every year.

One of these uses reflects the second innovative investment strategy: taking advantage of a publicly available resource through students' engagement with Virginia's Public Education Network (PEN). In the sophomore year course Tools for Discourse, students receive an Internet account with PEN that permits access to practicing teachers across the state. In the following year, when they take Computers and Media in Teaching, they participate in a newsgroup online conference, as well as mastering a variety of other technology tools for instruction. In their senior year, these technologies are explored within the context of specific subject matters. In the intern year, the schools in which they complete their internships are linked to PEN, allowing the intern, the supervising teacher, and the Curry faculty to confer via the electronic network throughout the teaching internship. By integrating a statewide, telecommunications network into preservice teacher education and the daily work of practicing teachers, the school was able to connect its university-based efforts with school-based changes that could, at no cost to either set of institutions, support their efforts to communicate well and improve their practice.

Development of Virginia's PEN actually started at UVA before it was taken on by the state department of education and was made possible by the school tapping into the university's Academic Computing Center, a key resource often ignored by schools of education. As one faculty member put it: "Traditionally, schools of education have not gone over to the computer center and developed a relationship. But teacher ed students pay the same share of expenses as engineering students, and deserve the same students. Computer centers need to give help and support to schools of education. . . . We couldn't do what we are doing without the technical expertise we find at the Computer Center" (Mergendoller, Johnston, Rockman, and Willis, 1994, p. 4.16).

Finally, Curry established technology partnerships with local schools providing useful field experiences for teacher education students while enriching the technological expertise of K–12 students and teachers. The tutoring that student teachers do in an after-school computer club is linked to their child case study, allowing them to try out their computer and teaching skills and research useful software for instruction, while also studying learning and teaching. Another practicum, tied to an instructional computing course, brought student teachers into classrooms to conduct computer-based projects with students, helping veteran teachers integrate technology into their classrooms.

The investment lessons that emerge from this case are several. First, it was critical that the work be organized as central to the enterprise of teacher education, for faculty and students alike, rather than organizing it at the margin of the enterprise and hoping it could poke its way into practice. It was supported not only through a sustained effort to access internal and external funds for hardware and software but also through support led by faculty who understood their colleagues and how the technology might be used, interdepartmental governance and faculty participation, and infusion throughout multiple courses and field experiences of the college.

Second, it was equally critical that the school look outside of itself to take advantage of other resources often ignored when programs behave like little red hens, trying to do everything themselves. The university's academic computing center and the state's Internet infrastructure were vital resources for this work that were readily available to support work both within the university and between the university and schools. The engagement of the schools in a mutually beneficial approach to training novice and veteran teachers while helping students was also a key factor, because the uses of technology—and incentives for surmounting barriers to use—were obvious once students and schools were benefiting. The partnership motif is a strong one in many of the essentials for transforming teacher education.

*Investing Resources in Candidates Who Are Likely to Succeed
and Stay in Teaching*

Not often considered when we think about investment of resources in teacher education is the question of whom these scarce resources should be invested in, given the societal purposes of teacher education. If teacher education is considered as not just a major students choose while making their way through college (a private choice and a private good) but as a profession that serves social goals and purposes, the question of selection into teacher education takes on new meaning.

Another question has to do with program effects: Are the investments these programs make actually value-added? Or might the successes of their graduates be largely a function of selecting high-ability entrants for the program? Framed yet another way, one may ask whether the kinds of programs we studied—intensive and rigorous in their expectations for study, commitment to clinical work, and ultimately to high performance in the classroom—could be implemented with less able or committed candidates.

For all of these reasons, we wanted to examine how the programs select candidates and with what outcomes. Every program we studied sent at least 90 percent of its graduates into teaching, and those that tracked retention several years later found a very high proportion of them (typically more than 75 percent) remaining in education. In our survey of graduates, we found that half identified themselves as teaching in urban schools, about twice as many as a national random sample of beginning teachers. These proportions were two-thirds or more for urban programs such as Alverno, Bank Street, and UC Berkeley.

All of the programs invest substantial effort in selecting candidates whom they feel have the capacity to become strong teachers. In addition to paper screenings for the usual indicators of academic ability (grades and in some cases test scores), all the programs ask candidates to write an essay about various aspects of their views of teaching, learning, and children, and most require in-person interviews.

However, the selection criteria are not always what one might expect. While places like UVA and Trinity look first for high academic achievement as measured by traditional indicators (both have students with average SAT scores well over 1100 and GPAs well over 3.2), they and all the other schools look for demonstrated commitment and potential teaching ability using their own indicators.

At UC Berkeley, which admits fewer than 20 percent of those who apply, candidates meeting high academic standards are overabundant. To choose a cohort, several people meet each candidate on interviewing days and later pool their views, seeking candidates who are child-centered and able to handle ambiguity and complexity. Next to its focus on children, "no one right answer" may be the program's guiding content. The faculty aim to attract "students willing to suspend their desire to learn the 'right way' to teach as quickly as possible while investing the time necessary to construct, for themselves, ways to put complex theory and research to work in their classrooms" (Black and Ammon, 1992). In addition to these ways of thinking, the program strives for diversity reflective of the urban schools it serves. When we were conducting our research, 50 percent of the program participants were students of color.

Bank Street also looks for certain kinds of thinking in its potential re-cruits. The admissions process includes multiple forms of evidence that uncover the candidates' experience and views as well as their academic preparation. These sources of evidence are aimed at assessing interper-sonal skills, attitude toward children, critical thinking ability, and strong commitment to continued learning and to education as a profession. The admissions process begins with an extensive written application form and review of previous academic record and of personal references. The appli-cation form includes questions seeking to understand the candidate as a potential "teaching person." Questions range from sentence completion such as "A child feels unhappy when . . ." to vignettes such as this one:

> A conversation between a ten-year-old and a student teacher:
>
> s.t.: What kinds of things make you mad?
> CHILD: I get mad when I know the answer and I raise my hand, and the teacher calls on somebody else.
> s.t.: Why does that make you mad?
> CHILD: Because then I figured out the answer for nothing.
>
> What are the issues in this situation? How would you respond?

Candidates are asked to write an autobiographical essay describing events that they feel are significant to the decision to enter the field of education. The application form also asks for educational background, references, experience working with children and adults, thoughts on other careers, reflections on learning experiences, and a statement of professional goals. The admissions process seeks students with a strong background in the lib-eral arts and sciences, good writing skills, evidence of analytic ability, and solid grades; however, standardized test scores are not required. The admis-sions director observed that "we have found that standardized tests don't really tell us anything about who is going to be a wonderful teacher."

The initial screening is followed by an onsite written essay on the day of an interview scheduled with one of the advisors. The interview gives candidates and advisors an opportunity to talk about the program, its expectations, and how it might best serve the interests and goals of the candidates and of the profession. Interviews are a chance to examine attitudes about children, families, and learning. Sometimes candidates who appear to have a superficial or romanticized vision of teaching are advised to visit schools, do some volunteer work, or take a course and return for a second interview later.

This intensive process might be viewed as suitable for only a very small program. Yet in the year of our study, more than six hundred applicants went through this process and more than three hundred enrolled the following fall. Faculty believe that a thorough and thoughtful admissions process helps the college and the candidates make better-informed selections of each other. As one long-time faculty member explained, "We have a responsibility to children and to the profession. It's better to take time in the selection process and avoid having to counsel people out of programs later on."

This care is a deciding factor for many candidates as well. As one student explained: "The application was so detailed that I trusted I would be taken seriously as an individual. They were really interested in who I was and why I wanted to teach. I felt that I had the opportunity to really find out what the profession was about and how I could be part of it."

At the University of Southern Maine, after applicants' transcripts and test scores are reviewed, faculty pay attention to their prior experiences, especially those involved with teaching and working with children, and to their responses to an essay question about learning and teaching. Then recruits who are still in the running must attend an open house describing the sites and sign up for interviews at the sites with school and university faculty before they can finally be selected into the program.

A more experiential approach is used at Alverno. Many candidates are nontraditional adult students who work and have children of their own and who are attracted to the college because of its social justice mission, because Alverno teachers are well respected and sought-out for jobs in Milwaukee, and because it favors a noncompetitive, effort-based, and supportive approach to education. Alverno does not give grades; it evaluates candidates on the basis of their achievement of each competency outlined in the curriculum. To achieve the diversity it seeks (25 percent of Alverno students are members of racial or ethnic minority groups, the highest proportion of any program in Wisconsin), Alverno recruits directly from Milwaukee high schools and from among paraprofessionals employed in the schools. Some recruits said they came to Alverno because they felt their low grades in secondary school would have precluded them going to other schools. At Alverno, they feel they have the chance to prove what they can do. Indeed, admission to teacher education is based on proven ability, effort, and commitment at several stages. This process yields so many insights on the process of learning to teach that it is worth describing here in some detail.

A faculty admissions and advancement committee handles all the decisions regarding admission and continuation in the program at all stages. Students can declare an education major as early as their freshman year. At the end of the first two semesters, students can apply to the preprofessional level of practice, which includes the first of four prestudent-teaching field experiences. At this point they need to present recommendations from their instructors and have completed among their courses a required human relations workshop and a portion of the math content requirement. After two more semesters and completion of two prestudent-teaching experiences, students can apply to be admitted to the professional level of the program. Here they must (1) show successful completion of the first two field experiences (and present letters of recommendation); (2) demonstrate the college's communication ability requirements at level three; (3) meet the statewide minimum cutoff scores on the reading, writing, and mathematics sections of the Preprofessional Skills Test; and (4) complete one of the several standard assessment exercises that are spread throughout the program, the Behavioral Event Interview and Self-Assessment. This hour-long interview gives students a chance to talk to a faculty member about their actions and thinking in relation to working with pupils. It focuses on stories elicited by questions ("Can you tell me about a time you came to a realization about children's development through an experience with a child?"). The students are then asked to use these cases as data for a self-assessment process focusing on the five advanced education abilities ("Where do you see yourself drawing upon ability X? Where do you see a need to strengthen this ability?"). The interview is audiotaped and students take the tape with them to complete a written self-assessment. They set goals for their next stage of development in their teacher education program and then meet for a second session with the faculty interviewer.

After completing two more semesters, including two more field experiences, students apply for admission to the full semester of student teaching. Here they must have successfully demonstrated communication ability at level four, completed all four prestudent-teaching experiences and another of the standard assessment exercises, Professional Group Interaction Assessment. Students also compile a portfolio that includes a videotape of their teaching together with a written analysis of that teaching in relation to the five advanced education abilities, cooperating teacher evaluations, and so forth. Candidates then participate in a half-day interview with principals and teachers from area schools who are part of a pool of more than four hundred educators who help assess readiness for student teaching. This approach focuses on what Alverno feels candidates really need to know in order to teach, and it results in a diverse, committed, and well-prepared group of graduates entering the field in high proportions.

Similarly, at Wheelock the admissions process values commitment to teaching and children over test scores, which are not a major factor in selection. Most candidates had at least B average in high school, but even more important all have had extensive child care experiences, whether as day care workers, camp counselors, community club leaders, or private tutors. The work, however, is rigorous and only those who are able, willing to work, and committed eventually become teachers. As one of the students, Angela, described her sophomore year, when she was taking Child Development as well as Principles of Inclusive Early Childhood Education, concurrently with Literacy and Numeracy: "The teachers expected so much. It was like they were weeding out who should be a teacher and who shouldn't. You had to work very hard and you had to do it all yourself. As I look back, I realize it helped me become a better teacher, but there were many times I wasn't sure I had what it takes to be a Wheelock graduate."

The experience in the two courses made Angela realize that teaching was going to be harder work than she imagined, that she would have to stretch herself to meet the challenges to be placed before her, that she had to rely on her own resources more than before, and that she needed to develop the ability to work well under pressure. Having faced these challenges, Angela felt she emerged from the experience with renewed strength and commitment: "In the end, I think they reempowered us after we almost all broke down. They reempowered us so we could empower children. After I finished the year, I felt I could do anything that anyone asked. I felt I was ready to be a Wheelock teacher."

Even given the strong processes of selection they engaged in, all of the programs were willing and able to provide intensive support, and if necessary weed out candidates who were not successful during the program. As stewards of the profession, they not only wanted to invest their resources in candidates who would become strong career teachers but also pledged to ensure that only those who could be responsible and effective teachers would enter the classroom.

What About Other Kinds of Programs?

We saw how careful selection and training in strong communities of practice were managed in the seven programs we studied. But is this degree of coherence and collaboration possible in the large schools of education that prepare so many teachers in the United States? In considering this question it is useful to note first that even though some of the programs we studied were relatively small, annual enrollment in teacher education ranged from three hundred to five hundred at Alverno, Bank Street, Wheelock, and the University of Virginia, all of which have managed to create well-integrated programs that carefully educate their candidates and have strong relationships with schools. But several of these institutions locate their primary mission in the education of teachers—a different proposition from that faced by many teacher educators in large state colleges, which may be less clear about their mission and poorly structured to overcome the fragmentation that plagues many traditional programs.

Fortunately, there are accounts of large colleges that have found ways to create the connections needed within and beyond the university to improve the education of teachers, often through vehicles such as the Center of Pedagogy envisioned by Goodlad's National Network for Educational Renewal. For example, Patterson, Michelli, and Pacheco (1999) document successful reform efforts that brought together education faculty, arts and sciences faculty, and school faculties around a common mission for teacher education at three distinct institutions preparing a large number of teachers: Montclair State University in Newark, New Jersey; Brigham Young University in Utah; and the University of Texas at El Paso. In many ways, their approaches resemble those of the programs we studied: developing a common vision, redesigning and connecting courses, creating school partnerships, and reshaping governance to include the parties that must work together.

It is also worth noting that colleges should consider what the optimal size might be for a program of teacher education to be successful in producing effective teachers and getting them to enter and stay in teaching. It is likely that somewhat smaller programs of higher quality could produce as many career teachers for the nation as the very large programs that have often functioned as "cash cows" with little selectivity or traction for long-term careers. As the National Commission on Teaching and America's Future (1996) noted, there is tremendous waste in the U.S. system of preparation, which invests too little in too many who progress along a leaky pipeline from possible interest in teaching to attrition both before and after they enter the profession. The report stated:

Many problems that undermine the creation of a strong teaching force are the product of mismanaged, uncoordinated systems that create snafus and inefficiencies at every possible turn. There is no way to comprehend what a hopelessly wasteful system of teacher preparation and recruitment we have in place without some understanding of how new teachers are prepared, hired, and introduced to the profession. All along the way, systems passively receive those who come to them rather than aggressively recruiting those who should apply; then they treat promising candidates with abandon, losing many along the way. . . . The first sieve is the pathway through traditional undergraduate teacher education, which many candidates enter not because they are committed to teaching but because getting a teaching credential seems like good job insurance [p. 34].

The commission noted that in many large undergraduate programs a substantial number of students have sought a degree in education without firm intentions of going into the profession or sufficient strong field experience to ensure that they can last and succeed if they do enter. Indeed, national data have suggested that only about 70 percent of undergraduate students who participate in teacher education programs actually enter teaching, and about 75 percent of them stay beyond three years—just over half of the cohort that entered preparation. By comparison, teachers prepared in five-year programs were found to enter and stay in teaching at a substantially higher rate (Andrew and Schwab, 1995), with more than 90 percent entering and more than 90 percent of them staying at least three years. This actually results in lower preparation cost to society per career teacher, once costs for recruitment, induction, and replacement due to attrition are taken into account (Darling-Hammond, 2000). (See Figure 10.1.)

The point of this analysis is not that all programs should become five-year models; clearly, many undergraduate programs and postbaccalaureate models do an excellent job of preparing teachers who enter and stay in teaching. The point is that colleges should evaluate how many teachers they can actually prepare well instead of using teacher education as a source of tuition to underwrite the costs of other programs.

Although many argue that colleges should boost the supply of teachers, there are actually more than enough newly prepared teachers each year to satisfy demand (more than 150,000 annually for the fewer than 100,000 slots that are filled by beginners). In 1999, for example, when U.S. schools hired 232,000 teachers who had not taught the previous year, fewer than 40 percent (about 85,000) had graduated from college the year before. About 80,000 were reentrants from the reserve pool of former

Figure 10.1. Average Retention Rate for Pathways into Teaching

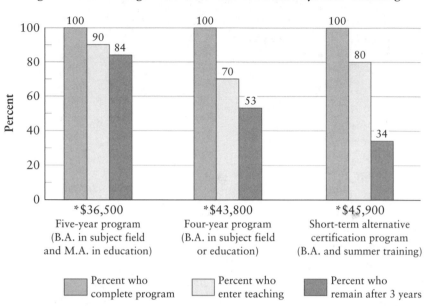

*Estimated cost per third-year teacher

teachers. Of the remaining 67,000, most were delayed entrants who prepared to teach in college but took time off to travel, study, work in another field, or start a family. In 2000, the 603 institutions counted in the AACTE/NCATE joint data system—representing about half of all teacher training institutions and about three-quarters of teachers in training—reported 123,000 individuals who completed programs that led to initial teaching certification. Thus the newly prepared pool that year was well above 160,000 (Darling-Hammond and Sykes, 2003).

The greater problem is retaining those who enter. This problem is related to the quality of preparation, since better-prepared teachers are much more likely to stay in teaching (Henke, Chen, and Geis, 2000; National Commission on Teaching for America's Future, 2003). Given that successful entry and continuation are higher where teachers are better prepared, colleges and policymakers should consider how to invest resources in ways that recruit individuals committed to careers in teaching and give them strong enough preparation so they can succeed and stay. These issues are explored in the final chapter.

DEVELOPING PROFESSIONAL POLICY

Not all the issues of teacher education quality can be handled by institutions transforming themselves. Of all programs in higher education, teacher education is among the most heavily affected by outside agents and policies. Other professional schools must also respond to forces external to the university because of their relationships with accrediting agencies, but teacher education feels the greatest impact of governmental regulation as well. In their efforts to regulate public education, state (and, recently, federal) agencies of government have increasingly sought to determine how teacher education programs will function. These influences reach to questions of curriculum, funding, admissions, testing, and accountability, among others. Furthermore, governmental management or mismanagement of labor markets for teaching has a strong effect on who can be recruited and how programs can be structured.

In what follows, I discuss several critically important areas of policy that influence the quality of teacher education, and ultimately of the teaching force itself: the effects of *standards* for licensing, accreditation, and certification; the *incentives* that are constructed for programs to improve their quality and for candidates to seek out and gain access to high-quality preparation; and the *labor market forces* that determine whether high-quality individuals will choose to enter teaching, where they will teach, and whether they will stay. I conclude with recommendations for a policy framework that can support high-quality teacher education and increase the odds that all teachers will have access to the knowledge they need to teach well.

Professional Standards

In recent years, new standards for teacher education accreditation and for teacher licensing, certification, and ongoing evaluation have been promoted as a lever for systemwide change in teaching (Darling-Hammond, Wise, and Klein, 1999). The National Commission on Teaching and America's Future (NCTAF, 1996) argued: "Standards for teaching are the linchpin for transforming current systems of preparation, licensing, certification, and ongoing development so that they better support student learning. [Such standards] can bring clarity and focus to a set of activities that are currently poorly connected and often badly organized. Clearly, if students are to achieve high standards, we can expect no less from their teachers and from other educators. Of greatest priority is reaching agreement on what teachers should know and be able to do to teach to high standards" (p. 67).

In organized professions, the major lever for professionwide transfer of knowledge and continuous improvement of preparation is the development and enforcement of professional standards through (1) professional accreditation of preparation programs; (2) state licensing, which grants permission to practice; and (3) certification (like board certification in medicine, psychology, and now, teaching), which is a professional recognition of high-level competence (Darling-Hammond, Wise, and Klein, 1999).

Such efforts represent "professional policy," an approach relying more on standard-setting by professional bodies than direct regulation by the state, on the theory that, where development and dissemination of professional knowledge is concerned, the most appropriate role for government is indirect. Because knowledge is always growing and its appropriate application is contingent on many factors, the process of developing and transmitting a complex knowledge base and ensuring its appropriate use is, many believe, better managed by members of the profession itself (Darling-Hammond, Wise, and Klein, 1999; Elmore and Fuhrman, 1993; Thompson and Zeuli, 1999).

Richard Elmore and Susan Fuhrman (1993) note: "As equality of opportunity comes to rest more squarely on the need for quality instruction, issues of how to enhance the professional competence of educators become more important. To ensure equal opportunity in today's context means enhancing, not limiting, the professional nature of teaching, and for that task state policy as it has been conceived in the past is hardly the best instrument. We need new ways of conceiving the state role and of the strategies at the state's disposal" (p. 86).

Professional policy delegates substantial authority to a profession while holding it more accountable for the outcomes of its actions. Professional policy emphasizes development of expertise to be used for problem solving rather than imposition of standardized prescriptions for practice that impede teachers' ability to meet the needs of the diverse learners they face. Together, standards for accreditation, licensing, and certification constitute a "three-legged stool" (NCTAF, 1996) that supports quality assurance in the mature professions. Although this three-legged stool has historically been quite wobbly in teaching, during the 1990s substantial efforts were made on all of these fronts and we saw some of their influences in our research.

Standard Setting Initiatives in Teaching

During the 1990s, efforts under way to develop and implement more meaningful standards for teaching included the move toward performance-based standards for teacher licensing, companion efforts to develop more sophisticated and authentic assessments for teachers, and development and integration of national standards for teacher education, licensing, and certification (Darling-Hammond, Wise, and Klein, 1999). These efforts were led by the National Board for Professional Teaching Standards (the National Board), an independent organization established in 1987 as the first professional body comprising a majority of classroom teachers to set standards and develop assessments for advanced certification of highly accomplished veteran teachers. The standards—and the associated portfolio assessments, which include teacher plans, classroom videotapes, commentaries about practice, and evidence of student work and learning—support a view of teaching as complex, contingent on students' needs and instructional goals, and reciprocal (that is, perpetually shaped and reshaped by students' responses to learning opportunities). By examining teaching in the light of learning, the board put considerations of effectiveness at the center of practice—a shift from the technicist era of teacher training and evaluation in which teaching was seen as implementation of set routines and formulas for behavior, unresponsive to either clients or curriculum goals.

Shortly thereafter, the Interstate New Teacher Assessment and Support Consortium (INTASC, 1992), a consortium of more than thirty states, began developing "National Board–compatible" licensing standards that also drew upon the new student learning standards being developed by such professional organizations as the National Councils of Teachers of Mathematics and English. The model standards for beginning teacher licensing—which outlined a core set of knowledge, skills, and dispositions supported by research on teaching and learning as central to teaching competence—were developed by a group of teacher educators, teachers, and directors of state education and certification under the auspices of the Council of Chief State School Officers. In 1994, the National Council for Accreditation of Teacher Education (NCATE) incorporated the performance standards developed by INTASC into its requirements, having previously strengthened standards for teacher education programs by emphasizing incorporation of research-based knowledge for teaching in the late 1980s.

The move toward *performance-based* standards by all three organizations placed the focus on what teachers should know, be like, and be able to do, rather than listing the courses a program should offer or that teachers should take in order to be awarded a diploma, license, or certificate. This shift toward performance-based standard setting is in line with the approach to licensing taken in other professions, which have used licensing tests and accreditation practices to clarify the criteria for determination of competence, placing more emphasis on the abilities professionals should develop than on the hours they spend taking classes.

The substantive connections among the three sets of standards form a continuum of development along the career path of the teacher, thus conceptualizing the main dimensions along which teachers can work to improve their practice. By furnishing vivid descriptions of high-quality teaching in specific teaching areas, "profession-defined standards provide the basis on which the profession can lay down its agenda and expectations for professional development and accountability; they clarify what the profession expects its members to get better at" (Ingvarson, 1998, p. 1).

The Standards at Work

In our case studies of exemplary programs, we observed how many of them were influenced by these standard-setting initiatives and used them to organize curriculum and assessment reforms. Although the programs were typically far out in front of the requirements of their states, in some cases state program approval standards also strengthened specific program elements.

INFLUENCE OF PROFESSIONAL STANDARDS. A critical element in the work of most of these programs was a set of expectations for teacher knowledge and skill that had been integrated into coursework, represented in the standards they used for evaluating clinical practice (for example, in student teaching), and codified in criteria for evaluating portfolios and performance assessments of candidates. The INTASC standards proved very helpful in this work. These standards were adopted or adapted in most of the states where the programs we studied were located.

The press toward performance-based standards was already growing across the country and the INTASC standards development panel built on the early work in several states, including Texas, where Trinity's work helped to inform the state's efforts. In Maine, the state launched an outcome-based teacher certification initiative in the early 1990s to move colleges toward a results-oriented approach to teacher education rather than a course-counting approach. The University of Southern Maine, selected as one of the state's three pilot programs, made the INTASC model standards the basis for developing outcomes and the criteria for evaluating its end-of-program portfolios. These criteria became the guideposts for the tightly integrated work of the program. The state later incorporated the standards into its expectations for all colleges.

In Wisconsin, the INTASC standards were incorporated into the state's program approval process through the work of the state teacher certification director and Alverno's education chair, both of whom were active on the panel that developed the standards (Ambach, 1996). Because of the state's involvement with INTASC and Alverno's many years of developing performance-based assessment in teacher education, the Wisconsin Department of Public Instruction initiated a major revision of the state code for teacher preparation and certification, which moved from specifying course content to requiring that each teacher education program outline the knowledge, skills, and dispositions it seeks to encourage in candidates and develop an assessment system demonstrating that they have been achieved. Similarly, in California, the INTASC standards were one foundation for the newly formulated California Standards for the Teaching Profession and guided reforms of program accreditation led by a professional committee headed by one of the leaders of Berkeley's DTE program. Thus, in synergistic fashion, teacher education leaders were helping to shape their state's standards while the standards supported their efforts to strengthen their programs.

In several cases, the colleges we visited had undertaken or were in the process of preparing for accreditation reviews by NCATE. These, we were told, helped them engage a broader range of school- and university-based faculty in conversation around the standards and how they played out in courses and learning experiences within and beyond the school of education. In at least two cases, the influence of the accreditation process was also fiscal: colleges of education were able to secure resources needed to strengthen their work as a side effect of preparing for NCATE accreditation.

How do standards like these actually shape what goes on in teacher education? An example from ETEP's outcomes is a case in point. Number three in the program's list of eleven desired outcomes reads: "The teacher plans and evaluates instruction based on knowledge of the learner, the subject matter, the community, the intended student outcomes, and the curriculum." Among the many kinds of knowledge, skills, and dispositions articulated as important for achieving this outcome are these:

> *Knowledge:* Understands learning theory, subject matter, curriculum development, student development, and motivation and knows how to use this knowledge in planning instruction to meet curriculum goals; knows how to take contextual considerations (instructional materials, individual student interests, needs and aptitudes, and community resources) into account in planning instruction that creates an effective bridge between curriculum goals and students' experiences.

> *Skills:* As an individual and a member of a team, selects and creates learning experiences that are appropriate for curriculum goals, relevant to learners, and based upon principles of effective instruction (e.g., that activate students' prior knowledge, anticipate preconceptions, encourage exploration and problem solving, and build new skills on those previously acquired).

> *Attitudes/Dispositions:* Values both long- and short-term planning; believes that plans must always be open to adjustment and revision based on student needs and changing circumstances [ETEP Outcomes, undated, p. 3].

Courses and assignments are developed around these statements of knowledge, skills, and dispositions to ensure that students have the chance to develop and demonstrate these abilities. Thus, for example, candidates in ETEP develop and teach curriculum units and lessons that are evaluated on the extent to which they meet the criteria described here. The outcomes provide a map for constructing the curriculum. In ETEP's case, the program's planning documents listed each of the eleven outcomes alongside the evidence used to evaluate its attainment through exhibitions, performance tasks, and other means. A twelfth outcome, proficiency in the use of technology, has since been added to these standards, to stimulate its infusion into coursework and fieldwork.

One reason we saw so many similarities among the programs we studied was that they were relying on common professional understandings of the knowledge base for teaching, incorporated into and further disseminated by standards of this kind. We observed how leaders in the teacher education community helped to conceptualize new standards for teacher licensing and how their efforts and those of state officials cause these standards to influence practice even more widely.

INFLUENCE OF STATE PROGRAM REGULATIONS. We also saw how some specific state efforts to create program approval standards influenced program designs in important ways. For example, long before most other states attended to issues of cultural and language diversity, California developed a CLAD credential for candidates preparing to teach culturally and linguistically diverse students, and enacted program standards for the coursework included in that credential as well as for core coursework to be offered to all candidates. Wisconsin required that all programs include student teaching placement in settings where candidates would work with diverse student populations, and included coursework to help them learn to teach these students well. These emphases were reflected in Berkeley's and Alverno's programs and in programs across these states—a case of standards moving the field forward in a more universal fashion.

Other state influences on improving teacher education could be seen in Wisconsin, where the Department of Public Instruction required cooperating teachers who work with student teachers to complete a course or workshop on mentoring student teachers and required one hundred hours of field experience prior to student teaching, which was lengthened to approximately eighteen weeks to match the public school calendar.

Continuing Problems in Implementing Teaching Standards

New teaching standards pose possibilities for raising the quality of teacher preparation (and they have proved useful in the efforts of high-quality programs to continue to improve their work), but standards cannot have widespread influence unless they are enforced. Performance-based standards, in particular, are difficult to evaluate unless good measures of performance are available. This continues to be an area in which teaching does not function as a profession, because standards are not consistent or uniformly applied for programs or for entrants to the occupation. Furthermore, although the National Board's efforts have created strong performance assessments of teaching, this kind of assessment is used for veteran teachers later in their careers and is not available for determining who can and should teach.

Although inroads have been made, there is still wide variation in expectations actually applied to teacher preparation programs, even among states that have, on paper, adopted versions of the same standards. As recently as 2001, some states required a college major or minor in the subject to be taught plus intensive preparation for teaching, including well-defined studies of learning and teaching and fifteen or more weeks of student teaching. Meanwhile, other states required no coherent program of studies in the field(s) to be taught, only a handful of education courses (not including the study of learning, curriculum, or content-specific pedagogy), and a few weeks of student teaching. One can argue that performance-based standards do not require the same input in terms of coursework and clinical experiences, but common sense suggests there are substantial differences in what teachers are likely to learn under these circumstances, and in most states there is no performance assessment of teaching skill that can be used to distinguish among the outcomes of diverse programs.

In addition to differences in the standards themselves, the extent to which they are enforced varies. Professional accreditation is voluntary in most states, and programs are typically approved by state education agencies, some of which have inadequate budgetary resources and person power to conduct intensive program reviews that would allow them to enforce high standards. During the 1990s, teacher education programs in some states were approved for more than fifteen years without any active external review.

In many of the forty states that have created alternative routes to certification, the programs offering such training are not subject to the same standards as traditional teacher education programs. Although some of these are well-constructed postbaccalaureate programs that ensure candidates have strong preparation in all of the areas they need to teach effectively, including well-supervised clinical training, others truncate coursework (focusing largely on classroom management and a few generic teaching tricks) and skip student teaching entirely, leaving new entrants with no models of good practice on which to draw in learning to teach.

It turns out that the urban school districts most likely to create alternative certification programs to solve problems of teacher demand also have relatively few resources to invest in teacher education. These districts typically do not have the financial or pedagogical resources to mount high-quality programs. Because they often have high turnover, there are relatively few expert mentor teachers to train novices, and they can rarely afford to free up many veteran teachers for intensive supervision. Districts with budget constraints also have a hard time making the case for investing thousands of dollars in preparing beginners, most of whom will leave for other occupations or suburban schools as soon as they are able. Thus even though alternative certification advocates voice hopes that these districts might have a stronger self-interest in teacher education than universities sometimes demonstrate, the quality of alternative programs is every bit as variable as that of traditional programs.

Even when state agencies identify weak programs, whether traditional or alternative, political forces within states make it difficult to close them down. A teacher education program can bring substantial revenue to a university or local community, and the availability of a large number of teaching candidates keeps salaries relatively low. As Dennison (1992) notes, "the generally minimal state-prescribed criteria remain subject to local and state political influences, economic conditions within the state, and historical conditions which make change difficult."

Finally, of course, there are many teachers who enter teaching on emergency permits or waivers without any teacher education at all. These candidates frequently do not meet even minimal standards when they enter, and researchers have found that pressure to get them certified in states where thousands are hired annually undermines the quality of preparation they ultimately receive. In California and Texas, among other states, unlicensed entrants have numbered in the tens of thousands annually, hired to teach to the least advantaged students who are thus denied the benefit of reforms of standards and preparation. Even if these candidates are required to make some progress toward a license each year by taking courses for teaching while they teach, the quality of preparation they receive is undermined (Shields and others, 2001).

Institutions that train emergency hires cannot offer the kind of tightly integrated programs we describe here in which candidates study concepts and implement them with guidance in supported clinical settings. They are forced to offer fragmented courses on nights and weekends to candidates who may never have seen good teaching and who have little support in the schools where they work. The part-time instructors who are often hired to teach these courses are not part of a facultywide conversation about preparation; nor do they have a sense of a coherent program into which their efforts might fit.

When these candidates work full-time, colleges often water down their training to minimize readings and homework and focus on survival needs such as classroom discipline rather than curriculum and teaching methods. Candidates often demand attention to classroom management and discipline techniques, without realizing that their lack of knowledge of curriculum and instruction causes many of the classroom difficulties they face (Shields and others, 2001). If they skip student teaching, colleges cannot weave good models of teaching into courses that would connect theory and practice, and candidates can only imagine what successful practice might look like.

Both recruits and employers find the outcomes of this kind of training less satisfactory than those of a more coherent experience that includes supervised clinical training along with more thoughtfully organized coursework (California State University, 2002a, 2002b; Shields and others, 2001). However, many districts hire untrained teachers even when prepared teachers are available because uncertified recruits earn less, and sometimes they are viewed as more compliant and easier to fire (Darling-Hammond and Sykes, 2003). In states where a large number of individuals enter teaching in this way, most programs are pressured to bend to this mode of entry, gradually eroding the quality of stronger programs.

Among the programs we studied, three of seven were in states where they (and other programs) experienced pressure to reduce the amount of time devoted to preparing teachers, admit candidates on emergency licenses who would require a fragmented program without student teaching, and short-circuit the clinical requirements that gave their other candidates the opportunity to learn to practice under supervision. They resisted these pressures, but the programs were keenly aware that they did so at a cost, and that other programs were not in a position to resist state, city, and market inducements to lower their standards. As Gideonse (1993) noted in an analysis of teacher education policy: "As long as school systems are permitted to hire under-prepared teachers through the mechanism of emergency certificates and their equivalent, teacher preparation institutions and the faculty in them will have reduced incentives to maintain standards by preventing the advancement of the marginally qualified to licensure. All the hype in the world about raised standards and performance-based licensure is meaningless absent a real incentive working on school districts to *recruit the qualified* through salary and improved conditions of practice, rather than being allowed to *redefine the available as qualified*" (p. 404, italics in the original).

Finally, standards for teaching candidates vary with the range of licensing examinations enacted in nearly all states during the 1980s and early 1990s. These too set very different standards of knowledge and skill in terms of what they assess and the kind of performance they require (National Research Council, 2001). In 2002, thirty-seven states required teaching candidates to pass tests of basic skills or general academic ability, thirty-three required them to pass tests of subject matter knowledge, and twenty-six required them to pass tests of pedagogical knowledge, primarily multiple choice in format (Youngs, Odden, and Porter, 2003). Only three states required performance assessments of actual teaching skill.

Although other professions control the content of licensure tests, teaching examinations are usually developed by testing companies or state agencies with little input from formal professional bodies. Where it is solicited, input from practitioners is usually limited to reviewing test categories and items. Teacher licensure tests are criticized for oversimplifying teaching, ignoring the complexities of instructional decision making, and adversely affecting racial minorities (Darling-Hammond, 1986; Haertel, 1991).

Creating Meaningful, Universal Standards for Teacher Education

This analysis points to the need to improve the standards and processes by which all programs of preparation, traditional and alternative, are evaluated, including creation of performance assessments that reflect competent teaching. The first issue is to develop a high-quality system for approving programs, one that is universally applied. In virtually all professions, candidates must graduate from an accredited professional school to sit for state licensing examinations that test their knowledge and skill. The accreditation process is meant to ensure that all preparation programs offer a common body of knowledge and structured training experiences that are comprehensive and up-to-date. Licensing examinations are meant to ensure that candidates have acquired the knowledge they need to practice responsibly. The tests generally include surveys of specialized information and performance components that examine aspects of applied practice in the field (lawyers must analyze cases and, in some states, write briefs or memoranda of law to address specific issues; doctors must diagnose patients via case histories and describe the treatments they would prescribe; engineers must demonstrate that they can apply specific principles to particular design situations; architects must present a portfolio of their designs. These examinations are developed by members of the profession through state professional standards boards.

COMING TO GRIPS WITH ACCREDITATION. Although required accreditation has been the major vehicle for transmitting knowledge and standards of practice across schools in fields such as medicine, law, and engineering, teacher education accreditation has been voluntary in most states. Only five states require schools of education to be nationally accredited; however, there has been progress in moving toward a system of professional standards for teacher education. Currently, forty-eight states plus the District of Columbia and Puerto Rico have partnerships with NCATE; twenty-five have adopted NCATE's unit standards as their own state standards, and the same number rely on NCATE's program review process in the subject matter areas. In seventeen states, all public schools of education (plus many private ones) are NCATE-accredited. In all, just over half of the nation's schools of education (seven hundred of the twelve hundred), educating about two-thirds of the country's entering teachers each year, are in the NCATE system.

Whereas advocates of accreditation are convinced that accreditation is necessary to create a common knowledge base and to leverage the resources for quality preparation that are available for other professional schools that have to meet clear standards, opponents complain about the costs and hassle involved in undergoing accreditation. Some university leaders do not welcome the idea of another professional school having a lien on resources created by outside accreditation. Some university leaders and faculty resent the lack of autonomy suggested by the existence of external standards. Many strained schools of education view accreditation as another bureaucratic hurdle they don't have time to implement appropriately.

Accreditation also poses local risks. A substantial proportion of institutions that volunteer for NCATE accreditation fail fully to achieve it on their initial attempt. (About 25 percent are conditionally approved or disapproved.) NCATE has been criticized by some for having standards that are too difficult to achieve and by others for having standards that are too low. Whereas many colleges that sat for accreditation report associated improvements in their faculty, resource base, curriculum design, and clinical work (see, for example, NCTAF, 1996, p.71; Williams, 2000), others have felt that the process did not stimulate major change in their institution. A paradox of the voluntary accreditation situation is that standards can never be raised beyond a certain level so long as institutions must decide whether or not to sit for accreditation.

It seems unlikely that the political and market pressures on state approval processes will allow states to exert standards high enough to put ineffectual preparation programs out of existence. It also seems unlikely that the standards exerted by national accreditation can be substantially increased—to insist, for example, on the kinds of program components and investments we observed in the programs we studied—until accreditation becomes required, as it is in other professions, rather than voluntary. Because accreditation may be the only policy lever capable of infusing common knowledge across the profession, a National Academy of Education (2005) report recommended that all programs of preparation, traditional and alternative, should be reviewed for national accreditation through a process that ensures they offer a coherent program with a strong, core curriculum and rich, well-supervised clinical experiences. Such a process, the academy argues, should take into account candidates' entry and retention in the profession as well as their demonstrated teaching skills through a performance assessment of teaching.

EVALUATING TEACHING PERFORMANCE. Interest in evaluating the outcomes of teacher preparation has led to a proliferation of teaching tests. Candidates must often pass as many as three or four tests to be admitted to preparation and licensed in a given state, and then take a batch of others if they move to a new state, thus making mobility more difficult. In addition, recent requirements under Title II of the Higher Education Act require reporting of the pass rate of a teacher education program on teacher licensing tests, and some states use this metric for program accountability. However, most teacher tests are multiple-choice assessments of basic skills or subject matter knowledge that do not measure much of what candidates learn in teacher education and do not furnish any evidence of whether they can actually teach. We found these tests meaningless in the work of the programs we studied. Being held accountable for such test scores does little or nothing to improve the quality of preparation for teaching practice, other than affecting entry and exit standards, sometimes in dysfunctional ways that have undermined programs in historically black colleges and diversity in the teaching force (see, for example, Irvine, 2003).

However, a few states require beginning teachers to complete subject-specific portfolios or other performance assessments to earn a teaching license. These assessments, modeled on those of the National Board for Professional Teaching Standards, more authentically measure candidates' ability to integrate knowledge of content, students, and context in making instructional decisions. For example, second-year teachers in Connecticut compile portfolios like those of the National Board, which reveal information about the logic and coherence of the teacher's curriculum plans, the appropriateness of their instructional decisions for students, the range of pedagogical strategies they use effectively, the quality of their assignments, their skill in assessing student learning, and their ability to reflect on their own teaching and make changes on the basis of evidence of student learning (Wilson, Darling-Hammond, and Berry, 2001). Teacher education programs in Wisconsin and California have borrowed from this strategy to embed similar portfolios in the teacher education process. The two states have looked to this kind of evidence as part of colleges' recommendations of candidates for initial licensure. Alverno and UC Berkeley are leaders in these initiatives.

One of these initiatives, the PACT (Performance Assessment for California Teachers) in California, was launched by the University of California campuses along with Stanford University, Mills College, San Jose State University, and San Diego State University in response to a state requirement that colleges use a teacher performance assessment as a basis for the initial license recommendation. The assessment requires student teachers or interns to plan and teach a weeklong unit of instruction mapped to the state standards; reflect daily on the lesson they've just taught and revise plans for the next day; analyze and supply commentaries of videotapes of themselves teaching; collect and analyze evidence of student learning; reflect on what worked, what didn't, and why; and project what they would do differently in a future set of lessons. Trained faculty and supervisors score these portfolios using standardized rubrics, with an audit procedure to calibrate standards. Faculties use the PACT results to revise their curriculum. In addition, both the novice teachers and the scoring participants describe benefits for teacher education and for learning to teach from the assessment and scoring processes:

> *The assessment piece* [of the PACT] *was good. . . . I could probably do this more often . . . really digging into their work and looking for what was going on. I should make that more of a habit next year than I have this year. (Prospective teacher)*

> *I think for me the most valuable thing was the sequencing of the lessons, teaching the lesson, and evaluating what the kids were getting, what the kids weren't getting, and having that be reflected in my next lesson . . . the teach-assess-teach-assess-teach-assess process. And so you're constantly changing—you may have a plan or a framework that you have together, but knowing that that's flexible and that it has to be flexible, based on what the children learn that day. (Prospective teacher)*

> *This* [scoring] *experience . . . has forced me to revisit the question of what really* matters *in the assessment of teachers, which in turn means revisiting the question of what really* matters *in the* preparation *of teachers. (Teacher education faculty member)*

[The scoring process] *forces you to be clear about "good teach-*
ing," what it looks like, sounds like. It enables you to look at your
own practice critically with new eyes. (Cooperating teacher)

It helped me as a teacher. Principals should learn it for their efforts
to help new teachers. (Cooperating teacher)

I have a much clearer picture of what credential holders will bring
to us and of what they'll be required to do. We can build on this.
(Induction program coordinator)

Some research suggests that use of portfolio assessments of this kind
can focus preparation programs on helping candidates attain important
teaching abilities (Tracz and others, 1994; Wilson, Darling-Hammond,
and Berry, 2001; Pecheone and Chung, 2006). Because the activities
teachers engage in center around authentic tasks of teaching that are
examined from the perspective of subject-specific standards applied in
the context of real students, they create a setting in which serious discourse about teaching can occur. Since evidence of the effects of teaching on student learning is at the core of the exercises, candidates and
assessors are constantly examining the nexus between teachers' actions
and students' responses. Making teaching public in a way that focuses
on the outcomes of practice can be the basis for developing shared norms
of practice across the profession (Shulman, 1998). Indeed, in Connecticut a shared set of understandings about good teaching and what good
teachers do emerged statewide as virtually all of the state's teachers
served as mentors, assessors, or candidates for the BEST portfolio assessments (Wilson, Darling-Hammond, and Berry, 2001). Such performance
assessments would be much more valuable than existing tests of basic
skills and isolated subject matter knowledge in giving useful feedback to
programs and in offering a tool for candidates and teacher educators to
look at practice together.

Incentives for Creating Stronger Programs

Policies that are effective combine the right mixture of pressure and support for change so as to increase the capacity for good practice among
the institutions that are the targets of the policy. Even though stronger,
more widely enforced standards for preparation programs and more useful and authentic assessments of teaching skills could yield guidance and

information as well as productive pressure for change, supports are also necessary. One set of supports has to do with teacher education funding—an adequate funding base for programs in general and a stream of funding that can allow the creation and institutionalization of school-university partnerships needed to support strong clinical practice. An adjunct to these supports is targeted funding for seeding the creation of high-quality teacher education programs featuring such partnerships in the urban areas where well-prepared teachers are most needed and least available.

Funding Teacher Education and Professional Development Schools

As noted earlier, requirements for teacher education accreditation often increase institutional investment in programs, as do reforms that capture the moral commitment of university presidents and provosts for educating teachers well. Government policy is also implicated in the low level of funding teacher education typically receives, because states generally provide support to public colleges and universities for programs of higher education, and they often allocate higher reimbursement ratios for programs in other professions than they do for programs of teacher education. We also found that, in some states, funds intended for teacher education programs were sent to the universities in a way that did not ensure they would actually be spent on those programs, and much of the intended funding leaked out of the pipeline before it reached them. Thus one area in which state action is needed is establishment of funding ratios comparable to what is provided for other clinically based professional programs, such as nursing or engineering, and targeting of those funds so that they are spent on preparing teachers.

An additional issue is the problem of collaboration between schools and universities when funding streams are targeted separately to each sector for specific purposes that do not include such innovations as professional development schools or other partnerships. Although more than a thousand PDS partnerships have emerged across the nation as sites for student teaching and development of good practice (Abdal-Haqq, 1998), they often lead a tenuous existence, on soft money or at the margins of institutions, and many have come and gone owing to the vicissitudes of changing budgets in school districts and universities. The sites we studied that had developed PDS models relied on university and district funds, as well as some outside grants. Some of them were quite successful in designing long-lasting models, but others experienced fluctuation in their partnerships because of funding issues.

Some states have sought to address these problems. In the 1990s, North Carolina created legislation to fund PDS partnerships launched by each university in the state. It encouraged all colleges to require and support a full year of clinical training for candidates, preferably in partnership schools. Like a few other states, it also required NCATE accreditation of all public colleges and universities and helped support the costs of acquiring accreditation, seeking to leverage change through higher standards and explicit supports for partnerships. As I describe shortly, North Carolina's package of reforms supporting stronger teacher education and recruitment was part of the reason for the sharp rise in student achievement the state experienced.

More recently, Maryland funded and required PDSs as part of its teacher education redesign initiative, using state funds and federal grants targeted to teacher education and professional development. Nearly four hundred PDSs were launched between the mid-1990s and 2004, designed to meet NCATE's standards for PDSs and the related INTASC standards embraced by the state and NCATE. By 2004, every college or university in the state had launched PDS sites, which served 92 percent of all teacher candidates in "extensive internships"; these sites also offered a substantial level of professional development for veteran teachers and teacher educators as well as novices. In an evaluation, early indications suggested that these initiatives were associated with stronger competence and retention of beginning teachers, which, the state noted, were in turn associated with reduced costs for induction and attrition (Maryland State Department of Education, 2004).

State and federal funding for such initiatives would help to institutionalize needed reforms of preparation and simultaneously improve key outcomes of teacher education: teacher entry, initial competence, and retention. Federal supports for PDSs would emulate the longstanding federal role under the Medical Manpower Act and the Health Professions Education Assistance Act, which support grants for training innovation and reimbursements for teaching hospitals through federal funding systems and third-party reimbursement formulas.

Seeding High-Quality Urban Teacher Education Programs

One critical factor in staffing the schools that are currently hardest to staff—those in poor urban and rural areas—is creating such high-quality programs where candidates are most needed. Teacher labor markets are in many ways still resolutely local. In many states, most teachers still teach in schools near where they grew up or went to college (Boyd, Lankford,

Loeb, and Wyckoff, 2005), and these locations are disproportionately suburban or small towns. Urban and rural schools must either lure applicants from other areas, which is often difficult, or enhance the pool of college graduates who grew up or went to school in these neighborhoods, suggesting a grow-your-own strategy for developing teachers to meet their needs.

Some cities have many higher education opportunities, but not all are affordable to local residents; nor do colleges necessarily have close ties with the district to facilitate an easy pathway from preparation to hiring. Thus many train candidates who have difficulty making their way through the cumbersome hiring morass that turns recruits away from city schools (NCTAF, 1996). The value of many alternate-route programs is that they finance and prepare candidates explicitly for a given district and streamline their hiring; thus the district reaps the investment benefits, and candidates know they will have a job. If these are high-quality programs, the bargain is a good one. If not, such pathways do not produce adequately prepared teachers who can succeed if they stay.

Federal grants, like those used in medicine to create "centers of excellence" and to develop community-based health facilities, could be offered to create or expand new model teacher preparation programs within cities where the problem is most severe. These programs would need to ensure a high-quality teacher preparation experience, attract local residents, and ensure a pipeline from preparation to hiring. Funding would be used both for program development and for tuition and living subsidies for candidates, tied to a service requirement in the local district. Ideally these programs would enable candidates to engage in practice teaching in PDSs that are particularly successful with urban and minority students, so that they learn effective practices rather than mere survival. Some programs might target both local residents and longtime paraprofessionals already knowledgeable about and committed to their communities, combining strong training targeted at local talent with strong incentives for hiring and retention in the district.

The cost of such an initiative would be modest. To create one hundred such programs located in the nation's largest cities, for example, by allocating $1 million annually to each program for five years, the total annual cost would be only about $100 million—a small fraction of the price of poor education and high attrition these cities normally bear. The models that emerge might include not only new forms of professional development schools used to develop state-of-the-art practices but also new applications of distance technology, new forms of collaboration between the private and public sectors, and new kinds of partnership among schools, districts, and the multiple universities (Darling-Hammond and Sykes, 2003). A critical goal would be to study the models that prove successful so as to disseminate the findings broadly and stimulate further reform.

Managing the Teacher Labor Market: Incentives for Recruiting and Distributing Well-Prepared Teachers

Almost all the structural conditions of U.S. schools exacerbate inequality in teachers' access to knowledge and students' access to knowledgeable teachers. The salaries that teachers can expect are lowest in the urban and poor rural school districts serving the most disadvantaged students with the greatest educational needs. The supports teachers will receive in the critical first years of teaching—both mentoring and physical supports such as adequate classrooms, materials, and supplies—are much less available in poorer districts, which then suffer greater turnover and must recruit a greater number of teachers. They often do this, ironically, by sponsoring backdoor routes and fast-tracks to teaching that only speed up the revolving door of candidates spinning through classrooms and being flung back out of the system.

Whereas many countries fully subsidize an extensive program of teacher education for all candidates, the amount of preparation secured by teachers in the United States is left substantially to what they can individually afford and what programs are willing and able to offer given the resources of their respective institutions. Although many U.S. institutions are intensifying their programs to prepare more effective teachers, they lack the systemic policy supports for candidate subsidies and programmatic funding that their counterparts in other countries enjoy. In states that have not developed induction programs or supports for teaching in high-need districts, programs are continually called upon to increase the production of new recruits who are then squandered when they land in an unsupportive system that treats them as utterly dispensable.

Lessons from Other Countries

Whereas the decentralized system of U.S. education tends to produce both exciting innovations and enormous inequality, some other nations take a more systemic approach to the development of teacher knowledge and skill that makes well-trained teachers more widely available to all students. For example, many European and Asian nations we might consider peers or competitors routinely prepare teachers more extensively, pay them more in relation to competing occupations, invest more in their induction, and give them more time for joint planning and professional development (Darling-Hammond, 2005b). They demonstrate that it is possible to develop an infrastructure for preparing high-quality teachers who can stay in teaching and continue to improve.

In the last two decades, many countries—including Australia, France, Finland, Germany, Hong Kong, Ireland, the Netherlands, New Zealand, Norway, Sweden, and Chinese Taipei (Taiwan)—as well as several provinces in Canada have moved most teacher education to the graduate level, adding in-depth pedagogical study and an intensive internship or practicum in schools to strong preparation in the disciplines (Cobb, Darling-Hammond, and Murangi, 1995; Erixon, Franberg, and Kallos, 2001; OECD, 1995). Interestingly, all of them now outperform the United States on international assessments, and they include most of the top-ranking nations in the recent international PISA (Program for International Student Assessment) evaluations, which focused on higher-order thinking and performance skills. (The United States ranked well below the median in mathematics and science, and just at the median in reading for fifteen-year-olds, even though it excluded far more students from testing than any of these nations.)

Finland is the greatest success story in these assessments, increasing its standing in all areas assessed to become first in the world in reading and scientific literacy and second (behind Hong Kong) in mathematics in 2003. The many articles about Finland's "secret" point to its dramatic overhaul of teacher education and teaching since the early 1990s, in a series of ongoing reforms based on continuous evaluation of its preparation system. Finland educates all of its teachers in master's degree programs that include strong content preparation and pedagogical preparation especially focused on learning to teach diverse learners well, including those with special needs, and to develop a reflective, inquiry-oriented approach to teaching.

Finnish universities sponsor "model schools" as well as other partnership schools where extended practica take place. All teachers complete a master's thesis that involves them in research on practice. Programs aim to develop "highly developed problem-solving capacity" that derives from teachers' deep understanding of the principles of learning and allows them to create "powerful learning environments" that steadily improve as they engage in a "cycle of self-responsible planning, action and reflection/evaluation" (Buchberger and Buchberger, 2004, p. 10). Spots in teacher education are highly competitive, and the government invests substantial funding in teacher education and research on teaching and teacher education (Mikkola, 2001). Salaries for teachers are equal across schools, with the exception of additional incentives for teachers who teach in hard-to-staff regions of the country.

Finland's strategic investments, though exceptionally intensive over a relatively short period of time, are not unique. In Germany, for example, prospective teachers earn degrees in two subjects and pass a series of essay and oral exams before they undertake two years of pedagogical training featuring teaching seminars combined with mentored classroom experience. Over the two years of internship, college and school-based supervisors observe and grade at least twenty-five lessons. At the end of this period, candidates prepare, teach, and evaluate a series of lessons, conduct a curriculum analysis, and undergo another set of exams before they are ready to teach. As one report noted of the system's rigorous standards and training, "In Germany, those who can, teach" (Waldrop, 1991).

In 1989, France undertook a sweeping overhaul of teacher education, motivated by the belief that elementary and secondary teachers needed to understand both subject matter and pedagogy more fully if their students were to succeed at more challenging learning. Now, after completing an undergraduate degree, prospective teachers apply for a highly selective two-year graduate program in a University Institute for the Preparation of Teachers. There they learn about teaching methods, curriculum design, learning theory, and child development while they conduct research and practice teaching in affiliated schools. Candidates are supported by government stipends, and they receive a salary in their final year of training, during which they take on a teaching position under supervision, much as a doctor does in a residency (Holyoake, 1993).

Japan also launched major reforms of teacher education in 1989, and Chinese Taipei (Taiwan) followed suit not long after. In both countries, the changes place more emphasis on graduate-level teacher education and add an intensive one-year internship to university training in education. After passing a highly competitive teacher appointment examination, beginning teachers are assigned to a school where they work with a master teacher who has release time to counsel interns. In these countries and others, teacher education is subsidized, and candidates pay little or nothing for this extensive training (Shimahara and Sakai, 1995; Cobb, Darling-Hammond, and Murangi, 1995).

Furthermore, teaching shortages are rare where salaries are competitive with those in other professional occupations. In Chinese Taipei, teachers' pay scale is pegged above that for civil service employees. Teachers receive a research allowance and 13.5 monthly payments, even though they don't work in summer and winter sessions. Primary and junior high school teachers earn tax-free income for working in the compulsory education system. In Japan, teachers' salaries are comparable to those of engineers and typically are 10–20 percent above those of other civil servants. The national government eliminates local disparities by providing 50 percent of teachers' salaries to bring them to the national level. Thus shortages are uncommon and seats in teacher education are highly competitive (Cobb, Darling-Hammond, and Murangi, 1995).

The practicum year in Japan, as in China, is also government-supported. By Japanese law, beginning teachers receive at least twenty days of in-service training during their first year in addition to sixty days of professional development on topics such as classroom management, computer use, teaching strategies, and counseling methods. Beginning teachers have a reduced teaching load, attend in-school training with "designated guidance teachers" twice a week, and receive out-of-school training weekly, including seminars and visitations to other schools. Master teachers have released time to counsel novices. For every two beginning teachers in a school, the local government assigns a full-time teacher to support induction activities. The national government covers half of all related personnel and out-of-school training costs (Cobb, Darling-Hammond, and Murangi, 1995).

New Zealand's Advice and Guidance Program for all beginning teachers during their initial two years in the classroom is similar, including in-classroom support from colleagues in the same curriculum area, opportunities to visit and observe experienced teachers, and meetings with senior staff and other beginning teachers (New Zealand Ministry of Education, 1995, p. 172). Primary schools that employ beginning teachers receive an additional 0.2 teaching entitlement per week for each new teacher's first year, to facilitate released time for the beginning teachers or senior staff working with them. At the secondary level, released time is allocated to the beginning teacher, who carries a 0.8 workload (Cobb, Darling-Hammond, and Murangi, 1995). Policies of this kind are foundations for learning to teach in many countries far less wealthy—and now, far higher achieving—than the United States. They demonstrate both the feasibility and the importance of getting serious about ensuring that teachers have access to the knowledge they need to teach well.

Policies for Supporting Teaching in the United States

U.S. efforts to reform teaching have resulted in high-quality learning opportunities for some teachers and innovative school designs for some students. However, systemic reforms that make these opportunities available to all have been more elusive. One thing the United States can learn from

other countries is how to build a policy infrastructure to make these opportunities widely available. This is especially critical given the dramatic
inequalities in students' access to well-prepared and well-supported teachers, strongly correlated with race and class, which exacerbate all the other
deep and long-standing inequalities in the American educational system.

It is no exaggeration to say that our nation is at a crossroads. We are
currently developing a sharply bimodal teaching force, just at a time when
the crucial importance of teacher quality has been recognized. Some children are gaining access to teachers who are more qualified and better prepared than in years past, but a growing number of poor and minority
children are being taught by teachers who lack training and are sorely unprepared for the task they face. This will turn the cracks into which many
children fall into chasms, despite the apparent drive to raise standards.

WHAT STATES CAN DO. To educate all our students to today's standards
requires a correspondingly high standard of commitment and competence
in the nation's teacher corps. Investment in teacher recruitment, support,
and retention, along with improvements in preparation and mentoring,
and equalization of resources have eliminated shortages and improved
teacher quality in some states and districts, with a corresponding rise in
student achievement. For example, during the late 1980s and 1990s Connecticut and North Carolina enacted some of the most ambitious teacher
legislation of any states. Both of these states, which serve large low-
income and minority student populations, coupled major statewide
increases in teacher salaries and improvement in teacher salary equity
with intensive recruitment efforts and initiatives to improve preservice
teacher education, licensing, beginning teacher mentoring, and ongoing
professional development.

Since then, North Carolina posted the largest student achievement gains
in mathematics and reading of any state in the nation, now scoring well
above the national average in fourth grade reading and mathematics,
although it entered the 1990s near the bottom of the state rankings. The
National Education Goals Panel also identified North Carolina as the state
most successful at closing the achievement gap between white and minority students during the 1990s (NEGP, 1999). Connecticut also posted significant gains during the 1990s. By 1998, Connecticut's fourth grade
students ranked first in the nation in reading and mathematics on the
National Assessment of Educational Progress, despite a substantial
increase in the proportion of low-income and limited English proficient
students it served during that time (NEGP, 1999). In addition, the proportion of Connecticut eighth graders scoring at or above proficient in

reading was first in the nation; Connecticut was also the top-performing state in writing, and the only one to perform significantly better than the U.S. average. A 1998 study linking the NAEP and the Third International Math and Science Study found that, in the world, only top-ranked Singapore outscored Connecticut students in science (Baron, 1999).

North Carolina's reforms, launched with omnibus legislation in 1983 and extended in subsequent reforms, boosted salaries in the mid-1980s and again in the 1990s; launched the North Carolina Teaching Fellows Program, which completely subsidized teacher education for thousands of able high school students; required schools of education to become professionally accredited by the NCATE; increased licensing requirements for teachers and principals; invested in improvements in teacher education curriculum, including the creation of PDSs to make sites available for yearlong student teaching practica; launched a beginning teacher mentoring program; and introduced the most wide-ranging set of incentives in the nation for teachers to pursue National Board certification. The state was recognized by the National Education Goals Panel report (NEGP, 1999) for having made among the greatest gains in mentoring for beginning teachers as well as the greatest achievement gains for students.

Connecticut's strategies were similar. The state's 1986 Educational Enhancement Act spent more than $300 million to boost minimum beginning teacher salaries in an equalizing fashion that made it possible for low-wealth districts to compete in the market for qualified teachers. The Education Enhancement Act and its companion legislation also increased licensing standards by requiring more intensive teacher preparation, including a major in the content area to be taught, and passage of basic skills and content tests, increased content pedagogical training, and preparation to teach reading and special needs learners. It eliminated emergency licensing, in part by enacting scholarships and forgivable loans to attract high-ability candidates into teacher education at the graduate and undergraduate levels and encourage candidates to teach in priority schools and shortage fields. It created a staged licensing process that included a beginning teacher program with individual trained mentors for all new teachers and student teachers and required ongoing professional development, including a master's degree for a professional license and continuing education for license renewal (Wilson, Darling-Hammond, and Berry, 2001).

Analysis of the outcomes of this initiative found that it eliminated teacher shortages and emergency hiring, even in the cities, and created a surplus of teachers within three years of its passage (Connecticut State Department of Education, 1990). By 1990, nearly one-third of the new teachers hired had graduated from colleges rated very selective or better in *Barron's Index of College Majors,* and 75 percent of them had undergraduate grade point averages of B or better (Connecticut State Board of Education, 1992). A report for the National Education Goals Panel (Baron, 1999) found that in districts with sharply improved achievement, educators cited the high and steadily increasing quality of teachers and administrators as a critical reason for their gains and noted that "when there is a teaching opening in a Connecticut elementary school, there are often several hundred applicants" (p. 28).

In addition to states that have created policy systems providing well-qualified teachers to their students, some urban districts have demonstrated that using a focused and comprehensive approach can make a major difference in teacher quality (see, for example, Darling-Hammond, 2005a, regarding San Diego; Elmore and Burney, 1999, regarding School District no. 2 in New York City; and Snyder, 2002, regarding New Haven, Connecticut). Although there is much that localities can do, the ultimate solution to current widespread inequities must include a strong federal role as well.

THE FEDERAL ROLE. Federal strategies for enhancing the supply of teachers have precedents in the field of medicine as well as teaching. Intelligent, targeted subsidies for preparation coupled with stronger supports at entry and incentives for equalization of salaries and working conditions could go a long way toward ensuring that all students have access to teachers who are indeed highly qualified. Since 1944, the federal government has subsidized medical training and facilities to meet the needs of underserved populations, fill shortages in particular fields, improve the quality of training, and increase diversity in the medical profession. The federal government also collects data to monitor and plan for medical manpower needs. This consistent commitment has contributed significantly to America's world-renowned system of medical training and care.

To address these needs, we need a comprehensive policy approach that provides a substantial, ongoing program of scholarships and forgivable loans to support individuals who prepare to teach in shortage fields and locations; investments in mentoring for beginning teachers to keep them in teaching; and incentives to reduce inequality in salaries and working conditions across schools and districts (Darling-Hammond and Sykes, 2003).

Increasing Supply in Shortage Fields and Areas

Although there is not an overall shortage of prepared and certified teachers in the United States, there are distribution problems caused by differential production of and demand for teachers across states and communities (heightened by funding disparities which make teaching in some locations much more appealing than in others). There are also differentials in production of teachers by field, in part caused by the varying opportunity costs for entering teaching for individuals skilled in high-demand and higher-paying fields such as math, science, and technology. Thus, even though most states have a surplus of candidates in fields such as elementary education, English, and social studies, there is an inadequate number of teachers in high-need areas such as mathematics, physical science, special education, bilingual education, and English as a second language (ESL).

Barring the unlikely eventuality that the United States begins to underwrite high-quality teacher education for all prospective teachers as some other nations do, these imbalances must at minimum be addressed by incentives to attract qualified teachers to schools and areas that have serious undersupplies. As it has in medicine for more than forty years, the federal government should launch a substantial, sustained program of service scholarships to underwrite teacher preparation for individuals who will teach in high-need fields and areas. Those desiring to teach math in an inner-city school, for example, would be prepared completely at government expense in high-quality programs. These service scholarships for preparing in undergraduate or graduate programs should be forgiven over the first four or five years of service in exchange for teaching in high-need fields and in high-priority schools serving a large proportion of low-income students, students of color, and language minority students. Because the chances of staying in teaching increase significantly after three years, the length of the service required would be important to the initiative's success.

Virtually all the positions currently filled by unqualified teachers could be satisfied in this way for only $800 million a year—less than what the United States currently spends in a single month in Iraq. Recent data suggest, for example, that the country may need to create incentives for up to forty thousand new teachers to fill positions currently held by unprepared teachers. If each candidate received up to $20,000, the money could cover full tuition at a public college or university for a one- or two-year master's program in teaching or for three or four years of undergraduate teacher education. Given that studies estimate losses in the billions of dollars each year resulting from early attrition from teaching (Benner, 2000), much of it a result of hiring underprepared teachers, this program would repay itself many times over.

Improving Teacher Retention

In addition to incentives for preparing to teach, it is critical to improve teacher retention, which creates the lion's share of teacher supply problems (NCTAF, 2003). About one-third of beginning teachers leave within five years, and the proportion is higher in many low-income urban and rural schools. Increasing the number of teachers prepared without addressing the high attrition rate is rather like pouring more water into a badly leaking bucket.

The costs of teacher attrition are enormous. One recent study estimated that, depending on the cost model used, districts spend between $8,000 and $48,000 for hiring, placement, induction, separation, and replacement for each beginning teacher who leaves (Benner, 2000). This study estimated that these costs in Texas alone ranged between $300 million and $2 billion per year. On a national scale, it is clear that teacher attrition costs billions annually that could more productively be spent on preparing teachers and creating better teaching conditions.

This kind of churn among novices also reduces overall education productivity, since teacher effectiveness rises sharply after the first one or two years in the classroom (Hanushek, Kain, and Rivkin, 1998; Kain and Singleton, 1996). It drains schools' financial and human resources. High-turnover schools must constantly pour money into recruitment and professional support for new teachers, many of them untrained, without reaping benefits from the investment. Other teachers, including the few who could serve as mentors, are stretched thin by the needs of their colleagues as well as their students (Shields and others, 2001). Scarce resources are wasted trying to reteach the basics each year to teachers who arrive with few tools and leave before they become skilled (Carroll, Reichardt, and Guarino, 2000). Most important, the constant staff churn consigns a large share of children in high-turnover schools to a parade of relatively ineffective teachers.

Teacher attrition is influenced by the extent and quality of initial preparation and mentoring as well as by working conditions and salaries. For example, teachers who receive student teaching are twice as likely to stay in teaching after a year, and those who receive the kind of preparation that includes learning theory and child development are even more likely to stay in teaching (Henke, Chen, and Geis, 2000; Luczak, 2004; NCTAF, 2003). Teachers who receive strong mentoring are also significantly more likely to stay (Luczak, 2004; NCTAF, 1996). A national teacher supply program should help to ensure that teachers receive strong preparation and supports in their early years, including a reduced teaching load, close fit between their qualifications and teaching duties, and mentoring from expert veterans.

Although many states and some districts have created induction programs, relatively few ensure that expert mentors in the same teaching field are made available for in-classroom support, the component of induction with the greatest effect on teacher retention and learning. The federal government should foster incentives for states to develop strong induction programs integrated with their licensure and certification requirements. Federal and state governments should support districts in creating programs that provide all beginning teachers with trained and qualified mentors in their teaching field who have released time to coach and model good instruction. To hone their professional skills, novice teachers should have reduced teaching loads that yield the time and opportunity to observe other teachers teaching, plan and confer with colleagues, work with their mentors, and reflect on their own teaching. These programs should be guided by sound assessment of teaching skills, like the performance assessments described earlier that reflect professional standards and help guide the learning process.

Improving the Conditions of Teaching

States and districts that have successfully solved teacher supply problems have purposefully worked to improve and equalize salaries, benefits, and working conditions. Too many urban districts are doubly disadvantaged in the competition for teaching talent. They have difficult living and working conditions, and they offer salaries below those of nearby suburban districts. As I have described, states that successfully raise and equalize salaries improve the access of urban schoolchildren to well-qualified teachers. School finance lawsuits in more than twenty states in recent years have raised the issues of students' unequal access to qualified teachers, and some states are beginning to develop new policies to address these complaints. The federal government can encourage more states to address these issues by sponsoring research on the success of various strategies and contexts. This might include systemic state strategies such as in Connecticut or North Carolina and local experiments with new performance-based compensation plans, like those now going on in Denver.

Experiments with extra pay for teaching in hard-to-staff schools (sometimes known as "combat pay") have generally proven ineffective, but some states and districts are exploring further innovation with compensation and working conditions that bear watching. For example, North

Carolina and New Mexico have instituted advancement on teacher salary schedules according to indicators of performance in teaching, such as National Board certification. California implemented $10,000 bonuses for National Board-certified teachers, with an additional $20,000 for such teachers in low-performing schools. This strategy was found to reduce inequalities in the distribution of board-certified teachers in comparison to other states (Humphrey, Koppich, and Hough, 2005). California also implemented its Teachers as a Priority Program, which sent resources to high-need schools to recruit and retain fully certified teachers through improving working conditions, adding mentors, reducing class size, and offering hiring bonuses. Unless these and other kinds of incentives are vigorously pursued, improvements in teacher education are not likely to influence the education of students in the schools where prepared teachers are not hired.

Finally, teachers are more likely to stay in schools where they feel they can succeed. In this regard, research stresses the importance of professional supports and redesigned schools to build learning opportunities for teachers and stronger teacher-student relationships that promote trust, motivation, commitment, and collective efficacy (Bryk and Schneider, 2002; Darling-Hammond, 1997). Many universities and schools seek to create these conditions in their PDS partnerships. Much more systematic work is needed to create schools designed for serious learning of adults and children throughout the educational system.

This broad policy agenda may seem ambitious, particularly in light of pronounced inaction in many states and the federal government over many years, but it is essential to address the contexts of teaching if we are to realize the benefits of investment in better-prepared teachers. In fact, the initiatives outlined here could be undertaken for less than 2 percent of the $350 billion tax cut enacted in May 2003 and, in a matter of only a few years, build a strong teaching force to last decades. Moreover, these proposals could save far more than they would cost. The savings would include the several billion dollars now wasted because of high teacher turnover as well as the costs of grade retention, summer schools, and remedial programs required because too many children are poorly taught. This is to say nothing of the broken lives and broader societal burdens that can be avoided if the nation ensures that all students have access to teachers who know how to help them become fully literate citizens of a knowledge-based society.

In the competition for educational investment, the evidence points strongly to the centrality of teacher quality to educational improvement. Although teacher education is only one component of what is needed to enable high-quality teaching, it is essential to the success of all the other reforms urged upon schools. Without thoughtful teachers who can implement new curricula, respond to assessments, evaluate student learning, and design successful learning experiences for students who learn in diverse ways, there is nothing that governments can do to improve student learning.

In terms of students' school success, their later employability, and their ultimate contributions to society, the benefits of investing in strong preparation for all teachers will repay the costs many times over. With carefully crafted policies that rest on professional standards, invest in serious preparation, and make access to knowledge a priority for all teachers, it is possible to imagine a day when all students will have access in every classroom to a "caring, competent, and qualified teacher working in a school organized to support his or her success" (NCTAF, 1996, p. vi). When that occurs, children will be substantially closer to securing what should be their inalienable right: the right to learn.

APPENDIXES

APPENDIX A: STUDY METHODOLOGY

THE RESEARCH USED A MIXED-METHODS, MULTIPLE CASE STUDY design to collect extensive data from interviews, observations, surveys, and document review about each of seven teacher education programs and the abilities of their graduates. The cases were purposively selected to be exemplars of programs that effectively prepare their graduates to teach the core concepts and central modes of inquiry of the disciplines so that they are deeply understood, and to teach diverse learners well.

Site Selection

The research team began by reviewing the literature for references to high-quality teacher education programs and by nominating programs known to members of the research team as having a strong reputation. This process resulted in a list of forty programs for initial consideration. With the information available, we reviewed programs against these criteria:

- The program prepares teachers to teach for understanding.
- The program prepares teachers to work with diverse learners successfully.
- The program prepares students for professional responsibility and for leadership, including commitment to the success of diverse learners and to working collegially with others to improve the quality of education.

This review reduced the number of programs to nineteen. We then sent the list of nineteen in a reputational survey to twenty-three teacher education experts, asking them to rate the listed programs and nominate others. The experts surveyed were asked to note the programs they felt were especially successful and rank-order their top five candidates, as well as identify any programs on the list they felt did not warrant selection.

We followed up to collect background information and outcome data for each program receiving multiple nominations from experts or the literature, including self-study data, surveys of program graduates, course evaluations, and articles written by faculty or outsiders. We also consulted leading educators in the local community to get firsthand information about program graduates. To be selected, a program had to have at least three kinds of testimonial and empirical evidence: testimonials about the outcomes of the program from teacher education experts who were part of a reputational sample or from regional practitioners (primarily principals and superintendents) who agreed that graduates are distinctively and consistently well prepared for "learner-centered" and "learning-centered" practice; evidence about program quality in the literature; and positive data on program outcomes and processes from surveys of graduates or other indicators collected by outside reviewers or program faculty for purposes such as self-study and accreditation.

From the fourteen programs that met these criteria, we selected seven to represent public and private universities in different parts of the country, educating both elementary and secondary teachers in different kinds of communities and in settings large and small. We wanted to study a diverse set of programs so that the findings might be more robust and useful for characterizing important features of programs that cut across contexts, as well as noting features that might be unique to a specific situation.

Focus of the Study

The focus of the study was descriptive, aiming to document the program goals, strategies, content, and processes used to recruit, select, and develop teachers. For each case, these central questions were included:

1. Why study this program? What are the goals and important features of the program, and what is the evidence of success? What evidence is there that recruits are sought after; that they enter and stay in teaching, especially in high-need schools; that their practice is effective for diverse learners; and that they take on leadership roles?

2. What are the program's goals, intentions, and design? What type of teaching does the program seek to help its students develop? What beliefs about teaching and teacher preparation undergird the program's design? What are the core features of the program? How is it structured, and why? Who are the students? How many? Where do they come from? How are they selected? What kinds of schools are they being prepared for?

3. What is the content of the program? What do students learn about learners and learning; about curriculum, teaching, and assessment strategies (including strategies for teaching students with diverse backgrounds and learning needs); about contexts and purposes for education? What

key ideas, areas of knowledge, and kinds of skills are deemed important for prospective teachers to learn? How do they encounter and work on these ideas? What kinds of formal and informal learning and practice opportunities are provided? How do these opportunities reinforce one another? How are students helped to confront their implicit views of teaching, learning (especially learning for deep understanding), and children (especially those different from themselves) and to consider other ideas and new knowledge? How are opportunities for inquiry and reflection built into the various aspects of the program? How are these scaffolded with a range of knowledge-building experiences? What do candidates learn as a result?

4. What are the processes of learning constructed by the program? What settings, activities, kinds of teaching, and other circumstances are created to support this learning? How are student-faculty relationships structured? How are courses and seminars structured and taught? (What is taught, when, and by whom? How are courses connected to one another and to clinical work?) How are clinical experiences organized and structured? What types of experience occur in what kinds of settings at what points in time? What are the goals? How are they managed to achieve these goals? What relationships with schools and school-based faculty have been developed? How are they managed to create learning experiences for prospective teachers? If PDS-type relationships have been created, how are they structured? How many students have access to this kind of experience? How do students talk about these experiences and their meaning for them? What is this set of experiences like from the viewpoint of those going through them?

5. What program supports make it work? Who are the faculty? What is the faculty-student ratio? What is their background and experience base? How did they come to do what they do in this program? What other human and material resources are important to the success of this program (for example, supervisors, cooperating teachers)? Are there financial aid supports for students? What about other tangible resources (funding, curriculum resources, and so forth)? What relationships have been constructed with other university departments, local schools, and community agencies?

6. What do graduates believe, understand, and do in their classrooms? How are diverse learners reached? How are they enabled to learn deeply? How is the practice related to what the teacher learned in preservice preparation?

7. What elements of the program context are salient to its success or challenges? What state and university policies and practices help or hinder

the work of this program? What are university policies regarding funding, accreditation, curriculum, admissions, and financial aid? What are state policies regarding licensing, program approval, innovation in higher education or K–12 education, and subsidies for candidates?

We wanted the case studies not only to carefully describe what the programs do and how they operate but also to look at how they deal with the core problems and tensions of teacher education. We identified several matters as worthy of attention:

o How the programs surface, confront, and deal with preexisting ideas about teaching and learning derived from the apprenticeship of observation, and how they transform beliefs about teaching and learning.

o How the programs create a productive "rub" between theory and practice.

o How the programs develop and integrate both subject matter knowledge and pedagogical knowledge, especially content pedagogy that fosters teaching for understanding—that is, teaching that helps students understand in depth the core concepts and modes of inquiry in the disciplines.

o How the programs help prospective teachers learn to think critically and diagnostically so that they can determine when particular theories and techniques are applicable, rather than merely applying routines.

o How the programs help prospective teachers move from being a student to becoming a professional who takes responsibility for others.

o How the programs prepare teachers for different contexts, including local schools and other schools they might teach in, such as schools that represent leading-edge practices that are not yet commonplace or schools that serve more high-need students, which often hire beginning teachers.

o How the programs balance their commitment to teacher education candidates and their obligations to children and the profession, including the need to support and screen candidates for teaching.

Data Collection

A research team was assigned to each program. Researchers were not assigned to review programs at the universities where they were employed. Data were collected over the period of a year for each program through a range of methods:

o *Review of program documents.* Some documents had already been collected for each program as part of the site selection process. They were augmented throughout the case study and included course catalogs, admission forms, syllabi, assignments, samples of candidate work (papers, performance tasks, and portfolios), accreditation documents, minutes of committee meetings and decisions, other descriptions of program plans and decisions, faculty publications about the program, and publications by other researchers about the program.

○ *Review of descriptive data on all teaching candidates for the previous three years,* including demographic information and information about teaching placements. These data were used to describe the program's students and their placements (and where available, their eventual teaching jobs), and the lists were also used for sampling interviewees and candidates to observe on the job.

○ *Interviews and focus groups with program participants.* At each site, interviews were conducted with approximately ten to twenty-five university teacher educators and administrators, depending on the size of the program, as well as with cooperating teachers in school sites. Interviews and focus groups were conducted with twenty to thirty students currently participating in each program. Students were generally selected at random for interviews, except where they had unique knowledge of a given program aspect and were selected for that reason.

Separate interview guides were used for each role group. In addition to specific questions about their individual courses, advisement, teaching, and assessment practices, teacher educators were asked about the program's overall goals, how they work to achieve these goals (as instructors, advisors, supervisors), and what they see as the strengths and weaknesses of the program. They were asked to evaluate the three traditional aspects of programs—subject matter learning, pedagogical learning, and supervised practice—and the connections among them, including specific opportunities candidates might have to learn and practice the specific elements of standards and objectives said to guide the program. Teacher educators were also asked how they know what candidates are learning and asked for evidence of this learning. Administrators were asked these questions and also asked for data about candidate characteristics, admissions, retention, and continuation in teaching, as well as what is done when a candidate does not meet the standards and must be further supported or counseled out.

Cooperating teachers were asked about their role, their view of the program's goals, their own goals when working with a student teacher, what they notice about students from the program in general and in comparison to students from other programs, how well prepared they view the students and graduates as being, and what they see as the program's and students' strengths and needs for improvement.

Students were asked about the program's goals, intentions, and processes; their agreement with them; their specific experiences in the program;
what they felt they were learning (and not learning) in courses and clinical settings, including evidence of this learning; and their assessment of
the program's general strengths and weaknesses.

○ *Observation of courses within the program.* Observations of key
courses were guided by a protocol designed specifically for observing
teacher education courses. Instructors were interviewed before and after
the course session observed about their intentions and interpretation of
what had transpired. Observations focused on the context of the course
(when the course falls in the program, how often it meets, nature of students and setting); content and organization of the session, including
connection to other material, courses, or clinical experiences students
encountered; teaching strategies and processes used to promote learning,
including the kinds of activities undertaken and questions posed; the roles,
responsibility, and involvement of participants; the relationship between
the ideas of the session and the practice of teaching; and the goals, standards, and assessments for students.

○ *Observations of other learning settings.* Candidates and university-
and school-based faculty were observed working together in supervisory
groups, advisement meetings, assessment conferences, and student teaching placements. Generally student teaching placements were selected
from a site where a program had a professional development school
partnership or another strong relationship, and observations throughout the school could be conducted. Faculty meetings, curriculum committee meetings, and planning meetings between small groups of faculty
were also observed to document the concerns and strategies of teacher
educators.

○ *Interviews with and selective observations of program graduates.*
Whenever possible, we randomly selected graduates to interview and
observe from the list of those remaining in the local region. Interviews followed the same protocol as that used with program participants, with the
addition of questions about current practices and views of preparedness
from the vantage point of being engaged in practice. These interviews
focused on graduates' philosophy of teaching; discussion of their classroom practice (including specific strategies and events observed in the
classroom by the researcher); how well prepared graduates felt for the
challenges of teaching; their appraisal of what specific courses and experience were most useful to them; and their continuing connections to the
program.

Generally, three graduates were selected for in-depth observation from a larger group who were interviewed. Graduates selected for observation typically had between one and three years of experience. The reason for the range of experience levels was that some evidence suggests the influence of preparation is more visible in the second and third years of teaching (and more recognized by teachers) than in the first year of teaching, when novices may feel overwhelmed. (However, it is worth noting that, although we certainly found second- and third-year teachers who were skilled and articulate about their preparation, we also found many first-year teachers who were already practicing with ease and sophistication, demonstrating much of what they had learned in their preparation.) Observation of classrooms was guided by a standard protocol following the same categories as that used for teacher education classes, but adapted to include evidence about activities and classroom management strategies for younger pupils.

○ *Surveys of program graduates.* Program graduates and a comparison sample of beginning teachers were surveyed about their views of how well prepared they were when they entered teaching, overall and across thirty-six separate dimensions of teaching, their feelings of self-efficacy, their classroom practices, their teaching experience and teaching context, and their demographic characteristics. These items were developed after reviewing other surveys of teacher education graduates used by more than twenty programs and were informed by the INTASC standards, those of the National Board for Professional Teaching Standards, and the literature about elements of teaching found to be important for teacher effectiveness. The survey items were piloted twice and fine-tuned each time. Faculty and administrators from each program were given the option of adding items to the surveys distributed to their graduates and graduates' employers. Four of the programs chose to add items.

The surveys were administered and analyzed by the Center for Educational Policy, Applied Research, and Evaluation at the University of Southern Maine. Surveys were mailed with postage-paid preaddressed return envelopes to all program graduates from the previous three years for whom an address could be supplied by the program. Surveys were also mailed to a comparison sample of beginning teachers with up to three years of experience. This group was randomly selected from a list of all members in the desired experience range furnished by the National Education Association, the nation's largest teacher association. A small monetary incentive of one dollar was included in the comparison-group mailing. The monetary incentive was not included in the research site mailings at the request of the program administrators. Follow-up postcards were mailed to all members of the sample approximately three weeks after the initial mailings. A total of 971 usable surveys were returned: 551 from graduates of the study sites and 429 from the comparison group sample.[1]

○ *Surveys of the employers of program graduates.* Each program was also asked to supply a list of principals who employed one or more program graduates during the previous three years. Surveys were mailed to these employers asking them about their view of candidates' preparedness as compared to other beginning teachers the principal employed and their abilities as teachers, and offering the opportunity for open-ended comment about the program.[2] The items paralleled the items used in the teacher surveys.

Data Analysis

Quantitative survey data were analyzed in several phases. (For details, see Silvernail, 1997.) First, item frequencies were reported for each survey item by site and group. Second, the survey structure was validated through a series of factor analyses employing the principal component method of extraction with varimax rotation. Items were retained with factor loadings of .40 and above, and factors were retained with Eigen values of 1.00 and above. The factor analysis resulted in identification of six factors for section A of the survey (perceptions of preparedness for dimensions of teaching), which included thirty-three of the thirty-six survey items in that section and accounted for 68 percent of the variance, with a full-scale alpha coefficient of .73. (See Chapter Three for further discussion of the factors.) These factors mirror the INTASC and NBPTS standards, suggesting a strong conceptual underpinning for the survey. Finally, comparison between the group of study programs and the comparison sample

---

[1] Some surveys were returned as undeliverable. The unadjusted response rates for all the programs were Alverno 59 percent, Bank Street 43 percent, Trinity 62 percent, UC Berkeley 68 percent, University of Southern Maine 52 percent, University of Virginia 44 percent, and Wheelock 43 percent. The unadjusted response rate for the comparison group of beginning teachers was 54 percent.

[2] Of 301 surveys mailed to employers, 44 percent were returned, with program breakdowns as follows: Alverno 46 percent, Bank Street 38 percent, Trinity 46 percent, UC Berkeley 52 percent, University of Southern Maine 49 percent, University of Virginia 25 percent, and Wheelock 70 percent.

was conducted using individual items and the factors. T-tests of mean difference were conducted for mean item ratings, and Z-tests of differences of proportions were conducted for item frequencies (for example, proportion of graduates feeling well prepared).

Qualitative data were analyzed beginning with the interview and observation protocols and aggregated through analytic memos organized around the research questions described earlier. These data were also integrated with findings from the quantitative survey data. Researchers developed themes based on the frequency of key ideas surfacing in interviews, observations, and documents, and they sought both triangulation and disconfirming evidence across respondents, data sources, settings, and events.

APPENDIX B: SURVEY RESULTS

Graduates were asked: "How well do you think your teacher preparation prepared you to do this?"

(Percentage answering "well" or "very well")	Comparison Group $N = 420$	Research Group $N = 551$
Teach the concepts, knowledge, and skills of your discipline(s) in ways that enable students to learn.	67	84**
Understand how different students are learning.	63	85**
Set challenging and appropriate expectations of learning and performance for students.	65	85**
Help all students achieve high academic standards.	55	76**
Develop curriculum that builds on students' experiences, interests, and abilities.	68	89**
Evaluate curriculum materials for their usefulness and appropriateness for your students.	58	79**
Create interdisciplinary curriculum.	56	82**
Use instructional strategies that promote active student learning.	78	91**
Relate classroom learning to the real world.	68	86**
Understand how students' social, emotional, physical, and cognitive development influences learning.	74	88**
Identify and address special learning needs and/or difficulties.	55	68**
Teach in ways that support new English language learners.	22	30**
Choose teaching strategies for different instructional purposes and to meet different student needs.	63	80**

Notes: *Z scores were calculated to evaluate the response differences between the two groups.*
$^*p < .05,$ $^{**}p < .01.$

(Percentage answering "well" or "very well")	Comparison Group N = 420	Research Group N = 551
Provide a rationale for your teaching decisions to students, parents, and colleagues.	62	79**
Help students become self-motivated and self-directed.	57	74**
Use technology in the classroom.	40	45
Develop a classroom environment that promotes social development and group responsibility.	70	86**
Develop students' questioning and discussion skills.	64	82**
Engage students in cooperative work as well as independent learning.	80	91**
Use effective verbal and nonverbal communication strategies to guide student learning and behavior.	74	79*
Teach students from a multicultural vantage point.	57	79**
Use questions to stimulate different kinds of student learning.	69	82**
Help students learn to think critically and solve problems.	62	85**
Encourage students to see, question, and interpret ideas from diverse perspectives.	54	77**
Use knowledge of learning, subject matter, curriculum, and student development to plan instruction.	70	86**
Understand how factors in the students' environment outside of school may influence their life and learning.	72	83**
Work with parents and families to better understand students and to support their learning.	45	63**
Use a variety of assessments (e.g., observation, portfolios, tests, performance tasks, anecdotal records) to determine student strengths, needs, and programs.	63	78**
Give productive feedback to students to guide their learning.	66	78**

(Percentage answering "well" or "very well")	Comparison Group $N = 420$	Research Group $N = 551$
Help students learn how to assess their own learning.	42	64**
Evaluate the effects of your actions and modify plans accordingly.	63	81**
Conduct inquiry or research to inform your decisions.	47	73**
Resolve interpersonal conflict.	43	60**
Maintain discipline and an orderly, purposeful learning environment.	56	65**
Plan and solve problems with colleagues.	45	72**
Assume leadership responsibilities in your school.	52	68**
Overall, how well do you feel your program prepared you for teaching?	65	86**

Notes: *Z scores were calculated to evaluate the response differences between the two groups.*
$^{*}p < .05, ^{**}p < .01.$

Graduates were asked: "How well do you think your teacher preparation prepared you to do this?"

(Percentage answering "well" or "very well")	Comparison Group N = 420	Alverno College N = 96	Bank Street College N = 62	Trinity University N = 69	University of California Berkeley N = 30	University of Southern Maine N = 85	University of Virginia N = 50	Wheelock College N = 159
Teach the concepts, knowledge, and skills of your discipline(s) in ways that enable students to learn.	67	94**	82**	77*	93**	75	86**	86**
Understand how different students are learning.	63	91**	82**	90**	90**	76**	72	89**
Set challenging and appropriate expectations of learning and performance for students.	65	94**	79**	93**	90**	76**	80**	84**
Help all students achieve high academic standards.	55	87**	59	85**	77**	66*	76**	79**
Develop curriculum that builds on students' experiences, interests, and abilities.	68	96**	97**	93**	100**	74	82**	90**
Evaluate curriculum materials for their usefulness and appropriateness for your students.	58	88**	87**	79**	100**	57	80**	78**
Create interdisciplinary curriculum.	56	91**	93**	92**	93**	78**	42*	80**
Use instructional strategies that promote active student learning.	78	96**	88*	93**	100**	89**	88*	90**
Relate classroom learning to the real world.	68	92**	84	93**	80	77*	82**	86**

Understand how students' social, emotional, physical, and cognitive development influence learning.	74	90**	88**	93**	93**	83*	72	94**
Identify and address special learning needs and/or difficulties.	55	68**	49	87**	60	51	66	78**
Teach in ways that support new English language learners.	22	30	21	38**	76**	16	10**	34**
Choose teaching strategies for different instructional purposes and to meet different student needs.	63	86**	64	84**	87**	75**	84**	78**
Provide a rationale for your teaching decisions to students, parents, and colleagues.	62	81**	82**	88**	97**	72*	82**	75**
Help students become self-motivated and self-directed.	57	81**	73**	86**	74**	61	58	79**
Use technology in the classroom.	40	85**	20**	64**	46	33	68**	24**
Develop a classroom environment that promotes social development and group responsibility.	70	86**	90**	87**	83*	78	80	88**
Develop students' questioning and discussion skills.	64	88**	90**	79**	90**	74*	80**	81**
Engage students in cooperative work as well as independent learning.	80	94**	95**	91**	97**	87	88	91**

Notes: Z scores were calculated to evaluate the differences in responses between members of the comparison group and graduates of each school sample.

* $p < .05$, ** $p < .01$.

(Percentage answering "well" or "very well")	Comparison Group N = 420	Alverno College N = 96	Bank Street College N = 62	Trinity University N = 69	University of California Berkeley N = 30	University of Southern Maine N = 85	University of Virginia N = 50	Wheelock College N = 159
Use effective verbal and nonverbal communication strategies to guide student learning and behavior.	74	86**	63	94**	70	70	78	82**
Teach students from a multicultural vantage point.	57	89**	87**	74**	87**	49	70*	85**
Use questions to stimulate different kinds of student learning.	69	87**	82**	82**	83*	71	84**	83**
Help students learn to think critically and solve problems.	62	92**	90**	90**	96**	74**	84**	82**
Encourage students to see, question, and interpret ideas from diverse perspectives.	54	88**	80**	85**	90**	59	72**	77**
Use knowledge of learning, subject matter, curriculum, and student development to plan instruction.	70	91**	80*	87**	100**	78	86**	84**
Understand how factors in the students' environment outside of school may influence their life and learning.	72	84**	77	93**	93**	71	78	89**
Work with parents and families to better understand students and to support their learning.	45	60**	66**	70**	60	43	39	80**

Use a variety of assessments (e.g., observation, portfolios, tests, performance tasks, anecdotal records) to determine student strengths, needs, and progress.	63	93**	68	90**	86**	79**	66	71*
Give productive feedback to students to guide their learning.	66	92**	68	88**	74	68	78*	76**
Help students learn how to assess their own learning.	42	88**	51	72**	63**	61**	50	59**
Evaluate the effects of your actions and modify plans accordingly.	63	92**	63	90**	93**	76**	84**	78**
Conduct inquiry or research to inform your decisions.	47	79**	69**	87**	93**	58*	78**	68**
Resolve interpersonal conflict.	43	69**	56*	67**	64**	49	44	61**
Maintain discipline and an orderly, purposeful learning environment.	56	59	47	80**	63	63	42	76**
Plan and solve problems with colleagues.	45	78**	69**	92**	87**	69**	64**	61**
Assume leadership responsibilities in your school.	52	82**	61	96**	74**	57	57	61**
Overall, how well do you feel your program prepared you for teaching?	65	92**	83**	93**	97**	83**	86**	85**

Notes: Z scores were calculated to evaluate the differences in responses between members of the comparison group and graduates of each school sample.

* $p < .05$, ** $p < .01$.

APPENDIX C: TEACHER EDUCATION PROGRAM STRUCTURES

Alverno College Elementary Education Program

The course of study in elementary education at Alverno College is divided into three levels, each one highlighting a stage in the development of the abilities of a professional teacher (see Exhibit C.1). The first three semesters (freshman year and the first semester of sophomore year) emphasize the *preprofessional* frameworks of the liberal arts disciplines while introducing some pedagogical ideas and experiences to students. During the preprofessional stage, students complete courses in the humanities and fine arts, natural sciences, mathematics, social sciences, general and developmental psychology, small-group interaction, and integrated communication. They also complete four professional education courses, a one-credit human relations workshop, courses on instructional design and educational computing, and their first of four pre-student teaching field experiences.

The middle three semesters of preparation, to which students are admitted on the basis of faculty recommendations and completion of specific ability validations and state-required tests, focus on *professional* teaching frameworks in relation to practice in the field. Students continue to take liberal arts courses while completing a series of three integrated language arts methods courses, and methods courses in the arts, social studies, science/ health, and mathematics. They also complete the three remaining pre-student teaching field experiences and a course on exceptional learners that includes an additional field experience.

The final two semesters are designated as the beginning of *professional practice*. During the third and final phase of the program, the students complete eighteen weeks of student teaching (two carefully chosen nine-week placements), a course in integrating the elementary curriculum, the student teaching seminar, and a culminating course in the philosophy of education where they engage in reflective scholarship.

363

Exhibit C.1. The Alverno College Elementary Education Program*

Semesters 1–3

Humanities and Fine Arts
Natural Sciences
Mathematics
Social Sciences
General and Developmental
 Psychology
Small-Group Interaction
Integrated Communication
Human Relations Workshop
Principles of Instructional Design
Introduction to Educational
 Computing
Field Experience 1

Semesters 4–6

Humanities and Fine Arts
U.S. History
Language Theory and Critical
 Thinking
Integrated Reading Curriculum 1, 2, 3
Methods (separate courses for Science,
 Social Studies, Arts, Mathematics)
Field Experiences 2–4
Exceptional Learner

Semesters 7–8

Integrating the Elementary Curriculum
Student Teaching and Seminar
Philosophy of Education
Coordinating Seminar

Note: *This list does not include courses taken in a student's specialty area.*

Bank Street College Childhood and Elementary and Early Adolescence Programs

The preservice programs that prepare early childhood, elementary, and middle school teachers at Bank Street College are master's degree programs that include thirty credits of graduate-level coursework plus twelve credits of fieldwork. Students have completed a bachelor's degree prior to entry; they then undertake a full academic year of advisement and practicum experiences, which incorporate several student teaching placements alongside intensive coursework focused on child development, language and literacy development, and content-specific teaching methods. Students who pursue their coursework in a concentrated fashion can complete the program in twelve to fifteen months. Most take two years to complete their degree. Some begin courses a year before they engage in the full year of student teaching and associated core coursework. Others start with the fieldwork year and begin teaching during the second year while they are finishing their course requirements.

Required courses at Bank Street are clustered into four major categories: development, foundations, teaching strategies, and curriculum design. There are many choices, but core requirements include courses in child development, teaching strategies, observation of children, family involvement, and curriculum development. Prospective middle-school teachers are as engaged in the study of children as are prospective early childhood and elementary teachers. The general outlines of the programs are displayed in Table C.1.

During the year of advisement and supervised field work, students take courses from each of these categories. Most courses are taken simultaneously with student teaching placements. Course assignments therefore typically include working with students, observing them, developing curriculum and trying it out, and working with parents. Students typically take a course in development and one of the curriculum courses during the summer prior to their advisement year because many cooperating teachers and advisors believe that it is easier for student teachers to start taking on teaching responsibilities in their placements if they have some background in these areas. If students are not yet in student teaching placements, their studies are connected to schools by conducting observations in classrooms and interviewing student or parents.

Trinity University

Trinity University's teacher education program combines academic rigor with the development of practical and innovative classroom skills in a five-year program culminating in a master of arts in teaching. It is a program grounded in a coherent vision of teacher education, anchored by a network of cooperative university-school partnerships, and aimed at producing teachers who will act, throughout their careers, as education change agents. The specifics of the Trinity program include:

- A required bachelor's degree in humanities for prospective elementary teachers and in one or more academic disciplines for secondary teaching candidates
- Undergraduate education coursework in areas such as child and adolescent development, education reform and policy, and schools and the community
- A minimum of 135 undergraduate hours in professional development school (PDS) settings
- Graduate-level coursework that continues to emphasize the connection between theory and practice
- A yearlong postgraduate (fifth-year) internship in a PDS under the tutelage of PDS mentors who serve as Trinity clinical faculty

Table C.1. Bank Street College Course Requirements

Early Childhood and Elementary Program	Early Adolescence Program
Child Development	Child Development with a Focus on the Upper-Elementary and Middle-School Years
Family, Child, and Teacher Interaction in Diverse and Inclusive Educational Settings	Group Processes in Adolescence and Issues in the Physical Development of the Early Adolescent
The Study of Normal and Exceptional Children Through Observation and Recording	The Study of Normal and Exceptional Children Through Observation and Recording
Curriculum in Early Childhood Education *or* Curriculum Development Through Social Studies	Curriculum Development Through Social Studies
Principles and Problems of Elementary and Early Childhood Education *or* Foundations of Modern Education	Assembly: Issues in Early Adolescence and Foundations of Modern Education
The Teaching of Reading, Writing, and Language Arts	Teaching Reading and Writing in the Content Areas for Elementary and Middle-School Classrooms
Language, Literature, and Emergent Literacy *or* The Uses of Language: A Perspective on Whole-Language Curriculum for Reading Programs	Children's Literature in a Balanced Reading Program *or* The Uses of Language: A Perspective on Whole-Language Curriculum for Reading Programs
Mathematics for Teachers in Diverse and Inclusive Educational Settings	Mathematics for Teachers in Diverse and Inclusive Educational Settings: Focus on the Upper-Elementary and Middle-School Years
Science for Teachers *or* Integrative Learning for Children in the Natural Environment	Special Study: Integrated Environment of the Hudson River
Arts Workshop for Teachers *or* Music and Movement: Multicultural and Developmental Approaches	Thinking and Learning in the Arts and Sciences: Physics for Kids
Supervised Fieldwork/Advisement (minimum two semesters)	Supervised Fieldwork/Advisement (minimum two semesters)

Fortuitously, at the same time as the humanities major was being developed, Trinity was in the midst of a universitywide curriculum reform effort. That work resulted in a new common curriculum for all Trinity students, which includes:

- A first-year seminar program (the topics of which change each year)
- A writing workshop
- Developing foreign language, computer, and mathematical skills
- Lifetime sports/fitness education
- Courses built around study in six substantive areas, what the university calls "six fundamental understandings": (1) Understanding the Intellectual Heritage of Western Culture (nine hours), (2) Understanding Other Cultures (three hours), (3) Understanding the Role of Values (three hours), (4) Understanding the World Through Science (seven to nine hours), (5) Understanding the Human Social Context (nine hours), and (6) Understanding the Aesthetic Experience (three hours).

The humanities major for education undergraduates fits neatly under the umbrella of the university's liberal arts requirements. Humanities at Trinity is structured around three strands of study: (1) Discovery and Innovation, which includes courses in art, sociolinguistics, mythology, world civilizations, music, religion, and comparative literature; (2) the City and Modern Life, encompassing classes in language, culture, society, art, literature, philosophy, sociology, and religion; and (3) Laws and Values, which spans politics, issues of law and justice, ethics, legal theory, and value conflicts in history.

Students select courses all of which are offered by the university's academic departments, from an extensive list of offerings. Many students specialize in a particular field, often achieving academic majors or minors in history, religion, or philosophy in addition to completing the general requirements for the humanities major.

An examination of the four-year transcript of a "typical" Trinity humanities major reveals, in addition to the required education courses:

- Thirteen courses in the social sciences and related fields, including history (American, European, and Asian), government, economics, philosophy, and religion

○ Eight science or science-related courses, including geology, anthropology, archaeology, and environmental science

○ Four English courses, including the Writing Workshop, and a course each in the British Masters, American Masters, and Shakespeare

○ Two mathematics courses, including calculus

Education coursework is structured in relationship to planned fieldwork with a specific theme for each year, moving from a focus on schools as organizations within communities, to teachers and teaching, to students as individuals, to an integrated perspective that puts these together (see Table C.2).

Table C.2. Education Coursework and Fieldwork, Trinity University

	Education Coursework	Fieldwork Connections
Year 1	School and Community	Observations in schools resulting in a school-based case study
	Current Issues in Education	School visits for research on a topic in education
Year 2	The Child in Society	Practicum 1: Study of the school; 3 hours/week with a PDS mentor assisting in the classroom
Year 3	Growing Up in America	Practicum 2: Study of teaching; close observation of many aspects of teaching while assisting in a PDS classroom
Year 4	Schooling in America	Practicum 3: Study of individual student needs; case study of a child completed while assisting in the classroom of a PDS mentor
Year 5	Curriculum, Teaching Inquiry, and Practice	Yearlong internship in a PDS under supervision of a mentor
	School Leadership, Supervision, and Evaluation	Plan and teach a curriculum unit Complete culminating research project on a problem of practice

University of California at Berkeley Developmental Teacher Education Program

The Developmental Teacher Education Program at Berkeley is a two-year postbaccalaureate[1] program that includes a year focused substantially on coursework and observation followed by a second year of intensive clinical experience with ongoing connected coursework. Professional preparation is integrated with the pursuit of a master's degree that culminates in an individually chosen research project relating developmental theory to teaching practice. Courses are sequenced to provide an opportunity for repeated consideration of teaching-related issues at higher levels of understanding over the two years.

Five student-teaching placements distributed over the two years make possible a gradual introduction to teaching through multiple placements in diverse settings where teaching issues can be addressed from increasingly higher levels of competence. The first two placements are each nine weeks in length, and the last three are each eighteen weeks in length, totaling seventy-two weeks of fieldwork, more than four times what most programs offer. Individual clinical supervision is provided by highly experienced staff. Although the introduction to teaching is gradual, the amount of supervision remains relatively constant over the five placements to support adequate reflection on teaching success and failure and to monitor the development of teaching competencies.

A small cohort of twenty to twenty-five students promotes establishment of collegial and cooperative relationships early in the teaching career. A weekly student teaching seminar that is flexibly organized promotes integration of theory and practice, small-group problem solving, and interaction between first- and second-year students. Research faculty participate as instructors, and there is an ongoing program of research and program evaluation.

Although the course list for the 1995–96 academic year (see Exhibit C.2) was different the year before and the year after, in fundamental ways DTE has not changed much in more than a decade. The sequence of development seminars, the multiple placements over the two years, and the use of the Bay Area Writing Project have remained intact. Although, as of this writing, the Lawrence Hall of Science is used less than in the

---

[1] California eliminated all undergraduate teacher education programs in 1970; thus, within the California context DTE is different because of its two-year time frame, rather than its postbaccalaureate design.

Exhibit C.2. UC Berkeley's
Developmental Teacher Education Program

Year One, Semester One
EP 211A: Human Development and Education—Cognitive and
   Language Development
EMST 235: Elementary Teaching in Math and Science
ELL 158: Foundations in Reading
EP 390C: First-Year Supervised Teaching

Year One, Semester Two
EP 211B: Human Development and Education—Individual and
   Social Development
SCS 283F: Education in Inner Cities
ED 289: Comprehensive Health Education
EP 390C: First-Year Supervised Teaching

Year Two, Semester One
EP 211C: Advanced Development and Education—Mathematics
   and Science
ELL 149: Foundations for Teaching Language Arts and Social Science
EP 390C: Second-Year Supervised Teaching

Year Two, Semester Two
EP 211D: Advanced Development and Education—Language Arts
ELL 246A: Teaching Linguistic and Cultural Minority Students
EP 207D: Assessment and Education of Exceptional Pupils in
   Regular Classes
EA263A: Education and Professional-Client Law
EP 390C: Second-Year Supervised Teaching

past owing to personnel changes there, new research faculty in elementary mathematics and science have taken a strong role in recent years. A new partnership with the Bay Area Arts Education Initiative (AEI), funded by the Ford Foundation, prepares teachers to integrate the arts more centrally into their teaching.

Another change is that the fifth and final field placement in DTE is now focused specifically on English language development. Pairs of DTE students not only assist regular classroom teachers with ELD but also design and operate after-school "ELD clubs" of their own for small groups of students. This emphasis reflects the impact of recent California policy initiatives that put a premium on preparing children for English-only (as opposed to bilingual) instruction. It is an opportunity for DTE students to consider how they can teach within that policy environment and still honor the home languages and cultures of English language learners.

Because of its unshakable convictions about the nature of teacher education, DTE is constantly changing. The changes, however, do not represent instability but rather steady, focused growth.

University of Southern Maine Extended Teacher Education Program (ETEP)

The University of Southern Maine's Extended Teacher Education Program (ETEP) is a nine-month, thirty-three-credit-hour graduate-level program that, at the time of this study, prepared approximately eighty students each year for certification in elementary and secondary schools. (Enrollment is now one hundred.) Candidates can continue on or return for graduate-level work to receive a master of teaching and learning (MTL) degree. The number of additional credits needed was eighteen at the time of our study; it is now thirteen. The success of the ETEP program has led to additional ETEP models since we completed this study: a two-year, less intensive version for prospective secondary teachers and two-year programs in elementary and secondary education that jointly award a traditional certificate and master's degree and certification in special education.

In the certification program, almost all fieldwork and much coursework take place in schools that are PDS partners in surrounding school district clusters. At the time of this study, they were Portland, Western Maine, Yarmouth, Wells/Ogunquit and Kennebunk, and Gorham. Recently, partnerships have been added in Southern Portland and a cluster of other districts in York County. Each of the five sites admits a cohort of fifteen to twenty students who progress through the internship as a group. The program follows the school calendar; candidates begin their placement when school starts for children and end it when school lets out, ensuring that they understand the entire cycle of the school year and participate as full members of the classroom teaching team.

This commitment to a practice-based program produces a grueling schedule. Along with student teaching each day in the classroom (recently reduced to 3.5 days per week in recognition of the intensity of the work), candidates take coursework almost every afternoon. In addition to the six-credit internship, they complete courses in literacy (six credits); Exceptionality and Life Span Development (six credits total); methods of teaching mathematics, science, and social studies (nine credits); and an internship seminar, which addresses learning, curriculum, and assessment (six credits). A typical student schedule is shown in Exhibit C.3.

The program is committed to a teaching approach that emphasizes ongoing, authentic assessment of student learning as the basis for making teaching decisions; use of a range of strategies appropriate to the needs of diverse learners; and intensive professional collaboration for the purpose of school reform. The eleven ETEP outcomes guide coursework and major assignments:

1. Knowledge of child and adolescent development and principles of learning

2. Knowledge of subject matter and inquiry

3. Instructional planning

4. Instructional strategies and technology

5. Assessment

6. Diversity

7. Beliefs about teaching and learning

8. Citizenship

9. Collaboration and professionalism

10. Professional development

11. Classroom management

Since we completed our research, a twelfth outcome, addressing technology proficiency, was added.

Exhibit C.3. University of Southern Maine ETEP Course Schedule

Monday	Tuesday	Wednesday	Thursday	Friday
Fall Semester				
Math and Social Studies Periodic Sessions 3:30–5:30 P.M.	Literacy and Writing 4:00–6:30 P.M.		Life Span Development and Exceptionality 4:00–6:30 P.M.	Internship Seminar 3:00–5:30 P.M.
Spring Semester				
Mathematics Methods 3:30–5:30 P.M.	Science Methods 3:00–4:30 P.M.		Social Studies Methods 4:00–6:30 P.M.	Internship Seminar 3:00–5:30 P.M.

University of Virginia BA/MT Program in Secondary Education

The UVA five-year teacher education program was launched in 1986, organized around the theme of "teacher as decision maker." Three major threads run throughout the program: technology education, special education, and multicultural education. Each cohort admits about one hundred students in their sophomore year. Four years later, they have completed the requirements for a bachelor's degree in a disciplinary field, a master's degree in teaching, and a teaching certificate in Virginia.

The first two years of undergraduate work are designed to help students develop knowledge and skills associated with a range of academic disciplines, including natural science, social science, humanities, foreign language, English composition, and fine arts. In the third and fourth years, students are expected to pursue one or more of these fields in greater depth and declare an academic major in one of them.

At the time of their application to the introductory course of the teacher education program (usually at the end of the freshman year), students must present a plan to take a distribution of courses, as part of the College Core Program, that will be completed during their first two years of study at the university. This includes twelve semester hours in the natural sciences and mathematics; ten hours in historical studies and social sciences; and six hours in the humanities, including literature, arts, philosophy, religion, and music, a demonstration of proficiency in a foreign language either through coursework or a placement test, and evidence of skill in English composition; and one semester hour in physical education.

All of these courses are part of the undergraduate core requirement for all undergraduates at the University of Virginia. Thus, any individual intending to pursue a teaching credential, whether at the elementary or secondary level, will meet these universitywide standards for the liberal arts degree. Further, all students preparing to teach at the secondary level must maintain a major in a subject matter field. Most students preparing to teach at the elementary level also choose a subject matter field for a major. Most individuals preparing to teach special education choose a major in psychology.

Because the program requires students to pursue their BA and MT degrees simultaneously over four years of the five-year program, students are continuously taking courses in their subject fields while pursuing professional studies. Though students in their freshman and sophomore years have not yet declared an academic major and will not formally be admitted to the teacher education program until the beginning of their junior year, they must complete a "permission to enroll" in the first course of the dual (BA/MT) program by the midpoint of their second year of college. This requirement begins to build the linkage between professional and academic skills. Taking advanced courses in specific disciplines concurrently with professional studies keeps the importance of subject matter foremost in students' minds. Each year of the program also has a thematic focus that guides the teacher education courses and associated fieldwork (see Table C.3).

Wheelock College Elementary Education Program

All of Wheelock's undergraduate teacher preparation programs have two distinct components: subject matter preparation and pedagogic mastery. The *subject matter* focus incorporates collegewide courses, traditional distribution requirements, and an academic art and science major. All students must satisfy the distribution requirement of thirty-six credit-hours by taking courses in arts and humanities (sixteen credits), natural sciences and mathematics (eight credits), social sciences (eight credits), and multiculturalism (four credits), developing problem-solving skills (four credits),

---

Table C.3. University of Virginia BA/MT Program Courses and Clinical Work

Courses	Clinical Work
Sophomore year	Teaching as a Profession
	Observations and interview in elementary and middle schools focused on schools as organizations
Junior year	Learning and Development
	Child case study
	The Exceptional Child
	Tutoring a special needs student
Senior year	Two courses in content-specific methods covering curriculum, instruction, and assessment
	Observe in classrooms
	Plan and teach lessons and a unit of instruction
Master's year	Contemporary Issues
	Field project in education
	Full-time student teaching

visual and performing arts (four credits), and human growth and development (eight credits). The major consists of thirty-two hours of course work in one of four interdisciplinary fields: arts, human development, humanities, or mathematics and sciences.

Each of the four majors is designed to meet two ends: to give students common interdisciplinary experiences and to allow them to develop individual interests and concentrations. The arts major offers multidisciplinary studies in music, theater, and the visual arts. Students gain a broad understanding in all three areas and then concentrate in one area for deeper understanding and competence. The human development major is the most popular major in the college. Rooted in the traditional disciplines of psychology, sociology, and anthropology, it offers students a common experience in the required eight-hour human development course and then the opportunity to focus on one of three perspectives: (1) personality and individual differences; (2) life span development; or (3) human ecology, the study of family, society, and culture. The humanities major is organized around the disciplines of history, literature, and philosophy. Students take courses that combine at least two of these disciplines and then select from courses that focus exclusively on one of them. The mathematics and science major profiles a basis for understanding three broad content areas: mathematics, physical sciences, and life sciences. Course work in this major emphasizes the connections among the disciplines and their relationship to the larger world. Though separate in disciplinary focus, all four majors are conceived in a multicultural perspective and offer a variety of multicultural courses and experiences.

Pedagogic study takes place in a set of required courses, including Principles of Inclusive Early Childhood Care and Education, and at least one course in literacy and numeracy. Two other courses, which may be taken in the sophomore or junior year, either before or in conjunction with the first of two required practica, are Multicultural Teaching and Learning, and Assessment of Young Children. Almost all courses are linked to supervised field placements, from the freshman year through to graduation.

The *supervised clinical practice* component of the program culminates in completion of two major field placements, one lasting 300 hours and the other 150 hours, in the last two years of study. Each of these is linked to an integrated curriculum course (Curriculum Development for Inclusive Early Childhood Settings) and a seminar. One focuses on children ages birth to five years and one on children ages K–3. At least one of the major practica must take place in a multicultural setting, and at least one setting must include special needs children. This integrated core is taught on a rotation by several faculty members each semester using a common syllabus. Students spend at least twenty-seven hours each week in their field placement sites assuming increasingly more responsibilities as the semester progresses for "managing the learning environment, using varied teaching strategies, facilitating play, developing an integrated curriculum, and relating to parents and other professionals" (course syllabus). The culminating experience is a senior capstone course on the history and philosophy of education that studies pedagogy, philosophy, and advocacy (see Exhibit C.4).

Exhibit C.4. Wheelock College Early Childhood Care and Education Program

College requirements:	26 credits—required courses
Distribution requirements:	32 credits in arts, humanities, and natural sciences, mathematics, social science, and multiculturalism
Major:	32 credits in one of four majors: arts, human development, humanities, or mathematics/science
Professional studies:	36 credits including individual courses in:

- Basic Principles of Early Childhood Education
- Human Development
- Literacy
- Numeracy
- Multicultural Teaching
- Assessment of Young Children
- Integrated core of:
  Curriculum Development for Inclusive Early Childhood Settings (2 courses: birth–5 years, K–3)

  Seminar + 300-hour practicum

  Seminar + 150-hour practicum

- Capstone

Electives:	8 credits in any discipline

REFERENCES

Abdal-Haqq, I. *Professional Development Schools: Weighing the Evidence.* Thousand Oaks, Calif.: Corwin Press, 1998.

Alexander, C., and Fuller, E. "Does Teacher Certification Matter? Teacher Certification and Middle School Mathematics Achievement in Texas." Paper presented at the American Educational Research Association Annual Meeting, San Diego, Calif., April 2004.

Allinder, R. M. "The Relationship Between Efficacy and the Instructional Practices of Special Education Teachers and Consultants." *Teacher Education and Special Education,* 1994, *17,* 86–95.

Alverno College Faculty. *Handbook for Cooperating Teachers of Alverno College Field Work Students and Student Teachers.* Milwaukee, Wisc.: Alverno College, 1992.

Alverno College Faculty. *Ability-Based Learning Program.* Milwaukee, Wis.: Alverno College Faculty, 1994.

Alverno College Faculty. *Handbook for Education Students, Part Two: Conceptual Frameworks.* Milwaukee, Wis.: Alverno College, 1995.

Alverno College Faculty. *Ability-Based Learning Program: Teacher Education.* Milwaukee, Wis.: Alverno College, 1996.

Alverno College Office of Research and Evaluation. *Self-Assessment in Key Teacher Education Assessments.* Milwaukee, Wis.: Office of Research and Evaluation, Alverno College, 1995.

Amarel, M. "Some Observations on a Model of Professional Training: The Developmental Teacher Education Program." *Genetic Epistemologist,* 1989, *17*(4), 31–34.

Ambach, G. "Standards for Teachers: Potential for Improving Practice." *Kappan,* 1996, *78*(3), 207–210.

Anderson, R., Greene, M., and Loewen, P. "Relationships Among Teachers' and Students' Thinking Skills, Sense of Efficacy, and Student Achievement." *Alberta Journal of Educational Research,* 1988, *24*(2), 148–165.

Andrew, M. "The Differences Between Graduates of Four-Year and Five-Year Teacher Preparation Programs." *Journal of Teacher Education,* 1990, *41,* 45–51.

Andrew, M., and Schwab, R. L. "Has Reform in Teacher Education Influenced Teacher Performance? An Outcome Assessment of Graduates of Eleven Teacher Education Programs." *Action in Teacher Education,* 1995, *17,* 43–53.

Anyon, J. "Schools as Agencies of Social Legitimation." *Journal of Curriculum Theorizing,* 1981, *3*(2), 86–103.

Armor, D., and others. *Analysis of the School Preferred Reading Programs in Selected Los Angeles Minority Schools.* Santa Monica, Calif.: RAND Corporation, 1976.

Ashton, P. "Motivation and Teachers' Sense of Efficacy." In C. Ames and R. Ames (eds.), *Research on Motivation in Education: Vol. 2. The Classroom Milieu.* Orlando, Fla.: Academic Press, 1985.

Ashton, P., and Crocker, L. "Does Teacher Certification Make a Difference?" *Florida Journal of Teacher Education,* 1986, *3,* 73–83.

Ashton, P., and Crocker, L. "Systematic Study of Planned Variations: The Essential Focus of Teacher Education Reform." *Journal of Teacher Education,* May–June 1987, pp. 2–8.

Ashton, P., and Webb, R. B. *Making a Difference: Teachers' Sense of Efficacy and Student Achievement.* White Plains, N.Y.: Longman, 1986.

Athanases, S. Z. "Teachers' Reports of the Effects of Preparing Portfolios of Literacy Instruction." *Elementary School Journal,* 1994, *94*(4), 421–439.

Bagley, W. C. *Classroom Management.* London: William Reese, 1910.

Baker, T. "A Survey of Four-Year and Five-Year Program Graduates and Their Principals." *Southeastern Regional Association of Teacher Educators (SRATE) Journal,* 1993, *2*(2), 28–33.

Ball, D. "With an Eye on the Mathematical Horizon." *Elementary School Journal,* 1993, *93*(4).

Ball, D., and Cohen, D. "Developing Practice, Developing Practitioners: Toward a Practice-Based Theory of Professional Education." In L. Darling-Hammond and G. Sykes (eds.), *Teaching as the Learning Profession: A Handbook of Policy and Practice.* San Francisco: Jossey-Bass, 1999.

Ballou, D., and Podgursky, M. "Teacher Training and Licensure: A Layman's Guide." In M. Kanstoroom and C. E. Finn (eds.), *Better Teachers, Better Schools.* Washington, D.C.: Fordham Foundation, 1999.

Bandura, A. *Social Foundations of Thought and Action: A Social Cognitive Theory.* Upper Saddle River, N.J.: Prentice Hall, 1986.

Banks, J. A. "Multicultural Education: Historical Development, Dimensions, and Practice." In J. A. Banks and C.A.M. Banks (eds.), *Handbook of Research on Multicultural Education.* San Francisco: Jossey-Bass, 2001.

Baron, J. B. *Exploring High and Improving Reading Achievement in Connecticut.* Washington, D.C.: National Educational Goals Panel, 1999.

Battenfeld, J. "Many 'Bonus' Teachers Bolt After First Year." Boston *Herald,* Jan. 26, 2001.

Baumgartner, F., Koerner, M., and Rust, F. "Exploring Roles in Student Teaching Placements." *Teacher Education Quarterly,* 2002, *29,* 35–58.

Begle, E. G. *Critical Variables in Mathematics Education: Findings from a Survey of the Empirical Literature.* Washington, D.C.: Mathematical Association of America, 1979.

Begle, E. G., and Geeslin, W. "Teacher Effectiveness in Mathematics Instruction." (National Longitudinal Study of Mathematical Abilities report no. 28.) Washington, D.C.: Mathematical Association of America and National Council of Teachers of Mathematics, 1972.

Benner, A. D. *The Cost of Teacher Turnover.* Austin: Texas Center for Educational Research, 2000.

Berman, P., McLaughlin, M., Bass, G., Pauly, E., and Zellman, G. *Federal Programs Supporting Educational Change, Vol. VII: Factors Affecting Implementation and Continuation.* Santa Monica, Calif.: RAND, 1977.

Betts, J. R., Rueben, K. S., and Danenberg, A. *Equal Resources, Equal Outcomes? The Distribution of School Resources and Student Achievement in California.* San Francisco: Public Policy Institute of California, 2000.

Biber, B. *What Is Bank Street? A Talk to Educators.* New York: Bank Street College, 1973.

Biber, B., and Windsor, C. B. *An Analysis of the Guidance Function in a Graduate Teacher Education Program.* New York: Bank Street College, 1967. (Also published in *Mental Health and Teacher Education,* 46th Yearbook).

Bird, T. "The Schoolteacher's Portfolio: An Essay on Possibilities." In J. Millman and L. Darling-Hammond (eds.), *The New Handbook of Teacher Evaluation: Assessing Elementary and Secondary School Teachers.* Thousand Oaks, Calif.: Sage, 1990.

Black, A., and Ammon, P. "A Developmental-Constructivist Approach to Teacher Education." *Journal of Teacher Education,* 1992, *43*(5), 323–335.

Bliss, T., and Mazur, J. "How INTASC Standards Come Alive Through Case Studies." Paper presented at annual meeting of American Association of Colleges for Teacher Education, Phoenix, Ariz., Feb. 1997.

Borko, H., and Mayfield, V. "The Roles of the Cooperating Teacher and University Supervisor in Learning to Teach." *Teaching and Teacher Education,* 1995, *11*(5), 501–518.

Bowles, S., and Levin, H. M. "The Determinants of Scholastic Achievement: An Appraisal of Some Recent Evidence." *Journal of Human Resources,* 1968, *3,* 3–24.

Boyd, D., Lankford, H., Loeb, S., and Wyckoff, J. "The Draw of Home: How Teacher Preferences for Proximity Disadvantage Urban Schools." *Journal of Policy Analysis and Management,* 2005, *24*(1), 113–132.

Boyer, E. *Scholarship Reconsidered.* Princeton, N.J.: Carnegie Commission for the Advancement of Teaching, 1990.

Bradley, A. "Pioneers in Professionalism." *Education Week,* Apr. 20, 1994, *13,* 18–21.

Bramald, R., Hardman, F., and Leat, D. "Initial Teacher Trainees and Their Views of Teaching and Learning." *Teaching and Teacher Education,* 1995, *11*(1), 23–31.

Bransford, J. D., Brown, A. L., and Cocking, R. R. *How People Learn: Brain, Mind, Experience,* and *School.* Washington, D.C.: National Academy Press, 1999.

Brown, A. L., and Campione, J. "Psychological Theory and the Design of Innovative Learning Environments: On Procedures, Principles, and Systems." In L. Schauble and R. Glaser (eds.), *Innovations in Learning: New Environments for Education.* Hillsdale, N.J.: Erlbaum, 1996.

Brown, C. A., Smith, M. S., and Stein, M. K. "Linking Teacher Support to Enhanced Classroom Instruction." Paper presented at annual meeting of American Educational Research Association, New York, 1995.

Bruner, J. S. *The Process of Education.* Cambridge, Mass.: Harvard University Press, 1960/1977.

Bryk, T., and Schneider, B. *Trust in Schools: A Core Resource for Improvement.* New York: Russell Sage Foundation, 2002.

Buchberger, F., and Buchberger, I. "Problem Solving Capacity of a Teacher Education System as Condition of Success? An Analysis of the 'Finnish Case.'" In F. Buchberger and S. Berghammer (eds.), *Education Policy Analysis in a Comparative Perspective.* Linz, Austria: Trauner, 2004.

Byrne, C. J. "Teacher Knowledge and Teacher Effectiveness: A Literature Review, Theoretical Analysis, and Discussion of Research Strategy." Paper presented at meeting of Northwestern Educational Research Association, Ellenville, N.Y., 1983.

California State University. *First System Wide Evaluation of Teacher Education Programs in the California State University: Summary Report.* Long Beach, Calif.: Office of the Chancellor, California State University, 2002a.

California State University. *Preparing Teachers for Reading Instruction (K–12): An Evaluation Brief by the California State University.* Long Beach, Calif.: Office of the Chancellor, California State University, 2002b.

Callahan, R. E. *Education and the Cult of Efficiency.* Chicago: University of Chicago Press, 1962.

Carnegie Task Force on Teaching as a Profession. *A Nation Prepared: Teachers for the 21st Century.* New York: Carnegie Forum on Education and the Economy, 1986.

Carroll, S., Reichardt, R., and Guarino, C. *The Distribution of Teachers Among California's School Districts and Schools.* Santa Monica, Calif.: RAND, 2000.

Carter, R., and Goodwin, L. "Racial Identity and Education." In L. Darling-Hammond (ed.), *Review of Research in Education, Vol. 20.* Washington, D.C.: American Educational Research Association, 1994.

Center for Educational Leadership. *Smart Schools for San Antonio's Future.* (Progress report, fall 1995). San Antonio, Tex.: Trinity University, 1995.

Clifford, G. J., and Guthrie, J. W. *Ed School.* Chicago: University of Chicago Press, 1988.

Cobb, V., Darling-Hammond, L., and Murangi, K. "Teacher Preparation and Professional Development in APEC Members: An Overview of Policy and Practice." In *APEC Education Forum: Teacher Preparation and Professional Development in APEC Members.* Washington, D.C.: United States Department of Education, May 1995.

Cochran-Smith, M. "Learning to Teach Against the Grain." *Harvard Educational Review,* 1991, *61*(3), 279–310.

Cochran-Smith, M., and Lytle, S. L. *Inside/Outside: Teacher Research and Knowledge.* New York: Teachers College Press, 1993.

Cochran-Smith, M., and Lytle, S. L. "Relationships of Knowledge and Practice: Teacher Learning in Communities." In *Review of Research in Education,* 1999, *24,* 249–306.

Coffman, L. D. *The Social Composition of the Teaching Population.* New York: Teachers College, Columbia University, 1911.

Cohen, D. K., and Hill, H. C. "Instructional Policy and Classroom Performance: The Mathematics Reform in California." *Teachers College Record,* 2000, *102*(2), 294–343.

Cohen, E. G., and Lotan, R. A. "Producing Equal-Status Interaction in the Heterogeneous Classroom." *American Educational Research Journal,* 1995, *32*(1), 99–120.

Coladarci, T. "Teachers' Sense of Efficacy and Commitment to Teaching." *Journal of Experimental Education,* 1992, *60,* 323–337.

Colberg, J., Trimble, K., and Desberg, P. *The Case for Education: Contemporary Approaches for Using Case Methods.* Boston: Allyn and Bacon, 1996.

Cole, M., and Cole, S. *The Development of Children* (2nd ed.). New York: Scientific American Books (dist. by Freeman), 1993.

Coleman, J. S., and others. *Equality of Educational Opportunity.* Washington, D.C.: U.S. GPO, 1966.

Conant, J. B. *The Education of American Teachers.* New York: McGraw-Hill, 1963.

Connecticut State Board of Education. *The Other Side of the Equation: Impact of the Teacher Standards Provisions of the Education Enhancement Act.* Hartford, Conn.: State Board of Education, 1992.

Connecticut State Department of Education. "Impact of Education Enhancement Act." *Research Bulletin,* school year 1990, no. 1. Hartford, Conn.: State Department of Education, 1990.

Cooper, E., and Sherk, J. "Addressing Urban School Reform: Issues and Alliances." *Journal of Negro Education,* 1989, *58*(3), 315–331.

Counts, G. S. *Dare the School Build a New Social Order?* Carbondale: University of Southern Illinois Press, 1932.

Crow, G. M., Levine, L., and Nager, N. "No More Business as Usual: Career Changers Who Become Teachers." *American Journal of Education,* May 1990, 197–223.

Cuffaro, H. *Experimenting with the World: John Dewey and the Early Childhood Classroom.* New York: Teachers College Press, 1995.

Darling-Hammond, L. "Teaching Knowledge: How Do We Test It?" *American Educator,* 1986, *10*(3), 18–21, 46.

Darling-Hammond, L. *Professional Development Schools: Schools for Developing a Profession.* New York: Teachers College Press, 1994.

Darling-Hammond, L. *The Right to Learn.* San Francisco: Jossey-Bass, 1997.

Darling-Hammond, L. "Teacher Quality and Student Achievement: A Review of State Policy Evidence." *Education Policy Analysis Archives,* 2000, *8*(1). http://epaa.asu.edu/epaa/v8n1.

Darling-Hammond, L. "Inequality and Access to Knowledge." In J. A. Banks and C.A.M. Banks (eds.), *Handbook of Research on Multicultural Education.* San Francisco: Jossey-Bass, 2001.

Darling-Hammond, L. "Access to Quality Teaching: An Analysis of Inequality in California's Public Schools." *Santa Clara Law Review,* 2003, *43,* 101–239.

Darling-Hammond, L. "The Color Line in American Education: Race, Resources, and Student Achievement." *W.E.B. DuBois Review: Social Science Research on Race,* 2004, *1*(2), 213–246.

Darling-Hammond, L. *Professional Development Schools (2nd ed.).* New York: Teachers College Press, 2005a.

Darling-Hammond, L. "Teaching as a Profession: Lessons in Teacher Preparation and Professional Development." *Phi Delta Kappan,* 2005b, *87*(3), 237–240.

Darling-Hammond, L., Ancess, J., and Falk, B. *Authentic Assessment in Action: Studies of Schools and Students at Work.* New York: Teachers College Press, 1995.

Darling-Hammond, L., and Ball, D. L. *Teaching for High Standards: What Policymakers Need to Know and Be Able to Do.* Philadelphia: Consortium for Policy Research in Education, University of Pennsylvania, copublished with National Commission on Teaching and America's Future (NCTAF), 1998.

Darling-Hammond, L., and Bransford, J. *Preparing Teachers for a Changing World: What Teachers Should Learn and Be Able To Do.* San Francisco: Jossey-Bass, 2005.

Darling-Hammond, L., Chung, R., and Frelow, F. "Variation in Teacher Preparation: How Well Do Different Pathways Prepare Teachers to Teach? *Journal of Teacher Education,* 2002, *53*(4), 286–302.

Darling-Hammond, L., French, J., and Garcia-Lopez, S. P. *Learning to Teach for Social Justice.* New York: Teachers College Press, 2002.

Darling-Hammond, L., and Hammerness, K. "Toward a Pedagogy of Cases in Teacher Education." *Teaching Education,* 2002, *13*(2), 125–135.

Darling-Hammond, L., Holtzman, D., Gatlin, S., and Heilig, J. V. "Does Teacher Preparation Matter? Evidence About Teacher Certification, Teach for America, and Teacher Effectiveness." *Education Policy Analysis Archives,* 2005, *13*(42). http://epaa.asu.edu/epaa/v13n42/.

Darling-Hammond, L., and Sclan, E. "Policy and Supervision." In C. Glickman (ed.), *Supervision in Transition.* Alexandria, Va.: Association for Supervision and Curriculum Development, 1992.

Darling-Hammond, L., and Snyder, J. "Authentic Assessment of Teaching in Context." *Teaching and Teacher Education,* 2000, *16*(5–6), 523–545.

Darling-Hammond, L., and Sykes, G. "Wanted: A National Teacher Supply Policy for Education: The Right Way to Meet the 'Highly Qualified Teacher' Challenge." *Educational Policy Analysis Archives,* 2003, *11*(33). http://epaa.asu.edu/epaa/v11n33/.

Darling-Hammond, L., Wise, A. E., and Klein, S. *A License to Teach: Building a Profession for 21st Century Schools.* San Francisco: Jossey-Bass, 1999.

Darling-Hammond, L., Wise, A. E., and Pease, S. R. *Review of Educational Research,* 1983, *53*(3), 285–328.

Darling-Hammond, L., and others. *Instructional Leadership for Systemic Change: The Story of San Diego's Reform.* Lanham, Md.: Scarecrow Education Press, 2005.

Davis, C. L., and Honan, E. "Reflections on the Use of Teams to Support the Portfolio Process." In N. Lyons (ed.), *With Portfolio in Hand: Validating the New Teacher Professionalism.* New York: Teachers College Press, 1998.

Decker, P. T., Mayer, D. P., and Glazerman, S. *The Effects of Teach for America on Students: Findings from a National Evaluation.* Princeton, N.J.: Mathematica Policy Research, 2004.

Delpit, L. *Other People's Children: Cultural Conflicts in the Classroom.* New York: New Press, 1995.

Dennison, G. M. "National Standards in Teacher Preparation: A Commitment to Quality." *Chronicle of Higher Education,* Dec. 2, 1992, p. A40.

Denton, J. J. "Early Field Experience Influence on Performance in Subsequent Coursework." *Journal of Teacher Education,* 1982, *33*(2), 19–23.

Denton, J. J., Morris, J. E., and Tooke, D. J. "The Influence of Academic Characteristics of Student Teachers on the Cognitive Attainment of Learners." *Educational and Psychological Research,* 1982, *2*(1), 15–29.

Dewey, J. *The Sources of a Science of Education.* New York: Liveright, 1929.

Dewey, J. *The Child and the Curriculum.* Chicago: University of Chicago Press, 1956. (Originally published 1902.)

Diez, M., Rickard, W., and Lake, K. "Performance Assessment in Teacher Education." In T. Warren (ed.), *Promising Practices: Teacher Education in Liberal Arts Colleges.* Lanham, Md.: University Press of America and Association of Independent Liberal Arts Colleges for Teacher Education, 1994.

Donovan, M. S., and Bransford, J. (eds.) *How Students Learn: History, Mathematics, and Science in the Classroom.* Washington, D.C.: National Academy Press, 2005.

Doyle, W. "Classroom Tasks and Students' Abilities." In P. L. Peterson and H. J. Walberg (eds.), *Research on Teaching.* Berkeley, Calif.: McCutchan, 1979.

Druva, C. A., and Anderson, R. D. "Science Teacher Characteristics by Teacher Behavior and by Student Outcome: A Meta-Analysis of Research." *Journal of Research in Science Teaching,* 1983, *20*(50), 467–479.

Duchastel, P. C., and Merrill, P. F. "The Effects of Behavioral Objectives on Learning: A Review of Empirical Studies." *Review of Educational Research,* Winter 1977, pp. 53–69.

Ebmeier, H., Twombly, S., and Teeter, D. J. "The Comparability and Adequacy of Financial Support for Schools of Education." *Journal of Teacher Education,* 1991, *42*, 226–235.

Ehrenberg, R. G., and Brewer, D. J. "Do School and Teacher Characteristics Matter? Evidence from High School and Beyond." *Economics of Education Review,* 1994, *13*, 1–17.

Elmore, R., and Burney, D. "Investing in Teacher Learning: Staff Development and Instructional Improvement." In L. Darling-Hammond and G. Sykes (eds.), *Teaching as the Learning Profession: Handbook of Policy and Practice.* San Francisco: Jossey-Bass, 1999.

Elmore, R., and Fuhrman, S. "Opportunity to Learn and the State Role in Education." In *The Debate on Opportunity-to-Learn Standards: Commissioned Papers*. Washington, D.C.: National Governors Association, 1993.

Enochs, L. G., Scharmann, L. C., and Riggs, I. M. "The Relationship of Pupil Control to Preservice Elementary Science Teacher Self-Efficacy and Outcome Expectancy." *Science Education*, 1995, *70*(1), 63–75.

Erixon, P., Franberg, G., and Kallos, D. (eds.). *The Role of Graduate and Postgraduate Studies and Research in Teacher Education Reform Policies in the European Union*. Umea Universitet, Sweden: European Network on Teacher Education Policies, 2001.

Evans, E. D., and Tribble, M. N. "Perceived Teaching Problems, Self-Efficacy and Commitment to Teaching Among Preservice Teachers." *Journal of Educational Research*, 1986, *80*(2), 81–85.

Evertson, C., Hawley, W., and Zlotnik, M. "Making a Difference in Educational Quality Through Teacher Education." *Journal of Teacher Education*, 1985, *36*(3), 2–12.

Featherstone, H. *A Difference in the Family: Life with a Disabled Child*. New York: Basic Books, 1980.

Feiman-Nemser, S. "Teacher Preparation: Structural and Conceptual Analysis." In W. R. Houston, M. Haberman, and J. P. Sikula (eds.), *Handbook of Research on Teacher Education*. New York: Macmillan, 1990.

Feiman-Nemser, S. "From Preparation to Practice: Designing a Continuum to Strengthen and Sustain Teaching." *Teachers College Record*, 2001, *103*(6), 1013–1055.

Feiman-Nemser, S., and Buchmann, M. "Describing Teacher Education: A Framework and Illustrative Findings from a Longitudinal Study of Six Students." *Elementary School Journal*, 1989, *89*(3), 365–378.

Ferguson, R. F. "Paying for Public Education: New Evidence on How and Why Money Matters." *Harvard Journal on Legislation*, 1991, *28*(2), 465–498.

Ferguson, R. F., and Ladd, H. F. "How and Why Money Matters: An Analysis of Alabama Schools." In H. Ladd (ed.), *Holding Schools Accountable*. Washington, D.C.: Brookings Institution, 1996.

Fetler, M. "High School Staff Characteristics and Mathematics Test Results." *Education Policy Analysis Archives*, 1999, 7. http://epaa.asu.edu/epaa/v7n9.

Figlio, D. N., and Getzler, L. S. "Accountability, Ability, and Disability: Gaming the System?" National Bureau of Economic Research, Apr. 2002.

Flexner, A., and Pritchett, H. S. *Medical Education in the United States and Canada: A Report to the Carnegie Foundation for the Advancement of Teaching*. New York: Carnegie Foundation for the Advancement of Teaching, 1910.

Floden, R. E., and Klinzing, H. G. "What Can Research on Teacher Thinking Contribute to Teacher Preparation? A Second Opinion." *Educational Researcher,* 1990, *19*(5), 15–20.

Fowler, R. C. *An Analysis of the Recruitment, Preparation, Attrition, and Placement of the Massachusetts Signing Bonus Teachers.* Salem, Mass.: Salem State College, 2001.

Freese, A. R. "The Role of Reflection on Preservice Teachers' Development in the Context of a Professional Development School." *Teaching and Teacher Education,* 1999, *15*(8), 895–909.

Freidus, H. "Contextual Learning: Portfolios as Connecting Teaching and Learning." Paper presented at annual meeting of American Educational Research Association, 1995.

French, R. L., Hodzkom, D., and Kuligowski, B. "Teacher Evaluation in SREB States. Stage I: Analysis and Comparison of Evaluation Systems." Paper presented at annual meeting of American Educational Research Association, Boston, Apr. 1990.

Friedlaender, D., and Frenkel, S. *School Equity Study Documentation.* Los Angeles: UCLA Institute for Democracy, Education, and Access, 2002.

Fullan, M. *Change Forces: Probing the Depths of Educational Reform.* London: Falmer, 1993.

Fuller, F. "Concerns of Teachers: A Developmental Conceptualization." *American Educational Research Journal,* 1969, *6*(2), 207–226.

Fuller, E. "Do Properly Certified Teachers Matter? A Comparison of Elementary School Performance on the TAAS in 1997 Between Schools with High and Low Percentages of Properly Certified Regular Education Teachers." Austin: Charles A. Dana Center, University of Texas at Austin, 1998.

Garcia, E. "Preparing Instructional Professionals for Linguistically and Culturally Diverse Students." In J. Sikula (ed.), *Handbook of Research on Teacher Education.* New York: Macmillan, 1996.

Gardner, H. *Frames of Mind: The Theory of Multiple Intelligences.* New York: Basic Books, 1983.

Garibaldi, A. "Preparing Teachers for Culturally Diverse Classrooms." In M. Dilworth (ed.), *Diversity in Teacher Education: New Expectation.* San Francisco: Jossey-Bass, 1992.

Gibson, S., and Dembo, M. "Teacher Efficacy: A Construct Validation." *Journal of Educational Psychology,* 1984, *76*(4), 569–582.

Gideonse, H. "The Governance of Teacher Education and Systemic Reform." *Educational Policy,* 1993, *7*(4), 395–426.

Glaser, R. *Testing and Assessment: O Tempora! O Mores!* Pittsburgh, Pa.: Learning Research and Development Center, University of Pittsburgh, 1990.

Glickman, C., and Tamashiro, R. "A Comparison of First-Year, Fifth-Year, and Former Teachers on Efficacy, Ego Development, and Problem Solving." *Psychology in Schools*, 1982, *19*, 558–562.

Goe, L. "Legislating Equity: The Distribution of Emergency Permit Teachers in California." *Educational Policy Analysis Archives*, 2002, *10*(42). http://epaa.asu.edu/epaa/v10n42.

Goertz, M., and Pitcher, B., *The Impact of NTE Use by States on Teacher Selection*. Princeton, N.J.: Educational Testing Service, 1985.

Goldhaber, D. D., and Brewer, D. J. "Does Teacher Certification Matter? High School Certification Status and Student Achievement." *Educational Evaluation and Policy Analysis*, 2000, *22*, 129–145.

Good, T. S., and Brophy, J. E. *Educational Psychology (3rd ed.)*. White Plains, N.Y.: Longman, 1986.

Goodlad, J. I. *A Place Called School: Prospects for the Future*. New York: McGraw-Hill, 1984.

Goodlad, J. I. *Teachers for Our Nation's Schools*. San Francisco: Jossey-Bass, 1990.

Goodlad, J. I. *Educational Renewal: Better Teachers, Better Schools*. San Francisco: Jossey-Bass, 1994.

Goodlad, J. I., Soder, R., and Sirotnik, K. A. *Places Where Teachers Are Taught*. San Francisco: Jossey-Bass, 1990.

Goodnough, A. "Winnowing Process Begins for Novice Teachers." *New York Times*, Nov. 22, 2000.

Gordon, E. W. "Coping with Communicentric Bias in Knowledge Production in the Social Sciences." *Educational Researcher*, 1990, *19*, 19.

Gore, J. M., and Zeichner, K. M. "Action Research and Reflective Teaching in Preservice Teacher Education: A Case Study from the United States." *Teaching and Teacher Education*, 1991, *7*(2), 119–136.

Graham, P., "Black Teachers: A Drastically Scarce Resource." *Phi Delta Kappan*, 1987, *68*(8), 598–605.

Gray, L., and others. *New Teacher in the Job Market: 1991 Update*. Washington, D.C.: Office of Educational Research and Improvement, U.S. Department of Education, 1993.

Grimmett, P., and MacKinnon, A. "Craft Knowledge and the Education of Teachers." In G. Grant (ed.), *Review of Research in Education, Vol. 18*. Washington, D.C.: American Educational Research Association, 1992.

Grossman, P. *The Making of a Teacher*. New York: Teachers College Press, 1990.

Grossman, P., and Schoenfeld, A. "Teaching Subject Matter." In L. Darling-Hammond and J. Bransford (eds.), *Preparing Teachers for a Changing World: What Teachers Should Learn and Be Able to Do*. San Francisco: Jossey-Bass, 2005.

Guskey, T. R. "The Influence of Change in Instructional Effectiveness upon the Affective Characteristics of Teachers." *American Educational Research Journal*, 1984, *21*, 245–259.

Haertel, E. "New Forms of Teacher Assessment." In C. Grant (ed.), *Review of Research in Education*, 1991, *17*, 3–29.

Hall, B., Burley, W., Villeme, M., and Brockmeier, L. "An Attempt to Explicate Teacher Efficacy Beliefs Among First Year Teachers." Paper presented at annual meeting of American Educational Research Association, San Francisco, Apr. 1992.

Hammerness, K., Darling-Hammond, L., and Bransford, J. "How Teachers Learn and Develop." In L. Darling-Hammond and J. Bransford (eds.), *Preparing Teachers for a Changing World: What Teachers Should Learn and Be Able to Do.* San Francisco: Jossey-Bass, 2005.

Hammerness, K., Darling-Hammond, L., and Shulman, L. "Toward Expert Thinking: How Curriculum Case Writing Prompts the Development of Theory-Based Professional Knowledge in Student Teachers." *Teaching Education*, 2002, *13*(2), 221–245.

Hanushek, E. "Teacher Characteristics and Gains in Student Achievement: Estimation Using Micro Data." *American Economic Review*, 1971, *61*(2), 280–288.

Hanushek, E. A. "The Trade-Off Between Child Quantity and Quality." *Journal of Political Economy*, 1992, *100*(1), 84–117.

Hanushek, E., Kain, J., and Rivkin, S. *Teachers, Schools, and Academic Achievement.* (Working paper no. 6691). Cambridge, Mass.: National Bureau of Economic Research, 1998.

Hanushek, E. A., Kain, J. F., and Rivkin, S. G. *Do Higher Salaries Buy Better Teachers?* (Working paper no. 7082). Cambridge, Mass.: National Bureau of Economic Research, 1999.

Hatano, G., and Inagaki, K. "Two Courses of Expertise." In H. Stevenson, H. Azuma, and K. Hakuta (eds.), *Child Development and Education in Japan.* New York: Freeman, 1986.

Hawk, P., Coble, C. R., and Swanson, M. "Certification: It Does Matter." *Journal of Teacher Education*, 1985, *36*(3), 13–15.

Haynes, D. "One Teacher's Experience with National Board Assessment." *Educational Leadership*, 1995, *52*(8), 58–60.

Hegarty, S. "Newcomers Find Toll of Teaching Is Too High: Among Those Quitting Are Non-Education Majors Thrust into Challenging Classrooms." St. Petersburg *Times*, Jan. 21, 2001.

Henke, R., Chen, X., and Geis, S. *Progress Through the Teacher Pipeline: 1992–93 College Graduates and Elementary/Secondary School Teaching as of 1997.* Washington, D.C.: National Center for Education Statistics, U.S. Department of Education, 2000.

Henry, M. "The Effect of Increased Exploratory Field Experiences upon the Perceptions and Performance of Student Teachers." *Action in Teacher Education,* 1983, *5*(1–2), 66–70.

Heubert, J., and Hauser, R. (eds.). *High Stakes: Testing for Tracking, Promotion, and Graduation.* (Report of National Research Council). Washington, D.C.: National Academy Press, 1999.

Hollins, E. "A Conceptual Framework for Selecting Instructional Approaches and Materials for Inner-City Black Youngsters." Paper commissioned by California Curriculum Commission, Sacramento, 1989.

Holmes Group. *Tomorrow's Teachers: A Report of the Holmes Group.* East Lansing, Mich.: Holmes Group, 1986.

Holyoake, J. "Initial Teacher Training: The French View." *Journal of Education for Teaching,* 1993, *19,* 215–226.

Hoover, N. L., and O'Shea, L. J. "The Influence of a Criterion Checklist on Supervisors' and Interns' Conceptions of Teaching." Paper presented at annual meeting of American Educational Research Association, Washington, D.C., Apr. 24, 1987.

Howard, R. D., Hitz, R., and Baker, L. "A National Study Comparing the Expenditures of Teacher Education Programs by Carnegie Classification and with Other Disciplines." *Action in Teacher Education,* 1998, *20*(3), 1–14.

Howey, K. R., and Zimpher, N. L. *Profiles of Preservice Teacher Education: Inquiry into the Nature of Programs.* Albany: State University of New York Press, 1989.

Humphrey, D. L., Koppich, J., and Hough, H. "Sharing the Wealth: National Board Certified Teachers and the Students Who Need Them Most." *Educational Policy Analysis Archives,* 2005, *13*(3). http://epaa.asu.edu/epaa/v13n3.

Ingvarson, L. "Teaching Standards: Foundations for Professional Development Reform." In A. Hargreaves, A. Lieberman, M. Fullan, and D. Hopkins (eds.), *International Handbook of Educational Change.* Dordrecht, Neth.: Kluwer Academic, 1998.

Ingvarson, L., and Marrett, M. "Building Professional Community and Supporting Teachers as Learners: The Potential of Case Methods." In L. Logan and J. Sachs (eds.), *Meeting the Challenge of Primary Schooling for the 1990s.* London: Routledge, 1997.

Interstate New Teacher Support and Assessment Consortium (INTASC). *Model Standards for Beginning Teacher Licensing and Development: A Resource for State Dialogue.* Washington, D.C.: Council for Chief State School Officers, 1992.

Irvine, J. "Beyond Role Models: The Influence of Black Teachers on Black Students' Achievement." Paper presented at Educational Testing Service, Princeton, N.J., May 1990a.

Irvine, J. *Black Students and School Failure: Policies, Practices, and Prescriptions.* New York: Praeger, 1990b.

Irvine, J. "Making Teacher Education Culturally Responsive." In M. Dilworth (ed.), *Diversity in Teacher Education: New Expectation.* San Francisco: Jossey-Bass, 1992.

Irvine, J. J. *Educating Teachers for Diversity: Seeing with a Cultural Eye.* New York: Teachers College Press, 2003.

Jackson, P. W. *Life in Classrooms.* Austin, Tex.: Holt, Rinehart and Winston, 1974.

Johnson, D. W., and Johnson, R. T. *Cooperation and Competition: Theory and Research.* Edina, Minn.: Interaction Book Co., 1989.

Kain, J., and Singleton, K. "Equality of Educational Opportunity Revisited." *New England Economic Review,* May–June 1996, pp. 87–111.

Kanstoroom, M., and Finn, C. E. (eds.) *Better Teachers, Better Schools.* Washington, D.C.: Fordham Foundation, 1999.

Katz, L. "Developmental Stages of Preschool Teachers." *Elementary School Journal,* 1972, *23*(1), 50–51.

Kennedy, M. "The Role of Preservice Teacher Education." In L. Darling-Hammond and G. Sykes (eds.), *Teaching as the Learning Profession: Handbook of Policy and Practice.* San Francisco: Jossey-Bass, 1999.

Kentucky Institute for Education Research. *The Preparation of Teachers for Kentucky Schools: A Survey of New Teachers.* Frankfort: Kentucky Institute for Education Research, 1997.

Kleinfeld, J. "The Use of Case Studies in Preparing Teachers for Cultural Diversity." *Theory into Practice,* Spring 1998, *37*(2), 140–147.

Kroll, L., and Black, A. "Developmental Theory and Teaching Methods: A Pilot Study of a Teacher Education Program." *Elementary School Journal,* 1993, *93*(4), 417–441.

Kunzman, R. "Preservice Education for Experienced Teachers: What STEP Teaches Those Who Have Already Taught." *Issues in Teacher Education,* 2002, *11*(1), 99–112.

Kunzman, R. "From Teacher to Student: The Value of Teacher Education for Experienced Teachers." *Journal of Teacher Education,* 2003, *54*(3), 241–253.

Laboskey, V. K. "Case Investigations: Preservice Teacher Research as an Aid to Reflection." In J. Shulman (ed.), *Case Methods in Teacher Education.* New York: Teachers College Press, 1992.

Laczko-Kerr, I., and Berliner, D. "The Effectiveness of Teach for America and Other Under-Certified Teachers on Student Academic Achievement: A Case of Harmful Public Policy." *Educational Policy Analysis Archives,* 2002, *10*(37). http://epaa.asu.edu/epaa/v10n37.

Ladson-Billings, G. "Preparing Teachers for Diversity: Historical Perspectives, Current Trends, and Future Directions." In L. Darling-Hammond and G. Sykes (eds.), *Teaching as the Learning Profession: A Handbook of Policy and Practice.* San Francisco: Jossey-Bass, 1999.

Lampert, M. *Teaching Problems and the Problems of Teaching.* New Haven, Conn.: Yale University Press, 2001.

Lieberman, A., and Grolnick, M. "Networks and Reform in American Education." *Teachers College Record,* 1996, *98*(1), 7–45.

Lortie, D. C. *Schoolteacher: A Sociological Study.* Chicago: University of Chicago Press, 1975.

Luczak, J. "Who Will Teach in the 21st Century? Beginning Teacher Training Experiences and Attrition Rates." Unpublished doctoral dissertation, Stanford University, 2004.

Lyons, N. *With Portfolios in Hand: Validating the New Teacher Professionalism.* New York: Teachers College Press, 1998.

Mandeville, G. K., and Liu, Q. "The Effect of Teacher Certification and Task Level on Mathematics Achievement." *Teaching and Teacher Education,* 1997, *13*(4), 397–407.

Maryland State Department of Education (MSDE). *Professional Development Schools in Maryland.* Baltimore: MSDE, 2004.

McDonald, J. P. *Teaching: Making Sense of an Uncertain Craft.* New York: Teachers College Press, 1992.

Melton, R. F. "Resolution of Conflicting Claims Concerning the Effect of Behavioral Objectives on Student Learning." *Review of Educational Research,* 1978, *48*(2), 291–302.

Mentzer, D., and Shaughnessy, T. "Hawthorne Elementary School: The Teachers' Perspective." *Journal of Education for Students Placed At-Risk,* 1996, *1*(1), 13–23.

Mergendoller, J. R., Johnston, J., Rockman, S., and Willis, J. *Case Studies of Exemplary Approaches to Training Teachers to Use Technology.* Novato, Calif.: Buck Institute for Education, 1994.

Midgley, C., Feldlaufer, H., and Eccles, J. "Change in Teacher Efficacy and Student Self- and Task-Related Beliefs in Mathematics During the Transition to Junior High School." *Journal of Educational Psychology,* 1989, *81,* 247–258.

Mikkola, A. "Finnish Teacher Education and Research." In P. Erixon, G. Franberg, and D. Kallos (eds.), *The Role of Graduate and Postgraduate Studies and Research in Teacher Education Reform Policies in the European Union*. Umea Universitet, Sweden: European Network on Teacher Education Policies, 2001.

Miller, L., and Silvernail, D. "Wells Junior High School: Evolution of a Professional Development School." In L. Darling-Hammond (ed.), *Professional Development Schools: Schools for Developing a Profession (2nd ed.)*. New York: Teachers College Press, 2005.

Moll, L. "Some Key Issues in Teaching Latino Students." *Language Arts*, 1988, *65*(5), 465–472.

Monk, D. H. "Subject Matter Preparation of Secondary Mathematics and Science Teachers and Student Achievement." *Economics of Education Review*, 1994, *13*(2), 125–145.

Monk, D. H., and King, J. A. "Multilevel Teacher Resource Effects in Pupil Performance in Secondary Mathematics and Science: The Case of Teacher Subject Matter Preparation." In R. G. Ehrenberg (ed.), *Choices and Consequences: Contemporary Policy Issues in Education*. Ithaca, N.Y.: ILR Press, 1994.

Munby, H., Russell, T., and Martin, A. K. "Teachers' Knowledge and How It Develops." In V. Richardson (ed.), *Handbook of Research on Teaching* (4th ed.). Washington, D.C.: American Educational Research Association, 2001.

Murnane, R. J. "Understanding the Sources of Teaching Competence: Choices, Skills and the Limits of Training." *Teachers College Record*, 1983, *84*(3), 564–569.

National Academy of Education. *A Good Teacher in Every Classroom: Preparing the Highly Qualified Teachers Our Children Deserve*. San Francisco: Jossey-Bass, 2005.

National Board for Professional Teaching Standards (NBPTS). *Toward High and Rigorous Standards for the Teaching Profession*. Detroit: NBPTS, 1989.

National Center for Education Statistics (NCES). *Digest of Education Statistics, 1996*. Washington, D.C.: U.S. Department of Education, 1996.

National Center for Education Statistics (NCES). *America's Teachers: Profile of a Profession*. Washington, D.C.: U.S. Department of Education, 1997a.

National Center for Education Statistics (NCES). *Condition of Education, 1997*. Washington, D.C.: U.S. Department of Education, 1997b.

National Center for Education Statistics (NCES). *Inequalities in Public School District Revenues*. Washington, D.C.: U.S. Department of Education, 1998.

National Center for Education Statistics (NCES). *Contexts of Elementary and Secondary Education—Indicator 28—Inclusion of Students with Disabili-*

ties in Regular Classrooms. Washington, D.C.: U.S. Department of Education, 2002.

National Commission on Teaching and America's Future (NCTAF). *What Matters Most: Teaching for America's Future.* New York: NCTAF, 1996.

National Commission on Teaching and America's Future (NCTAF). *No Dream Denied: A Pledge to America's Children.* Washington, D.C.: NCTAF, 2003.

National Education Goals Panel (NEGP). *Reading Achievement State by State, 1999.* Washington, D.C.: U.S. GPO, 1999.

National Research Council. *Testing Teacher Candidates: The Role of Licensure Tests in Improving Teacher Quality.* Washington, D.C.: National Academies Press, 2001.

New Zealand Ministry of Education. "Teacher Training and Professional Development Practices in New Zealand." In L. Darling-Hammond, V. Cobb, and K. Murangi (eds.), *APEC Education Forum: Teacher Preparation and Professional Development in APEC Members.* Washington, D.C.: U.S. Department of Education, 1995.

Nieto, S. *The Light in Their Eyes.* New York: Teachers College Press, 1999.

Olsen, D. G. "The Quality of Prospective Teachers: Education vs. Noneducation Graduates." *Journal of Teacher Education,* 1985, *36*(5), 56–59.

Organization for Economic Cooperation and Development (OECD). *Education at a Glance: OECD Indicators.* Paris: OECD, 1995.

Ortiz, A., and Maldonado-Colon, E. "Reducing Inappropriate Referrals of Language Minority Students in Special Education." In A. Willig and H. Greenberg (eds.), *Bilingualism and Learning Disabilities.* New York: American Library, 1986.

Paine, L. "Orientation Towards Diversity: What Do Prospective Teachers Bring?" (Research report 89-9). East Lansing, Mich.: National Center for Research on Teacher Education, 1990.

Parkay, F. W., Greenwood, G., Olejnik, S., and Proller, N. "A Study of the Relationship Among Teacher Efficacy, Locus of Control, and Stress." *Journal of Research and Development in Education,* 1988, *21*(4), 13–22.

Patterson, R. S., Michelli, N. M., and Pacheco, A. *Centers of Pedagogy: New Structures for Educational Renewal.* San Francisco: Jossey-Bass, 1999.

Pecheone, R., and Chung, R. "Evidence in Teacher Education: The Performance Assessment for California Teachers (PACT)." *Journal of Teacher Education,* 2006, *57*(1), 22–36.

Perkins, D. "What Is Understanding?" In M. S. Wiske (ed.), *Teaching for Understanding.* San Francisco: Jossey-Bass, 1998.

Peterson, P. L., and Clark, C. M. "Teachers Reports of Their Cognitive Processes During Teaching." *American Educational Research Journal,* 1978, *15*(4), 555–565.

Price, J. "Action Research, Pedagogy and Change: The Transformative Potential of Action Research in Pre-Service Teacher Education." *Journal of Curriculum Studies,* 2001, *33*(1), 43–74.

Raudenbush, S., Rowen, B., and Cheong, Y. "Contextual Effects on the Self-Perceived Efficacy of High School Teachers." *Sociology of Education,* 1992, *65,* 150–167.

Raymond, M., Fletcher, S., and Luque, J. *Teach for America: An Evaluation of Teacher Differences and Outcomes in Houston, Texas.* Stanford, Calif.: CREDO, Hoover Institution, Stanford University, 2001. www.rochester.edu/credo.

Richardson, V., and Placier, P. "Teacher Change." In V. Richardson (ed.), *Handbook of Research on Teaching* (4th ed.). Washington, D.C.: American Educational Research Association, 2001.

Riggs, I., and others. "Impacting Elementary Teachers' Beliefs and Performance Through Teacher Enhancement for Science Instruction in Diverse Settings." Paper presented at annual meeting of National Association of Research in Science Teaching, Anaheim, Calif., Apr. 1994.

Rivkin, S. G., Hanushek, E. A., and Kain, J. F. *Teachers, Schools, and Academic Achievement.* (Working paper no. 6691, revised). Cambridge, Mass.: National Bureau of Economic Research, 2000.

Roeser, R. "Bringing a 'Whole Adolescent' Perspective to Secondary Teacher Education: A Case Study of the Use of an Adolescent Case Study." *Teaching Education,* 2002, *13*(2), 155–178.

Rose, J. S., and Medway, F. J. "Measurement of Teachers' Beliefs in Their Control over Student Outcome." *Journal of Educational Research,* 1981, *74,* 185–190.

Ross, J. A. "Teacher Efficacy and the Effect of Coaching on Student Achievement." *Canadian Journal of Education,* 1992, *17*(1), 51–65.

Ross, S. M., Hughes, T. M., and Hill, R. E. "Field Experiences as Meaningful Contexts for Learning About Learning." *Journal of Educational Research,* 1981, *75*(2), 103–107.

Sanders, W. L., and Horn, S. "The Tennessee Value-Added Assessment System (TVAAS): Mixed-Model Methodology in Educational Assessment." *Journal of Personnel Evaluation in Education,* 1994, *8,* 299–311.

Sanders, W. L., and Rivers, J. C. *Cumulative and Residual Effects of Teachers on Future Student Academic Achievement.* Knoxville: University of Tennessee Value-Added Research and Assessment Center, 1996.

Schalock, D. "Research on Teacher Selection." In D. C. Berliner (ed.), *Review of Research in Education,* Vol. 7. Washington, D.C.: American Educational Research Association, 1979.

Schön, D. A. *The Reflective Practitioner: How Professionals Think in Action.* New York: Basic Books, 1983.

Schubnell, G. O. "Hawthorne Elementary School: The Evaluators' Perspective." *Journal of Education for Students Placed at Risk,* 1996, *1*(1), 13–23.

Seligman, M., and Darling, R. B. *Ordinary Families, Special Children.* New York: Guilford Press, 1989.

Sergiovanni, T. J. *Building Community in Schools.* San Francisco: Jossey-Bass, 1999.

Shavelson, R., and Dempsey-Atwood, N. "Generalizability of Measures of Teacher Behavior." *Review of Educational Research,* 1976, *46,* 553–612.

Shields, P. M., and others. *The Status of the Teaching Profession 2001.* Santa Cruz, Calif.: Center for the Future of Teaching and Learning, 2001.

Shimahara, N. K., and Sakai, A. *Learning to Teach in Two Cultures: Japan and the United States.* New York: Garland, 1995.

Shulman, L. S. "Knowledge and Teaching: Foundations of the New Reform." *Harvard Educational Review,* 1987, *57*(1), 1–22.

Shulman, L. "Toward a Pedagogy of Cases." In J. Shulman (ed.), *Case Methods in Teacher Education.* New York: Teachers College Press, 1992.

Shulman, L. "Portfolios in Historical Perspective." Presentation at Portfolios in Teaching and Teacher Education Conference, Cambridge, Mass., 1994.

Shulman, L. "Just in Case: Reflections on Learning from Experience." In J. Colbert, K. Trimble, and P. Desberg (eds.), *The Case for Education: Contemporary Approaches for Using Case Methods.* Boston: Allyn and Bacon, 1996.

Shulman, L. S. "Theory, Practice, and the Education of Professionals." *Elementary School Journal,* 1998, *98*(5), 511–526.

Silvernail, D. *Results from Surveys of Graduates of Exemplary Teacher Education Programs and the Employers of These Graduates.* University of Southern Maine: Center for Educational Policy, Applied Research, and Evaluation, 1997.

Sizer, T. *Horace's School: Redesigning the American High School.* Boston: Houghton Mifflin, 1992.

Slavin, R. E. *Cooperative Learning: Theory, Research, and Practice.* Upper Saddle River, N.J.: Prentice Hall, 1990.

Smylie, M. A. "The Enhancement Function of Staff Development: Organizational and Psychological Antecedents to Individual Teacher Change." *American Educational Research Journal,* 1988, *25,* 1–30.

Snyder, J. "Knowing Children, Understanding Teaching: The Developmental Teacher Education Program at the University of California–Berkeley." In L. Darling-Hammond (ed.), *Studies of Excellence in Teacher Education:*

Preparation at the Graduate Level. Washington, D.C.: American Association of Colleges for Teacher Education and National Commission for Teaching and America's Future, 2000.

Snyder, J. "New Haven Unified School District: A Teaching Quality System for Excellence and Equity." In A. Hightower, M. Knapp, J. Marsh, and M. McLaughlin (eds.), *School Districts and Instructional Renewal.* New York: Teachers College Press, 2002.

Stein, M. K., and Wang, M. C. "Teacher Development and School Improvement: The Process of Teacher Change." *Teaching and Teacher Education,* 1988, *4,* 171–187.

Stodolsky, S. S. "Teacher Evaluation: The Limits of Looking." *Educational Researcher,* 1984, *13*(9), 11–18.

Strauss, R. P., and Sawyer, E. A. "Some New Evidence on Teacher and Student Competencies." *Economics of Education Review,* 1986, *5*(1), 41–48.

Sunal, D. W. "Effect of Field Experience During Elementary Methods Courses on Preservice Teacher Behavior." *Journal of Research in Science Teaching,* 1980, *17*(1), 17–23.

Teitel, L. "The Impact of Professional School Partnerships on the Preparation of Teachers." *Teaching Education,* 1992, *4*(2), 77–85.

Thompson, C. L., and Zeuli, J. S. "The Frame and the Tapestry: Standards-Based Reform and Professional Development." In L. Darling-Hammond and G. Sykes (eds.), *Teaching as the Learning Profession: A Handbook of Policy and Practice.* San Francisco: Jossey-Bass, 1999.

Tikunoff, W. *Applying Significant Bilingual Instructional Features in the Classroom.* Rosslyn, Va.: National Clearinghouse for Bilingual Education, 1985.

Toppin, R., and Levine, L. "'Stronger in Their Presence: Being and Becoming a Teacher of Color." Paper presented at American Educational Research Association Annual Meeting, San Francisco, Apr. 1992.

Tracz, S. M., Sienty, S., and Mata, S. "The Self-Reflection of Teachers Compiling Portfolios for National Certification: Work in Progress." Paper presented at annual meeting of American Association of Colleges for Teacher Education, Chicago, Feb. 1994.

Tracz, S. M., and others. "Improvement in Teaching Skills: Perspectives from National Board for Professional Teaching Standards Field Test Network Candidates." Paper presented at annual meeting of American Educational Research Association, San Francisco, Apr. 1995.

Tschannen-Moran, M., Woolfolk Hoy, A., and Hoy, W. K. "Teacher Efficacy: Its Meaning and Measure." *Review of Educational Research,* 1998, *68*(2), 202–248.

Tyack, D. *The One Best System.* Cambridge, Mass.: Harvard University Press, 1974.

U.S. Department of Education. *The Secretary's Report on Teacher Quality.* Washington, D.C.: U.S. Department of Education, 2002.

Van Zandt, L. "Assessing the Effects of Reform in Teacher Education: An Evaluation of the MAT Program at Trinity University." Paper presented at annual meeting of American Educational Research Association, New York, Apr. 1996.

Van Zandt, L., and Harlan, N. "A Professional Development School Improves Teacher Preparation: Twain Meets Trinity in Texas." *Middle School Journal,* May 1995, 11–16.

Villegas, A., "Assessing Teacher Performance in a Diverse Society." In L. Goodwin (ed.), *Assessment for Equity and Inclusion: Embracing All Our Children.* New York: Routledge, 1997.

Waldrop, T. "Before You Lead a German Class, You Really Must Know Your Stuff." *Newsweek,* 1991, *118,* 62–93.

Walsh, K. *Teacher Certification Reconsidered: Stumbling for Quality.* Baltimore, Md.: Abell Foundation, 2001. http://www.abellfoundation.org.

Watkins, B. "Education School Reform Group Set to Endorse Plan That Would Alter Teacher Training, Public Schools." *Chronicle of Higher Education,* 1990, *36*(21), A15–A20.

Wenglinsky, H. *How Teaching Matters.* Princeton, N.J.: Educational Testing Service, 2000.

Wenglinsky, H. "How Schools Matter: The Link Between Teacher Classroom Practices and Student Academic Performance." *Education Policy Analysis Archives,* 2002, *10*(12). http://epaa.asu.edu/epaa/v10n12/.

Wheelock College Catalog, 1995–96. Boston: Wheelock College, 1995.

Wideen, M., Mayer-Smith, J., and Moon, B. "A Critical Analysis of the Research on Learning to Teach: Making the Case for an Ecological Perspective on Inquiry." *Review of Educational Research,* 1998, *68*(2), 130–178.

Wiley, D., and Yoon, B. "Teacher Reports of Opportunity to Learn: Analyses of the 1993 California Learning Assessment System." *Educational Evaluation and Policy Analysis,* 1995, *17*(3), 355–370.

Williams, B. C. *Reforming Teacher Education Through Accreditation: Telling Our Story.* Washington, D.C.: National Council for the Accreditation of Teacher Education and American Association of Colleges for Teacher Education, 2000.

Wilson, S. M., Darling-Hammond, L., and Berry, B. *A Case of Successful Teaching Policy: Connecticut's Long-Term Efforts to Improve Teaching and*

Learning. Seattle: Center for the Study of Teaching and Policy, University of Washington, 2001.

Wilson, S. M., Floden, R. E., and Ferrini-Mundy, J. *Teacher Preparation Research: Current Knowledge, Gaps, and Recommendations: A Research Report Prepared for the U.S. Department of Education.* Seattle: Center for the Study of Teaching and Policy, 2001.

Wright, S. P., Horn, S. P., and Sanders, W. L. "Teacher and Classroom Context Effects on Student Achievement: Implications for Teacher Evaluation." *Journal of Personnel Evaluation in Education,* 1997, *11*(1), 57–67.

Youngs, P., Odden, A., and Porter, A. C. "State Policy Related to Teacher Licensure." *Educational Policy,* 2003, *17*(2), 217–236.

Zahorick, J. A. "The Effect of Planning on Teaching." *Elementary School Journal,* 1970, *71,* 143–151.

Zeichner, K. *Educating Teachers for Cultural Diversity.* East Lansing: National Center for Research on Teacher Learning, University of Michigan, 1992.

Zeichner, K. M. "Traditions of Practice in U.S. Preservice Teacher Education Programs." *Teaching and Teacher Education,* 1993, *9*(1), 1–13.

Zeichner, K. *Ability-Based Teacher Education: Elementary Teacher Education at Alverno College.* Washington, D.C.: American Association of Colleges of Teacher Education, 1998.

Zeichner, K. M., and Gore, J. "Teacher Socialization." In W. R. Houston, M. Haberman, J. P. Sikula, and Association of Teacher Educators (eds.), *Handbook of Research on Teacher Education.* New York: Macmillan, 1990.

Zeichner, K. M., and Liston, D. P. "Teaching Student Teachers to Reflect." *Harvard Educational Review,* 1987, *57*(1), 23–48.

Zumwalt, K. "The Need for a Curricular Vision." In M. C. Reynolds (ed.), *Knowledge Base for the Beginning Teacher.* New York: Pergamon Press, 1989.

ABOUT THE AUTHOR

Linda Darling-Hammond is the Charles E. Ducommun Professor of Education at Stanford University, where she served from 1998 to 2004 as faculty sponsor for the Stanford Teacher Education Program. Darling-Hammond is also founder and co-director of the Stanford Educational Leadership Institute and the School Redesign Network. She was the founding executive director of the National Commission for Teaching and America's Future, the blue-ribbon panel whose 1996 report, *What Matters Most: Teaching for America's Future,* catalyzed major policy changes across the United States to improve the quality of teacher education and teaching. Darling-Hammond began her career as a public school teacher and has cofounded a preschool and day care center as well as a public charter high school, with which she continues to work closely. Her research, teaching, and policy work focus on issues of teaching quality, school reform, and educational equity. Among her more than two hundred publications are *Teaching as the Learning Profession* (coedited with Gary Sykes), recipient of the National Staff Development Council's Outstanding Book Award for 2000, and *The Right to Learn,* which earned the American Educational Research Association's Outstanding Book Award for 1998.

NAME INDEX

A

Abdal-Haqq, I., 328
Allinder, R. M., 66
Altman, R., 171
Ambach, G., 317
Ancess, J., 123
Anderson, J., 222
Anderson, R. D., 33, 65, 66
Andrew, M., 275, 311
Anyon, J., 223
Armor, D., 65, 66
Ashton, P., 20, 31, 65
Athanases, S. Z., 114, 139, 140

B

Bagley, W. C., 78
Baker, L., 278, 301
Baker, T., 275
Ball, D., 89, 105, 189, 190, 193, 235, 278, 287
Ballou, D., 6
Bandura, A., 68
Banks, J., 224
Baron, J. B., 336
Baumgartner, F., 100
Baumwall, L., 42–43
Begle, E. G., 32
Benner, A. D., 338, 339
Berliner, D., 29
Berman, P., 65, 66
Berry, B. A., 325, 327, 336
Betts, J. R., 21, 23
Biber, B., 194, 286, 297
Bird, T., 139
Black, A., 208–209

Blackstone, P., 269–270
Bliss, T., 114
Borko, H., 36
Borunda, M., 263
Bowles, S., 28
Boyd, D., 329
Boyer, E., 176, 296
Bradley, A., 114, 140
Bramald, R., 36
Bransford, J. D., 9, 11, 36, 68, 80, 83, 84, 95, 119, 157, 163, 269
Brewer, D. J., 21, 28, 31–32
Brimberg, S., 167
Brockmeier, L., 66
Brown, A. L., 11, 36, 38, 68
Brown, C. A., 286
Bryk, T., 341
Buchmann, M., 36
Burley, W., 66
Bush, G.H.W., 19
Byrne, C. J., 31

C

Callahan, R. E., 78
Carl, E., 43
Carroll, S., 339
Carter, R., 223
Champione, J., 38
Charney, R. S., 142
Chen, X., 14, 312, 339
Cheong, Y., 66
Chung, R., 34, 66, 232, 327
Clark, C. M., 116
Clifford, C. J., 6
Cobb, V., 332, 334
Coble, C. R., 21, 22, 33

Cochran-Smith, M., 85, 107, 108, 146
Cocking, R. R., 11, 36, 38
Coffman, L. D., 78
Cohen, D., 89, 105, 170, 193, 235, 286, 287
Cohen, E. G., 38
Coladarci, T., 66
Colberg, J., 119
Cole, M., 123, 124
Cole, S., 123, 124
Coleman, J. S., 28
Conant, J. B., 6
Cooper, E., 223
Corrigan, D., 289
Counts, G., 240
Cozart, S., 219–221
Crocker, L., 20, 31
Crow, G. M., 247, 294
Cuffaro, H., 142, 239–240

D

Daly, B., 217–219
Danenberg, A., 21, 23
Darling, R. B., 267
Darling-Hammond, L., 9, 15, 21, 22, 23, 24, 25, 30, 34, 66, 79, 80, 83, 84, 95, 114, 116, 118, 119, 123, 139, 157, 163, 223, 232, 242, 269, 275, 278, 289, 311, 312, 314, 315, 322, 323, 325, 327, 331, 332, 334, 336, 337, 341, 399
Decker, P. T., 29
Delpit, L., 234, 235, 242, 251
Dembo, M., 66
Dempsey-Atwood, N., 115
Dennison, G. M., 321
Denton, J. J., 100
Desberg, P., 119
Dewey, J., 11, 77, 78, 79, 142, 190
Diez, M., 132, 298
Donovan, M. S., 9
Doyle, W., 115
Druva, C. A., 33
Duchastel, P. C., 116

E

Ebmeier, H., 278
Eccles, J., 66
Ehrenberg, R. G., 28
Elmore, R., 314
Enochs, L. G., 66
Erixon, P., 332
Etzioni, A., 142
Evans, E. D., 66
Evertson, C., 20, 21, 31

F

Falk, B., 123
Featherstone, H., 267
Feiman-Nemser, S., 36, 42, 97
Feldlaufer, H., 66
Feldman, D., 173
Ferguson, R. F., 21, 22, 28
Ferrini-Mundy, J., 20, 21
Fetler, M., 21
Figgins, M., 215, 216, 236–238
Figlio, D. N., 257
Finn, C., 20
Fletcher, S., 29
Flexner, A., 12, 13, 281
Floden, R. E., 20, 21, 116
Forresta, A., 174
Franberg, G., 332
Freese, A. R., 103
Freire, P., 237
Frelow, F., 34, 66
French, J., 242
French, R. L., 116
Frenkel, S., 25
Friedlaender, D., 25
Fuhrman, S., 314
Fullan, M., 281, 282, 290
Fuller, F., 23, 118

G

Garcia-Lopez, S. P., 242
Garibaldi, A., 115
Garofalo, J., 199–200, 219
Gatlin, S., 21, 22, 30

Gaulman, B., 14
Gear, C., 269
Geeslin, W., 32
Geis, S., 14, 312, 339
Getzler, L. S., 257
Gibson, S., 65, 66
Gideonse, H., 322
Gingrich, N., 20
Glaser, R., 77
Glazerman, S., 29
Glickman, C., 66
Goe, L., 21
Goldhaber, D. D., 21, 31–32
Goodlad, J. I., 6, 20, 94, 97, 281, 285, 290, 293
Goodwin, L., 223
Gordon, E. W., 234
Gore, J. M., 97, 107
Grant, L., 123, 246–248
Gray, L., 275
Greene, M., 65, 66
Greenwood, G., 66
Gregg, M., 70–73, 223
Grimmett, P., 235
Grossman, P., 34, 89, 193, 204
Guarino, C., 339
Guskey, T. R., 66
Guthrie, J. W., 6

H

Haertel, E., 139, 323
Hall, B., 66
Hall, G. S., 47
Hammerness, K., 114, 119
Hanushek, E. A., 19, 28, 42, 339
Hardman, F., 36
Harlan, N., 180–181
Hatano, G., 11
Hauser, R., 257
Hawk, P., 21, 22, 33
Hawley, W., 20, 21, 31
Haynes, D., 114, 140
Hegarty, S., 14
Heilig, J. V., 21, 22, 30

Henke, R., 14, 312, 339
Henn-Reinke, K., 195
Henry, M., 100
Heubert, J., 257
Hill, H. C., 286
Hill, R. E., 100
Hitz, R., 278, 301
Hodzkom, D., 116
Hollins, E., 115
Holtzman, D., 21, 22, 30
Hoover, N. L., 116
Horn, S., 19
Hough, H., 341
Howard, R. D., 278, 301
Howey, K. R., 20, 97, 98, 275
Hoy, W. K., 65
Hughes, T. M., 100
Humphrey, D. L., 341

I

Inagaki, K., 11
Ingvarson, L., 114, 316
Irvine, J., 115, 325

J

Jackson, P. W., 35, 40, 114
Jahr, J., 190–192, 223
Johnson, A., 229–230
Johnson, B., 248–251
Johnson, D. W., 68
Johnson, R. T., 68
Johnston, J., 302, 304
Jordan, R., 165–166

K

Kain, J. F., 19, 42, 339
Kallos, D., 332
Katz, L., 118
Kennedy, M., 35, 37, 114
King, J. A., 33
Klein, S. A., 139, 314, 315
Kleinfeld, J., 119
Kleinman, J., 264–265
Klinzing, H. G., 116

Koerner, M., 100
Kopp, J., 252, 258–259, 269, 270–271
Koppich, J., 341
Kroll, L., 208–209
Kuligowski, B., 116
Kunzman, R., 96
Kutz, E., 237

L

Laboskey, V. K., 103
Laczko-Kerr, I., 29
Ladd, H. F., 28
Ladson-Billings, G., 223, 235
Lageman, E., 77, 78
Lake, K., 132
Lampert, M., 38–39
Lankford, H., 329
Lavrack, E., 14
Leat, D., 36
Levin, H. M., 28
Levine, L., 247, 294
Liston, D. P., 107
Little, J. W., 147
Loeb, S., 330
Loewen, P., 65, 66
Lortie, D. C., 35, 36
Lotan, R. A., 38
Luczak, J., 14, 339
Luque, J., 29
Lyons, N., 144
Lytle, S. L., 85, 107, 108

M

Macedo, D., 237
MacKinnon, A., 235
Maldonado-Colon, E., 115
Marrett, M., 114
Martin, A. K., 36
Mata, S., 140
Mayer, D. P., 29
Mayer-Smith, J., 99
Mayfield, V., 36

Mazur, J., 114
McDonald, J. P., 38, 39
Medway, F. J., 66
Melton, R. F., 116
Mergendoller, J. R., 302, 304
Merrill, P. F., 116
Merritt, G., 219
Michelli, N. M., 310
Midgley, C., 66
Miller, L., 289
Miller, S., 222
Mitchell, L. S., 50, 78
Moll, L., 115
Monk, D. H., 32, 33
Moon, B., 99
Morelli, M., 217, 238
Morris, J. E., 100
Morroca, M., 266–267
Mott, A. M., 211
Munby, H., 36
Murangi, K., 332, 334
Murnane, R., 28–29

N

Nager, N., 247, 294
Nieto, S., 242

O

Odden, A., 323
Olejnik, S., 66
Olsen, D. G., 20
Ortiz, A., 115
O'Shea, L. J., 116

P

Pacheco, A., 310
Paige, R., 6
Paine, L., 36
Parkay, F. W., 66
Patterson, R. S., 310
Pease, S. R., 79
Pecheone, R., 327
Perkins, D., 103, 113, 114

Peterson, P. L., 116
Placier, P., 36
Podgursky, M., 6
Porter, A. C., 323
Price, J., 107
Pritchett, H., 12–13, 281
Proller, N., 66

R

Raudenbush, S., 66
Ray, M., 206–207
Raymond, M., 29
Reichardt, R., 339
Richardson, V., 36
Rickard, W., 132
Riggs, I. M., 66
Rivkin, S. G., 19, 42, 339
Rockman, S., 302, 304
Rodriguez, M., 150, 223
Roeser, R., 114, 119
Rose, J. S., 66
Rose, R., 237
Roskelly, H., 237
Ross, J. A., 66
Ross, S. M., 100
Rowen, B., 66
Rueben, K. S., 21, 23
Russell, T., 36
Rust, F., 100

S

Sanders, W. L., 19
Sawyer, E. A., 21, 22
Scantini, P., 198
Schalock, D., 115
Scharmann, L. C., 66
Schneider, B., 341
Schoenfeld, A., 34
Schön, D. A., 37, 84
Schwab, R. L., 275, 311
Sclan, E., 116
Sedenka, S., 204–205
Seligmann, M., 267

Sergiovanni, T. J., 128
Shavelson, R., 115
Sherk, J., 223
Shields, P. M., 24, 321, 322, 339
Shulman, L. S., 34, 80, 88, 89, 104, 106, 114, 119, 120, 144, 150, 327
Sienty, S., 140
Silvernail, D., 59, 289
Singleton, K., 339
Sirotnik, K. A., 97
Sizer, T., 139
Slavin, R. E., 68
Smith, M. S., 286
Sneed, M., 195
Snyder, J., 70, 116, 118
Soder, R., 97
Stein, M. K., 286
Stern, D., 237
Stodolsky, S. S., 115, 146
Strauss, R. P., 21, 22
Strezpek, J., 216
Sunal, D. W., 100
Swanson, M., 21, 22, 33
Switzer, A., 170
Sykes, G., 312, 322, 331, 337

T

Tamashiro, R., 66
Taylor, T., 260, 269, 270
Teeter, D. J., 278
Teitel, L., 289
Thompson, C. L., 314
Thorndike, E. L., 77, 78
Tikunoff, W., 115
Timson, M., 171–172
Tooke, D. J., 100
Toppin, R., 294
Tracz, S. M., 114, 140, 327
Tribble, M. N., 66
Trimble, K., 119
Tschannen-Moran, M., 65, 68
Twombly, S., 278
Tyack, D., 78

V

Van Zandt, L., 180–181, 295
Villegas, A., 115
Villeme, M., 66

W

Waldrop, T., 333
Walsh, K., 28
Watkins, B., 289, 290
Webb, R. B., 65
Weinburger, T., 166, 167
Wenglinsky, H., 33
Wheelock, L., 46, 78
Wideen, M., 99
Wiley, D., 286
Williams, B. C., 324
Willis, J., 302, 304
Wilson, S. M., 20, 21, 325, 327, 336

Windsor, C., 286, 297
Wise, A. E., 79, 139, 314, 315
Woolfolk Hoy, A., 65
Wright, S. P., 19
Wyckoff, J., 330

Y

Yoon, B., 286
Young, E. F., 78
Youngs, P., 323

Z

Zahorick, J. A., 116
Zeichner, K. M., 20, 97, 107, 223, 224
Zeuli, J. S., 314
Zimpher, N. L., 20, 97, 98, 275
Zlotnik, M., 20, 21, 31
Zumwalt, K., 82

SUBJECT INDEX

A

AACTE/NCATE joint data system, 312

Accreditation standards, 323–325, 329

Action research, 146–151

"Adaptive experts," 10–11

African American students, 223–224. *See also* Diverse learners; Minorities

Albemarle High School, 219–220

Alliance for Better Schools (San Antonio), 56

Alverno College Faculty, 46, 134

Alverno College program: candidate selection in, 307–309; clinical experience of, 156, 157; described, 7, 45; developing skills for teaching diverse learners in, 248–251; exhibitions of performance curriculum of, 132–136; guided approach used in, 297–298; *Handbook for Education Students* (1995) of, 208; high quality of, 283; institutional incentives used in, 295; learning assessment/development tools used in, 204; modeling teaching strategies approach by, 195–196; multicultural study approach of, 235–236; perceptions of preparedness by graduates of, 65; performance tasks used in, 105; portfolio used in, 140; social justice field placement approach by, 226–228; teacher education model used in, 45–46

"Apartheid schools," 24

Apprenticeship of observation: creating objectives of, 193–195; modeling process of "thinking like a teacher," 197–200; modeling teaching strategies, 195–196; problem of, 35–37

Assessment: based on professional standards, 277; developing tools for learning, 204–207; emphasis on process of, 82; practice of, 118–119; practice of self-assessment, 135–136; of teaching performance, 325–327. *See also* Performances of understanding

Autobiography, 108–109

B

Bank Street College program: action research done at, 148; candidate selection in, 306–307; child development/learning theories basis of, 86, 120–123; comments by graduates on, 43, 45; connecting to home and school communities approach of, 267–268; contexts and purposes of education courses of, 94, 95; coursework and clinical work used by, 102–103, 120–123; curricular thinking facilitated in, 209–211; curriculum materials/ design development in, 212; described, 48–49; developing skills for teaching diverse learners in, 246–247;

Bank Street College program, *continued*
 guidance approach of, 297; helping students develop learning strategies, 268–270; institutional incentives used in, 294; lab school model used by, 161–162, 163–174; learning assessment/development tools used in, 205–206; managing dialectic between students and subjects in, 190–192; O and R course of, 120–123; partnership schools with, 169–174; PDS model used in, 155, 161–162, 163–174; pedagogical knowledge included in, 89, 90; perceptions of preparation by graduates of, 60; portfolio use in, 141–142; race, class, gender, and social inequality issues discussed in, 245–246; responding to students' needs approach in, 263–267; School for Children, 49, 50, 161–162, 163–169, 210; social action commitment of, 238–240; teacher education model used in, 48–51; *Young Geographers* of, 211

Barron's Index of College Majors, 337

Bay Area Writing Project (Berkeley), 52, 203–204

Behavioral learning theory, 77–78

Berkeley's Lawrence Hall of Science, 52, 203, 300

BEST portfolio assessments, 327

Brackenridge Forum (Trinity University), 285

Building Community in Schools (Sergiovanni), 128

Bureaucratic organization theory, 78

C

California: distribution of underqualified teachers in, 23*fig*–24; PACT (Performance Assessment for California Teachers), 326–327; portfolio assessments used in, 325–326; teacher bonus strategies implemented by, 341; Teachers as a Priority Program, 341

California State University, 275, 322

California, Williams v., 25, 26, 27

Carnegie Foundation for the Advancement of Teaching, 12

Carnegie Task Force on Teaching as a Profession, 20, 281

The Case for Education (Colberg, Trimble, and Desberg), 119

Case methods: child case study using, 120–128; other uses of, 128–131; overview of, 103–104, 119–120

Center of Pedagogy, 310

Certification. *See* Teacher certification

The Child and the Curriculum (Dewey), 190

Child development: child study coursework, 139–146; field placements and ecological perspective on, 232–235; teaching education programs based on, 86–88

Chinese Taipei (Taiwan), teacher education, 333–334

Chrysanthemum lesson, 266–267

CLAD credential, 319

Class issues, 242–246

Classrooms: assuming graduated responsibility during, 159–160; creating new apprenticeship of observation in, 193–200; example of managing dialectic between students/subjects in, 190–193; guided observations of, 157–159, 168, 217–221, 297. *See also* Clinical experience

Clinical experience: analyses of teaching and learning during, 104–105; assuming graduated responsibility during, 159–160; benefits of using, 277; case writing of, 103–104; creating new apprenticeship of observation, 193–200; developing curricular perspective of subject matter, 207–221; developing teachers through, 156–161; examining students' thinking in the disciplines, 200–207; example of managing dialectic between students and subjects, 190–193, 217–221; guided field placements for social justice teaching, 224–234; guided observations of, 157–159, 168, 297; interweaving coursework and, 99–103; overview of, 152–156; performance tasks included in, 105–106; preparing for placements, 161; school-university partnership for, 161–163; Trinity PDS model used for, 177–181; University of Southern Maine's SMP model used for, 181–185. *See also* Classrooms; PDS (professional development school) model; Teacher education programs

"Combat pay," 340

Complexity problem, 38–40

Connecticut: Educational Enhancement Act (1986), 336; State Department of Education, 336; student achievement gains in, 335–336, 337

Coursework: child study, 139–146; interweaving clinical work and, 99–103; knowledge base included in, 27–34, 77–97, 84*fig. See also* Subject matter; Teacher education content

Curricular thinking: developing habits of, 207–211; developing materials and designs to facilitate, 211–217

Curriculum education: developing perspective on subject matter, 207–221; problem of using superficial, 279; sociocultural context of, 82; strong core curriculum used in,

276; subject matter knowledge and design of, 82; teacher education program inclusion of, 93–97. *See also* Subject matter; Teacher education content

Curry School of Education. *See* UVA (University of Virginia) BA/MT program

D

Dare the Schools Build a New Social Order? (Counts), 240

Decision making: reflective, 83; understanding of learning for, 81

Democracy and Education (Dewey), 142

A Difference in the Family (Featherstone), 267

Diverse learners: analyzing and understanding student needs, 263–267; combining practice with research and theory to teach, 259–263; comprehensive approach to teaching, 254–257; connecting to the home and school communities of, 267–268; developing skills for teaching, 246–251; ELL (English language learners), 65, 338; helping students develop strategies guiding learning, 268–271; importance of reaching, 252–254; learning to teach so all students learn, 257–271. *See also* Learners; Minorities; Multicultural study

DTE (Developmental Teacher Education). *See* UC Berkeley, DTE (Developmental Teacher Education) program

E

ELL (English language learners): lack of preparedness for teaching, 65; lack of teachers for, 338

Enactment problem, 37–38

Equity education: for diverse learners, 246–251; integrated approach to multicultural study, 235–246; learning to teach for social justice, 223–235

"Equity" pedagogy, 224

ERIC bibliographic system, 148

ETEP program. *See* University of Southern Maine, ETEP program

Evaluation. *See* Assessment

Evidence of practice, 68–73, 69*t*

Exhibitions of performance: Alverno College program curriculum of, 132–136; University of Southern Maine curriculum of, 136–139

Experimenting with the World (Cuffaro), 142

F

Feedback: emphasis on process of, 82; as part of assessment practice, 118; student improvement through teacher, 139

Field placements: Alverno approach to, 226–228; ecological perspective on child development approach to, 232–235; social justice teaching and guided, 224–225; Trinity approach to, 230–232; UC Berkeley approach to, 225–226; Wheelock approach to, 228–230

Finland's "model schools," 332–333

Flexner Report (1910), 12, 281

Fluvanna High School, 217–219

Fordham Foundation, 12

French teacher education programs, 284, 333

G

Gender issues, 242–246

Goodlad's National Network for Educational Renewal, 310

Gorham School District, 136–139, 213

Graduated responsibilities, 159–160

Guided observation approach, 157–159, 168, 297

H

Handbook for Education Students (Alverno College), 208

Hawthorne Elementary School (San Antonio), 176

Health Professions Education Assistance act, 329

Higher Education Act Title II, 325

Holmes Group, 20, 53, 162, 174, 281, 284, 286, 301

How People Learn (Donovan and Bransford), 9

I

"Inquiry stance," 107–108, 277

Institutional development: building connections to the field, 288–289; designing incentives for high-quality preparation, 293–301; integrating work of universities and schools, 290–292; investing resources in strong candidates, 305–309; making teacher education investments in, 278–280; of market incentives to improve quality, 280–282, 331–342; strategies for improving preparation and, 282–283; of stronger standards, 280; transforming teacher education through, 281–282; wise resource investment, 301–309

Institutional incentives: high-quality preparation through, 293–301; promotion, tenure, and scholarship, 295–297; for staffing teacher education, 297–301; supporting teacher education, 294–295

INTASC (Interstate New Teacher Assessment and Support Consortium), 54, 80, 81, 143, 315–316, 317, 329

International Studies Academy (San Antonio), 150

Internship. *See* Clinical work

ISA (International School of the Americas), 177

J

Jackson-Keller Elementary School, 176–177

Jackson-Via Elementary School, 155

Japanese teacher education, 333, 334

Journals, 107

K

Kentucky Institute for Education Research, 275

Knowledge base: on conceptualization of teaching, 80–85, 84*fig*; on contexts and curriculum, 93–94; on contexts and purposes of education, 94–95; on curriculum development and assessment, 95–97; learning theories on, 77–80; subject matter, 30–34, 81–82, 88–93. *See also* Learning; Pedagogical knowledge; Performances of understanding

L

Lab school model: Bank Street College's School for Children, 161–162, 163–169; Bank Street partnership schools, 169–174; evolution of, 174–185; professional development schools' evolution of, 174–185; Trinity's PDS network, 175–181

Labor market. *See* Teacher labor market

Latino students, 223–224. *See also* Diverse learners; Minorities

Lawrence Hall of Science (Berkeley), 52, 203, 300

Learner-centered teaching, 7–8, 189–190

Learners: ELL (English language learners), 65, 338; knowledge of, 85–88; teaching decisions based on understanding of, 81. *See also* Diverse learners

Learning: analyses of teaching and, 104–105, 131; developing tools for assessing/developing, 204–207; helping students develop strategies guiding, 268–271; knowledge of, 85–88; opportunities for reflection on, 106–107; preconceptions regarding, 36; teaching decisions based on understanding of, 81; three fundamental principles of, 9–10; three "problems" in learning to teach, 35–40; within professional community, 109–112. *See also* Knowledge base

Learning disabled students. *See* Diverse learners

Learning theories: behavioral, 77–78; bureaucratic organization, 78; on knowledge base of teachers, 77–80; teaching education programs based on, 86–88

Learning to teach: "the apprenticeship of observation" problem of, 35–37; challenges of, 35; to diverse learners, 246–251; an integrated approach to multicultural study, 235–246; pedagogies confronting problems of, 103–106; problem of complexity, 38–40; problem of enactment, 37–38; so all students can learn, 257–271; for social justice, 223–235. *See also* Teaching

Learning-centered teaching: described, 7–8; teacher understanding and use of, 189–190

Literacy: Reading the World and the World (Freire and Macedo), 237

Living on the Boundary (Rose), 237

Locus of control, 67*t*

Longitudinal Study of American Youth (LSAY), 32, 33

M

Making of a Teacher (Grossman), 193
Mark Twain Middle School (San Antonio), 176, 180
Maryland State Department of Education, 329
Massachusetts State Task Force on Teacher Preparation, 285
Medical education study (1908–1910), 12, 281
Medical Manpower Act, 329
Mentor teaching: impact on teacher retention, 339–340; Trinity's experience with, 179
Midtown West Elementary School, 123, 171–172
Milwaukee Public Schools, 156, 288
Minorities: diverse learning issues for, 246–271; equity education and, 223–251; increasing PDS success with, 330–331; teacher education candidate selection and, 307–308. *See also* African American students; Diverse learners; Latino students
Multicultural study: commitment to social action as part of, 238–242; using integrated approach to, 235–238; willingness to include race, class, gender, and social inequality issues, 242–246. *See also* Diverse learners; Social justice teaching

N

National Academy of Education, 83, 95, 324–325
National Academy of Sciences, 9
National Assessment of Educational Progress (NAEP), 33, 336
National Board for Professional Teaching Standards (NBPTS), 80–81

National Center for Education Statistics (NCES), 257, 278
National Commission on Teaching and America's Future (NCTAF), 15, 53, 279, 315, 330, 339, 342
National Commission on Teaching and America's Future report (1996), 310–311, 314
National Commission on Teaching and America's Future report (2003), 312
National Council for the Accreditation of Teacher Education (NCATE), 81, 302, 316, 324, 329
National Councils of Teachers of English and Mathematics, 81
National Education Association, 59
National Education Goals Panel (NEGP), 335, 336, 337
National Educational Longitudinal Studies of 1988 (NELS), 22
National Longitudinal Study of Mathematical Abilities, 32
National Network for Education Renewal, 281, 285, 286, 310
National Research Council, 322
National Teacher Examinations (NTE), 22
New York City. P.S. 234, 169–170, 190
New Zealand's Advice and Guidance Program, 334
North Carolina teacher legislation, 335, 336, 340–341

O

Oakland Unified School District, 222
Observation: creating new apprenticeship of, 193–200; guided, 157–159, 168, 297
Observation logs, 107
Ordinary Families, Special Children (Seligman and Darling), 267

Organization for Economic Cooperation and Development (OECD), 11

P

PACT (Performance Assessment for California Teachers), 326–327

PDS (professional development school) model: described, 154–155, 156; developing teachers through guided clinical experience of, 156–161, 297; future potential of, 289; increasing use with minorities and urban students, 330–331; integrating work of universities and schools using, 290–292, 295–296; objectives of, 163; recommendations for increasing funding of, 328–329; relationship between elementary schools and, 155; school-university partnerships, 162–163; teacher working conditions of, 341; Trinity's PDS network/clinical work, 175–181; University of Southern Maine's use of, 181–185. *See also* Clinical experience; School-university partnerships

"Peace Treaty" (class rules), 72

"Pedagogical amnesia," 106

Pedagogical knowledge: confronting problems of learning to teach, 103–106; "equity," 224; as multicultural teaching model, 237–238; School for Children approach to, 167–168; student learning within content-specific, 201–204; subject matter versus, 30–34; teacher education inclusion of, 88–93; teaching effectiveness and requirements for, 27–34; UVA's courses approach to, 89–90, 198. *See also* Knowledge base

PEN (Public Education Network) [Virginia], 219, 303

Perceptions of preparedness survey: described, 59; findings on feelings of efficacy, 65–68, 67t; findings on locus of control, 67t; findings of, 60, 61t–65, 64t; samples used in, 59–60

Performance tasks, 105–106

Performance-based standards, 316

Performances of understanding: action research to promote, 146–151; analysis of learning and teaching demonstrating, 131; case methods demonstrating, 103–104, 119–131; exhibitions of performance, 132–139; focus on performance, 116–117; integration of knowledge and skills in practice, 117; multiple measures of, 117–118; opportunities for practice, 118–119; teaching portfolios to demonstrate, 106, 114, 139–146; utility of, 113–116. *See also* Assessment; Knowledge base

PISA (Program for International Student Assessment), 332

Portfolios (teaching), 106, 114, 139–146, 325–326

Preparing Teachers for a Changing World: (Darling-Hammond and Bransford), 83

Professional community: learning within, 109–112; reform through development of, 286–292; teaching as collaborative activity of, 83. *See also* Teachers

Professional standards: assessment based on professional, 277; continuing problems in implementing, 319–323; creating meaningful and universal, 323; influence of, 316–319; INTASC teacher certification, 143–144, 315–316, 317, 329; move toward performance-based, 316; NCATE accreditation, 324, 329;

Professional standards, *continued*
overview of, 314–315; setting
initiatives in teaching, 315–316;
state program regulations and, 319,
335–337; weak accreditation, 280.
See also Teacher certification
Promotion incentives, 295–297
Public policies: federal, 337; improving conditions of teaching, 340–
342; improving teacher retention,
339–340; to increase supply in
shortage fields/areas, 337–338;
lessons from other countries, 331–
334; state program regulations,
319, 335–337; supporting teaching
in the U.S., 334–337

R

Racial issues, 242–246
RAND study, 66
Reflection: decision maker's use of, 83;
as part of assessment practice, 118;
self-reflection, 108–109
Reflective essays, 107
Research: action, 146–151; diverse
learning using practice, theory, and,
259–263
Research inquiries, 107–108
Robert E. Lee High School, 177

S

Scholarship incentives, 295–297
Scholarship Reconsidered (Boyer), 296
School for Children (Bank Street College), 49, 50, 161–162, 163–169,
210–211
School-based case studies, 128
School-university partnerships:
addressing special needs students
through, 263; Bank Street's experience with, 169–174; benefits of,
277; for clinical experience, 161–
163; evolution of lab school and,
174–185; Trinity's PDS network of,

175–181; University of Southern
Maine's experience with, 181–185.
See also PDS (professional develop-
ment school) model
Self-assessment, 135–136
Self-efficacy, 65–68, 67t, 68
Self-reflection, 108–109
Smart Schools for San Antonio's
Future, 175
SMP (Southern Maine Partnership),
181–185
Social action commitment, 238–242
Social inequality issues, 242–246
Social justice teaching: guided field
placements for, 224–225; impor-
tance of preparation for, 223–224.
See also Multicultural study
The Sources of a Science of Education
(Dewey), 11, 77
Southern Maine Partnership, 175,
285, 288. *See also* University of
Southern Maine (USM), ETEP pro-
gram
Southwestern Bell, 177
Special education students. *See* Diverse
learners
The Spirit of Community (Etzioni),
142
Standards. *See* Professional standards
State program regulations, 319, 335–
337
Student achievement: Connecticut
gains regarding, 335–336, 337;
links between teacher qualifications
and, 21–22; socioeconomic status
impact on, 24*fig*
Student performance: subject matter
knowledge and link to, 32–34;
teacher feedback and improved,
139
Students: diverse learning of, 246–
271; ELL (English language learners), 65, 338; impact of socioeconomic status of, 24*fig*;

learning-centered teaching of, 7–8, 189–190; managing dialectic between subjects and, 190–192, 217–221; teacher's effect on learning by, 19; three fundamental principles of learning by, 9–10

Subject matter: creating apprenticeship of observation on, 193–200; developing curricular perspective on, 207–221; examining students' thinking in the disciplines, 200–207; examples of managing dialectic between students and, 190–192, 217–221; learning-centered approach using, 189–190; writing standards for content, mechanics, and goals, 191–192. *See also* Coursework; Curriculum education

Subject matter knowledge: curriculum design and, 82; importance of, 81–82; pedagogical versus, 30–34; sociocultural context of, 82; student performance link to, 32–34; teacher education inclusion of, 88–93

T

Teach for America (TFA), 29–30

Teacher accreditation, 323–325, 329

Teacher certification: CLAD credential, 319; effective teaching relationship to, 24–27, 29–30; increasing shortage in specific fields/areas, 337–338; INTASC standards for, 143–144, 315–316, 317, 329; North Carolina teacher legislation on, 335, 336; problem of weak standards for, 280; proposed evaluation recommendations for, 325–327; *Williams* v. *California* lawsuit over, 25–26. *See also* Professional standards; Teacher qualifications

Teacher Corps, 282

Teacher education: average retention rate of candidates, 312*fig*; challenges of contemporary, 7–11; comments from graduates about, 43–44; common components of powerful, 41; common practices of, 276–277; dilemmas of, 34–35; getting knowledge to teachers through, 13–16; importance of coherence in, 97–99; increasing demands/expectations for good, 4–6; preparing teachers for responsive practice, 11–13; process of, 97–112; recommendations for increasing funding of, 328–329; teacher satisfaction with, 275–276; why it matters, 20–34. *See also* Teacher education programs; Transforming teacher education

Teacher education content: conceptualization of teaching knowledge, 80–85; contexts and purposes of education, 94–95; knowledge of contexts and curriculum, 93–94; knowledge of subject matter and pedagogy, 88–93; learning theories and child development elements of, 86–88; pedagogical learner knowledge built through, 85–88. *See also* Coursework; Curriculum education

Teacher education models: Alverno College program, 45–46; Bank Street College program, 48–51; Trinity University program, 55–57; UC Berkeley, DTE program, 51–53; University of Southern Maine, ETEP program, 53–55; UVA, BA/MT program, 57–59; Wheelock College program, 46–48

Teacher education process: continuous opportunities for reflection on learning/teaching, 106–109; creating foundation for learning in professional community, 109–112;

Teacher education process, *continued*
importance of coherence to, 97–99;
integrating theory and practice,
99–103; pedagogies confronting
problems of learning to teach,
103–106

Teacher education programs: accreditation of, 323–325, 329; average
retention rate for pathways into
teaching, 312*fig*; the challenge of
looking for, 6–7; critiques of, 279;
distinctive models used for, 45–59;
evidence of practice in, 68–73, 69*t*;
general state of national, 310–312;
graduates' feelings of efficacy from,
65–68; graduates' perceptions of
preparedness from, 59–65; incentives for creating stronger, 327–
331; institutional investments and
university context of, 278–280;
integrating work of universities and
schools, 290–292; seeding high-
quality urban, 329–331; selection
of candidates to, 305–309; staffing,
297–301; supporting university,
283–286; value of studying successful, 16–17. *See also* Clinical
experience; *specific individual
programs*; Teacher education

Teacher effectiveness: link between
qualifications and, 24–27, 29–30;
market incentives undermining
quality and, 280–282; pedagogical
requirements and, 27–34; pedagogical versus subject matter knowledge and, 30–34; verbal ability
predictor of, 28–29

Teacher labor market: improving conditions of teaching, 340–342;
improving teacher retention,
339–340; incentives to improve
teacher quality, 280–282; increasing supply in shortage fields/areas,
337–338; lessons from other countries, 331–334; public policy to
support teachers in, 334–337

Teacher qualifications: debate over
effective teaching and pedagogical,
27–34; effective teaching and, 24–
27; link between teachers' effectiveness and, 22–23; links between
student achievement and, 21–22;
relationship among API scores,
student SES, and, 24*fig*. *See also*
Teacher certification

Teacher salaries, 340–341

Teachers: as adaptive experts, 10–11;
impact on student learning by, 19;
improving retention of, 339–340;
incentives for recruiting/distributing quality, 331–342; increasing
shortage in specific fields/areas,
337–338; satisfaction with teacher
education by, 275–276; strategies
for improving compensation of,
340–341; "thinking like a teacher"
modeling for, 197–200; unequal
distribution of well-qualified,
23–24. *See also* Professional community

Teaching: analyses of learning and,
104–105, 131; as collaborative
activity of professional community,
83; debate over teacher knowledge
and effective, 27–34; evaluating
performance of, 325–327; improving conditions of, 340–342;
"inquiry stance" toward, 107–108;
mentor, 179, 339–340; new mission/approaches to, 9–10; opportunities for reflection on, 106–107;
perceived as intuitive, 8; preconceptions regarding, 36; problem
of enactment and expectations for,
115; reality of effective, 8; responsive practice of, 11–13; teacher
qualifications and effective, 24–27;
three "problems" in learning

process of, 35–40. *See also* Learning to teach

Teaching Children to Care (Charney), 142

Teaching English So It Matters (Stern), 237

Teaching portfolios, 106, 114, 139–146, 325–326

Teaching strategies: developing repertoire of, 82; modeling, 195–196; "thinking like a teacher" modeling to develop, 197–200

Technology investment, 302–304

Tenure incentives, 295–297

Texas Middle School Conference, 141

"Thinking like a teacher" modeling, 197–200

Third International Math and Science Study, 336

Thomas B. Fordham Foundation, 20

Title II (Higher Education Act), 325

Trainers of Teacher Trainers, 282

Transforming teacher education: building connections to the field, 288–289; by designing incentives for high-quality preparation, 293–301; designing institutional incentives for education, 293–301; developing community for preparing teachers, 286–292; infusing technology in education, 302–304; institutional investment and university context of, 278–280; integrating work of universities and schools, 290–292; investing resources in strong candidates, 305–309; nature of the problem, 277–282; strategies for institutional change, 282–283; supporting university teacher education programs, 283–286; through wise investment of resources, 301–309. *See also* Teacher education

Trickle-down theory of knowledge, 79

Trinity University program: action research done at, 149–150; Brackenridge Forum and, 285; child study coursework of, 128; clinical experience in, 177–181; combining practice, research, and theory in, 260–261; comments by graduate about, 44; coursework and clinical work mix of, 100–101, 102, 128; curriculum materials/design development in, 212, 213–214; described, 7, 55; evidence of practice in, 70; foundation of learning through, 111; institutional incentives used in, 295–296; lab school model used in, 175; mentor teaching in, 179; modeling teaching strategies approach by, 195; PDS initiatives launched by, 154; PDS network of, 175–181; pedagogical knowledge included in, 89; perceptions of preparedness by graduates of, 65; portfolio use in, 140–141; reform measures taken by, 284–285; Smart Schools for San Antonio's Future developed by, 175; social justice field placement approach by, 230–232; subject matter knowledge included in, 91; teacher education model used in, 55–57

U

UC Berkeley, DTE (Developmental Teacher Education) program: action research done at, 147; candidate selection in, 305–306; child study coursework of, 124–128; combining practice, research, and theory in, 260; coursework and clinical work used in, 102; curricular thinking facilitated in, 208–209; described, 7, 51; evidence of practice in, 70, 71; examining students' thinking as part of, 200, 201–204;

UC Berkeley, DTE program, *continued*
graduate's comment about, 44;
guidance approach used in, 299–
301; INTASC standards used in,
317; learning theories/child development basis of, 86–87; PDS in,
155; pedagogical knowledge
included in, 89–90; perceptions of
preparedness by graduates of, 65;
race, class, gender, and social
inequality issues discussed in,
242–245; reforms enacted by,
284; social justice field placement
approach by, 225–226; student
comments on, 15; teacher education model used in, 51–53
UCLA lab school, 162
*Uniquiet Pedagogy: Transforming
Practice in English Classrooms*
(Kutz and Roskelly), 237
University of Chicago lab school, 162
University programs. *See* Teacher
education programs
University of Southern Maine (USM),
ETEP program: child study coursework at, 128; community case
study used at, 129; coursework and
clinical work used in, 102, 128;
curriculum materials/design development in, 212–213; described, 53;
exhibitions of performance curriculum of, 136–139; foundation of
learning through, 111; guidance
approach used in, 298, 299; institutional incentives used in, 296–
297; INTASC model standards
used in, 317; learning assessment/
development tools used in, 204–
205; learning theories/child development basis of, 87–88, 128; learning to teach diverse students as part
of, 258–259; ongoing improvement
efforts by, 276; PDS initiatives

launched by, 154; PDS model used
in, 181–185, 290, 291–292; pedagogical knowledge included in, 89,
90; portfolio used in, 140, 143;
professional standards used in,
318; reform measures taken by,
284, 285; teacher education model
used in, 53–55; technological
investment in, 302–304. *See also*
Southern Maine Partnership
U.S. Congressional Office of Technology, 302
U.S. Department of Education, 6, 21,
28
UVA (University of Virginia) BA/MT
program: action research done at,
148–149; case methods used in,
129–130; child study coursework
of, 128; combining practice,
research, and theory in, 260;
coursework and clinical work mix
of, 100, 101; curriculum materials/
design development in, 213–217;
described, 7, 57; evidence of practice in, 70; foundation of learning
through, 110; graduated responsibility approach in, 159–160;
guided observation approach used
in, 159; helping students develop
learning strategies, 270–271; learning theories/child development elements of, 87–88; master teacher
practicum focus of, 101; multicultural study approach of, 236–238;
PDS school model used in, 155,
162; pedagogical knowledge
included in, 89–90, 198; perceptions of preparedness by graduates
of, 65; portfolio use in, 143; self-
reflection as part of, 108–109; subject matter knowledge included in,
91–92; teacher education model
used in, 57–59

V

Valero Energy, 177
Virginia's Public Education Network
    (PEN), 219, 303

W

Wheelock College program: action
    research done at, 147; candidate
    selection in, 309; child study
    coursework of, 123–124; combin-
    ing practice, research, and theory
    in, 261–263; described, 7, 46–47;
    guidance approach used in, 298;
    learning theories/child development
    basis of, 86, 87; modeling teaching
    strategies approach by, 196; out-of-
school community organizations
    case study of, 129; PDS model used
    in, 155, 174–175; reform measures
    taken by, 285–286; social action
    commitment of, 240–242; social
    justice field placement approach by,
    228–230; teacher education model
    used by, 46–48
"The Wheelock Way," 48, 196
William Monroe High School, 219
Williams v. California, 25, 26, 27

Y

YMCA, 175, 231
Young Geographers (Bank Street
    College), 211

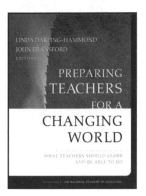

Preparing Teachers for a Changing World

What Teachers Should Learn and Be Able to Do

Linda Darling-Hammond
and John D. Bransford

624 pages / Cloth
ISBN: 0-7879-7464-1

"The knowledge base for teacher preparation and teaching is maturing and becoming very relevant to practice. This state-of-the-art compendium is essential reading for teacher educators committed to preparing professionals who can teach so that all children will, in fact, learn."
—Arthur E. Wise, president, National Council for Accreditation of Teacher Education

Based on rapid advances in what is known about how people learn and how to teach effectively, this important book examines the core concepts and central pedagogies that should be at the heart of any teacher education program. Stemming from the results of a commission sponsored by the National Academy of Education, *Preparing Teachers for a Changing World* recommends the creation of an informed teacher education curriculum with the common elements that represent state-of-the-art standards for the profession.

Written for teacher educators in both traditional and alternative programs, university and school system leaders, teachers, staff development professionals, researchers, and educational policymakers, the book addresses the key foundational knowledge for teaching and discusses how to implement that knowledge within the classroom. *Preparing Teachers for a Changing World* recommends that, in addition to strong subject matter knowledge, all new teachers have a basic understanding of how people learn and develop, as well as how children acquire and use language, which is the currency of education. In addition, the book suggests that teaching professionals must be able to apply that knowledge in developing curriculum that attends to students' needs, the demands of the content, and the social purposes of education: in teaching specific subject matter to diverse students, in managing the classroom, assessing student performance, and using technology in the classroom.

The ideas and suggestions outlined in this book have far-reaching implications for educational policy, classroom practice, and staff development and will go a long way toward informing the next generation of teachers.

John D. Bransford is Centenniel Professor of Psychology and Education and co-director of the Learning Technology Center at Vanderbilt University. He is co-chair of the National Academy of Education's Committee on Teacher Education.

Collaborating editors *Pamela LePage, Karen Hammerness,* and *Helen Duffy* served as staff of the National Academy's Committee on Teacher Education.

A Good Teacher in Every Classroom

Preparing the Highly Qualified Teachers Our Children Deserve

Linda Darling-Hammond
and Joan Baratz-Snowden, Editors

112 pages / Paper
ISBN: 0-7879-7466-8

What kind of experiences do children need in order to grow and learn? What kind of knowledge do teachers need in order to facilitate these experiences for children? And what kind of experiences do teachers need to develop this knowledge? *A Good Teacher in Every Classroom* addresses these questions by examining the core concepts and central pedagogies that should be at the heart of any teacher education program, and it recommends the policy changes needed to ensure that all teachers gain access to this knowledge. This book is the result of a blue-ribbon commission sponsored by the National Academy of Education.

With two million teachers entering the workforce in the next decade, *A Good Teacher in Every Classroom* offers a blueprint for educating this new generation of teachers. The book is filled with solid recommendations for helping new teachers develop a basic understanding of education, teaching, and learning. And, it explains why and how teachers must learn to connect with different cultures, develop curriculum that meets students' learning needs, manage common behavior problems, and assess academic progress.

Joan Baratz-Snowden is director of Educational Issues at the American Federation of Teachers (AFT). She was vice president for Education Policy and Reform and for Assessment and Research at the National Board for Professional Teaching Standards.

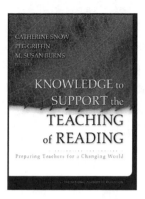

Knowledge to Support the Teaching of Reading

Preparing Teachers for a Changing World

Catherine Snow, Peg Griffin, and M. Susan Burns, Editors

336 pages / Cloth
ISBN: 0-7879-7465-X

Reading and literacy has been a cornerstone of the education platforms of the last several presidential administrations. At the same time, there has been a movement to improve the quality of teaching and come to agreement on a core knowledge base for the teaching profession. While it's now recognized that basic reading proficiency is key to student success in all content areas, many teachers have not been specifically grounded in the fundamentals of reading theory and practice, especially if their area of expertise is in another discipline.

This book presents recommendations for the essential knowledge new teachers need to know about the development, acquisition, and teaching of language and literacy skills. This volume is the first to offer recommendations for this core knowledge base from the esteemed National Academy of Education.

Based on the scholarship and renown of Catherine Snow and the National Academy of Education, this book will become the definitive guide to reading and literacy preparation for teacher education, and its recommendations will be widely adopted. Whether you are a teacher educator, reading specialist, staff developer, classroom teacher, or an educational administrator, you will find Catherine Snow's recommendations relevant and essential to your own professional development and those with whom you work.

Catherine Snow is the Henry Lee Shattuck professor of education at the Harvard Graduate School of Education. She is an expert on language and literacy development in children, focusing on how oral language skills are acquired and how they relate to literacy outcomes. She has recently chaired two national panels for the National Academy of Sciences and the Rand Reading Study Group.

The Right to Learn

A Blueprint for Creating Schools That Work

Linda Darling-Hammond

Winner of the AERA Outstanding Book Award in 1998

416 pages / Paper
ISBN: 0-7879-5942-1

Using in-depth interviews with dozens of teachers and studies of many successful schools, Darling-Hammond provides a vision of exceptional learner-centered schools and describes the policies and practices that are needed to create these schools on a systemwide basis.

"Darling-Hammond's central claim is well worth listening to. She argues that American students do so poorly by comparison with students in other industrialized countries not because we don't give them enough work, but because our teaching is less thoughtful, and because we are obsessed with bureaucratic processes rather than educational outcomes."
—*The New York Times Book Review*

"In *The Right to Learn*, Linda Darling-Hammond gives readers a comprehensive, thoughtful look at the condition of American schooling and sets forth proposals for its improvement. . . . This well-organized and meticulously documented book presents an agenda for re-creating public education." —*Washington Post*

"This is a very fine work—well argued, comprehensive, and authoritative. It will be treated as a Bible—or, more properly, a Constitution—by those seriously engaged in the improvement of American public education."
—Howard Gardner, professor of education, Harvard University, and author of *Leading Minds*

"If only I could get every American who claims to be concerned about our schools to read this thorough, readable, and brilliant book. Linda Darling-Hammond knows our schools as no one else does—as a scholar, hands-on researcher, practitioner, concerned citizen, and parent. She crosses all the boundaries that so often divide us. And all sides of her diverse strengths show in her work and in this extraordinary book. As a reader you'll love it, and you'll come away wise as well."
—Deborah Meier, senior fellow, Annenberg Institute of School Reform, author of *The Power of Their Ideas*, and principal, Mission Hill School, Boston

Teaching as the Learning Profession
Handbook of Policy and Practice

Linda Darling-Hammond, Gary Sykes, Editors

Winner of the NSDC Outstanding Staff Development Book in 2000

464 pages / Cloth
ISBN: 0-7879-4341-X

Leading educational thinkers and researchers deliver an in-depth overview of the issues and challenges facing the teaching profession today. This book is the first in over a decade to synthesize the most important research in the fields of teaching and teacher education. The authors present case studies of innovative approaches to school improvement, principles for better staff development, proposals for the reform of unions, and practical advice on recruitment, licensing, diversity, leadership, and other inventive forms of teacher-to-teacher learning.

"This book teaches us that, if the improved learning we require for all students in a democracy is to be accomplished, both the policymakers and the professionals must take joint responsibility to craft a new alliance. . . . Readers of this book will discover that within its pages lies an impressive array of findings, analyses, interpretations, and proposals that can guide the needed efforts to design such settings. *Teaching as the Learning Profession* is far more than a superb book title. It is a mandate for the stakeholders in whose hands lies the future of America's teachers, and through them, the future of America's students."
> —from the foreword by Lee S. Shulman, president,
> The Carnegie Foundation for the Advancement of Teaching

"It's common knowledge—and common sense—that the quality of teaching strongly affects student achievement. *Teaching as the Learning Profession* rightly advocates enhancing instructional quality by providing teachers with meaningful professional learning opportunities that allow them to continually improve their practice and enable their students to excel."
> —Sandra Feldman, president, American Federation of Teachers

"No education topic is more important than how to raise the quality of teaching in America's schools. This book eloquently makes the case for reshaping teacher preparation and professional development to enhance student learning."
> —Bob Chase, president, National Education Association

Gary Sykes is professor of educational administration and teacher education at Michigan State University.

A License to Teach
Raising Standards for Teaching
Linda Darling-Hammond, Arthur E. Wise, and Stephen P. Klein

240 pages / Paper
ISBN: 0-7879-4680-X

"It's hard to find an official who doesn't say teacher quality is a key issue in education reform—and it's even harder to find one willing to do something responsible about it. No more excuses. *A License to Teach* tells us why we need to get it right in the first place and how to do it. It is the best source on the subject we have."
—Albert Shanker, former president, American Federation of Teachers

"This timely and important book presents a new and demanding vision of preparing teachers for America's public schools. It effectively critiques new efforts underway that are challenging what teachers need to know and how and who is licensed to teach. *A License to Teach* is a must-read for anyone interested in today's quality education debate."
—Keith Geiger, former president, National Education Association

The authors provide a comprehensive blueprint for developing a better system of teacher licensing. They detail the essential components of that plan—from establishing rigorous professional standards to developing performance assessments, as well as institutional accreditation, advanced certification for individual teachers, and appropriate internships. Rich with examples of real-life standards, exams, assessments, and other useful tools, *A License to Teach* not only shares the wisdom of professionals who are experienced in setting accreditation and certification standards, but offers important advice on how to prepare and evaluate aspiring teachers for the challenges of their profession.

Arthur E. Wise is president of the National Council for Accreditation of Teacher Education (NCATE). *Stephen P. Klein* is a senior research scientist at the RAND Corporation.

Child Case Studies — SLP — P. 120

Alverno — Non-graded
   General Ed. Abilities
   Professional Ed. Abilities   -132-33

We would have to shut down for a
year and retrain to adopt this system.
Then it would be rejected by F. G. Silas

U. S. Marine —
      P. 136 — Killer Quote

Portfolio assessment, Proc. of Mastery,
Public performs — just not Wa. Co.

      Active French , P. 147

To me, the biggest "problem" w/our program is placements. At present, (p.152) — Killer quote —

My contribution to discussion.

I want our students to have Excellent placements — I saw this with Mike S. I lived it (opportunities Table).

This is our biggest failure.

Seems a strike mismatch
between the "Mission for
Truth" (P.9) and the mission
put forth by Fed. govt. And
local districts (but not yet
state).

Programs are undeniably
Constructivist.

Also — placements are made
to match constructivist properties
(P. 50)

Take away — Placements
are our biggest problem.
Also: Oregon schools are whole